iii

PREFACE

Books about history are numerous enough in all conscience. But most of them are books which try to make history more complex, recondite, and uninteresting — books forbidding and even terrifying. This is an attempt to bring out certain of the richer meanings of history, to explain in some detail its objects and difficulties, and to make clear its proper standards; and yet while doing this to illustrate its wonderful variety, and to show how engrossing its pursuit may be made. The volume is written by an amateur of history in the hope that it may aid other amateurs. When I say that I am in amateur standing I do not mean that my affection for history is of recent date or has not passed through several phases. It began when I was a child in an Illinois farmhouse, reading Macaulay and Parkman (for the family library was sizable and austerely serious) on the rainy days that meant a relief from labor; and it has continued ever since. At first my liking for history was simply for the stories it told and the scenes it painted. A little later, as a newspaperman, I tried to apply some of it to current events. Later still I have had the task of teaching it. I have come to wish both that more people read history, and that more of them did so with feeling and passion, not as a means to a limited end. I have come to wish also that history was a little freer — that readers and writers alike would abstain from fettering it with dogmas, and let it be as varied, mutable, catholic, and progressive as so great a branch of literature ought to be. Here I have tried, without worrying about that pseudo-philosophic jargon upon Historismus, frames of reference, patterns of culture, and cyclical phases of causation which I no more understand than do most of its users, to provide a very Doric entrance to the historical domain. I have tried to help some general readers to realize how much history has been written for them; what a wealth of talent and even genius has been poured into it; what a tremendous conquest of perplexities and obstacles it represents; and how pregnant with ideas the best of it is.

Once historical study in America was tremendously alive. If it were as alive and energetic today as it should be, we would have in this country two enterprises which do not exist. We would have a popular historical magazine, published monthly, written for the multitude and not the learned few, and full of articles relating the past (particularly the American past) to the present. We would also have some organization which made a systematic attempt to obtain, from the lips and papers of living Americans who have led significant lives, a fuller record of their participation in the political, economic, and cultural life of the last sixty years; a period in which America has been built into the richest and most powerful nation the world has ever seen, and socially and economically has not only been transformed but re-transformed. For both these enterprises there is a plain and even acute need. Once upon a time American magazines published a wealth of historical material. They publish it no longer, and some medium is required to bring its wealth of human interest back to the bosom of the ordinary well-educated man. We have agencies aplenty to seek out the papers of men long dead. But we have only the most scattered and haphazard agencies for obtaining a little of the immense mass of information about the more recent American past — the past of the last half century — which might come fresh and direct from men once prominent in politics, in business, in the professions, and in other fields; information that every obituary column shows to be perishing. The lack of these agencies, which might easily be established and should both be highly

THE GATEWAY
TO HISTORY

ALLAN NEVINS

1938

D. C. HEATH AND COMPANY

BOSTON   NEW YORK   CHICAGO   ATLANTA
DALLAS   SAN FRANCISCO
LONDON

successful, is unfortunate in itself, and unfortunate also as a symbol of the widespread indifference to history.

With great kindness, several of my colleagues in Columbia University have read part or all of the proofsheets of this volume: Professors W. L. Westermann, Austin Evans, Robert L. Schuyler, Geroid Tanquary Robinson, and Frank L. Tannenbaum. They have saved me numerous errors and helped me remedy several omissions. Professor Henry Steele Commager of New York University has given me the benefit of his wide knowledge and acute critical sense. Two graduate students in Columbia University, Mr. Sidney Ratner and Mr. Harold Jonas, have furnished helpful comments and suggestions. To all these men I owe my warm thanks.

ALLAN NEVINS

April 2, 1938

CONTENTS

THE GATEWAY TO HISTORY

CHAPTER ONE

IN DEFENCE OF HISTORY

EVERYONE recalls the majestic exordium of Webster's reply to Hayne. "Mr. President," he began, "when the mariner has tossed for many days in thick weather, and on an unknown sea, he naturally avails himself of the first pause in the storm, the earliest glance of the sun, to take his latitude and ascertain how far the elements have driven him from his true course." In that sentence Webster indicated one of the cardinal utilities of history. Mankind is always more or less storm-driven; and history is the sextant and compass of states which, tossed by wind and current, would be lost in confusion if they could not fix their position. It enables communities to grasp their relationship with the past, and to chart on general lines their immediate forward course. It does more. By giving peoples a sense of continuity in all their efforts, and by chronicling immortal worth, it confers upon them both a consciousness of their unity, and a feeling of the importance of human achievement. History is more than a mere guide to nations. It is first a creator of nations, and after that, their inspirer. Without it this world, a brilliant arena of human action canopied by fretted fire, would indeed become stale, flat, and unprofitable, a congregation of pestilent vapors.

By looking either at the past or the present we can see how vitally history serves its purpose as a womb or matrix of nations. The strongest element in the creation of any human organization of complex character and enduring strength is the establishment of common tradition by the narration of its history.

Members of a religion may be knit together by their gospel, but even that must contain historic elements; while members of a nation are knit together above all else by a common history — by learning of their past. The Greek who thrilled over Thermopylae, the Roman exulting in the tale of Caesar's conquests and triumphs, the Briton reading of the assault on Badajoz, the American following the epic story of Western pioneering, all have responded to the same emotion. When Treitschke resolved to revive the national spirit of the Germans he began by writing their history; when Vienna wished to hinder the growth of patriotism among the Czechs it threw obstacles before the publication of Palacký's history of Bohemia. To give a people a new sense of their future we need first the historian who will give them a new sense of their past. The school text that told the story of Valley Forge, the rhetorical page of Bancroft, helped immeasurably to make America a nation. Today Communist Russia is being welded together by a Communist version of history, and Fascist Italy and Nazi Germany by Fascist and Nazi histories. "Laws die, books never" — and the nation-builder may well say that he cares not who writes the laws of a country if he can write its history.

But if history is a maker of nations, her rôle as their inspirer is almost equally great. Clio, as the quotation on our title page reminds us, was the first of the Muses; and while she began as minstrel and wonder-teller, she soon became instructress. It is in that part that she has chiefly impressed the modern world. "All learners, all inquiring minds of every order," writes Carlyle, "are gathered round her footstool, and reverently pondering her lessons as the true basis of wisdom." But there is more than wisdom in her inspiration. All thoughtful men tend in some degree to identify themselves with the figures and forces of history. They realize that each individual mind is one more incarnation of a universal mind. We can understand history only as we understand that it was wrought by men and women basically like ourselves; that what Shakespeare and Napoleon achieved, what Caesar Borgia and Ivan the Terrible perpetrated, what Hasdrubal and Gustavus Adolphus dared and endured, are illustrations of the powers, debasements, and fortitudes of our common human nature. This universal nature gives value to our lives, and from it we may select the best. The grandeur of history sheds a grandeur upon ourselves. In the largest accomplishments of the past we feel that we have a share. "We sympathize in the great moments of history, in the great discoveries, the great resistances, the great prosperities of men; because there law was enacted, the sea was searched, the land was found, or the blow was struck, *for us*, as we ourselves would have done in that place or applauded." [1]

Poetry, philosophy, drama, all have a dignity of their own; but it is inferior to the dignity of history, for each is dependent upon history for a great part of its materials. As the distillation of everything that humanity has suffered, dared, failed, and vanquished, history is indeed the deepest philosophy, the truest poetry. Seated at the roaring loom of time, for six thousand years man has woven a seamless garment. But that garment is invisible and intangible save where the dyes of written history fall upon it, and forever preserve it as a possession of generations to come. Call it a department of literature or knowledge as you will — it is both — the work of historians will be most read when men are roused to a sense of their own dignity; when great events wake them to their most serious and responsible temper. Two thousand years ago Lucian was writing: "From the beginning of the present excitements — the barbarian war, the Armenian disaster, the succession of victories — you cannot find a man but is writing history; nay, everyone you meet is a Thucydides, a Herodotus, a Xenophon." It was no accident that the convulsion of the World War fostered such an interest in history that for a time the number of books devoted to it in English exceeded the titles in fiction; that on the

[1] Emerson's *Works*, Concord Ed., II, 4

heels of that war, when men groped for some guiding conception of the course of civilization, appeared the most-widely read volume of its kind in modern times, H. G. Wells's *Outline of History*.

II

Modern history, in spirit and method, is largely a product of the eighteenth century Enlightenment; and it was just as that Enlightenment began to merge in the Industrial Revolution that the United States was born. Various writers, such as Lord Morley in his *Voltaire*, have pointed out how great a part historical writing and reading played in the mature phases of the Enlightenment. The literate generation contemporary with the American and French Revolutions, in Western Europe and the United States, was steeped in history. When the eighteenth century ended no gentleman's library was complete without Thucydides, Livy, and Tacitus, and few cultivated men could not discuss the historical works of Voltaire, Hume, Gibbon, and Robertson. Henry Adams in his life of John Randolph of Roanoke speaks of the "literary standards of the day" to which Randolph's education conformed: "He read his Gibbon, Hume, and Burke; knew English history . . ." Even at an earlier period three historical works — Raleigh's eloquent *History of the World*, Bishop Burnet's *History of the Reformation*, and above all, Fox's *Book of Martyrs*, had been widely diffused throughout the American colonies. The last-named was so frequent a companion to the Bible that it may be said to have transported history to the common body of readers. But these three books are all upon an inferior historical plane; and as the Enlightenment widened its appeal to the intellectual aristocracy of the time, it brought in more select works. The men who took the leadership of our young republic were well acquainted with the first great modern historical classics. Law was no doubt their primary study, but history maintained a place close beside it.

Thus it is that we find George Washington after the Revolution ordering from England a small library of historical works — Robertson's *Charles V* and *History of America;* Voltaire's *Charles XII* and Sully's *Memoirs;* lives of Peter the Great, Louis XV, and Gustavus Adolphus; and histories of Rome and Portugal.[1] Thus it is that we find John Adams, in discussing the qualifications of a Secretary of State, writing a little later: "He ought to be a Man of universal Reading in Laws, Governments, History." [2] Thus it is, again, that we find Chancellor Kent confessing in his autobiography that in 1782, at Poughkeepsie, he varied his study of law by reading Smollett's and Rapin's histories of England. "The same year I procured Hume's *History*, and his profound reflections and admirable eloquence struck most deeply on my youthful mind." Alexander Hamilton's library included not only Greek and Roman historians, but well-thumbed sets of Gibbon, Hume, and Robertson. It is safe to say that few well-educated Americans, editors, theologians, and attorneys as well as politicians, failed at this time to regard history as a necessary discipline even if they did not take to it as a delight. Most of them would have agreed with Jefferson, himself a lover of Hume, Voltaire, Robertson, and later Hallam, in what he wrote of the proper nature of Virginia's educational law:

But of the views of this law none is more important, none more legitimate, than that of rendering the people the safe, as they are the ultimate, guardians of their own liberty. For this purpose the reading in the first stage, where *they* will receive their whole education, is proposed, as has been said, to be chiefly historical. History, by apprizing them of the past, will enable them to judge of the future; it will avail them of the experience of other times and other nations; it will qualify them as judges of the actions and designs of men; it will enable them to know ambition under every guise it may assume; and knowing it, to defeat its views.[3]

[1] Paul Leicester Ford, *The True George Washington*, pp. 203–204
[2] *Statesman and Friend: Correspondence of John Adams with Benjamin Waterhouse*, p. 57
[3] *Notes on Virginia* (Jefferson's *Works*, Memorial Edition, II, 206, 207)

The spell which history exercised over the aristocratic and intellectual groups of America remained undiminished for a long generation. Hear young Charles Sumner, for example, writing a friend just after his graduation from Harvard in 1830. "I have marked out to myself a course of study which will fully occupy my time — namely, a course of mathematics, Juvenal, Tacitus, a course of modern history, Hallam's *Middle Ages* and *Constitutional History*, Roscoe's *Leo* and *Lorenzo*, and Robertson's *Charles V* . . . ." [1] Even pioneer America felt that history befitted the leader, and after the log cabin campaign Webster spent a wearisome day deleting the names of Greek heroes and Roman consuls from William Henry Harrison's inaugural address.

But to fulfill its proper purpose in a country like the United States, history had to become democratized. That feat required a group of great talents, but it was performed. It is a salient fact of American literature, and one of the most creditable chapters in our cultural record, that from 1830 to 1870 history stood as one of the most popular literary forms — that it was continuously and strongly popular. Prescott's *Conquest of Mexico* sold 5,000 copies in four months in the United States, and then went through edition after edition; his *Conquest of Peru* sold 7,500 copies in England and America in the same brief period, then commencing a career that is still far from ended. The works of Bancroft and Motley, of Parkman and Irving, had equal or greater currency. Indeed, Irving's life of Washington, the ablest study of the Revolution made up to that time, was one of the great successes of American publishing prior to the Civil War. Even volumes which might have seemed destined to a slender public, such as Ticknor's dry *History of Spanish Literature*, reached a large fraction of the readers of the day. When it is recalled that meanwhile the histories of Macaulay and Carlyle were not merely brought out by authorized publishers, but pirated in huge cheap editions

[1] E. L. Pierce, *Memoir and Letters of Charles Sumner*, I, 80–82

and scattered in myriads through the land, while translated histories like Rollin's sold widely, we can comprehend why the American mind retained a distinct historical bias during most of the century. We can understand why a philosopher like Fiske turned to history as the best medium for disseminating his ideas; why novelists like Mark Twain and Edward Eggleston wrote formal histories as well as fiction; and why in the greatest days of the *Atlantic, Century,* and *Harper's,* history occupied a prominent place in their tables of contents.

This popularity, beyond question, has been followed by a period of comparative deliquescence. Since Parkman published his last history in 1892, and Fiske in 1899, no writer can be named who has rivalled their appeal. Successful books there have been in large numbers. But the greatest of the latter-day historians in many respects, Henry Adams, complained that he was hardly read at all, and it took thirty years for his history of the United States from 1801 to 1817 to reach a second edition. While the work of John Bach McMaster and James Ford Rhodes, begun in the eighties, commanded a substantial sale, it never reached so large a fraction of the literate population as did Prescott and Motley. Since the World War the greatest successes in serious literature have been biographical, and the sale of extended histories — histories in sets — has declined to very slender proportions.

For both this broad appeal of history during the half-century 1835–85, and its comparative decline in popularity in the half-century 1885–1935, manifold reasons may be assigned. It is conventional to say that history in its era of ascendancy was highly literary in character, more literary than today. But this does not wholly express the difference. To be sure, Macaulay, Carlyle, and Froude, Prescott, Parkman, and Motley were masters of style whose literary gifts — that is, whose powers of description, exposition, and narration — amounted in four of the six to genius, and in the other two to very rare talent. It would be difficult to point to any British or American histories since 1885 of equally sustained literary power. But the subjects and methods of these writers had much to do with their "literary" excellence.

They belonged, like Gibbon and Robertson before them, to the great age of historical exploration. In their day the field of history lay spread before mankind like a huge half-completed map, full of mountain ranges, seas, and plains still to be traversed and measured. It appealed to the imagination, for it offered tasks of vast scope and rich color, and at every new turn held novelty and adventure. Gibbon was a veritable Columbus, who travelled across wider reaches than any predecessor, and showed the decline of one world and the rise of a new one. Macaulay in his history of the momentous transition from Stuart to Hanoverian England and the rise of a new democratic state, and Parkman in his chronicle of the conflict which determined that North America should have a British and not a French civilization, were like Humboldt and Livingstone, mapping huge new territories. The readers of Prescott's story of the Spanish conquest of the New World experienced much the same emotions as those who followed the feats of Frémont and Stanley. They were the first who ever burst into that historical domain, and they saw a great panorama unrolled as from a mountain top. The period in which these historians wrote might well be called the age of wonder in history, and its special rapture can never be regained.

These eminent literary histories, moreover, appertained to a simpler age in another sense. It was an age in which men felt that they held more of the key to the universe than educated men can believe they hold today. To the Victorians in Britain and America all moral and scientific values seemed to be coming within grasp. The domain of physics was ruled by Newton. The globe was fast being conned and triangulated to its farthest corners. The doctrines of evolution and natural selection answered the chief riddles of biology, psychology, and sociology. Historians did not need to be writers of many ideas, for simple ideas — which were all that even Macaulay, Carlyle, and Prescott offered — sufficed. They did not need to integrate their histories with a complex set of sciences, for science seemed to have little complexity. In a simple, direct world simple, direct historians, writing in the temper of democratic, progressive, rationalist peoples, could be sure of understanding and acceptance. It was an acceptance all the more enthusiastic when they none too subtly flattered the preconceptions of their readers, as they usually did: — Macaulay with his Whig bias their democratic preconceptions; Motley, Froude, and Parkman their Protestant preconceptions; Carlyle their moral preconceptions and their worship of work and efficiency; Freeman and John Fiske their belief in the endless linear progress of man.

In one respect not so obvious the simplicity of the age tended to the popularization of history. In the United States and Europe the first three-fourths of the nineteenth century was primarily an age of political interests, while the period which followed it became — at least in intellectual circles — primarily an age of economic and sociological interests. If this statement sounds extreme, it is at least accurate to say that after the middle of the nineteenth century economic and sociological factors received increasing attention as compared with political topics. Now political history, which is comparatively easy to write and to read, appeals alike to the well-educated and the semi-educated. But history which gives due weight to both social and economic elements is, on the contrary, seldom appreciated save by the fully educated, and not a little of it is appreciated only by specialists. Particularly is this true so long as the social and economic elements in history are unskilfully and pedantically treated by writers who still lack finished models and well-settled rules, as till lately has been the fact. In short, it seemed easier in the middle of the nineteenth century to combine instruction with entertainment — it was easier — than in the middle of the twentieth century.

Most Americans, Britons, Frenchmen, and Germans in the

age of Lincoln, Gladstone, Thiers, and Bismarck instinctively believed that the central focus of men's attention, in current affairs and historical study alike, should be the state, its fortunes and misfortunes. Hence it was that Macaulay's stirring portrayal of the evils of James II's reign, the crushing of Monmouth's rebellion, the rising tide of anger against real temporal and threatened ecclesiastical tyranny, the "glorious revolution" of 1688, the vicissitudes of William and Mary's reign, seemed admirable history to his own and the succeeding generation. Macaulay's fourth chapter, while social history of a rare kind, is a small part of the whole. Hence it is that Thierry's *Norman Conquest*, dealing with the English dissensions under Harold, with Stamford Bridge, with William's invasion, the battle of Hastings, and the ensuing conquests, confiscations, and administrative acts of the Conqueror, seemed perfect history to our forefathers. Today most men believe that the central focus of their attention should be *society*, not the state, and society is more complicated and formless than politics. Good history is correspondingly harder to write, and unless done with consummate art, harder to read.

It is sometimes said that history was more widely read a century ago than today because, good books being fewer, it encountered less competition. But in so far as the literature of books goes, this is not merely a dubious but a false assertion. The nineteenth century was a century of great novelists, great essayists, and great poets. Men of Macaulay's time did not turn to history because there was little else to read; they had Thackeray, Dickens, and Trollope; Tennyson, Browning, and Swinburne; De Quincey, Bagehot, and Arnold. Men of Parkman's day did not read him because of a paucity of American books; they had Howells, James, and Mark Twain; Longfellow, Lowell, and Whittier. The quarter in which history meets a really novel degree of competition in our day is the journalistic quarter — the field of current discussion.

Readers, like other consumers, demand a balanced diet; they

will accept but so much poetry and so much prose, so much entertainment and so much wisdom. History, though by no means without entertaining values, is to be classified primarily as serious matter; and for serious matter men in the turmoil of today turn largely to the discussion of contemporaneous problems in newspapers, reviews, and books. To a far greater extent than in the more placid Victorian days they are prone to feel that history is a dead field, that it concerns itself with a lifeless past, and that for the purposes of earnest, living men it is often useless enough to deserve Henry Ford's epithet — "bunk." Particularly since the vast upheaval of the World War, they wish a discussion of current issues. Having read enough books and articles upon unemployment and corporation control, upon disarmament and neutrality, upon the Supreme Court and the Securities Commission, upon Nazi Germany and Communist Russia, to feel well informed, they turn for recreation to fiction, and for refreshment to essays and poetry. The present has become so exigent that the demands of the past seem tame and colorless.

This is of course a temporary attitude; but even if evanescent, it is unjust to history. The political present, the economic present, the sociological present, cannot be understood without knowledge of the past. The attitude is not wholly unjust to the latter-day race of historians. Most of them have failed to solve the problem of uniting human appeal with the new stuff of history; the problem of bringing insight, imagination, and eloquence to bear upon the more refractory materials that now go into their crucibles. But it is unjust to history as a whole. Who can understand Nazi Germany without knowing something of Germany of the Weimar Constitution, Germany of the Kaisers, and back of that the Germany of Jena and Leipzig? Who can understand Franklin D. Roosevelt's New Deal without studying Woodrow Wilson's New Freedom, the elder Roosevelt's New Nationalism, and back of that the democratic ideals of Lincoln, Jackson, and Jefferson? The more exigent the present day the more exigent also the past, for they are indissolubly united. But this necessity of studying the origins of present-day forces and tendencies in bygone times is far from being the only reason why history is essential even to the man who tries to fasten his eyes narrowly upon what is current and practical. A knowledge of history is needed, in addition, to throw the present into perspective. We can endure the current economic boom or depression better if we comprehend what preceded and followed 1837 and 1873. We can take a clearer view of Mussolini if we are familiar with the career of Napoleon III. It throws the course of the Japanese in China into better definition to know something of the time when the savage horsemen of Tamerlane rode across the roof of the world.

History has also suffered, by a natural paradox, from overproduction. The period in which it bore its greatest names was also a period in which it had many fewer small names, many fewer mediocre practitioners, than in late years. As a branch of literature it then demanded passports of talent from all entrants. It has tended too largely to become a mere branch of learning; and in that field the only passports are diligence and accuracy, which are too often synonymous with plodding dulness. The Artisans of history have multiplied beyond all proportion to the Artists. Far more historical works are printed, sold (or not sold), and put on library shelves, than when history was most read. A multitude of books, chiefly petty in scope and pettier in aim, stream from presses to be forgotten. The very size of the shallow stream, the brawling clamor it wakes in reviews, its brackish taste when sampled, repel many readers from history altogether. Nothing could do more for widespread historical reading than some reform by which fewer men would take up their pens, and these few would do so later in life, or at any rate not until intellectually mature and fully trained in their craft. Failing this, history would at least benefit by a more discriminating terminology. As a fairly clear line is drawn between poetry and verse (even Kipling modestly called his compositions by the latter name), so such a line might be drawn between history on one side, and chronicles, compilations, and monographs on the other. We could then speak of Parkman's histories, but, to select a writer long dead and of greater stature than most, of Hildreth's chronicles.

But most of all, history has suffered in recent years from confusion of aims and standards. It has passed through what John Richard Green and John Bach McMaster thought a mere age of transition into an age of utter revolution, and has not yet quite oriented itself. Of course all literary forms which possess any vitality manifest their constant changes of mode and temper. Poetry moves from a classical age to a romantic age; the novel is wrested from the realistic school by the naturalistic school. But history has been altered simultaneously and radically not only by this type of change, but by another of very different character.

It was inevitable that it, like other prose of the nineteenth century, should alter from a romantic to a realistic mood, from the rich coloring and adventurous pace of Macaulay, Prescott, and Parkman to the sober tones of Mommsen, Freeman, and Henry Adams. Such a change was part of the spirit of the time. It kept pace with the change from Byron and Keats to Browning and Meredith. But history differs from pure literature in being closely interconnected not only with the spirit of the time, but with the whole body of the social sciences. When these underwent their tremendous expansion and development in the latter half of the nineteenth and early twentieth centuries, history had to expand, develop, and change with them. While the old history did not cease to be a true history, men perceived that it was only part of the truth. The new wine had to be poured into new bottles, and historians fell to quarreling as to their shape if they were not to break. Lovers of old traditions and standards even denied that men should attempt, in any greater degree than Von Ranke or Guizot, the analysis of economic institutions, the dissection of social structure. Enthusiasts for the application of social science to history simultaneously, and with equal folly, denied that politics, war, and diplomacy held any weighty place in history at all — that they were more than the spume and bubble on the river of human development. This lack of settled standards not only bewildered some writers of history, but encouraged many readers to underrate its importance. They asked "What is history?" and picking up the latest magazine, would not pause for an answer.

But out of confusion slowly emerges integration; little by little the new bottles are being shaped for the new wine. As the limitations of the old history are more charitably weighed and the limits of the new history more sharply appraised, it is being found that the truly sound specimens of both are not far apart. It is also being found that the best history is a combination of old and new. Henry Adams wrote history as political in character as Von Ranke, as much devoted to *Staatsrecht;* but the first six chapters of his greatest work are a social history (descriptive, not analytical, to be sure) of transcendent merit. William Roscoe Thayer's *Cavour* would be classified as a political history. But no sociological historian could be more thorough in displaying the vast and complex network of forces, social, religious, and economic, local, national, and international, through whose warring confusion Cavour had to fight his way to his goals. Nor could any psychological historian do better in measuring the fluctuating tides of opinion, prejudice, and sentiment, and the fierce uneven growth of nationalist feeling in Italy. If we think of intellectual history, Henry Osborn Taylor's *Medieval Mind* unites sympathy with the scientific spirit in as notable a union, and with as vigorous a grasp, as anyone could demand; while in such a chapter as "The Spotted Actuality" he shows a very modern realism. These men are "old" historians, and yet they are new. Such active present-day historians as the younger Trevelyan know how to combine the old standards of brilliant narrative, as in his Garibaldi volumes, with the new standards of scientific breadth, as in his Queen Anne volumes. The establishment of accepted norms is possible and will come. Meanwhile the confusion is at least a sign of healthy growth; and when it ends history will be the richer and stronger for it.

The history written in the future will necessarily be eclectic in the best sense. Because the full truth is the only real truth, history as a whole will make all possible use of science — of statistics, sociology, economics, psychology, geography — to present a complete and exact picture of the past. Because the state is usually the greatest common denominator of society, and is often its highest expression, history will never neglect political movements. Because even business cannot be interpreted solely by statistics of prices and profits — because ruined men weep and suddenly enriched men dance — the best historian will still look deep into the human heart. Because narrative power is indispensable to the highest kind of history, future historians will still tell romantic, heroic, and heart-rending stories, and still have their heroes, their villains, and their yet more interesting mixtures of the heroic and the villainous.

III

Meanwhile we possess the serried shelves of the great historians of the past, a department of letters as rich and noble as any other, and as deathless as the writings of the great poets or philosophers. Their work is not a dead record. Instead, it pulses with fire. Again and again great events have found a historian who knew how to paint with unfading colors, so that intervening time melts away between us and his scene. We are still moved by the sight of Nebuchadnezzar, his hair tangled on his shoulders, his uncombed beard hanging down his swart chest, his nails sharp as eagle's talons, returning sane at last to the gates of Babylon. We still thrill to the shout of Xenophon's Ten Thousand as, reaching the crest of their final hill, they at last descry the dark line of the Euxine Sea. We catch the crash of brazen impact, the crackling of flames, and the yells of rage and pain as Antony's five hundred ships close with the Octavian fleet, and then we see the purple sails of Cleopatra puff in the breeze as she signals the Egyptian vessels to flee with her. We watch Diocletian, leaving his huge palace at Spalato and driving to his massive ampitheatre, take the salute of two bands of doomed criminals before, rushing upon one another with sword and spear, they open the gladiatorial show. We see the thin English line at Crécy halting at Edward's sharp word, planting their pointed stakes in the mud, drawing bow to ear, and suddenly darkening the air with clothyard arrows that crumple the French host in front. And so the story marches down with its ever-widening sweep until we see Wolfe reciting the Elegy below Quebec, Pitt bidding his servant roll up the map of Europe, Lincoln sinking back unconscious in his arm-chair in Ford's theatre, Bismarck presiding over the Congress of Berlin, the German tide rolling through Brussels in 1914; until, with a start, we face the events of only yesterday — Woodrow Wilson struggling to found a League of Nations, and Lenin founding a Communist state.

On these serried shelves there is fare for every taste and nutriment for every mind. There are perhaps lovers of rich and picturesque description who have never read Herodotus's pages telling how the Arabians collected frankincense from trees guarded by winged serpents, how the Scythians boiled meat without firewood, and how the Carthaginians carried on a dumb commerce with certain African tribes. There are perhaps lovers of tense and harrowing narrative who have never followed the chapter in which Thucydides relates how the Athenian expedition came to utter ruin before Syracuse. There are perhaps men who like a panoramic picture of a world-shaking struggle, yet who have never perused Livy's detailed and engrossing story of how Hannibal massed an army in Spain, marched it across the Alps, and bringing it into the plains of Italy, defeated one Roman army after another until he stood at the gates of the desperate capital. The potential readers of history who have missed these works are to be pitied. We could better lose a thousand current novels than any one of the three. Some men, again, may like a picture of a dark age painted in dark colors. If they wish to feed a taste for the sensational they need only turn to Tacitus. Himself an eye-witness of the reign of terror in the last three years of Domitian, he saw only the worst side of imperialism; and figuring Tiberius as another tyrant of the Domitian stripe, he has retold us every horrible tale of the emperor's misdeeds.

Those who prefer the quieter side of history, a study of works and days, may find it in a long shelf of works, from the portraiture of national life and manners in Xenophon's *Education of Cyrus* and in Tacitus's *Germania* down to Elie Halévy's masterly presentation of every aspect of British life in his *English People in 1815*, and Lamprecht's vivid and scholarly volumes on the cultural development of Germany. For those interested in the intellectual and spiritual history of mankind an equal treasury of material exists. They may begin with James H. Breasted's study of *The Dawn of Conscience*, describing the full emergence of a sense of social morals in Egypt five thousand years ago, with W. Robertson Smith's *Religion of the Semites*, and with Gilbert Murray and G. Lowes Dickinson on the history of the Greek mind and spirit; and from this they may come down to such historians of the modern mind as Taine, Lecky, Brandes, and Vernon Parrington. Some may prefer history of the highly analytical order, with ample introduction of statistical and sociological data; such history as we encounter in Leroy-Beaulieu on Russian economic changes, or in the works of J. B. and Barbara Hammond on the town laborer and rural laborer in England. Some may like institutional history, which Maitland has shown may be made witty and entertaining. Others, again, may like history written so closely around some central figure, as in Parkman's *Frontenac and New France*, or

Mommsen's chapters upon Rome in Caesar's day, that it almost becomes biography. Every department of history spreads an ample feast to those who will but seek it out.

No nation, it is pleasant to note in this connection, has done more in the last fifty years to add to the amplitude and vitality of its own historical record than the United States. Great single names, unless license be taken to call Rhodes and Henry Adams great, are indeed lacking. But for this deficiency our writers have largely atoned by a wealth of monographic work, not a little of it brilliant, more of it searching, and still more of it impressively thorough. It is seldom realized, even by the well-read, how much remained to be done forty years ago — what great areas of the American past stood untouched, what other areas were like raw, new-broken prairie. Our best historians, Prescott, Motley, and Parkman, had not turned to national history at all; Bancroft had but reached the threshold of that field; the history of the West, the period since the Civil War, the history of business, of thought, and of institutions all remained to be written. Theodore Roosevelt only forty years ago could speak of the great inviting reaches that beckoned to authors.[1] They could paint anew, he declared, the labors of the colonists to plant civilization in the Indian-haunted forests. They could describe almost for the first time the backwoodsmen with their long rifles and light axes hewing their way to the Mississippi; the endless march of white-topped wagons across plain and mountain to the Pacific. "They will show how the land which the pioneers won slowly and with incredible hardship was filled in two generations by the overflow from the countries of western and central Europe. The portentous growth of the cities will be shown, and the change from a nation of farmers to a nation of business men and artisans, and all the far-reaching consequences of the rise of the new industrialism. The formation of a new ethnic type in this melting-pot of the nations will be told. The hard materialism

[1] In *Works*, National Ed., XII, 23, 24; "History as Literature"

of our age will appear, and also the strange capacity for lofty idealism which must be reckoned with by all who would understand the American character." Most of this has been done, and part of it with compelling interest. The remainder will rapidly be accomplished. The history written of and by Americans in the last generation not only illuminates our past, but suffuses a glow which more than anything else — more than the work of sociologists, economists, or political experts — lights up our immediate future. The American who ignores it has neglected the most vital part of his education.

Were history as nearly static as some branches of learning, it would be a drab affair; but it is alive in every sense. It is most of all alive in this, that it is constantly being reborn like a phoenix from its own ashes. As mankind lengthens its record, perspectives steadily change. The lenses through which we look at the past must be refocussed from generation to generation. What seemed wisdom to our fathers is often folly to us; what is intensely dramatic to our age may seem naïve or banal to the next. While the best history is perdurable, there is a sense in which every generation needs to have history rewritten anew for it; and in this fact lies much of the challenge and fascination which historical activity will always have to thoughtful men. The history written in any age insensibly bodies forth the form and spirit of that age; a succession of histories is a record of the stages through which thought and feeling have passed. We shall try to show in this volume that history in its protean forms touches the realm of ideas at more points than any other study, and that in the best of its forms it is compact as much of ideas as of fact. There was a profound and not merely superficial meaning in the last instructions Napoleon left for the King of Rome: "Let my son often read and reflect on history; this is the only true philosophy." [1]

[1] August Fournier, *Napoleon the First: A Biography*, one-volume edition (1903), p. 743

CHAPTER TWO

HISTORY VERSUS THE DOGMATISTS

BECAUSE history has been approached from many different points of view, it has received more amusingly varied definitions than even the novel. The cynic's definition of it as a *mensonge convenu,* a lie agreed upon, may harmonize with the statement attributed to Disraeli that he preferred romances to history because they told more truth; but it is a piece of baseless flippancy. It is precisely the fact that historians are always ready to disagree with each other which makes any persistence of lies in history — that is, true history — unlikely. Carlyle, approaching the subject from his special predilection, which emphasized the rôle of the individual, termed history the essence of innumerable biographies. But obviously it is a good deal more than that; it takes account of many forces which are not personal at all. John Cotter Morison defined it as "the prose narrative of past events, as probably true as the fallibility of human testimony will allow." Good so far as it goes, that definition is too pedestrian to be wholly satisfactory. Conversely, a familiar modern statement that history is the record of everything in the past which helps explain how the present came to be, is too philosophical and priggish. It emphasizes too much the utilitarian rôle of history, which we often wish to read without any reference whatever to the present — even to get entirely away from the present.

History is any integrated narrative or description of past events or facts written in a spirit of critical inquiry for the whole truth. A definition which attempts to be more precise than this is certain to be misleading. For above all, it is the historical point of view, the historical method of approach — *that is, the spirit of critical inquiry for the whole truth* — which, applied to the past, makes history. It will not do to lay down a more exclusive formula. There are as many different schools and theories of history as the schools of philosophy, of medicine, and of painting. But it will be agreed that a newspaper report of some current event, a debate in Congress, a diplomatic exchange between France and Germany, is not history, because it cannot be written as an inquiry into the *whole* truth. Only superficial sources of information, generally speaking, are open to newspapermen. It will also be agreed that a Democratic or Republican campaign-book reviewing events of the four years just preceding publication is not history; it is not written as a *critical* inquiry into the truth. A careful historical novel, like Charles Reade's *Cloister and the Hearth*, holds many historical values. But it will be agreed that it is not history, for it is not written primarily as an inquiry into past *truth* at all, but primarily to entertain and please by an artistic use of the imagination.

It is important not to be dogmatic on the subject; for one of the primary requisites for enjoying and understanding history is a catholic acceptance of its many types and forms. The varieties of history are almost as numerous as the really great writers of history. In many instances these writers, having adopted firm convictions and founded schools, have been deplorably contemptuous of one another. No reader should be misled by their occasional displays of professional narrowness or ill-nature. Macaulay wrote in his diary for December 7, 1849, when his first volumes had just appeared, that he had a more just conception of history and understood its nature more fully than Hume, Voltaire, or Gibbon; though at the same time he admitted that Thucydides wrote much better history than he did.[1] But Macaulay's own contemporaries disagreed

---

[1] George Otto Trevelyan, *Life of Lord Macaulay*, II, 174

bitterly as to his merits. Lord Acton records that, conversing at different times with Stubbs and Creighton, and with the eminent German historians, Mommsen and Harnack, he found that they agreed that Macaulay was the most gifted historian of modern times. Yet other contemporary historians denied in the strongest terms that he was more than a very second-rate writer. Carlyle, speaking as a moralist, declared that his *History of England from the Accession of James II* was "a book to which 400 editions could not lend any permanent value, there being no depth of sense in it at all and a very great quantity of rhetorical wind and other ingredients, which are the reverse of sense." A more moderate critic, Frederic Harrison, later asserted that Macaulay's conception of history was grievously erroneous; that he was a mere painter of lively pictures, whose narrative came closer to romance than fact. Yet Carlyle, sure that his own historical methods were just, fared as badly at other hands. Prescott angrily pronounced his *French Revolution* "perfectly contemptible."

A humorous exaggeration has sometimes crept into these broadsides fired by historians at one another. Carlyle remarked that Henry Hallam's *Literature of Europe in the 15th, 16th, and 17th Centuries* was a mere "valley of dry bones"; and Hallam meanwhile confessed to Tennyson of Carlyle's *French Revolution* that "I have tried to read it but I can't get on, the style is so abominable." Even American historians have been savagely critical of one another. James Ford Rhodes, primarily an analytical historian, entertained a low opinion of the historical methods and achievements of John Bach McMaster, primarily a descriptive historian. In turn, Albert J. Beveridge believed that Rhodes's *History of the United States From the Compromise of 1850* was shallow in thought, sectionally biassed, unfair to Stephen A. Douglas and the Southern leaders, and ill-written.[1] Every strongly-individual historian sets up his own

[1] For an extremely amusing excoriation of one historian by another, see W. A. Dunning's analysis of the defects of James Schouler's volume on the Civil War; *Truth in History and Other Essays*, pp. 173–178.

standards, and few historians of the first rank will admit that a different conception of historical aims is as good as their own. But many of these attacks have no more real validity than Francis Jeffrey's famous verdict on Wordsworth's *Excursion*, *"This will never do!"* The reader should cultivate a taste for different varieties of history, varying as widely as *War and Peace, Humphrey Clinker, The Talisman, L'Assomoir, Treasure Island,* and *Swann's Way,* all novels and all good ones, vary in form and aim.

It is indeed the tremendous variety which historical literature presents which constitutes one of its principal charms. To limit that variety, to crib and cabin history within narrow bounds, would constitute the greatest injury that pedants could do it. If the reader's passing mood or consistent taste demands brilliant irony, piquant epigram, a style as stately as an army with banners, and the dexterous management of a mighty panorama of peoples and empires, Gibbon waits upon the shelves. If it demands not irony or stateliness but eloquence, enthusiasm, a headlong rush of language, a vivid succession of scenes lit up as by a succession of lightning-flashes, there are Michelet and Carlyle. If it calls for systematized erudition, inexorable logic, a scientific attention to the arrangement of facts in neat categories, there are Von Ranke and Gardiner. If the reader demands adventure and suspense, he may follow Cortez and Pizarro as Prescott shows them picking their way amid deadly perils; or, if a broader setting and mightier issues be demanded, he may read Hodgkin's fascinating history of the barbarian invasions. If he wishes the sombre coloring of the forest on his page, there is Parkman; if the rich sparkle of court and palace, there are Froude's pictures of Elizabeth at Hampton Court and Windsor, and Guizot's of the French monarchs at Fontainebleau and Versailles. If he calls for a searching narrative of a great political movement, in which minute research is combined with power of bold generalization, he may turn to Theodore Mommsen's history of the great struggle which felled the Roman Republic and created the Empire.

There are happily all sorts and conditions of history — factual and interpretive; popular and learned; history as minutely erudite as Stubbs's monotonous page, as lively as Lytton Strachey's; history that presents an economic interpretation of the past, and history that gives ideas and acts a more elevated motivation; history that is concerned with statistics and history concerned with ideas. The true lover of history will reject none, but try rather to take what is good from each. Neither will he, in spite of definitions, reject fiction and poetry as often having a legitimate relationship with history — as sometimes almost falling within its bounds. Gogol's magnificent *Taras Bulba* is not formal history; but there is no work in Russian or English which will give the student so vital and accurate an impression of the grim Cossack struggle against Mohammedan Tartars and Catholic Poles in the sixteenth century — and needless to say, no account written in such beautiful prose. It is safe to say that the general conception of several reigns in English history has been moulded much more powerfully by Shakespeare's historical dramas than by any formal historian; and while the great poet rearranged many events to suit himself, his genius pierced nearer the essential character of Richard II and Henry V than mere students of documents have done. After the reader has mastered all that Lecky and Trevelyan have to tell him of the eighteenth century in England, he will still have to con Fielding's *Tom Jones*, with its crowded stage of characters disposed about the central figures of Allworthy, Blifil, Jones, and Squire Western, its wealth of observation upon manners, dress, and speech, and its accurate reproduction of the ideas and ideals of the age. In a sense it and *Humphrey Clinker* are materials for the social historian; in another sense they are *history*, their pages containing much that no social historian can redistil into his own volume.

II

One of the most potent causes of intolerance among historians has lain in the old and essentially futile dispute as to whether history is a science or an art. It is essentially futile because the answer depends upon the definition given the word science, and disputants seldom agree upon that definition. It is futile also because of the profound truth stated by T. H. Huxley in his *Letters:* "Literature and science are not two different things, but two sides of the same thing." As Von Ranke, one of the chief founders of the so-called scientific school, stated, history is both a science and an art. There is nothing irreconcilable in the two. Darwin's *Voyage of the Beagle* is sufficiently scientific to please the zoölogist who cares nothing about art, and more than sufficiently artistic to please the literary man who cares little for geology or biology. History makes demands upon science in that it must perform every possible office of research and criticism. It makes demands upon art in that, if it is to reach many readers or endure for many years, it must have vital attractions of form, style, and spirit. Like Darwin's book, a really consummate history, the work of Mommsen or Fustel de Coulanges or Sir J. G. Frazer, unites art and science indissolubly.

We can understand this better, and can approach a true comprehension of the word science in this connection, if we note that historical writing involves three elements. One is the element of factual inquiry and sifting — that is, research. This should be strictly scientific in its use of highly exact principles to accumulate, observe, and weigh data; it is scientific, that is, in method. The second element is that of interpretation. Having accumulated his facts, the historian must discover their logical connection with each other, the laws which rule them and their significance for the period studied and for our own time. In this second element lie broad possibilities for the establishment of a scientific set of deductions. But here

the word science is used in a different sense; a scientific generalization from a large number of historical facts has the same
quality as a generalization from a large number of zoölogical
facts. It is an attempt to set up a general law resting on the
weight of evidence. Darwin not merely accumulated a mass of
data bearing on the differences among species; he tried to establish a law explaining the differences. A scientific historian
who studied revolutions would not merely accumulate a vast
mass of data on these human upheavals; he would try to formulate some laws common to all. Finally, the third element in
historical writing is presentation — the narration, description,
and exposition required to set forth the results of research and
interpretation.

A superficial observer might say that the first two elements
are scientific, and the third literary. But as a matter of fact,
all three are scientific and all three literary. Presentation,
while primarily an art, involves that complex and exacting
science termed Rhetoric. It must also be scientific in temper;
it must not understate or overstate. As for the first two elements, they should have their aesthetic side. If research unites
precision and ingenuity as it should, it achieves a beauty as
pleasing as a fine mathematical demonstration — and Edna St.
Vincent Millay tells us that "Euclid alone has looked on beauty
bare." Similarly, the element of interpretation draws upon the
imagination, and all exercises of the imagination, even for
scientific ends, are aesthetic. It will be generally conceded
that Sir Henry Maine's *Ancient Law* is an impressive work of
history not for any beauty of imagery or diction, for it lacks
that, but because the superb dexterity and force with which
it draws from a tangled array of facts certain well-substantiated
laws excites our admiration. A finished intellectual demonstration may excite the aesthetic sense as the powerful, smooth-
spinning dynamo excited Henry Adams's. Thus it is that some
passages in Buckle charm by their sheer intellectual grasp and
power. A truly great history unites a whole series of scientific
qualities; it also unites a whole series of artistic qualities.

The group of intolerant critics who deny history any scientific standing whatever must rest their case upon an excessively narrow definition of the word science. It is obvious, of course, that history is not a science in the sense in which physics, chemistry, and astronomy deserve that term. For one reason, these sciences are strictly impersonal, while history is violently personal; stars and molecules have no loves and hates, while men do. For another, these studies aim at the discovery of laws that exist quite out of time, and that repeat themselves consistently with the repetition of a given set of circumstances. It is a law of chemistry that the combination of hydrogen and oxygen in fixed proportions will always produce water. It is a law of physics that every mass tends toward every other mass with a force varying directly as the product of the masses, and inversely as the square of their distances apart. History, far from attempting to discover laws that exist out of time, is only a more or less generalized description of some segment of a time-process. If it is not in time it is not history. Moreover, historical events never precisely duplicate themselves. It is commonly said that history repeats itself (and Max Beerbohm adds that "historians repeat one another") but this is wrong. G. K. Chesteron was quite correct when he wrote that the great lesson of history is that mankind never profits by the lessons of history. Unfortunate as this sometimes is, mankind can say with truth that its situation at any given moment differs in vital particulars from any previous situation, however parallel in outline. That has always been true, and will always be true.

Hence it is that we can have no precise laws in history as we have precise laws in physics, chemistry, and mathematics; that history can never be a science in that highly rigid sense. The historian labors under heavy difficulties as compared with some physical scientists. The chemist, for example, can boast a superior apparatus for ascertaining truth. In formulating the laws which govern an element, he can repeat his experiments thousands of times with all factors precisely the same, or with endless variations of factors. The historian has no control of phenomena in the blowpipe or test tube sense. He may be greatly puzzled by Stephen A. Douglas's motives in hastening on the Civil War by introducing the Kansas-Nebraska Act; but he cannot call Douglas before another Congress of 1854 to test his theories. He cannot summon Luther before another Diet of Worms, with another Charles V presiding, to test his suppositions as to their conduct. Conclusions as to human beings, with "their instincts immature, their purposes unsure," must always lack precision — and ours would be a dull world if they did not.[1]

But science, as the word is more properly understood, is not confined to physics and chemistry, to such matters as the table of the elements and the laws of heat and motion. It includes biology, which is incapable of discovering laws of a purely timeless and mathematical character. Both zoölogy and botany deal with living matter, and they therefore share with history a new, difficult, and fascinating dimension. Physics, treating of stars, pendulums, and falling tennis-balls, can inform us of the laws of dynamics. But when science deals with the motions of leaping tigers, skimming swallows, and diving tadpoles, it must include with the laws of dynamics certain new elements. Matter behaves in unpredictable ways because it is alive, and this unpredictability colors the whole subject. The zoölogist and botanist can no more abolish the time-element than the historian can. Apart from the minor phenomena of individual behavior, they find themselves facing the major phenomena of progression and evolution. The old mathematical laws are not abrogated, but are transcended. A scientist in these fields has to do on a small and simple scale what the historian will gradually do with much larger and more complex phenomena — he

---

[1] Students will profit from the treatment of this subject — the limitations of experiment — by a reading of John M. Keynes's *The Scope and Method of Political Economy*, and from the pages upon "Reason in Social Science" in Morris L. Cohen's *Reason and Nature*.

will formulate conclusions as to tendencies, and lay these down as laws. Some tendencies, both in biology and in history, are more enduring than others, and so come nearer to laws of the timeless kind. Obviously history cannot demonstrate so many uniform and enduring conclusions as biology, but in essentials it is as much a science, and no more a science.[1]

Few observers will deny that generation after generation history is becoming more of a science in the broad sense of the word. The steady accumulation of data, together with our increasing ability to classify and analyze facts bearing upon individual psychology, communal psychology, economic changes, and the growth of institutions and mores, enables us to lay down more "laws" and to do so less tentatively. It is true that they are still few and for the most part feeble; but then mankind has a recorded past of only about six thousand years. Historians have discovered, for example, certain uniform tendencies governing movements of religious enthusiasm. They are the same for the rise of Christianity, the rise of Mohammedanism, the rise of Mormonism; for the Crusades and the Great Awakening. On such a subject the historian derives much aid from psychologists like William James (cf. *The Varieties of Religious Experience*) and other scientists. Laws which seem to govern the growth, flowering, and decline of certain forms of capitalism can also be outlined with more

---

[1] But note that even the new physics and new chemistry seem more lawless than some scientists had thought. J. N. W. Sullivan writes (*Atlantic Monthly*, Vol. 155, No. 1, January, 1935) that the more men probe into the ultimate constitution of matter the more they are puzzled. "It appears that the behavior of these ultimate constituents of matter is not strictly determined. So far as we can make out, they will sometimes do one thing and sometimes another, although the surrounding circumstances remain exactly the same. The best we can do is to say what the chances are that they will do one thing rather than another. We can replace exact prediction by statistics, as a life insurance actually does. . . . Some of our leading scientific authorities hold that the ultimate processes of nature really are indeterminate, that the strict sequence of cause and effect hitherto assumed by science is merely an idea based on insufficient experience."

clarity than a generation ago. Here the economists, as in the treatment of the economic cycle, have helped history to find a way. And in a few fields where the sociologist and historian (who usually fight like cat and dog) can really ally themselves, the social tendencies of history are being adumbrated if not formulated. Take the previously mentioned field of the great politico-social revolutions. Historians have made bold to lay down general laws which hold good for the English, American, French, and Russian Revolutions alike. They begin, for example, with the rule that revolutions originate not where populations live in utter wretchedness, but where they live in comparatively good and (though pricked by sharp hardships) progressively better conditions.

It is self-evident that the biologist holds many advantages over the historian in the accumulation of his facts. He can do much to control environment; he can rule out chance and eliminate abnormal individuals; he can repeat his experiments, using plants, fruit flies, and guinea pigs, with great rapidity. The historian may watch Middletown for a generation, but he cannot isolate it under a glass bell or increase the tempo with which it changes. Yet this is a difference in the conditions of work, not in the basic character of the work. Both historian and biologist are dealing with life in time, and have to grapple with factors that are a mixture of the scrutable and inscrutable; for this reason history is at bottom as much a science as biology. Nor must we push too far the statement that history never repeats itself. While no situation reproduces itself in detail, many reproduce themselves, as we have said, in outline. Any tariff fight brings a body of lobbyists to Washington and a movement for logrolling; every great war in Europe arouses furious partisanship in America; every wave of hard times gives vitality to radicalism. The statesman should be the last person to underrate the scientific element in history, for much of his success will depend upon his proper scrutiny of it.

III

If some extremists minimize too much the rôle of science or law in history, others greatly exaggerate it. A considerable number of writers swallow unreservedly the mechanical view which considers it a regular process of evolution, a series of inevitable results proceeding from clear causes. Its principal phenomena seem to them nearly as predictable a growth as the succession of plant-forms in a cut-over tract of woodland. They hold that certain great facts and forces bring on other forces as logical, almost inescapable, sequels. These historians exhaust their ingenuity to prove that the establishment of the Norman Empire was bound to occur; that all the elements were present in England and Normandy to produce it, and that if William the Conqueror had not done it, someone else would. William, they hold, played about as important a part as Rostand's Chantecler, who thought that his crow evoked the sunrise. They maintain that the growth of the medieval papacy was an equally inevitable process. They urge, again, that the Reformation resulted from the evolution of certain economic, social, and intellectual forces, and that it produced Luther — that Luther did not produce it; had Luther never lived, someone else much like him would have arisen. They argue at length that the American Civil War, as a collision between two economies and two cultures, was an evolutionary event, not a cataclysm. Chance played no part in it, and given the main forces of the day, it was absolutely logical.

The holders of this view can point to many striking facts to support their emphasis upon the scientific basis of history. They assert, for example, that America owed its discovery not to Columbus but to various inventions and forces which would have effected it at that very time had Columbus never lived. Pedro Alvarez de Cabral, sailing from Portugal to India in 1500, was blown westward to the coast of Brazil; he might well have taken Columbus's place in history. And had it not been

Cabral, the improvements in navigation, the irresistible thrust of commerce, would soon have produced somebody else.

But this view can be pushed to the point at which it becomes demonstrably false. It underrates the powerful rôle which fortune or accident plays in history. After all, events frequently present themselves not as a logical chain, but a fortuitous string of occurrences, affected by chances of a thousand kinds. A sudden illness; a change in weather; the loss of a document; a man's or woman's whim suggested by a mere accident — these have altered the very face of history. "For want of a shoe the horse was lost," and the battle and the kingdom. It has been said by H. A. L. Fisher that the destiny of Egypt was changed by the fact that in 1884 Sir Evelyn Baring (Lord Cromer) had a severe cold which temporarily cost him his voice, so that at Cairo he could not impress upon Gordon all the instructions he was to follow at Khartoum. Like Shakespeare, we may call the chances of history Providence, which shapes our ends rough-hew them how we may; like the Orientals, we may call them Kismet. But President Franklin D. Roosevelt was right when, facing an audience at the Harvard Tercentenary during the great depression, he told them that they ought to wear their worries with a difference; for they knew enough history to realize that misfortune, like fortune, seldom comes from the quarter in which it is apprehended.

The most prominent of the fortuitous chances of history is the intermittent appearance of commanding personalities, of great men. We need not accept the whole view of the school of historians founded by Thomas Carlyle; the school which makes little of the "dull multitude" and much of the "hero," and protests with asperity against the Darwinian view of history as altogether too mechanical. Carlyle was shocked by the materialism inherent in the doctrine that the masses stumble upward to a better order by a process of evolution. He believed that a living spirit guides the race, and that this spirit is best embodied in the great leaders — whether the hero as soldier, the hero as saint, or the hero as man of letters. All wholesome aspiration, in the opinion of Carlyleans, must look up to the wisdom of these select archetypes; it is unwholesome to rely upon "blind laws" as agencies of progress. An opposite view is expounded by writers like John Richard Green and John Bach McMaster, who write history in terms of whole peoples, not select leaders. The greater truth is probably with them, and with their belief that the "hero" is usually important not in himself but as an expression of the *Zeitgeist*. But into this hoary quarrel we need not at the moment enter. It is sufficient to say that the Carlylean gospel, though often pushed too far, has a decided element of truth in it. As Sir Charles Oman states, it is easier to go wrong by denying the importance of the hero's rôle than by exaggerating it.[1]

For beyond doubt some personalities have been — to use Oman's word — "cataclysmic." It is easy to conceive that Philip of Macedon might have left behind him a son as weak as Oliver Cromwell left in his son Richard. Had he done so, had there been no Alexander the Great, history would have recorded no Macedonian conquest of Asia Minor and Persia, no establishment of Greek kingdoms as far east as the Oxus, no clearance of the way for the Roman Empire, and no such annexation of Egypt and Syria to the Western world as was the fact for eight hundred years after Alexander's death. The course of all ancient and medieval history would have been profoundly different. Suppose, on the other hand, that Cromwell's son and heir had possessed the genius of Alexander. What might not have been the dominating rôle of England in Western Europe in the years following 1658? A still more striking illustration of the "cataclysmic" personality is afforded by Mahomet. The founder of Islam profoundly influenced the course of world history, and he is the only Arabian who ever did so. What was there in the relatively monotonous

[1] Sir Charles Oman, "Cataclysmic History," address to the 23rd annual meeting of the British Historical Association

and unambitious history of the Arabian tribes in the fifth and sixth centuries to suggest that they would suddenly become leaders in a great world movement? What cultural, religious, and political factors existed in the Arabic peninsula when this son of a poor Mecca trader appeared which would make his spectacular career an inevitable response to social law? Almost none; the only general factor which helps to explain Mahomet was a religious ferment which, with the advent of Christianity and Judaism, had seized upon part of Arabia just before his birth. On the whole, he was as unaccountable a phenomenon of nature as an earthquake or a tornado. And history presents not a few such cataclysmic personalities — Peter the Great, Napoleon, Lenin.

The true path is a middle path. By careful research we can attempt to decide what part of history is due to evolution or law, and what part is explicable in terms of a natural process — and unquestionably this is a much larger part than was once supposed. The remainder, we can say, is due to chance, or at any rate is inexplicable. As we ascertain more facts about the past, and as we bring various modern sciences, such as psychology, economics, and sociology, to bear upon them, we are able to assign more of history to the operation of known principles. That is, we are able to increase its scientific character. We can thus analyze the great natural processes of history much better than Gibbon or Voltaire; historians a century hence will be able to analyze them much better than we. The chief interest of history lies in accounting for past events by a reasoned array of causes, and in refusing to admit that mere fortuity produced them until we have no alternative.

What caused the rapid spread of Christianity after the sudden conversion of Saul of Tarsus on the road to Damascus in A.D. 34 or 35? Was it sheer bad fortune, as many pagans thought? Was it Providence acting in ways inscrutable to man, as the church fathers taught? Of course we know that it was neither. Gibbon gives us a partial list of the true causes. He enumerates the facilities of communication created by the Roman Empire; the zeal of many Jews for the new religion; the widespread acquaintance of the ancient world with the doctrine of the immortality of the soul; the virtues of the first Christians; and the persecutions by Roman officials, making the blood of the martyrs the seed of the church. A fuller acquaintance with historical causes has enabled later writers to elaborate upon Gibbon's list. They enumerate the wide diffusion of Judaism and Jews, furnishing a ready soil; the close kinship between Hellenistic syncretism and Christian doctrine; and the vigorous expansion of Mithraic religion, whose ceremonies — baptism to remove sins, anointment, a sacred meal of bread and water, the use of consecrated wine — strongly resembled some of the rites used by Christians. Yet when we have taken account of these and other logical causes, one non-logical element remains. What if Saul had never undergone the experience, mystical or pathological, on the Damascus road? For Saul by his personal force revolutionized the ideas held by the leaders of the Church upon its future development. He took a movement that might easily have been restricted to the reformation of Judaism, and transformed it into a great new evangel which, as Jesus had apparently intended, was fitted for worldwide acceptance. But for the "cataclysmic" personality of Saul, what might Christianity have been like?

So we may follow various movements through history. We can today account by logical and orderly causes for much that formerly seemed mysterious. We can show that the Saracens were not turned back merely because Charles Martel was a better soldier than Abd-el-Rahman at Poitiers in A.D. 732, but for better and far more complex reasons. We can explain the rise and fall of feudalism without reference to individuals or to accidental events. We can account by logical social causes for the development of Jacksonian democracy, and can reduce the credit to be assigned to its idol and exemplar, Andrew Jackson himself. Scientific history is constantly advancing in its work of making the past more logical, orderly, and comprehensible. But when scientific research and interpretation have done their utmost, we must still give a powerful emphasis to chance and to the "cataclysmic" personality.

IV

Just as there are dogmatists who exaggerate the domain of the scientific in history and dogmatists who deny it any domain at all, so there are dogmatists who would hem in the field of historical presentation by narrow rules. They would have the historian write in a certain way or not at all. The demand most frequently advanced by such writers is that history be kept absolutely impartial and unbiassed. In the preface to his highly detailed life of Lincoln, Albert J. Beveridge states that absolute disinterestedness can and should be secured. "Facts when justly arranged interpret themselves," he remarks. "They tell the story." This is an echo of what Lord Acton said of Von Ranke's emphasis upon absolute impartiality: "He taught us to be critical, *to be colorless*, to be new."

In answer to this it may be confidently affirmed that no important history has yet appeared which did not reveal some bias, and that in the very greatest of histories the element of partiality is strong. Even Beveridge did not dare say that "facts interpret themselves"; he wrote that "facts *when justly arranged* interpret themselves." But when the same facts can be arranged in an order tending to prove that Lincoln in 1854-56 was more statesmanlike than Douglas (as Lord Charnwood arranges them), or in an order indicating that Douglas was more the statesman (as Beveridge arranges them), who shall say which is the *just* arrangement? Facts cannot be selected without some personal conviction as to what is truth, and cannot be arranged without the same conviction — and this conviction is a bias. In historical writing, as in current politics, what seems to one man a principle may seem to equally honest students a mere prejudice. Ulrich B. Phillips and Frederic

Bancroft were in possession of much the same body of facts regarding slavery; they were both thoroughly honest, and determined to tell the uncolored truth as they saw it; but one arrived at friendly, the other at hostile conclusions upon slavery as an institution. The best answer to Beveridge's rash statement is his own book. Every true historian has a mind formed by practical experience and observation, and Beveridge's was highly formed. He held likes and dislikes, trusts and distrusts, convictions and disbeliefs; some topics especially interested him, and some bored him. A Westerner, reared in a State which united Northern and Southern blood, of progressive and expansive temperament, he responded more readily to Douglas's desire to throw open the West on a popular-sovereignty basis than to the Free Soil demand for restrictions on Western settlement. The mental thrust and firmness which had made him a political leader carried these predilections over to give a sharp individuality to his history.

Of course it is important that the historian have what the French call an *intelligence déliée*, a mind free from conscious prejudices. Some pseudo-historical writers take pleasure in absolutely closed minds. Mr. Hilaire Belloc's, for example, is barred and shuttered against any ray of light on matters touching the Catholic Church; he delights in his prejudices, and writes for other willfully prejudiced minds. Other pseudo-historians know precisely what they are going to write before they examine the evidence. It is impossible to examine Mr. Walter Millis's *Road to War* conscientiously without feeling that the author did not so much arrange his judgments to fit the data as he arranged the data to fit his preconceived judgments. Fortunately it is seldom impossible to draw a clear line between honest conviction on the one side and prejudice or preconception on the other; for it is not difficult to detect the warping of evidence which the latter involves. Conviction rules out absolute impartiality, but nevertheless aims at truth. An examination of the work of the greatest historians shows that it not merely lacks absolute objectivity, but owes much of its greatness to its conviction.

Macaulay would assuredly have penned a history of England much poorer in color, narrative power, and portraiture had he not written as a Whig, an earnest officer of a party in whose rapid rise he played his part as member of Parliament and Cabinet Minister. To be sure, he sometimes carried his adjectives and epigrams too far, giving a certain basis for the criticism that his work is "a huge Whig pamphlet"; but this was the excess of an honest quality. Grote's history of Greece was originally conceived as an answer to the extreme Tory views expressed by Mitford in his earlier history. He held advanced democratic ideas, he had helped carry the Reform Bill to enactment, and he wished to right the wrong which he believed Mitford had done to free institutions. No small part of the warmth and inspiration of his work flows from his close sympathy with democratic tendencies in Greece and ardent dislike of Greek aristocracy. No reader of Gibbon needs to be told that he was strongly biassed in the sense of holding intense convictions. The most vital pages of the *Decline and Fall*, the section most frequently read, are the famous fifteenth and sixteenth chapters ("Progress of the Christian Religion" and "Conduct of the Roman Government Toward the Christians"); where, under the veil of a grave and deliberate irony, he arraigns Christianity as the principal dissolvent of ancient civilization. An equally important conviction was his firm belief, which modern research has shown to be mistaken, that the Byzantine Empire was weak and miserable, and that the degeneracy, cruelty, and factionalism associated with the very name Byzantium made the study of events at Constantinople of minor importance. This conviction, which at points became a prejudice, weakens the whole later part of Gibbon's history.[1] But who would care to read a Gibbon who possessed no strong convictions, who aimed at absolute objectivity even if he sacrificed color and

[1] See James Cotter Morison, *Gibbon*, pp. 144 ff.

drama, and whose personality counted for nothing in his history?

Illustrations of the same truth may be found among our own historians. Parkman held powerful innate convictions of a racial and religious character. He believed English civilization superior to French; the Protestant religion more favorable to free institutions than the Catholic. His history of the contest for North America makes it clear that he deemed the victory of the English-speaking folk a profound blessing. He never pushed this conviction across the line of prejudice, or failed to do justice to either French or Catholic. His *Jesuits of North America* is on the whole a magnificent tribute to the missionaries of that creed, and he brings out all the heroic qualities of La Salle, Frontenac, and Montcalm. But the underlying conviction flows as a strong pulse through all his books. The same racial and religious beliefs give color and energy to much of Prescott's work. When we turn to Bancroft, we encounter a different form of bias, for he felt a passionate American nationalism, and an equally powerful devotion to egalitarian democracy. As J. Franklin Jameson has said, all his histories voted for Jackson. And similar illustrations might be multiplied by reference to the modern historians of Continental Europe. Heinrich Von Treitschke, successor of the "colorless" Von Ranke as Prussian state historian, was an ardent believer in German unity, who resigned his chair at Freiburg when Baden joined Austria in the Austro-German War, and went to Berlin. He held a profound belief in a centralized monarchy, in the Prussian ideal of the state, and in the conquering mission of Germany. These beliefs, expressed with sincerity and high ability, colored his *Deutsche Geschichte* more to its advantage than its disadvantage.

Impartial annalists and monograph-writers we may have; but the impartial historian, using the noun in its highest signification, does not exist. If history became impartial in the sense of lacking conviction it would be a poor affair. The only completely unbiassed historian is one whose works are not on the shelves of libraries — the Recording Angel; and doubtless he has convictions which to Satan, as Mark Twain irreverently suggested, would seem prejudices. The chief difficulty with history which sacrifices conviction to an exaggerated ideal of impartiality is that it often falls into a cold, colorless, and timid character. Such history is likely to lack large architectural elements, for nothing imparts structure to a book like the attempt to prove a thesis. It is likely to lack fervor; likely to lack proportion. It will frequently fail to distinguish between what is important and what is unimportant because it has no fixed standard of measurement; and it will frequently refuse to pass even elementary moral judgments, though a great historian is always a great moralist. It was an "objective" historian who wrote the unconsciously humorous sentence: "The Turks sawed the Commandant and his wife in halves, and committed other grave breaches of international law." Perhaps the most striking example of the completely impartial historian in English is Samuel Rawson Gardiner. His work has almost every merit that laborious research, taken alone, can give it; and it treats the most controversial period in English history from an absolutely non-partisan standpoint. But he is so flat and colorless that his readers have dwindled to a handful, and most of his history of England 1603–56 is now completely out of print. What influence has his impartial biography of Cromwell exercised in comparison with Carlyle's book on the same leader, full of the strongest basic opinions? Carlyle's powerful book has formed almost the whole modern conception of Cromwell.

Here again, as in writing of scientific history, we have to take care with our definitions. The historian should avoid bias in the sense of prejudice; he should court it in the sense of honest conviction. That conviction should follow, not precede, a study of the evidence, and be formed during and by the historian's researches. In brief, the author should approach his evidence as a judge, but should present it as a guarded and honest advocate. It is his duty to form judgments, but even more his duty to avoid *prejudging* the evidence. Beyond question even Von Ranke, the leading exponent of colorless history, did not succeed in being wholly objective; much of his work was unconsciously written from the standpoint of the conservative reaction of his time in Prussia. When he criticized George Bancroft's democratic point of view, Bancroft might have retorted in kind. Beyond question no writer can wholly emancipate his mind from the coloring influence of time, environment, education, current ideals, personal ambitions, and national trends. But that does not exempt him from the duty of striving to attain the greatest possible degree of objectivity and impartiality. Truth is promoted by a clash of honest judgment. After Mitford and Grote have had their say, a Bury or a Droysen finds his ground better cleared and his ideas illuminated by their controversy. After the clash of Clarendon and Carlyle on the character of Cromwell, C. H. Firth can draw a more accurate portrait. But the clash of mere prejudice retards the truth.

It is a defeatist gospel which would have the historian, on the ground that he can never wholly purify his mind from preconceptions, abandon the attempt altogether, and commit himself instead to a philosophy in accordance with which he will deliberately write. Charles A. Beard has urged that American scholars turn to "the task of exploring the assumptions upon which the selection and organization of historical fact proceed," not with the object of reducing the rôle of assumption, but with that of enlarging and emphasizing it.[1] The implication is that one set of assumptions would be chosen as sounder than another set, and an effort would be made to organize historical writing upon this set of preconceptions. This is the doctrine to which historical writing has bowed under state pressure in Nazi Germany and Fascist Italy; it is a doctrine which regards

---

[1] See Charles A. Beard, "That Noble Dream," *American Historical Review*, XLI, 74–87 (October, 1935).

truth as purely relative and pragmatic. Those who have a higher ideal of truth will, while admitting that their effort to attain it is often doomed to failure, never give up the attempt. Historians have often come close — human frailties considered — to unprejudiced truth in the past; they can often do so in the future.

V

Under the general heading of style the dogmatist has also had his say, chiefly in condemning a highly literary treatment of history. Should the historian cultivate literary art, even arti-fice? Or is it the business of history simply to be "scientific," "scholarly," and "exhaustive," to disdain ornament in an ef-fort to bring the dry white light of truth to bear upon the past? One would think a decision in favor of literary art might be taken for granted. Yet it has had its enemies, some of them writers of prominence. "If economics is the dismal science," asserted Freeman, "history is and ought to be the dull science." An almost equally sweeping statement has been made by James Harvey Robinson.[1] A large school of plodding research workers in history not merely disdain literary "brilliance," but condemn it as pernicious — as leading to subtle perversions of the truth. Their ideal of history is not Mommsen, Guizot, or Macaulay, but the slow, heavily-documented page of William Stubbs, the laborious array of marshalled facts in Herbert L. Osgood, the grim drabness of Heinrich von Sybel's monograph on the Cru-sades. Their hostility to art or inability to achieve it led Philip Guedalla to speak of the style of modern historians in England and America as an occupational disease; the style of the smooth, monotonous French historians as one long Taine without a turning.

Literary artifice is indeed often carried too far by the more popular historians. It results in invented conversations, par-ticularly frequent in much popular biography; in invented or

[1] So, also, by that admirable and highly respected historian Charles M. Andrews

twisted details, thrown in for color; and in the over-dramatiza-
tion of situations. It must also be remembered that the degree
of literary art possible, or legitimate, depends greatly upon the
subject. The history of charities in the United States, the
financial history of England or France, are not themes which
offer scope for stylistic ornament or eloquence. On the other
hand, Thierry's history of the Norman invasion would almost
kindle the dullest pen. But even with dull subjects, literary
skill adds not merely to readability, but to historical values.
It supplies the difference between a clear and a murky landscape. A comparison of Von Holst's dull constitutional history
of the United States with F. W. Maitland's sparkling, graceful
writings on the legal history of Britain will quickly demonstrate
this fact. Scholarliness and thoroughness are high ideals, but
scholarliness combined with literary skill constitutes an ideal
far higher. In almost any subject some literary values exist —
Gladstone could render a speech on the fiscal affairs of England
fascinating; Woodrow Wilson and Walter Bagehot made their
semi-historical analyses of Congressional and Parliamentary
Government almost as interesting as romantic history. The
methods by which historical masters develop these values are
as interesting as the methods by which they extract the truth
from an obscure document, or decide between two contradic-
tory pieces of evidence.

There is a sense in which the highest kind of historical truth
cannot be found without literary art, and in which every historical writer must cultivate his artistic faculties as a means of
ascertaining truths. It requires imagination to penetrate the
past. The historian who best understands Hannibal, as Sidney
Smith wrote, is the man who sees the brilliancy of Hannibal's
single eye; the best record of his campaigns will be written by
the writer who audibly hears the clash and jingle of the rings
stripped from Roman dead that Hannibal's messenger emptied
on the floor of the Carthaginian Senate after Cannae. The
historian who best understands De Soto's exploration of the

Southwest is the man who feels with his own hand the warmth of the sluggish Mississippi as De Soto plunges his arm into it over the side of his boat. It requires imagination to fuse the materials of history into a malleable whole, glowing with life. Realities are seldom dull; they seem so simply because some writers bring a dull mind and heart to them.

In this sense we may well quarrel with James Harvey Robinson's harsh statement of the literary restrictions which should hedge in the historian. "Fiction and Drama," he declares in *The New History*, "are perfectly free to conceive and adjust detail so as to meet the demands of art, but the historian should always be conscious of the rigid limitations placed upon him. If he confines himself to an honest and critical statement of a series of events as described in his sources, it is usually too deficient in vivid authentic detail to make a satisfactory story." Certainly if the historian can attain vividness only by inventing statements, he had better leave vividness out. He should not give excuse for such a gibe as Mark Twain's at the reconstructed dinosaur, "three bones and a dozen barrels of plaster." But Mr. Robinson went entirely too far in saying that the sources are "usually" too meagre to permit of vivid authentic detail. That is true of much (by no means all) medieval history; it is emphatically not true of later times. Memoirs, letters, diaries, public documents, newspapers, provide for the greater part of modern history a wealth of vivid detail. Moreover, a great deal of vivid detail is usually *inherent* in the situation itself and in the environment, social and physical — detail of the most authentic kind. The truly imaginative historian perceives this authentic detail, his more prosaic fellow does not. The gulf of difference that lies between the neglect and the masterly use of such detail may be briefly illustrated in the two following extracts — the first from a mere compiler, the second from a historian of high literary talent:

Braddock's expedition had set out from Turtle Creek on the Monongahela on the ninth of June — twelve hundred men. The objective point was Fort Duquesne, "which can hardly detain me above three or four days," remarked the dull curmudgeon. No scouts were thrown out; they walked straight into the ambuscade.[1]

It was the tenth of June before the army was well on its march. Three hundred axemen led the way, to cut and clear the road; and the long train of packhorses, wagons, and cannon toiled on behind, over the stumps, roots, and stones of the narrow track, the regulars and provincials marching in the forest close on either side. Squads of men were thrown out on the flanks, and scouts ranged the woods to guard against surprise; for, with all his scorn of Indians and Canadians, Braddock did not neglect reasonable precautions. Thus, foot by foot, they advanced into the waste of lonely mountains that divided the streams flowing to the Atlantic from those flowing to the Gulf of Mexico — a realm of forests ancient as the world. The road was but twelve feet wide, and the line of march often extended four miles. It was like a thin, long parti-colored snake, red, blue, and brown, trailing slowly through the depth of leaves, creeping round inaccessible heights, crawling over ridges, moving always in dampness and shadow, by rivulets and waterfalls, crags and chasms, gorges and shaggy steeps. In glimpses only, through jagged boughs and flickering leaves, did this wild primeval world reveal itself, with its dark green mountains, flecked with the morning mist, and its distant summits pencilled in dreamy blue. The army passed the main Alleghany, Meadow Mountain, and Great Savage Mountain, and traversed the funereal pine-forest afterwards called the Shades of Death. No attempt was made to interrupt their march, though the commandant of Fort Duquesne had sent out parties for that purpose. A few French and Indians hovered about them, now and then scalping a straggler or inscribing filthy insults on trees; while others fell upon the border settlements which the advance of the troops had left defenceless. Here they were more successful, butchering about thirty persons, chiefly women and children.[2]

No memoir or diary of Braddock's march supplies such details as the stumps, roots, and stones of the narrow track, the

---

[1] Julian Hawthorne, *History of the United States*, Vol. I
[2] Parkman, *Montcalm and Wolfe*, Ch. VII

parti-colored snakelike column, red, blue, and brown, the omnipresent shade and dampness of the shaggy primeval forest, the glimpses through flickering June leaves of distant summits pencilled in dreamy blue. They were inherent in the situation and Parkman's imagination extracted them. They give his paragraph a vitality — a reality — that lift it to a plane of the highest truth; a truth far greater than Julian Hawthorne's, chained to a few flat facts. Parkman's history shows just how, even when sources are meagre, the "vivid authentic detail" which Dr. Robinson thought out of reach may often be supplied; and it shows how literary art, with its triple support of imagination, vivid language, and graceful periods, is not merely a valuable ally of history, but is indispensable to its highest attainments.

CHAPTER THREE

PRIMITIVE MATERIALS FOR HISTORY

THERE IS a vivid page in one of James Ford Rhodes's essays which is full of suggestion as to the variety and antiquity of materials for history. He relates how, spending a day at the great Pyramids, he first filled his eyes and mind with the novelty of the spectacle; and then, his initial curiosity satisfied, "found nothing so gratifying to the historic sense as to gaze on these most wonderful monuments of human industry, constructed certainly 5,000 years ago, and to read at the same time the account that Herodotus gave of his visit there about 2,350 years before the date of my own." [1] That evening, going to his modern and garish Cairo hotel, he took up the latest issue of the London *Times*. It contained an account of the annual meeting of the Royal Historical Society, including a report of a carefully-prepared address by the president on Herodotus, pointing out the value of the Greek writer as a model to modern historians. This newspaper report was reinforced by an editorial article upon the merits of Herodotus and the lessons he conveyed to current European writers. "I ended the day with the reflection of what a space in the world's history Herodotus filled, himself describing the work of 2600 years before his own time and being dilated upon in 1894 by one of the most modern of nineteenth century newspapers." In this page are mentioned at least four different types of material for history — the great Pyramids, hoary with fifty centuries; the first truly illustrious chronicler of ancient times; the proceedings of a historical

[1] James Ford Rhodes, *Historical Essays*, pp. 35 ff.

society; and a modern newspaper. In addition, Rhodes's own paragraph is a bit of material interesting to the social historian.

The two basic elements in history are a body of more or less trustworthy materials, and a critical method applied to them. History was not born — it could not be born — until both these elements came into existence.

Of the latter, the critical spirit, we shall have much to say later, and it is necessary here only to make a brief general statement. Everyone with much experience of the world knows how difficult is the ascertainment of truth even in matters of immediate record. We are soon taught how hard it is to trust the letter we receive from a real-estate agent, a politician, even, alas! some friends. Coming from a public meeting, we are astonished by the garbled account published in the newspapers. If we have passed forty, we find acquaintances writing self-justificatory memoirs over which we shake our heads. It is often difficult to obtain an exact account of even a simple transaction witnessed by a large body of observers; courtroom trials are constantly proving the fact. Ingenious psychologists like Hugo Munsterberg have arranged that some disturbance should occur unexpectedly before the eyes of watchers, have demanded written narratives of it, and have shown that the records differ in an astonishing degree. The happenings in Ford's Theatre just after the shot which killed Lincoln, though observed by a large audience, have been the theme of angry dispute. After the Wall Street bomb explosion of September, 1920, several of the nine eye-witnesses testified that numerous vehicles had been in the block, one declaring he had counted nine; three witnesses asserted positively that they had seen a red motor-truck carrying the bomb! Yet it was finally proved that only two vehicles were in the block, and that the explosion occurred on a small horse-cart. If the truth about what happened under so many eyes in Ford's Theatre and at noonday on Wall Street is difficult to obtain, what about the truth of events in 1775, or 1492, or 55 B.C.? A critical attitude toward the materials of history is absolutely indispensable.

Hence it is, as Lord Acton declared, that it is far more important to possess the historical spirit — a doubting, critical mind, which demands proofs and verification — than to have a mass of historical learning. The beginning of wisdom in history is doubt. Its votaries should be imbued with the mental toughness of Bret Harte's M'liss, who, told in school that Joshua had bidden the sun to stand still and it had obeyed him, shut her astronomy with a loud snap and defiantly asserted: "It's a damn lie. I don't believe it." The true historical scholar is not the man who spills facts out of every pocket, who can tell instantly when Nicholas of Cusa lived and what were the contents of the Constitutions of Clarendon — matters on which an encyclopaedia can furnish more precise and interesting information. It is the man who, confronted with facts, assertions, and testimony offered with varying degrees of authority, knows how to test them, discard what seems false, and evaluate what seems true.

True history was impossible until this skeptical attitude had been sufficiently developed for application to myth, tradition, and the firmer materials of history. Although the admiration of James Ford Rhodes and the London *Times* for Herodotus was not misapplied, it must be admitted that the Greek was woefully lacking in this spirit. His work is a storehouse of mingled fact and fable, a strange mixture of intelligent first-hand observation and uncritical credulity. In his rich and fascinating narrative the myths of the Greeks, the hearsay tales of other ancient peoples, are often swallowed whole. He accepts the old legends of Croesus, of Proteus, of Battus, and of Labda in childlike spirit. With unquestioning faith, for example, he describes the reputed visit of the great Athenian sage, Solon, to the court of Croesus at Sardis — a visit which perhaps took place, for the Lydian king was a munificent patron of arts and letters. Herodotus tells how Croesus asked Solon whom he considered the happiest man of his acquaintance, expecting the complimentary answer "Croesus"; but how Solon resolutely abstained from flattery, remarking that no life could be called happy until it ended, and that the best examples of felicity were furnished by men like Tellus, who had died victoriously in battle. He further narrates that years later, when Croesus had lost his kingdom to Cyrus and was awaiting death in the flames, he remembered this conversation with the Athenian, and cried out: "Solon, Solon, Solon!" — which cry, being explained to Cyrus, won him a pardon. It is a pretty tale — but is it true? Herodotus felt an uncritical reverence for all that pertained to religion, and accepted sacred or moralistic stories as easily as medieval historians swallowed the miracles of the saints.

To be sure, even in Herodotus we find some beginnings of skepticism and the historical spirit. He presents certain materials for what they are worth. Describing the temple of Jupiter Belus in Babylon, and writing, "In the time of Cyrus there was likewise in this temple the figure of a man, twelve cubits high, entirely of solid gold," he hastily adds: "I myself did not see this figure, but I repeat what the Chaldeans report concerning it." He also takes the picturesque legend of Io, and gives us to understand that the Greeks and Phoenicians presented it in two radically different versions. According to the Greeks, Io was vestal or priestess of Hera at Argos. Zeus fell in love with her, and when Hera's jealousies were excited, tried to avoid them by transforming her into a cow. After some complications, Hera sent a gadfly which drove Io into Egypt, where she was restored to her original form, and became the mother of Epaphus — one of a line of heroes. But the Phoenicians told a more realistic story. They declared that Io was simply a wayward young woman of Argos who became the paramour of a Phoenician sea-captain; she eloped with him, wishing to conceal her pregnancy, and was carried in his ship to Egypt, where she gave birth to a son. Of course neither story has historical value, and by setting them side by side Herodotus perhaps intended to show this.

But it is in Thucydides, writing a short generation later than Herodotus, that the historical spirit first appears. He made essentially the same critical demands upon history as those which animate modern writers, and pursued much the same objects. His aim, he declared, was to give an accurate narrative of important and interesting events, and to teach lessons of value for the future — to hold the lamp of the past at the stumbling feet of mankind. Approaching the Peloponnesian War in this spirit, his method was one of thorough research, skeptical examination, and patient verification. When dealing with the conflict, in which he had fought and been cashiered, he relied primarily upon personal observation and the questioning of eye-witnesses; but for preceding events he had to use other writers. In his first pages he assails these early compilers and chroniclers for their indolence and credulity. His own ruling principle, as he asserts, was very different, and he has given us a classic statement of the importance of a critical attitude:

And with reference to the narrative of events, far from permitting myself to derive it from the first sources that came to hand, I did not even trust my own impressions, but it rests partly on what I saw myself, partly on what others saw for me, the accuracy of the report being always tried by the most severe and detailed tests possible. My conclusions have cost me some labor from the want of coincidence between accounts of the same occurrence by different eye-witnesses, arising sometimes from imperfect memory, sometimes from undue partiality for one side or the other. The absence of romance from my history will, I fear, detract somewhat from its interest; but if it be judged useful by those inquirers who desire an exact knowledge of the past as an aid to the interpretation of the future, which in the course of human things must resemble if it does not reflect it, I shall be content. In fine, I have written my work, not as an essay to win the applause of the moment, but as a possession for all time.[1]

[1] Richard Crawley's translation, Bk. I, Ch. 1

Since Thucydides blazed the way, true history has never deviated from the high-road that follows the line of his thorough and skeptical method.

II

But before critical methods can be applied, we must first have the materials for history; and as James Ford Rhodes's paragraph suggests, the earliest of these materials antedated Herodotus not merely by centuries, but tens of centuries. The accumulation of these materials is one of the great romances of man's activity on the planet. For ages it was an exceedingly slow process, and for many centuries even after written history began the materials grew but slowly and clumsily. In the ancient world it was only for a comparatively brief time and in a few places that really large bodies of material ever existed. Then in the middle ages came a long period of poverty and darkness. Only in late modern times have materials become voluminous. Indeed, their first production and preservation in large quantities came near to coinciding with that Age of Enlightenment of which we have hitherto spoken as the parent of modern history. Lord Acton, in his inaugural lecture at Cambridge in 1895, spoke of the immense change that had occurred even within a century, so that "where Hallam had no diplomatist but Barillon, his successors command the correspondence of ten countries." He spoke, and justifiably, of an entirely new era in history — the documentary age. As a prelude to the examination of the critical tests used in historical study, let us review briefly the romance of which we have spoken — the romance of man's accumulation of data upon his own past.

The sources for history, originally confined to few and simple categories, have gradually become more complex in character and will continue to do so. They may now be listed in half a dozen broad groups. One is made up of physical remains, of which James Ford Rhodes's Pyramids are a salient example. Another comprises such orally transmitted material as legends, ballads, sagas, and traditions — material of the type so undiscriminatingly used by Herodotus. A third is the more elementary and durable kinds of representative material, such as chiselled stones, stamped coins, woven tapestries, vases, and sculptures. Then come hand-written materials, including papyri, bricks bearing cuneiform writing, vellum or parchment manuscripts, and modern documents; and after this of course that vast group of materials made up of printed books and papers. The motion-picture film and phonograph-record may well come to be counted in a sixth category. To these must be added that great primary source of historical material, personal observation — either by the writer, or by people whom he interviews. It is not often realized how many of the great historians have dealt with events which passed in part under their own eyes, in part under the eyes of men they could easily consult. Among them have been not only Herodotus and Thucydides, but such other ancient writers as Polybius, Sallust, and Tacitus; such early modern writers as Guicciardini, Davila, Grotius, Clarendon, and Burnet; such late modern writers as Hanotaux, Treitschke, Winston Churchill, James Schouler, and James Ford Rhodes. The writing of contemporaneous history has its special difficulties, but also its rich advantages and rewards.

The picturesque possibilities of the first source listed above, physical remains, are too seldom realized. Their variety is immense — historic sites, roads, aqueducts, pyramids, fortifications, buildings ruined or whole, furniture, pottery, implements, weapons, and museum pieces of a hundred kinds. Usually they throw more light upon social and economic history than upon political history; usually, also, they are more valuable for the descriptive than the analytical elements in history. But even those who write of rulers and generals sometimes owe much to them. Thucydides in his accounts of battles displays a minute acquaintance with the topography of the fields. Even Livy made some slight use of them. He speaks of the breastplate dedicated by Cossus in 428 B.C. which he saw hanging in the temple of Jupiter Feretrius in Rome, much as a modern British historian might draw some significant fact from the armor of the Black Prince still sombrely depending in Canterbury Cathedral. A long list could be made of writers who in recent times have found physical remains rich in value. Even Parkman, writing the history of a region still largely wild and unpeopled, visited every battle-site and familiarized himself with every important bit of terrain. But it will suffice to quote what one scholar has written of Edward Freeman: [1]

He was an accurate observer, not only of the broad features of a country but of its ancient roads and earthworks, its prehistoric monuments, and its earlier and especially its ecclesiastical buildings. No man was better versed in the distinctive styles of Christian architecture, or had a better general knowledge of the earthworks from the study of which he might hope to correct or corroborate any written records, and by the aid of which he often infused life and reality into otherwise obscure narrations. . . . He visited every spot upon which the Conqueror is recorded to have set his foot, compared many of the strongholds of his followers with those they left behind them in Normandy, and studied the evidence of Domesday for their character and possessions. When writing upon Rufus he spent some time in visiting the afforested district of the New Forest, and sought for traces of the villages and churches said to have been depopulated or destroyed. . . . When he attended a provincial congress and had listened to the description of some local antiquity, some mound, or divisional earthbank, or semi-Saxon Church, he at once strove to show the general evidence to be deduced from them, and how it bore upon the boundaries or formation of some Celtic or Saxon province or diocese, if not upon the general history of the kingdom itself. . . . He thus did much to elevate the pursuits of the archaeologist, and to show the relation they bore to the far superior labours of the historian.

The largest single branch of the study of remains is archaeology, and it of course has many subbranches. A dis-

[1] James Bryce, *Biographical Studies*, pp. 266, 267, quoting George T. Clark

cussion of even the outlines of archaeological work in one of these fields — in the archaeology of primitive man, for example, or classical archaeology — would fill a large volume; and it is sufficient to say here that the rise of archaeology has run parallel with the rise of modern history, and that the same scientific spirit animates both. The discovery of Herculaneum in 1720 and Pompeii in 1748 opened the great age of classical archaeology; and during the lifetimes of Voltaire, Hume, and Gibbon the naïve antiquarian spirit which had at first dominated the study was rapidly supplanted by more adequate methods. Two men, the Count de Caylus, whose seven-volume work on antiquities appeared in 1752–54, and J. J. Winckelmann, whose history of ancient art was published a decade later, may be called respectively the prophet and founder of historical archaeology in the classical domain. Winckelmann enunciated the famous theory that the character of artistic creations is always in harmony with the spirit and events of their times. Britons were the first to undertake a well-organized and systematic exploration of ancient sites in Greece and Asia Minor, the splendid achievements of two scholars, Stuart and Revett, who issued a four-volume work on the antiquities of Athens, inspiring the Society of Dilettanti to send out an expedition to continue their work. It was as a result of this early British interest that Lord Elgin at the beginning of the nineteenth century removed the Parthenon sculptures to the British Museum. What Heinrich Schliemann later did for history at Troy, Mycenae, and Tiryns, what Sir Henry Layard did in Asia Minor, and what Sir Flinders Petrie in Egypt, is common knowledge.

Archaeology is of course a science in itself, its work to be performed by men who have received long training in that profession alone. Now and then, as the names of Stéphane Gsell and James H. Breasted remind us, an eminent historian will appear who is also an eminent archaeologist, but in general each study is a jealous mistress. The findings of specialists in some branches of archaeology are adding so rapidly to our knowledge of the past that the historian must depend upon expert judgment. It used to be held, for example, that the Mayas did all their carving with tools of obsidian, nephrite, and other stone; but recent workers have offered strong evidence that the Mayas had entered the bronze age and used copper implements as well.[1] The feats accomplished in our Southwest in ascertaining the precise time when the beams of the dwellings of prehistoric tribes were hewn and put in place, feats made possible by the new tree-dating method, are very remarkable. And when the expert archaeologist is also an expert ethnologist, he can sometimes do a great deal to penetrate the curtain that separates history from pre-history.

Lewis H. Morgan, for example, the father of American ethnology and an enthusiastic student of archaeology, undertook to reconstruct the extinct society of the Mound Builders from their half-obliterated embankments. His boldness excited the wonder of his contemporaries.[2] "If anyone were to say that, given a mound octagonal in shape, on the banks of a river, constructed in an age long gone by, science would tell us what sort of people had built it, the purpose for which it was built, how these people lived, where they came from, what sort of houses they constructed, how they defended themselves against their enemies, how many of them there were, and what became of them in the end — we should be inclined to imagine that any answers must be reached by guesswork" — so commented the *Nation*.[3] "But these are the questions proposed by Mr. Morgan, and . . . the process by which he resolves them is as strictly scientific as chemical analysis." Of course Morgan arrived only at what he called approximate solutions. He concluded that the Mound Builders were Indians who had reached the "middle status" of barbarism, like the Indians of the South-

[1] Cf. Theodore A. Willard, *The Lost Empire of the Itzaes and the Mayas* (1933).
[2] See Morgan's "Houses of the Mound-Builders," *North American Review*, July, 1876.
[3] N. Y. *Nation*, September 28, 1876

west, Old Mexico, and Central America. They came from
beyond the Mississippi to the Northwest. They had practised
communism and dwelt in houses of adobe brick — joint tenements with a ground floor ten to twelve feet high, closed up
solidly on the first floor externally for defence. In the Middle
West adobe was out of the question; and hence they built
their tenements on huge mounds, ten or twelve feet high, the
tenements themselves being made of wood with sloping walls
covered with mud or mortar. These made strong fortresses.
Since no traditional knowledge of these Mound Builders persisted among tribes east of the Mississippi, they must have
been ancient. Since the number of such remains is small, the
tribesmen must have been few. The Mound Builders finally
perished or withdrew, according to Morgan, because a warm
climate is necessary to a vigorous form of Indian communal
life. Of course in the sixty-odd years since Morgan wrote, his
conclusions have been modified, especially by newer evidence
that many mounds are mortuary or sacrificial; but his work
was extremely shrewd and illuminating for its time.

Yet while archaeology is a field for the expert, and for the
latest expert at that, this fact does not exempt the historical
student from doing careful labor of his own if he finds a topic
which involves archaeological lore. The example of Prescott
in writing his chapters on Mexican culture before the Conquest
is instructive. The ground in his day had been very imperfectly explored. Casting aside many pretentious writings as
mere moonshine speculation, he found Humboldt almost the
only authority of any solid value. After reading all the secondary works, he himself went to the primary sources. That
is, he studied the documentary collections of Lord Knares-
borough, the volumes of the *Antiquités Mexicaines*, the accounts,
whether manuscript or printed, of the early Spanish chroniclers,
and the works of all the keen-eyed travellers in Mexico and
Yucatan from Bernal Diaz to the moderns like John L. Stephens.
As he had given thorough study to the coins of Ferdinand and

Isabella's day, so now he spent equal effort upon the astronomy of the Aztecs. We find him writing: "Finished notes on the hieroglyphical part of the chapter — a hard, barren topic. And now on the astronomy — out of the frying-pan into the fire. I find it, however, not so hard to comprehend as I anticipated. Fortunately, the Aztec proficiency does not require a knowledge of the *Principia*. Still it was enough to task all my mathematics, and patience to boot. . . ." After nearly a century Prescott's chapters on Aztec culture yet stand in little need of revision, and the pains which he took carry a plain lesson.

To any understanding of the vague twilight beginnings of history, or of ancient times, the study of remains is fundamental; and if for later ages it holds a place subordinate to other materials, it is nevertheless important. The discerning eye will often find in architectural monuments the key to a whole age. Ruskin's *Stones of Venice* effectively illustrates his belief that the buildings and art of a people express their morals, their spiritual emotions, their manners and customs, and their national ideals; Henry Adams's *Mont St.-Michel and Chartres* uses two great shrines to penetrate to the soul of an era. No imaginative student of medieval times can visit Carcassone or Rothenburg without a blinding new illumination, while the spirit of the eighteenth century is preserved forever in the crescents and triangles of Bath. For a critical evaluation of remains, some students will need a knowledge of art, others of costume, others of weapons, and still others simply the ability to distinguish between a Telford and a Macadam road. A memorable statement of the way in which history lies written, half blotted, half plain, upon the very face of a great city, occurs in Victor Hugo's *Notre Dame de Paris:*

There is the Paris of Catherine de Medicis at The Tuileries, the Paris of Henry II at the Hôtel-de-Ville — two edifices which are still in fine taste; the palace of Henry IV at the Place Royale — a brick front, faced with stone, and roofed with slate, real tricolored houses; the Paris of Louis XIII at Val-de-Grâce — of architecture crushed and squat, with basket-handled vaults, big-bellied columns, and a humpbacked dome; the Paris of Louis XIV at the Pantheon — St. Peter's at Rome ill-copied, and the building has been awkwardly heightened, which has by no means rectified its lines; the Paris of the [First] Republic at the School of Medicine, a poor Greek and Roman style . . . ; the Paris of Napoleon at the Place Vendôme — sometime sublime, a brazen column composed of melted cannon; the Palace of the Restoration at the Bourse or Exchange — a colonnade very white, supporting a frieze very smooth; the whole square costing twenty millions of francs.

To each of these characteristic structures is allied, by similarity of style, manner, and disposition of parts, a certain number of houses scattered over the different quarters of town, which the eye of the connoisseur easily distinguishes and assigns to their respective dates. When a man understands the art of seeing, he can trace the spirit of an age and the features of a king even in the knocker on a door.

Even in a land so young as the United States the study of remains is an invaluable pillar of history. It is a gratifying fact that Americans, who used to let such monuments of the past as John Hancock's splendid house on Beacon Hill, Federal Hall in New York, and the first skyscraper in Chicago (the Home Insurance Building) perish without a qualm, have learned to appreciate the historical — or at least the sentimental — worth of such relics. Today we not only preserve Lincoln's birthplace and Mark Twain's boyhood home with pious care; we have erected skilful reproductions of colonial Williamsburg, the Harrodsburg fort, Old Salem on the Sangamon, Sutter's Fort at Sacramento, and the log-cabin settlement of Norwegian pioneers at Decorah, Iowa. We have a museum at Doylestown, Pa., which preserves specimens of agricultural apparatus, another at New Bedford devoted to whaling, and even one at Oshkosh which specializes in the products of fancy-work. A wealthy industrialist otherwise indifferent to history has brought to Greenfield, Michigan, the original laboratory of Thomas A. Edison at Menlo Park, the office in which Luther Burbank worked at Santa Rosa, California, a steam manufacturing plant

of the eighties, an old blacksmith shop, and an old country
store. Woodwork, hangings, and furnishings of American domestic interiors for various periods are to be found in numerous
museums. One may step into the authentic domestic atmosphere of the seventies as he enters the reproduction of Theodore
Roosevelt's birthplace, with much of his parents' furniture intact, in New York City.

III

Folklore and ballads are among the most beautiful and allur-
ing of the sources of history. They have the dewy freshness
of the morning of the human race upon them, for they have
sprung in the main from times and communities innocent of
written literature. The ballad in particular, which often throws
a bright prismatic light upon manners, customs, beliefs, and
primitive emotions, is the composition rather of a folk than of
an individual; it rose from the heart and lips of a whole people.
Like the fairy tales or *märchen*, much balladry goes back of
historic times to the immemorial past of European peoples.
Resemblances of story, incident, tone, and style all unite the
Scottish, Provençal, Scandinavian, Italian, German, and Slavic
folk-song and folk-tale and point to an extreme antiquity. Of
course, originating in the improvised song of the rustic dance
or warriors' feast, and then handed down through long centuries by shepherds, servants, nurses, and other simple folk,
the more ancient ballads contain no direct historical facts.
But the spirit of the long-gone peasant folk breathes in their
measures. As Andrew Lang wrote, they are "a voice from
secret places, from silent peoples, and from old times long dead."
They bind the Tennessee mountaineer to the Scottish borderer;
they bind both to peoples who migrated from Asia to Europe
in ages long forgotten; and for this reason as well as for the
spirit and eloquence which made Chevy Chase stir Sir Philip
Sidney like a trumpet, they hold an unfailing magic.
Even the more recent ballad compositions usually contain

little explicit and authentic fact, but they are none the less valuable. Was there really a Sir Patrick Spens? Was he actually wrecked in the Orkneys? How much explicit truth resides in the ballad of Chevy Chase, which obviously contains incidents drawn from the real battle of Otterburn? It appears that this ballad is full of confusion, and indeed is founded upon confusion. Henry Morley writes: "In the warfare against English settlements in France a raid was called by the French allies of Scotland a *chevauchee*, and by a common process, that name was corrupted into Chevy Chase. It lives yet among schoolboys as a 'chivy.' Now, since there are in Northumberland Cheviot Hills, as well as an Otterburn, Chevy Chase was interpreted into the hunting of the Cheviot. The old ballad of the 'Battle of Otterburn,' of 'Chevy Chase'—the battle of the *chevauchee* which was its cause—was therefore recast as 'The Hunting of the Cheviot,' always with some confused sense of identity between one incident and the other. The battle of Otterburn is an incident that arose out of a hunting on the Cheviots." But despite the absence or vagueness of fact, the *spirit* which breathes in the border ballads is highly valuable to the historian.

Legends, in the most technical sense, are a branch of folklore relating to a sacred person, place, or incident.[1] The early Christian church, for example, produced stories of the saints which were sometimes primarily historical and sometimes even at the outset primarily fabulous. Successive tellers altered and expanded them; different priests or clerks embroidered them to suit local ideas and preferences; and finally chroniclers gathered and repolished the whole. The result was a wild though charming medley of facts and inventions. Chief among the early chroniclers was James of Varagium, who late in the thirteenth century compiled his *Golden Legend*, a work still read. He has had many successors, some credulous, and some as scholarly as Sabine Baring-Gould, whose revised *Lives of the*

[1] For Henri Bergson's classic distinction between the *fabulatory* function and the *verificatory* function, see R. Klebansky, ed., *Philosophy and History*, pp. 27 ff.

Saints fills sixteen volumes. Analogous legends have grown up in the Pagan, Moslem, Jewish, and other faiths.

But in the popular sense "legend" of course has a much broader significance. It refers to any narrative which professes to be historical, but which is actually traditional and imaginative in character. The Talmudic stories, the cycles of Arthur and Roland, the traditional tales of the Catskills which Irving transmuted into the pure gold of "Rip Van Winkle" and "The Legend of Sleepy Hollow," all the personages of that poetic world which embraces the city of Troy, the Forest of Broceliande, and the Halls of Tara, with such cruder personages as Mike Fink of the Western waters, may be included under the one name. Sometimes, like the ballads and *märchen*, legends represent a strange survival from the distant past. The story of St. George's rescue of the daughter of the king of Libya obviously derives from the more ancient tale of Perseus the dragon-slayer. At the one extreme a legend may be pure myth, like the tale of the witch under the water in the poem *Beowulf*. At the other extreme it may embody a large percentage of fact, like the legends of Hengist and Horsa, or of the Norse discoverers of America. In still other instances the mixture of fact and fancy may defy analysis and leave savants debating endlessly. Though six centuries before Christ Stesichorus exclaimed that Helen never really came in the beached ships to Pergamum, we know that there was a Troy and that it was besieged. Though such a commanding hero as the Roland of the great Song never existed, we know there was an obscure Count of Brittany who three centuries before the Song fell in the defiles of the Pyrenees at Roncesvalles. On the granite of hard fact grows the moss of legend, and even pure myth contains its grains of stony reality. Though *Beowulf* is an invention, it mentions the historic incident of the raid of Hygelac's Vikings on the Frisian coast.

Some effort has been made to draw a line between legends of secular heroes, and legends of sacred persons and places, and to assign greater historical value to the former. But this distinction is far from being definite, as anyone may prove by a little reading on the heroes Theseus or Hercules. One recent student of comparative folklore, Lord Raglan, concludes after a survey of both the classical and medieval bodies of traditional narrative that they are all derived from dramatic ritual, not from historical fact. The whole body of popular literature he regards as a detritus of mythical stories connected with religious rites. The rites perished, but the stories remained, repeated endlessly by rote. This theory, which he ably defends, may really account for many folk-heroes, like those of Thebes and Troy. That is, the hero of legend may in numerous instances have originally been an actor in a dramatic ritual, not a leader in real life. But this denial of the historical value of all legendary stories is far too sweeping. We know that there was an actual Roland who was killed in the Pyrenees in 778 A.D.; we know that an actual Marko Kraljevitch fought the Turks and died in battle in 1394. Both these men became heroes of legend, and the folk-tales furnish us unquestionable bits of fact about them. In legend, indeed, we find values that become the greater the nearer we approach to modern times, and the further we leave primitive social conditions behind. Lord Raglan contends that an illiterate and primitive people cannot preserve the memory of an historical event for more than 150 years. But as inroads are made upon illiteracy and the primitive, legends can preserve fact for much longer periods. It may often be debatable fact, but taken in a body it cannot be spared by history.

Such works of comparative folklore as Sir J. G. Frazer's *Golden Bough*, though written chiefly from a religio-sociological standpoint, have suggested many ideas and supplied much valuable material to the student of ancient history. Sabine Baring-Gould's tales of the saints cannot be neglected by the student of medieval culture. Not even American historians can ignore legends and ballads. The story of the earliest discovery of the continent is unquestionably to be found in Icelandic sagas, which in their first written form were founded on oral tradition. The principal sources are two, the *Saga of Eric the Red*, and the *Tale of the Greenlanders*. The former, written not later than the close of the thirteenth century and possibly in its early years, seems to be founded upon a fairly direct and reliable tradition. The *Tale of the Greenlanders*, known to have been written late in the fourteenth century, is less trustworthy — it plainly represents an oral tradition in process of dissolution. But there are some elements in the *Eric Saga* which are not plausible, while there are bits in the *Tale* which may well be authentic. The task of excluding what is inaccurate and combining and collating what is accurate in the Icelandic Sagas is, like the treatment of most legends, one in which experience and a full knowledge of historical backgrounds count for much. Experts have thus far not agreed, in dealing with Leif's voyages to America, upon the question whether Vinland lay as far south as Cape Cod or as far north as Labrador; or whether the *vinber*, for that matter, were wild grapes or cranberries. But they have agreed upon points important to American historians.

For both pre-Columbian and post-Columbian times, again, Indian legends possess an historical coloring which gives them genuine utility. Though ordinarily worthless in what they state of heroes or sacred persons, they supply much information upon tribal organization, migrations, and customs. Their full interpretation of course demands the ethnologist's equipment. In our more recent history the legends of pioneer settlements, mining camps, lumbermen, and the cowboys of the western range, whether in prose or ballad, are by no means devoid of light upon social and cultural history.

Perhaps the clearest illustration of the way in which legend merged with the first important writings upon history is to be seen in Livy. His great work, beginning with the landing of the legendary Aeneas, and coming down to the establishment of the republic, is based primarily upon annalists, who in turn had drawn in large part upon the flimsiest kind of popular legend and upon family traditions. For the regal period of Roman history these annalists had possessed little else upon which to draw. The Gauls who burned Rome in 390 B.C. had destroyed the records of the city, and subsequent chroniclers perforce contented themselves with myths, ballads, oral tales embroidered generation after generation, and treacherous reminiscences. Modern scholars can hardly feel certain of the reality of a single incident in all this glittering mass of material. They cannot be positive that such persons as Numa Pompilius, or Ancus Martius, or Servius Tullius, ever breathed; they *are* positive that the tales of their conquests, reforms, and institutions have but a vague relationship to truth. They can easily discern the fables which ultra-patriotic Romans invented to lend a spurious grandiosity and splendor to the petty and checkered beginnings of the republic. After these beginnings, the filio-pietistic myths became intermixed with more dependable data. The historian finds in the fragments we possess of the old annals extremely brief notices, precisely dated and rather archaic in style, of arresting events — wars, treaties, consecrations of temples, and so on. Obviously these were taken from the first written records — the records kept by the pontiffs and aediles, and by certain families. Such annalists as Q. Fabius Pictor, called the father of Roman history, filled in this bare framework from the rich stores of legendary stuff at hand. The resulting composition, judged by present-day standards, was a weird affair. But it held grains of wheat among the chaff. Had later annalists only applied critical methods to it, they might have given Rome the beginnings of true history. But they refused, and a school of rhetoricians arose who even dressed up the traditions with new exaggerations and interpolations.

Livy's second to fifth books inclusive, embracing Roman history down to the evacuation of the city by the Gauls, are not only founded upon the annalists but exemplify the worst methods of using traditional material. His preface admits the unsafe character of the early traditions. "Such things as are reported either before or at the foundation of the city, more beautified by poet's adornments than grounded upon faithful records, I mean neither to assert nor deny," he remarks. He adds that the whole history previous to the Gallic sack is obscure because of its great antiquity, the paucity of monuments and writings, "the only faithful remembrancers of times past," and the destruction of the priestly and civic records. But while these statements are critical, his handling of the annalists' work is not. He made no effort to go behind their writing even where other evidence existed; nor did he compare different annalists, as he should. Moreover, for whole books his history gives no references to authorities, contenting itself with such phrases as "they say" or "ancient writers declare." The work is a compilation, in whose later chapters the materials are so imperfectly fused that inconsistences and contradictions are by no means rare. In contrast with it, readers who wish to learn how a scientific treatment of legendary materials can separate the gold from the dross need only turn to the first chapters of Mommsen.

IV

Our third category, that of representative materials not written in the ordinary sense, began (if we exclude the cave-paintings of remote prehistoric ages) with inscriptions — inscriptions baked upon clay, chiselled upon stone, or engraved upon metals. Even in very ancient times it was seen that such inscriptions were extremely useful for the study of history. Great Greek orators, like Demosthenes and Aeschines, cited them as evidence for their arguments. Herodotus used them repeatedly, and his record of the battle of Plataea is drawn in part from the inscription on the bronze base of the golden tripod dedicated at Delphi after the victory. Thucydides and still more frequently Polybius used them. Dionysius of Halicarnassus, who wrote his *Antiquities of Rome* just before the commencement of the Christian Era, mentions several important inscriptions as sources, two dating from the regal period and one from the early years of the republic. It is one of Livy's faults that when he might have used such sources freely, he ignored them. In Greece the systematic collection of inscriptions was begun by certain scholars at an early date. Philochorus made a compilation of them about three hundred years B.C., and Polemus one in the second century B.C.; still others were made by Aristodemus, Craterus of Macedon, and lesser men.

When the Revival of Learning dawned upon Europe and renewed men's interest in ancient literature, the study of inscriptions revived also. Early in the fifteenth century an imposing number of them were copied by Cyriac of Ancona, one of the most enthusiastic of Renaissance antiquarians; an Italian scholar who devoted his travels in Italy, Greece, Egypt, and Syria not merely to the collection of manuscripts, coins, and works of art, but to the study of incriptions and the sketching of roads, walls, buildings, and other physical remains. But for him all knowledge of many monuments and inscriptions would have perished utterly. He had contemporaries who did much, and successors who did more. By the beginning of the nineteenth century, thanks to traveling scholars of many lands — Italian, French, German, English — a large stock of Greek and Roman inscriptions had been accumulated. The time was ripe for competent hands to compare, arrange, and edit this information; and the work was undertaken for Greek inscriptions by the eminent German scholar, Augustus Boeckh.

It was Boeckh who raised Greek epigraphy to the position of a science, one of the most useful handmaidens of ancient history. The Royal Academy of Sciences in Berlin made no mistake when in 1818 it chose him to classify and annotate the known inscriptions in one systematic work. The first volume of his monumental *Corpus Inscriptionum Graecarum* appeared in 1828, the second in 1833, and the third and fourth, in which he was aided by other scholars, in 1853 and 1856. These four volumes permanently established the methods of Greek epigraphy. For Boeckh's own time they constituted a masterpiece of lucid arrangement, erudition, scholarly care, and brilliant generalization. In his treatise on the public economy of Athens, Boeckh also gave the world a masterly application of the principles of epigraphy to historical study. But of course his collection was merely a beginning. The liberation of Greece from Turkey and the development of archaeological research resulted in a far more systematic exploration of famous sites, and the exhuming of huge numbers of new inscriptions. Boeckh's four volumes had contained approximately ten thousand. In 1871 the Berlin Academy began the preparation of a new Corpus, still being published under canons of the highest scholarship. By 1880 the number of Greek inscriptions known to scholars was estimated at nearly thirty thousand, and today it very probably exceeds fifty thousand.

The variety, color, and instructiveness of the Greek inscriptions are far greater than the amateur would suppose. Dating as far back as the middle of the seventh century B. C., they comprehend not merely political and religious affairs, but commercial and private relations. Among the political materials, the decrees of rulers, representative bodies, and popular assemblies are extremely numerous; so numerous for the Athenian state in the fifth and fourth centuries B.C. that a complete compilation of them "is like turning over the minutes of the Athenian Parliament." They include also the laws of such statesmen as Draco, and such bodies as the Amphictyonic Council; treaties between the various Greek cities; awards by arbitral authorities in disputes between states; accounts of public expenditures; records of the armies and navies; and even royal letters — such as that which Lysimachus wrote to the Samians, printed in Boeckh's work. An interesting series of inscriptions deals with the conditions under which colonists

were sent out by the various cities. Among the religious inscriptions are those which decree festivals and prescribe an
elaborate ritual for their observance; which give rules for the
appointment, discipline, duties, and rewards of priests; which
pertain to auguries and sacrifices; which deal with the lease
of sacred lands; and which contain prayers or imprecations
in tombs and temples. Certain Delphian inscriptions illustrate
the enfranchisement of slaves under the form of sale to a god.
The innumerable private inscriptions deal with leases, mort-
gages, athletic competitions, and honors to individuals.

While the earliest Latin inscriptions, with few exceptions,
run back only to the first part of the fourth century B.C., for
the republic and empire they are quite as important as Greek
inscriptions. It is interesting to note that the first man to
make extensive use of them in historical study was Rienzi,
the celebrated orator and reformer, who about the middle of
the fourteenth century prepared a description of the Eternal
City which cited them very effectively. Early in the fifteenth
century the antiquarian Poggio Bracciolini prepared a collection of inscriptions, and after that date such compilations appeared at frequent intervals. The careless or unscrupulous
methods of many students, permitting gross inaccuracies and
still grosser inventions, made Latin epigraphy an unscientific
and dangerous study until the nineteenth century. Forgers like
Pirro Ligorio of Naples palmed off false texts on the world in the
most brazen fashion. But in this field as in so many others,
the eighteenth century showed itself the parent of a truly scientific method. The critical and systematic handling of Latin
inscription began most notably with Marini, who published an
epochal work in 1795, and whose principles were followed by
his disciple, Count Bartolomeo Borghesi. The Berlin Academy
followed up its success in the field of Greek inscriptions with
careful plans for a similar Corpus in Latin; and it found an
even greater editor in Theodor Mommsen. He and William
Henzen brought out in 1863 the first volume of the *Corpus*

Inscriptionum Latinarum, which is still being continued by
German scholars.

Though to a great extent the Roman inscriptions parallel
those of Greece, important differences exist. Erectors of public
structures of many kinds — bridges, aqueducts, temples, and
other buildings — were usually permitted to engrave their
names upon them, and these *tituli operum publicorum,* with
their dates, supply much information upon the growth of public
facilities and the aspect of ancient cities. Boundary stones
show political limits. The *Fasti,* or lists of consuls and other
leading magistrates, are an interesting source of information.
One of the most striking of all inscriptions is the famous Monu-
mentum Ancyranum, the record of his own exploits which
Augustus graved in Greek and Latin upon the walls of a temple
at Ancyra in Asia Minor. Constitutions, decrees, laws, and
documents connected with public worship are numerous. From
Pompeii have come many inscriptions painted or drawn on
street-walls — advertisements, election handbills, and notices of
highly diverse and often indecent character. And private documents, incised upon bronze, lead, or ivory tablets, are for obvious reasons more numerous for Rome than for Greece.[1]

Not only the riches, but the difficulties and problems of inscriptions are greater than the amateur would suppose. The
date of inscriptions has first to be determined. This can sometimes be done by internal evidence furnished by the subject,
event, or person treated. It can sometimes be fixed, with
general accuracy, by the dialect or style. Finally, the approximate date can often be ascertained simply from the form of
the letters and the manner of their execution. In Greek inscriptions carved before 450 B.C. the characters have a stiff and
angular outline, while for the Periclean Age they possess a graceful though simple form. Inscriptions of this later period, more-

[1] Discoveries of Roman inscriptions in recent years in Cyrenaica have
thrown much illumination upon imperial administration under Augustus;
see Francis Cumont, *Journal des Savants,* March, 1927, pp. 126 ff.

over, are usually written in such fashion that the letters are
aligned vertically as well as horizontally. The Greek alphabet
also underwent notable changes. After the archonship of
Euclides in 403 B.C., the Athenians used a fuller alphabet than
that which Ionia had theretofore employed. In the Macedonian
period appeared the use of apices, a stroke or curved line, as
an ornament of letters. In the period of the Roman domination,
a sharp distinction can be made between the Greek inscriptions of the Augustan Age, which are clear and handsomely
designed, and those of the subsequent empire, which rapidly
degenerate. Similarly, in dealing with Roman inscriptions it
has been possible to lay down clear and detailed rules for supplying dates. The Latin alphabet again varied from age to
age — the old Z as the seventh letter was replaced in the fourth
century A.U.C. by G; in Cicero's time two new letters were
added from the Greek; and the Emperor Claudius unsuccess-
fully attempted to make still further additions. Changes in
the form of letters were numerous, and these paleographical
alterations can be given a fairly certain chronology.

Since the alphabet, the outline of the letters, and the style
of execution count for so much in the proper interpretation
of inscriptions, it is obvious that the utmost care in copying
them is indispensable. Many early collectors were more enthusiastic than precise. Others, as we have noted, were thoroughly
dishonest. Here, as in every other branch of historical materials, forgers early appeared. The Pirro Ligorios of the fifteenth, sixteenth, and seventeenth centuries did much injury
to history until in the nineteenth century the severely critical
methods of modern epigraphists and paleographers exposed
them. Of course the invention of photography has greatly
benefited exact scholarship.

V

For the purposes of history, coins may be considered almost a
branch of inscriptions. They also go far back into the past —

in the classical world, to about 700 B.C., gold apparently having been first coined in Lydia, and silver in Aegina, from which lands coinage spread with great rapidity throughout the Hellenic part of the Mediterranean world. For the ancient world coins were issued in great profusion, and their varieties were steadily increased during medieval and early modern times. By 1880 the European museums possessed several hundred thousand different varieties of coins and medals, and the number held in classified collections today can hardly be less than half a million. So enormous an array of "monuments" of past times is naturally of value to the study of politics, economics, art, and religion. Their usefulness for history as well as their aesthetic interest was recognized, indeed, by those same scholars of the Renaissance who first clearly perceived the value of inscriptions. Petrarch collected coins, and made presents of some of his best to the Emperor Charles V. Many early critics of the classics illustrated their commentaries by reproductions of coins. In 1517 an Italian, Andrea Fulvio, published an album of portraits of illustrious figures of the ancient world taken from coins and gems, his *Illustrium Imagines*. Such albums soon became numerous. So did historical or pseudo-historical works illustrated by reproductions of coins; a whole series of them produced by Hubert Goltz of Antwerp in the latter half of the sixteenth century is still remembered for its commingling of genuine with fraudulent coins, for Goltz invented pieces to suit his own purposes, and even created consuls and generals who never lived. Fulvio Orsini, a famous collector of antiquities and gems, issued in Rome in 1577 an epochal work on Roman silver coins from his own collection; but though he was a man of profound learning and of stricter rectitude than Goltz, many spurious or wrongly-described coins marred his pages. Adolph Occo, whose work on imperial Roman coins appeared at Antwerp in 1577, can be credited with a more scholarly and reliable treatise.

But the truly scientific study of numismatics goes back to about the same period as that of inscriptions. It hardly became possible until great national collections, larger than any in private hands, had grown up. J. H. Eckhel, its first exponent, was curator of the imperial collection in Vienna. He has been called the Father of Numismatics, for his eight-volume work, the *Doctrina Numorum Veterum* (1792–98), gave the study of ancient coins an expert and critical basis. His erudition, judgment, and accuracy were such that even now his writings are valuable to students, his material being regarded as a starting-point in the study of classical coins, and his principle a model for other students. Since his time the study of coins has of course become highly specialized. In our own day the numismatics of nearly every ancient and modern people of importance — the United States, alas, is not one — has been made the subject of a special treatise. There are books on Merovingian coins, Anglo-Saxon coins, Byzantine coins, Russian coins, Chinese coins, Papal coins, and many more — and some contain a surprising amount of historical information.

To political history coins seldom contribute much new information beyond the supplying or correction of dates; their value to such history, in general, lies simply in *illustrating* it. It is true that in a few lands for a few periods we must rely largely upon coins for what little information we possess. The records of the Graeco-Bactrian kingdom established about 256 B.C., and comprising a considerable part of Central Asia, for example, have been pieced out chiefly from coins discovered in Afghanistan and surrounding areas. They furnish a list of names of rulers whose succession can be fixed with general accuracy. But early coins seldom offer much precise information, for they disclose only that certain states or princes issued money at certain dates. Later coins, whose inscriptions and devices present more facts, also deal for the most part with peoples and times for which other sources supply far fuller and clearer information; they corroborate this information, but they rarely alter or extend it. When they do, it is chiefly by fixing details of chronology, or by expanding our knowledge of royal genealogies. The pedigree of more than one royal house has first been traced by a set of coins. In economic history, the *spread* of coins is often significant. Discoveries of Greek coins in the Mediterranean basin, of Roman coins in India, help fix the extent of ancient trade areas.

But the illustrative value of numismatics, for students of political history alone, is striking. In the vast museum exhibits of coins we possess contemporaneous or almost contemporaneous effigies of most of the great rulers and captains of the world from Alexander the Great down to our own time. Painters did little to supply portraiture to history until the later part of the Middle Ages; sculptors, though active in both ancient and medieval times, gave the world far fewer portraits than the coin-makers, and often so idealized them that they lack authenticity. "There is no more delightful companion in historical reading," justly writes one student, "than a cabinet of coins and medals. The strength and energy of Alexander, the ferocity of Mithridates, the philosophic calmness of Antoninus, the obstinate ferocity of Nero, and the brutality of Caracalla, are as plain on the coins as in the pages of history." He goes on to say that in the Dark Ages numismatic portraits lost their individuality, but regained it with the revival of art. For the later Middle Ages and Modern times "we can form a series of portraits more complete and not less interesting than that of the ancient period." Engraved gems and cameos often afford useful information; and everyone knows that for a century the stamps of the world have carried many admirably engraved portraits.

Religious as well as political history, particularly that of the Greeks, is illuminated by coins. All Greek coins until the death of Alexander, or virtually all, were stamped with sacred subjects alone. In later times the reverse of the coin was usually devoted to sacred images or emblems. But for these representations, modern scholarship would have encountered immense difficulty in forming a complete and satisfactory set of the effigies under which the Greek divinities were represented. While ancient statues and reliefs of good workmanship and preservation do not exist in sufficient numbers for this purpose, coins fill all the gaps. Many of them, indeed, supply effigies of divinities which are not merely good, but excellent. The mythology of the Romans is less fully illustrated, but numerous coins nevertheless bear images which refer to the religious traditions of the early decades of the city. And as we should expect, coins also fix many geographical elements in history. They often supply invaluable information as to the position of towns on ocean or streams, as to the race and allegiance of the inhabitants, and as to natural productions — for these last are sometimes represented on ancient money. Finally, coins convey much as to the progress of art and architecture.

Even textiles may have much the same historical values as coins, sculptures, and inscriptions. Something of the history of Oriental lands has been wrought into the traditional designs of their rugs, and experts can tell at a glance whether the pattern reflects the austerity of the Sunni or the freedom of the Shiah branch of the Moslems. The most famous piece of embroidery in history is doubtless the so-called tapestry of Bayeux, which is not a tapestry at all, but a long-stitch embroidery in crewels on a long, narrow strip of linen cloth. Executed late in the eleventh or more probably early in the twelfth century, it represents various episodes in the conquest of England by William the Conqueror. Though tradition ascribed it to no less a personage than Queen Matilda and her maids, it is difficult to believe that they undertook so laborious a work on materials so coarse. It is much more likely that it was done in England by needlewomen employed at the expense of those Normans upon whom William had bestowed rich grants of English lands, and was sent by them as an offering to the Bayeux Cathredal. But whatever its origin, it furnishes almost invaluable illustrations of the arms, modes of fighting, and general customs of the time of the Norman Conquest.

Few manuals of English history are so brief as to omit mention of it or reproductions of some of its scenes. Freeman terms it "the highest authority on the Norman side," adding that it presents "hardly any of the inventions, exaggerations, and insinuations of the other Norman authorities."

Primitive materials for history, we have called these various forms of non-literary data; but while they are primitive in the sense of lacking subtlety and detail, in another sense some of them are far indeed from primitive. The New Zealander of Macaulay's illustration, taking his stand to sketch the broken arch of London Bridge, would find nothing primitive in such physical remains as a locomotive or dynamo, such representative materials as an Aubusson tapestry, a painting by Turner, or a coin by St. Gaudens. Mr. Dooley, dropping once into historical vein, closed his catalogue of American progress by a list of the representative materials which illustrate it. "I have seen America spread out fr'm th' Atlantic to th' Pacific, with a branch office iv th' Standard Ile Company in ivry hamlet. I've seen th' shackles dropped fr'm th' slave, so's he cud be lynched in Ohio. . . . An' Corbett beat Sullivan, an' Fitz beat Corbett. . . . An' th' invintions . . . th' cotton gin an' th' gin sour an' th' bicycle an' th' flying machine an' th' nickle-in-th'-slot machine an' th' Croker machine an' th' sody fountain an' — crownin' wurruk iv our civilization — th' cash raygister." It would be more correct to say that these are the broader, simpler materials for history, adumbrating and illustrating it rather than offering means for presenting it in detail. But they are essential parts of the mass of evidence upon which historians must rely. They are important elements in the immense flood-system which drains the past for the benefit of the present, not to be ignored because they flow apart from what is today the great central stream of historical evidence, the written or printed word. To that central stream we must now turn.

CHAPTER FOUR

ONE MIGHTY TORRENT

IN THE BEGINNING was the written word — so the historian would amend the ancient text. It was the fact of writing that was all-important; and in placing inscriptions in a different category from writings upon more perishable materials, we must not draw any deep line of division between them. Men learned to write on skins, clay, bark, and papyrus quite as early as on stone or metal, and they still write on them all. The adoption of parchment and paper as media for writing is important simply as it made written records far fuller and far more abundant. Browning's lines on Saul are full of historical truth in their expression of the unconquerable desire of mankind to record the past in manifold forms:

> Is Saul dead? In the depth of the vale make his tomb — bid arise
> A gray mountain of marble heaped four-square, till, built to the skies,
> Let it mark where the great First King slumbers: whose fame would ye know?
> Up above see the rock's naked face, where the record shall go
> In great characters cut by the scribe, — Such was Saul, so he did;
> With the sages directing the work, by the populace chid, —
> For not half, they'll affirm, is comprised there! Which fault to amend,
> In the grove with his kind grows the cedar, whereon they shall spend
> (See, in tablets 'tis level before them) their praise, and record
> With the gold of the graver, Saul's story, — the statesman's great word
> Side by side with the poet's sweet comment. The river's awave

With smooth paper-reeds grazing each other when prophet-winds
  rave:
So the pen gives unborn generations their due and their part
In thy being!

Far back in neolithic days, primitive man — man a stage
beyond the string-knotting savage — learned to make rude
pictures which would convey simple ideas and record events.
Still earlier, no doubt, the chieftains and rich men of various
tribes had placed distinctive marks upon their property to
identify it: strokes embodying a rough sketch or emblem. Out
of these beginnings grew more flexible systems for identifying
facts and objects by symbols. Gods came to be represented
by their sacred animals; upper Egypt was represented by a
conventional lily; famine by a picture of an emaciated man
with protruding ribs. As culture advanced, men learned to
use these pictographs and ideographs to transmit really complex ideas and considerable bodies of information. But they
were long puzzled, no doubt, by the difficulty of presenting
an abstraction, or even a concrete object for which no comprehensible picture could be made. Easy enough to sketch a
man; but how indicate that he was a father, a son, a husband?
In this difficulty, ingenious minds struck upon the utility of a
punning similarity of sounds. The Egyptian word for "son"
was almost identical in sound with the word for "goose"; what
more natural than to indicate the idea of a son by a sketch of
a goose? It was as if in English the sketch of an eye served to
represent the pronoun I. Having thus begun to make symbols
not for objects and ideas but for sound, the ancient scribes
drew close to the invention of the alphabet.[1] Pictographs and
ideographs gave way to a *transitional* mode of writing, in which
they were mingled with symbols which represented a sound or
syllable alone. Half a dozen different peoples developed this
transitional system of conveying intelligence: the Egyptians,

[1] See E. Clodd, *The Story of the Alphabet;* Sir W. Flinders Petrie, *The
Formation of the Alphabet.*

the Sumerians and Babylonians, the Hittites, the Chinese, the Aztecs, and the Mayas.

Historians of Western civilization have of course made us most familiar with the transitional scripts of the Egyptians and Babylonians, which go far back into antiquity. In Egypt we find pictographs and ideographs — that is, hieroglyphs — well developed even in the First Dynasty, when annual records of events were kept in them. The hieroglyphs, written rapidly upon papyri sheets, soon became a series of scrawls which followed the original symbol about as closely as the letters in modern cursive handwriting imitate the printed capitals. Such running-hand or "hieratic" writing became well developed under the First Dynasty. In Babylonia the pictographs had to be impressed upon clay tablets, stiffer and more refractory than paper, and for this purpose sharp-pointed writing instruments were employed. The rudely-scratched symbols were ranged in vertical columns. As scribes wrote faster and faster, the pictographs and ideographs became more abbreviated, and were soon impressed, not incised, with a three-sided graving tool which left a wedge-shaped or cuneiform mark. This emergence of cuneiform writing paralleled the emergence of the hieratic or cursive writing in Egypt; but in Babylonia the cuneiform marks wholly superseded the pictorial symbols, while in Egypt the hieratic writing did not. By the same process of evolution in both lands the introduction of syllabic symbols gradually provided a transitional mode of writing, halfway to the alphabet proper.

The use of papyrus supposedly dates back about as far as 4000 B.C., and we actually possess an historical papyrus which contains an account of the reign of King Assa, 3580–3536 B.C. Of the cuneiform tablets of Babylonia, we possess specimens which were written far back in the third millennium before Christ. As early as 2400 B.C. legal records and public accounts were being systematically kept on such tablets. Large collections of Egyptian papyri, some of them believed to be not less than four thousand years old, have been made by European and American libraries and museums, and are constantly being enlarged. None of the historical books written in hieroglyphics, for such books existed, have survived, but the world possesses an abundance of other hieroglyphic material. It likewise possesses huge collections of Babylonian tablets, commercial, legal, and religious, ranging from 3000 B.C. to the second century of the Christian era. Our knowledge of very early Babylonian literature — legends, hymns, incantations, epics — is exceptionally full; other tablets give us a very considerable understanding of social conditions, economic and cultural life, and legal procedure; and the annals and the commemorative inscriptions make it possible to trace much of the political history of the country from an early period. The era of modern scientific exploration for historical material in Egypt began with Napoleon's invasion, and the transportation of the Rosetta stone to Paris for decipherment; in Babylonia, with Sir Henry Rawlinson's translation of the inscription on the Behistun rock in 1834, and his opening of the first Babylonian mound at Birs Nimrud in 1844.

The alphabet proper — our own highly conventional form of writing, with no essential connection between sound and symbol — is of uncertain origin. Some scholars would trace it to the Egyptian or Babylonian systems of transitional writing; some to the Minoan writing in Crete; some to the syllabic system of writing in Cyprus; and some to the Phoenicians. One writer, Sir W. Flinders Petrie, holds that it developed from a series of conventional signs employed for commercial purposes throughout the whole Mediterranean area in earliest times. What is certain is that the beginnings of the alphabet date much further back than men recently supposed. Inscriptions discovered by Petrie in the Sinai Peninsula in 1916, which appear to be purely alphabetic, go back at least as far as the sixteenth century B.C.; long antedating the famous Moabite stone of the ninth century B.C. which, written in the Semitic alphabet, was until lately believed the earliest known example of such writing. Over these Sinaitic inscriptions, again, scholars have quarreled. Some hold the writing to be Egyptian in origin; some declare that it is independent of Egypt, and ancestral to the Semitic alphabet. The Greeks may possibly have adapted their alphabet (which in essentials is also ours) at a remote time from some such source, independent of any other. But it is far more probable that they derived it from Semitic origins. We have inscriptions in the Greek alphabet which belong to the eighth — perhaps even to the ninth — century B.C. This carries us as far back as Hesiod, and almost as far as Homer, who is supposed to have composed the *Iliad* about 950 B.C., perhaps himself reducing it to a written text.

No Greek documents exist which have the antiquity of the oldest Egyptian papyri or Babylonian tablets; in fact, none were produced in Greece until much later. Nevertheless, Cretan records have been found which prove the existence of written documents in that island at a date of very respectable antiquity. One record narrates that when an Egyptian envoy visited Byblos about 1080 B.C., but unhappily neglected to bring presents with him, the official documents of Crete were brought out to prove to him that earlier Egyptian deputations had offered valuable gifts. As a result the Egyptians apologized and made amends by sending various presents, including five hundred sheets of papyrus, evidently for writing purposes. Historians would give much for a glance at these first written archives of Crete, far back beyond Homer.

II

But the written word is of little use to students of history until it is collected into systematic repositories; until fact is added to fact, document to document, book to book. The librarian must aid the scribe in preparing the ground for annalist and historians to till. So early was this fact perceived that priests and rulers began to form libraries soon after hieratic and cuneiform writing became important. A few decades ago it was supposed that the two libraries of Rameses II (1300– 1236 B.C.) mentioned by Diodorus Siculus were the first insti- tutions deserving the name; if indeed even they were not the stuff that legends are made from. Now we know that they did gloriously exist; papyri have been found which, though of later date than Rameses, came from these collections. We know that they were deservedly the most famous of the early ancient libraries. But we also know that collections of books and docu- ments went back in Egypt to a much earlier time. Egyptian inscriptions refer to the library of Khufu, a monarch of the Fourth Dynasty, and to that of Khafra, Fourth Dynasty builder of the second pyramid. The very spot on which stood the library of Ikhnaton (who died about 1350 B.C.) is now known. In Babylonia, too, rich and extensive libraries had been col- lected long before Greece became a centre of civilization. Just how early they appeared cannot be ascertained, but Assur- banipal, whose reign ended about 625 B.C., made one of the greatest collections known before modern times.

The last of the great Assyrian kings, Assurbanipal gathered at Nineveh tablets containing not less than ten thousand separate works and documents; this royal library preserving not only the records of his reign, but a collection of Babylonian literature. It was the British archaeologist Layard who found its remains, two large rooms filled with tablets. Later dis- coveries extended the number of titles. Most of the collection is now housed in the British Museum. Important supple- mentary discoveries were afterwards made at the sacred city of Nippur, which Assurbanipal had restored, by an American expedition. J. P. Peters, H. V. Hilprecht, and others un- covered a series of rooms where, stored neatly on shelves, lay more than 20,000 clay tablets. Like those at Nineveh, they had been systematically arranged and catalogued, and though this library was at least partly an adjunct to a temple school, they may have been open to the public. In addition to these

royal and ecclesiastical libraries, still other Babylonian collections existed. Many of the surviving cuneiform tablets pertain to business affairs, and were as systematically collected
and preserved as the records of business corporations today.
They show that in Hammurabi's day, more than two thousand
years B.C., Babylonian production and commerce had been
thoroughly organized by that keen business sagacity which has
marked the Semitic race ever since.

As the civilizations of the Mediterranean basin developed,
papyrus makers, clerks, authors, and libraries increased in
number, until long before the Christian era the written materials for literature and history had become fairly abundant. In
Greece we hear, though vaguely, of a library collected by
Peisistratus, and prized and increased by the Athenians after
his death; a library which according to the writer Aulus Gellius, was carried off to Persia by Xerxes, and later brought
back. We hear also of a library belonging to Polycrates of
Samos, and of another at Heraclea Pontica about the beginning of the fourth century B.C. It is certain that Aristotle had
an excellent library, which passed through interesting vicissitudes after his death, and was finally carried to Rome by Sulla
about 82 B.C. We know also that after Aristotle libraries
multiplied so remarkably in Greece that Cicero speaks of an
infinite multitude of books there. Book collecting became
fashionable. It is said that when the Goths seized Athens in
267 A.D. they threw together a huge pile of books, which they
were about to burn as containing dangerous magic, when one
aged leader cried: "Let the Greeks have their books. So long
as they waste their days with these idle toys, we need never
fear that they will give us any trouble in war."

The effulgent centre of all critical and historical work in the
silver age of Greek literature was Alexandria, where Ptolemy I,
the Louis XIV of that era, founded an imposing library. Ptolemy II continued and completed it, and also built a daughter-
library, called the Serapeion. Though these were partly

displays of royal magnificence, they proved of priceless utility to ancient scholars. No such literary workshops existed anywhere else, for estimates of their contents range from 200,000 to 700,000 volumes. They continued to be the marvel of the learned world during early Christian times. A long-popular tradition assigns the shame of their destruction to the Islamic forces of Amru and the Caliph Omar, who thought them wicked if contrary to the Koran and superfluous if in harmony with it. But Gibbon long ago pointed out that Omar could not have burnt them because they did not then exist; the early Christian leaders had been far more destructive than the Moslems! Still other large libraries flourished in Egypt in the time of the Ptolemies. Great quantities of papyri have been dug by modern archaeologists from the mounds covering ancient towns and cities, and from cemeteries. One of the discoveries made in this way was the long-lost work of Aristotle on the Athenian Constitution.

No important libraries, with perhaps one or two exceptions, existed in Rome until the last century of the republic. But by the time of Cicero both public and private libraries were numerous. He owned a much-valued collection, as did his friend Atticus. Well-organized publishing houses, some of which employed numerous copyists, were at work multiplying volumes. These houses — the Sosii in Horace's day, for example — produced hundreds and even thousands of copies of a popular author; and books became so cheap that Juvenal refers to a poor fellow living in a garret who possessed a number. Wealthy Romans prided themselves upon their groaning shelves, or rather drawers. Licinius Lucullus, for example, whose name is still synonymous with luxury, confiscated large numbers of Greek books in his Eastern campaigns (67 B.C.) and housed them magnificently. As Plutarch says, the generosity with which he let men use them redeemed the meanness with which he had acquired them. His reading rooms and grounds were thrown open to all students, and Greeks repaired thither "as to an abode of the Muses." Seneca speaks of the ostentation with which his wealthy contemporaries covered their walls with book-presses of ivory or inlaid wood and their tables with expensive volumes. "Nowadays a library takes rank with a bathroom as a necessary ornament of a house," he declared; but he sneered at the men who yawned among their thousand titles, and whose chief delight was in their rich bindings and rubrics.[1]

The public libraries of Rome came in with the empire. Julius Caesar planned to build one, for which the learned Terentius Varro collected and assorted many volumes. Cicero has eulogized the villa which housed this library and which was used by Varro as a place of retired study. "What noble discussions used to take place in that building! What writings were composed there! What ideas were originated there! The laws of the Roman people, the memorials of our ancestors, the consideration of all wisdom and all learning, were the topics dwelt on . . ." But Caesar did not live to complete the undertaking, and Varro's books were scattered by Mark Antony. The first public library in the city was founded soon after Caesar's murder by Asinius Pollio, who had returned from a victorious campaign against the Illyrians (39 B.C.). A little later Augustus opened a more famous library, with two collections of books, one Greek and one Latin, in a structure called the Porticus Octaviae. Later still, to commemorate the victory at Actium, he established another large library of Greek and Latin works on the Palatine Hill, reached by a colonnade leading past the temple on that eminence. The very names of the first librarians of these institutions have come down to us. Horace refers to one collection in a warning to plagiarists:

> Bards should draw inspiration from themselves,
> And not from Palatine Apollo's shelves.

As time passed, the number of Roman libraries increased; and about the end of the first century A.D. we meet a great new

[1] In *De Tranquillitate Animi*

landmark in the development of means for historical study — the first true public record office. This was the Library of Ulpius Trajanus, which contained many state records as well as ordinary volumes. The Emperor Trajan deposited in it the ivory tablets and the linen books which held the records of the senatus consulta and other official bodies. The collection, removed about two hundred years later to the Baths of Diocletian, remained in use until the great storm of the barbarian invasions burst upon Rome in the latter part of the fifth century.

By the decade 360–370 A.D. the city of Rome possessed no fewer than twenty-eight public libraries, while such towns as Milan and Tibur (Tivoli) also had valuable collections. Some of the most important combined the function of library with that of a discussion-club for learned men. A scene in which Aulus Gellius played a part — one that holds an instant appeal for present-day students — has been summarized by a modern writer as follows:

One very hot day he and some friends were outside the Temple of Hercules at Tibur, drinking melted snow. A discussion arose as to the wisdom of the practise. One of the party declares that not only did many of the physicians disapprove of snow-water, but that Aristotle had expressed a like opinion. To prove his case he goes to the temple library for Aristotle's treatise. In imagination we can see him in this room. It is small, evidently designed for the storing of books and not for use as a reading-room. Presses run around the walls, and probably there is an additional press in the middle of the room. He must refer to the catalogue, then to the numbered press, and run his eye over the tickets hanging from the ends of the rolls stored in it — doing, in fact, precisely what a reader in an open-shelf library does today. Finding his Aristotle, he rejoins his friends — because he seems to have been allowed to take books out of the library room — unties the straps, removes the colored envelope, unrolls the manuscript, and triumphantly displays to the disputants the convincing passage. The same writer also mentions a discussion in the Tiberian library, and says that a grammatical difficulty was settled by consulting a book in the Temple of Peace, in the Forum of Vespasian.[1]

[1] Ernest A. Savage, *The Story of Libraries and Book-Collecting*, p. 19

III

The great black line which closed the history of ancient libraries was drawn in blood and ashes during the century 450–550 A.D., when nearly all the book collections in the Italian peninsula, whether public or private, were destroyed. But happily many libraries still survived in the eastern part of the Roman world. When Constantine transferred the seat of his empire to Byzantium and founded Constantinople, many Roman bibliophiles and scholars followed him to the East. The spirit of history went with them. On the Golden Horn they were joined by Greek scholars. Constantine lost little time in searching for books both Christian and pagan, and before his death had gathered an imperial library of about 7,000 volumes. His son Constantius and other successors augmented it until it became impressive. Julian the Apostate founded another library, this time non-Christian, and gave it all his books. Meanwhile, many of the religious institutions of the East became fairly safe centres for the preservation of books and documents. The monasteries of Mount Athos bore throughout medieval and modern times a peculiar fame for their collections. Early in the nineteenth century a British traveller, Robert Curzon, who went to Mount Athos to search for ancient books, found in the twenty monasteries of that single peninsula about 2,000 MSS on vellum and 5,500 on paper — not to mention more than 20,000 printed volumes. These Eastern monasteries were one of the principal sources from which Italian book-collectors of the Renaissance gathered their treasures. And even after the World War a writer could declare: "The Balkan provinces and Russia hold great masses of Greek and Slavonic MSS as yet very incompletely known."

For centuries the world's principal storehouse of written materials, historical, literary, and scientific, its great nursery of learning, was the Byzantine Empire. Constantinople did not fall until 1453, and long before that date the savants of the

Western world were busy studying there, while its collectors were seeking for ancient manuscripts and bringing back whole cargoes of Greek and other books. The transfer had reached sweeping proportions before turban and scimitar stormed the walls. So much had been carried westward that historians like John Addington Symonds deem it unlikely that the works of any of the more important ancients perished in the capture. For that matter, the enmity of the Turks for books has been much exaggerated, and they gladly continued the sale of manuscripts to Frankish infidels. It is impossible, as Frederic Harrison says, "to see how our knowledge of ancient literature or civilization could have been recovered if Constantinople had not nursed through the Middle Ages the vast accumulations of Greek learning in the schools of Alexandria, Athens, and Asia Minor . . .; if indefatigable copyists had not toiled in multiplying the texts of ancient Greece." Once carried out of the East, the manuscripts were likely to be safe. It was the great ones of the earth who did most in sending emissaries to rescue them; and these princes and prelates, regarding a Greek manuscript as a rare jewel, locked most of them up in libraries where they were less exposed to dispersion and maltreatment than ever before. Latin manuscripts, though less highly esteemed, were also protected.[1]

A second great channel through which the learning of the ancient world was poured down into late medieval times was the Saracenic power. The speed and energy with which the Arabs conquered much of the East, all of North Africa, and most of Spain, is one of the marvels of the Middle Ages. But almost equally marvelous was the taste for learning displayed by many of the Arabic conquerors. While secular writings were still little valued by Christian folk, and even reprobated, men in Arabia, Syria, and Islamic Egypt read them with avidity. Moreover, the learned Moslems showed a strong predilection for scientific works, which were long neglected even by such

[1] M. R. James, *The Wanderings and Homes of Manuscripts*, pp. 22, 23

Christians as paid attention to pagan history, poetry, and philosophy. It was no accident that the Arabs of Spain gave Western Europe its first knowledge of most of Aristotle's works. A long line of Saracenic book-collections can be traced, spanning the medieval world from the far West to the farther East. Haroun Al-Raschid, ruler of Bagdad's shrines of fretted gold, patronized scholars and treasured manuscripts. We hear of libraries at Bassora; at Cairo, where the Fatimids collected ten thousand volumes only to see Saladin scatter them; at Tripoli; and above all, at Cordova.

It seems difficult to believe that Moorish writers did not indulge in a little Oriental magnification in their pictures of the rich culture of tenth century Andalusia. They speak of seventy public libraries. They describe the magnificence of the central collection in Cordova, where the sovereign Alhakem founded an academy, sent out agents to scour the East for Greek treasures, and at one time employed three hundred scholars in translating them into Arabic. This library at its height is said to have contained 600,000 titles. But after full allowance for any exaggeration, it is undeniable that Moorish Spain in that century was the chief well-spring of culture in Western Europe.

Meanwhile, in various nooks throughout the Christian West many scattered books and papers survived the tidal wave of barbarian invasion and the storms of local violence. Scholars here and there cherished a few volumes — Boethius more than a few. Some Western monasteries preserved them, for while these institutions often suffered severely from the general lawlessness, they were long the safest of all repositories. When St. Benedict founded the abbey of Monte Cassino in 528, he enjoined the monks to read constantly to save themselves from idleness. This abbey, despite destructive onslaughts by the Lombards and later the Saracens, kept many books intact. In the eleventh century its monks transcribed numerous important works, pagan as well as Christian; in Boccaccio's day it still owned many volumes, though he wept at seeing their neglect;

and long afterward Ernest Renan discovered there unpublished manuscripts of value. From St. Benedict in 528 to Renan in 1849 is a far cry, but the abbey had spanned it!

As the Benedictine order spread over much of Europe, it established libraries and centres of study; in England, for example, at York, Canterbury, Whitby, Glastonbury, Wearmouth, and Croyland. Another founder of monasteries, Cassiodorus, encouraged his monks to study and transcribe the classics, and thus, as Hodgkin writes, "utilized the vast learning of the convent for the preservation of divine and human learning, and for its transmission to later ages." Ireland of the sixth century, full of monasteries, schools, and other Christian institutions, was also rich in books. In various parts of Western Europe the Franciscans, pledged to poverty, first departed from the strict interpretation of their vow by taking up book-collecting. They and other mendicant orders often showed a creditable energy in building libraries; and Richard de Bury, after visiting their convents, speaks of finding "heaped up amidst the utmost poverty the utmost riches of learning." Some monasteries did history and letters an unwitting service. Valuing old manuscripts of classical origin simply as paper for their own writings, they erased the script and used the pages for religious material. These palimpsests can easily be restored by the devices of modern chemistry. Some of them, particularly in Italy, have yielded important materials — "lost" fragments of Cicero's *Republic*, orations by him and others, works of the rhetorician Fronto, and so on. Early in the last century the head of the Vatican Library, exploring what was still an almost untouched field, gave the world some delightful surprises of this sort.

Thus gradually the medieval world acquired the material for secular schools, for research, and for historical writing. The early English churchman Benedict Biscop (628–690), founder of the monastery at Yarrow, labored diligently to collect books, bringing them from Rome on six occasions and at least once making a special trip. Dying, he urgently enjoined his friends to preserve the "most noble and rich library" he had brought together; and his successor Ceolfrid made important additions to it. On this library the Venerable Bede largely founded his *Ecclesiastical History of the English People*, the first great monument of English historical writing. One of Bede's pupils, Egbert, became Archbishop of York, and established on the model of Yarrow a school and library. Ranging among the volumes in this collection, the scholar Alcuin acquired his vast and varied erudition; and in due time he became director of the school at York. Thence he was called to be head of the greater school supported by Charlemagne, who in 782 proclaimed that he had undertaken "the task of reviving, with the utmost zeal, the study of letters well-nigh extinguished through the neglect of our ancestors." The richest phase of the Carolingian Renaissance had begun. It was one of the palace scholars, a close friend of Alcuin's, the versatile Einhard, who wrote in imitation of Suetonius's lives of the Caesars the chief monument of Frankish historiography, his *Life of Charlemagne*. Some critics would credit him also with authorship of part of the Frankish annals.

Before the death of Charlemagne in 814, the means for historical and other literary work had been securely established in his dominions. The light that had been held aloft in Ireland in the sixth century, and that had flared up in England during the seventh and eighth, was now burning brightly on the Continent. During the ninth century, while Britain was being harried by the Danes, a vigorous intellectual life flourished at the Carolingian court and in the great French and German abbeys; a life stimulated by scholars from Ireland, England, and Italy. The author of *The Wanderings and Homes of Manuscripts* has told in a few words what this ninth century accomplished for future students of history:

There is immense activity, literary and artistic, afoot at the Court of Charlemagne and his successors. The German abbeys — e.g., Lorsch, Fulda — and cathedral schools (Mainz, Bamberg, etc.) are full of scribes and teachers. Irishmen who know Greek flock to the Continent, driven from home by Danish invasion; such are Johannus Scotus Erieugena, and Sedulius Scotus. They haunt Liège, Laon, Aix-la-Chapelle, and penetrate to Italy: at Tours the handwriting called the Carolingian minuscule, the parent of our modern "Roman" printing, is developed, though not at Tours alone. At Corbie, Fleury on the Loire, St. Riquier by Abbéville, Rheims, and many another center in northern and Eastern France, libraries are accumulated and ancient books copied. Of St. Gall and Reichenau the same may be said. The archdeacon Pacificus (d. 846) gave over two hundred books to the cathedral, where many of them still are; and at Monte Cassino, the head house of the Benedictine order, books were written in the difficult "Beneventane" hand.[1]

By the thirteenth century the book-trade of Western Europe had become enormous. It still found its centre in Paris, where it was passing from the control of monastic scribes into that of tradesmen or stationers; men who made a livelihood by transcribing books, and who sometimes hired a corps of professional copyists. Towards the close of the century the trade took on specialization. Bologna, for example, with the most renowned school of law in Europe, turned out legal texts and commentaries, both ecclesiastical and civil. Picardy and Artois manufactured quantities of illustrated romances, containing such legends as those of Arthur and Lancelot, which familes of wealth bought to pass the long winter evenings. Thus we reach the fourteenth century, when old books were copied in far greater number than ever before; when, as we have seen, the East was scoured by emissaries of wealth and scholarship to obtain its manuscripts; and when more new books were written than ever, for this was the century of Petrarch and the dawn of the Renaissance. And just beyond it lay the fifteenth century, when the Age of Manuscripts ended, and the Age of Printed Books began; the century of Gutenberg, Aldus, and Caxton.

[1] M. R. James, *op. cit.*, p. 36

IV

The medieval annalist could perform his service to history with such materials as his own memory afforded; aided sometimes by monastic or private archives, sometimes even by an interested court official. But before the more ambitious chronicler of medieval days could accomplish his work, libraries of some scope had to be built up; and ere the true historian could make his bow, the world had to have at least the rudiments of our great modern libraries and archives. The story of their development is full of significance for all lovers of history.

The annalist, in the strictest meaning of the word, always filled a highly limited function. Perhaps the best examples are supplied by Britain. From about the beginning of the seventh century, the Anglo-Saxon Church was accustomed to draw up formal tables which indicated the date of Easter over certain periods of years; and in these Paschal tables, each annual date was followed by a blank space in which church dignitaries or monastic scribes might briefly note all important events. Early annalists, using oral information and the scanty records at hand, set down in these spaces a concise record. Their practise having obvious value, missionaries carried it from the British Isles to the Continent. Gradually in both areas the record expanded and grew more satisfactory. The Carolingian Renaissance gave us such important works as the *Annals of Einhard*, the *Annals of Lorsch*, and the *Annals of St. Bertini*, officially compiled as a record of the acts of Charlemagne and the rulers who preceded and followed him.

In time the best of such annals became worthy of the name of chronicles. That is, they became much broader in scope. Chronicles, though in general still impersonal, sketchy, and founded upon vaguely-indicated sources, are distinguished from annals by their comprehensive character; they relate to a whole nation or a large aspect of history, instead of to one locality, one religious body, one court, or at most one phase of national affairs. *The Anglo-Saxon Chronicles* are thus a general history of the Danish Wars, their most ancient portion having been written in the ninth century, and the whole composed at Canterbury, Evesham, and various other places by various writers. Alfred the Great has been credited with inspiring the composition of this national chronicle as distinguished from local annals, and may even have revised the part describing his own campaigns. Obviously, the chronicler had to search more widely than the annalist for materials and tap a larger range of sources. One of the prime difficulties in dealing with chronicles, indeed, is to ascertain just what were the chief sources, and how much value should be assigned to each. Compelled in this way to find resources outside his own office or monastic hall, the chronicler demanded more books, more papers, more advisers and helpers than the annalist; he demanded the library and the archive, the librarian and archivist.

The development of historical study from the Renaissance onward thus moves *pari passu* with the development of libraries and archives, and the history of these institutions is inextricably intertwined with that of historical scholarship. The first important history of scientific temper written in England was David Hume's. It is significant that in 1752 Hume was appointed head of the Advocates' Library in Edinburgh, a post small in emoluments but rich in opportunities for literary work. By 1753 he was preparing for his great historical endeavor. He wrote his friend Clephane that he felt completely settled in life. He had an income, a house, reputation, and independence; what more could he ask? "A wife? That is not one of the indispensable requisites of life. Books? That is one of them; and I have more than I can use." Without the Advocates' Library, we should never have had a Hume's *History of England*. Gibbon wrote the first three volumes of his *Decline and Fall* amid all the literary accumulations of London, and collected there the materials (including a large private library) for the

three final volumes; Voltaire wrote his most ambitious historical works with the aid of the libraries of Paris and Berlin. It was
no accident that historical writing in the United States first
flourished in the shadow of the libraries at Cambridge (where
the Harvard Library was begun in 1638) and in Boston (where
the Athenaeum was established in 1807). Nor was it an accident that several distinguished American historians — John
Fiske, Justin Winsor, Reuben Gold Thwaites — were also librarians.

Since historical writing in its modern character began only
about two centuries ago, we should expect to find the great
modern libraries comparatively young; and it can be truly said
that none was beyond its infancy five hundred years ago, and
that the best did not attain great scope or vigor until the
eighteenth century.

The Vatican Library, which ranks first in the variety, antiquity, and value of its manuscript collections, really began with
the return of the Papal Court from Avignon after the Great
Schism — that is, was a creation of the fifteenth century; and
it was still a tiny collection of only 2,527 volumes when Sixtus
IV gave it an ornate abode and appointed its first librarian in
1475. So well did Platina, the librarian, exert himself, that
only six years later it counted 3,500 volumes. Yet it grew but
slowly. Montaigne has left a description of it just a hundred
years later (1581), when it was contained in five or six rooms.
"I was taken to every part thereof," he writes, "by a gentleman who invited me to make use of it as often as I might desire." Sixtus V began in 1586 the erection of the handsome
structure in which the Vatican books are still housed, and
thereafter it enjoyed almost uninterrupted prosperity. Early
in the seventeenth century the archives were separated from
the library proper. The one serious disaster was the seizure of
nearly all the early manuscripts and the finest illuminated books
by the French in 1798; but after Waterloo these treasures were
restored. For centuries access to the library was difficult;

until 1881 it contributed less toward historical study than any other great collection. But under Leo XIII commendable advances were made in opening not only the printed books but the manuscripts, and, with some severe restrictions, the Vatican archives, to research; while since his time still more has been done. Within recent years (1927–29) a new catalogue has been compiled by Vatican officials and American librarians working together, upon the best principles of American library practice.

The Bibliothèque Nationale, now probably the largest library in the world, was first established in France as the king's library, and had no real importance until the time of Louis XI; indeed, one of the royal collections was actually bought at the beginning of Charles VII's reign by the Duke of Bedford, and carried away to England. But various monarchs took pride in the collection, and by 1500 so many volumes had been acquired by purchase or seizure that it was a really splendid collection — one of the "four marvels of France." At this time it was at Blois. But about 1520 Francis I, desiring a library nearer his court, established one at Fontainebleau, under the charge of one of the best scholars in his realm. He required that one copy of every work printed in France be sent to his collection, and though at first the rule was more often evaded than obeyed, the time came when it was enforced. In 1544 the Fontainebleau collection absorbed the library at Blois, and some twenty years later the whole body of books and manuscripts was removed to Paris. Here by steady growth it ceased to be the king's private possession and became a general court library. The great Colbert, as superintendent of royal buildings, obtained control of it in 1661, and his wise and energetic administration raised it from about 17,000 to about 50,000 volumes. Historians may remember gratefully that Colbert required provincial officials to search for books and documents illustrating French history and politics, and directed them to copy what they could not buy. It was under Colbert, too, that systematic cataloguing began to make the books more useful to scholars.

Before the seventeenth century closed the library was opened to students twice a week, though this generous rule did not long endure. By 1715 the collection amounted to about 70,000 volumes.

Throughout the vicissitudes of the eighteenth century the Bibliothèque continued to grow, until 1790 found it with more than 150,000 volumes, in addition to opuscules and manuscripts. Then the Revolution brought an astonishing expansion. Books poured in from seized estates and dissolved monasteries. Within a few years the collection more than doubled. Now renamed the national instead of royal library, it retained that title under the first and second empires. During the Napoleonic régime appropriations were increased, the Belgian librarian Van Praet labored amain to make his treasures valuable to scholars, and the conquests of the Emperor brought books from all over the continent. Though most of these had to be returned after the peace of 1815, by that date the Bibliothèque possessed an easy primacy. Its growth thereafter was enormous; in 1927 it boasted of 4,400,000 printed books and more than 120,000 manuscripts. From Van Praet's time onward the library had been open every weekday to students using its historical and literary treasures.

The British Museum, almost as large as the Bibliothèque and so much better classified and administered that French scholars have been known to cross the Channel and use it in preference to their own, can also be traced back to a small royal collection. This was formed by Henry VII, and slowly increased by his Tudor and Stuart successors. During the Commonwealth a few friends preserved the puny collection intact, and it was handed over to Charles II unharmed. Under William and Mary it received its first eminent librarian, Richard Bentley. His strict enforcement of a much earlier rule (1662) enabling the library to claim a copy of every work published under the British flag brought in about a thousand volumes. The early Hanoverians took little interest in these printed treasures, and

George II presented them to the nation in 1757. Meanwhile, two other important libraries had grown up in England. One was the Cottonian, especially notable as having been established for historical objects. It was founded by Sir Robert Cotton, a younger contemporary of Shakespeare, who spent money lavishly for historical materials — chronicles, records, charters and other state papers, as well as survivals of the old monastic collections. His array of public documents, many of them priceless originals, was scrutinized with a rather hostile eye by the public authorities; some of them jealous because they needed his papers for official purposes, some fearful lest he sell state secrets. But historical scholars, including Bishop Burnet, used them. The other great English collection was the Harleian Library, founded by Robert Harley, Earl of Oxford, who was roughly a contemporary of Pope's (1661–1724). It included the collections of Stow, the historian of London, and of Fox, whose history of the martyrs so edified our Puritan forefathers. Harley's son, the second Earl of Oxford, continued the accumulation of manuscripts, charters, rolls, prints, and books. They, like the Cottonian books and papers, were gathered primarily to furnish materials for the study of English history.

Finally, in 1753, the Harleian manuscripts, though not the books, were bought by the government. This was the year in which Sir Hans Sloane bequeathed to the nation his books, manuscripts, and rarities, the nucleus of the British Museum, for the nominal sum of £20,000. The Cottonian, Harleian, and Sloane collections were at once united, and four years later the gift of George II united the royal library with them. At the beginning of 1759, in the midst of one of the greatest periods of victory in the annals of the British Empire, the consolidated collections were thrown open to the public under the name of the British Museum. At once bequests and donations began to enlarge the Museum. Many of them were rich in materials for British history and biography. Though the government was long parsimonious in its appropriations, at Victoria's accession the Museum contained about 240,000 volumes, and by 1865 it held 640,000. This was in the midst of the great era of Victorian historiography, when Froude, Freeman, Stubbs, Carlyle, Milman, and others were most active; and they all relied heavily upon the collection. By 1927 the library contained some 3,200,000 books, a vast array of pamphlets, and about 56,000 manuscripts. Of all the great libraries, it has unquestionably been the most useful to historical scholarship.

The principal American collection, the Congressional Library, is by far the youngest of the major libraries, but the generosity with which the government has supported it promises to render it preëminent at no distant date. Founded in 1800, the efforts of Albert Gallatin and Samuel Latham Mitchill had made it a valuable though small collection by 1814, when it was destroyed in the British capture of Washington. After the war, Jefferson's library of some 6,700 volumes was bought by the government for $23,000 as the basis for a new collection. By the middle of the century the library held more than 50,000 volumes. Though a fire in 1851 destroyed more than half of it, most of Jefferson's books fortunately survived; and Congress spent such generous sums for replacements that before the Civil War opened it was larger than ever. At the close of this conflict the library of the Smithsonian Institution, about 40,000 volumes, chiefly scientific, was combined with the Congressional Library. Thenceforward its progress was more rapid and sustained than that of any rival. Two able administrators, A. R. Spofford and Herbert Putnam, led in building it up; Congress appropriated funds for purchases on an unprecedented scale; and it became the chief repository for papers of distinguished Americans. Under acts of 1834 and later, it purchased those of Washington; in 1848 those of Jefferson, Madison, and Hamilton; in 1849 those of Monroe; while by purchase or gift it has since acquired those of many other public men.

A great building, the most costly and ornate ever devoted to books, was opened in 1911; and though it was designed to hold 4,000,000 volumes, it became so crowded that by 1935 it was necessary to begin a great addition. Strongest in history, politics, and law, the Congressional Library is better adapted to historical work than to any other purpose, and has for a generation been the chief focal point of research in the American past.

It is impossible to say anything here of other national libraries only less important than those just briefly described — the great State Libraries in Berlin and Munich; the National-bibliothek in Vienna; the State Library at Leningrad, declared by some authorities to be the largest on the globe, with not fewer than 5,000,000 volumes and 240,000 manuscripts; and the Lenin Memorial Library in Moscow, with more than three million volumes. We can merely mention the numerous libraries rich in unique books, like the Laurentian Library in Florence, the Bibliothèque Mazarine in Paris, and the John Rylands Library in Manchester; the great municipal collections all over Europe, the Americas, and Australasia, of which the New York Public Library plainly stands first; the many university libraries, like the Bodleian at Oxford, the Sorbonne, those of the Universities of Berlin, Vienna, Warsaw, and Leningrad, and the even more extensive collections at Harvard, Yale, Columbia, and the University of Chicago; and such treasuries of manuscript material as the Huntington Library at San Marino, California. It is sufficient to say that since the invention of printing the fast-increasing production of books has scattered libraries throughout the civilized world. In far-off New Zealand, in young lands like Argentina and California, in what a few generations ago was the hermit nation of Japan, collections of books exist far richer than those known to the eighteenth-century historians of Western Europe. The extent and variety of the modern collections, in fact, impose upon historical study one of its chief present-day characteristics — its specialization.

V

But modern historical work rests upon a triple base, and books, whether manuscript or printed, are but one of its supports. The other two are public archives, and collections of private papers. Until the later decades of the eighteenth century, most historical works of modern times were based upon book-material, for little else was available. Yet until government documents were made available for study upon a broad scale, no student could write critically or exhaustively of political transactions. Until the letters, memoranda, and diaries of individual leaders were thrown open on a comparable scale, no man could write expertly of the rôle of personalities in any movement or conflict. A brief examination of the steps by which such aids to historical composition became available will throw much light on the progress of historiography.

Among modern governments Great Britain's has shown the most enterprise in collecting, arranging, and throwing open to study its official records. "Both from an earlier date and on a larger scale than other nations," according to competent American authorities,[1] it has displayed a conscientious zeal in protecting, cataloguing, and giving use to its archives. Few lands have suffered so little from invasion or civil war as England, and her internal tranquillity has done much to keep her papers intact. Yet even Britain's records remained largely inaccessible to the historian until the beginning of the nineteenth century.

For many centuries every department of the British government, administrative, legislative, and judicial, kept its own records. They were used, in random and unsystematic fashion, by a few specially favored historical workers in the seventeenth and eighteenth centuries, but their contents were unclassified, unexplored, and largely unknown. At last, in 1800, a Record

[1] George Matthew Dutcher and others, *A Guide to Historical Literature*, pp. 477, 478

Commission was appointed by Parliament, which with other royal commissions and committees began examining the records, publishing lists of documents, and even making calendars or abstracts of the most important. These lists were sufficiently well done to have permanent usefulness. For example, students of Irish history will always find of basic importance the three volumes (1813–25) of "Reports from the committee appointed by His Majesty to execute the measures recommended in an address to the House of Commons respecting the public records of Ireland." The Record Commission was shortly publishing important papers in full; such as the proceedings of the Privy Council from 1386 to 1542, which it issued in seven volumes in 1834–37. Altogether, before it went out of existence in 1869, this single body published almost a hundred volumes, and did much to drive highways into the *terra incognita* of official papers. Meanwhile, as early as 1786 the British Government had set up a state printing establishment which made possible a careful supervision of printed documents. This was the Stationery Office, which still acts as printer, publisher, and bookseller for government departments, and whose publications have long been divided into two general groups: parliamentary papers, or "blue books," and non-parliamentary papers.

Then in 1838 the British Government blazed a path for other nations to follow by establishing the first central repository for archives, competently administered, and open to all students of the past. A law of that year created the Public Record Office, and made the Master of the Rolls its head. From the beginning he was custodian of practically all the judicial records of the realm; while fourteen years later an Order in Council placed all administrative records under his authority. The Public Record Office pushed on with the work begun by the Record Commission in publishing lists, calendars, and complete documents from the archives. For a century its gray stone home, quietly placed between Chancery and Fetter Lane just off roaring Fleet Street, has been a magnet for historical students from all parts of the planet, and especially of the English-speaking world. Americans find here much of their own early history. The records brought from the Colonial Office include the papers of the Committee on Trade and Plantations down to the severance of the thirteen colonies from the Empire. The records brought from the Foreign Office begin with 1782, when it was established, and contain a wealth of material on Anglo-American relations. A great part of the important manuscripts in the British archives have now been printed entire, or calendared so fully that the abstracts relieve the student from the necessity of consulting the originals.

In the year that the Record Commission ceased work (1869), Queen Victoria appointed a Royal Commission on Historical Manuscripts, its chairman being the Master of the Rolls, which has become famous throughout the domain of historical studies. Its duty was to inquire as to the existence of private manuscripts and papers, "a knowledge of which would be of great utility in the illustration of history, constitutional law, science, and general literature." Everyone knew that the older families of the kingdom possessed immense stores of manuscripts. In 1870 the Commission issued the first of its long shelfful of reports, to which it is steadily adding. The calendar of the Cecil MSS, owned by the Marquis of Salisbury and more valuable for the time of Elizabeth than any in London, fills fourteen volumes. The papers of the Marquis of Ormonde, at Kilkenny Castle, have been abstracted in ten volumes; the Stuart MSS in Windsor Castle, the property of the king, in seven volumes; and the American MSS in the Royal Institution, four volumes. Many finds of sensational historical and literary value have been made. At first defective in scholarship, the reports have long since become models of their kind; and they are indispensable to any working library of European, Imperial, or American history. To cite but one of many items interesting to Americans, the diaries of the first Earl of Egmont are full of material on the establishment and development of Georgia — the work of Oglethorpe, the activities of the two Wesleys, Indian relations, immigration, the progress of settlement, and so on. Indeed, American colonial history could not have been properly written without the work of the Commission.

Many of the searches of the Commission were made in the nick of time. Increasing changes in the distribution of wealth in Great Britain have brought about a rapid breakup of estates, and the sale of libraries and muniments. Numerous collections of family papers, especially those containing autographs of value, have been sold piecemeal; others have been bought in bulk and transported abroad. The Commission reported in 1926 that "the number of collections that have actually been reported on and cannot now be traced is no longer inconsiderable, but in these cases our reports supply to some extent their place."

The publication of Parliamentary debates naturally began in the country which was the mother of Parliaments. The first systematic and satisfactory collection made in England was the work not of the government but of an eminent journalist — William Cobbett's *Parliamentary History of England from the Earliest Period to the year 1803*. It supplanted various earlier works by private hands; *D'Ewes's Journals of the Parliaments of Queen Elizabeth*, for example, and *Grey's Debates . . . 1667–1694*, as well as the more ambitious *Parliamentary or Constitutional History of England, 1066–1660*, issued in twenty-four volumes in the middle of the eighteenth century. Cobbett's enterprise was continued from 1803 by Thomas C. Hansard, whose father was government printer, under the title of *Parliamentary Debates;* and the reports continue to be generally called *Hansard's Debates*.

French archival practice, unlike British, has been based upon a decentralization of materials, and has been imitated by most nations of continental Europe. As the result of a policy carefully formulated in 1789, the national archives have been preserved in well-classified groups in the Hôtel de Soubise in Paris. Each of the departments has meanwhile guarded its separate archives as scrupulously as have the American States, while municipal and communal records have also been kept separately. In some respects France has led the world in the critical study of official documents — especially medieval documents — as sources for history. The first great textbook in this field (that is, in diplomatics) was the work of the Benedictine scholar Jean Mabillon, whose *De Re Diplomatica* was published in 1681. The best-known institution for cultivating diplomatics, the École des Chartes, founded in Paris in 1821, has ever since been an unapproached centre for documentary and paleographical studies. In this way France has been kept fully supplied with archival experts. All the French collections, national, departmental, and local, have been well explored since the Revolution; a part of the material has also been inventoried, though some of this has been done so badly that the lists have been withdrawn from circulation.

Germany has her Reichsarchiv at Potsdam, and long had separate archives for all the states of the country. Italy has seventeen different repositories, one for each of the ancient divisions of the country; the Tuscan archives at Florence being particularly important. Of course the Vatican has its separate archives, impressive in extent and value. Switzerland and the Netherlands possess national archives at Berne and The Hague respectively, and separate cantonal and state archives as well. Both in Germany and Austria the government has given support to the study of diplomatics, and Italy has not neglected it.

The United States held the inglorious distinction of having been one of the last great Powers to provide itself with a central building and administration for its national records. After the Civil War, as wealth and population increased, and as Federal functions grew at the expense of the state, the mass of documents in Washington rapidly became prodigious. Yet even in

1900 it remained the general rule that each bureau and office retained all its past records; a rule modified only by a partial concentration into departmental collections, and the deposit of a few groups of papers in the Congressional Library. Thus widely scattered and ever more voluminous, the records were grossly neglected. They were constantly being damaged by dampness, heat, insects, and careless handling, fires repeatedly destroyed valuable files, and many documents were thrown away as valueless. One Cabinet officer sold 400 tons of official records as junk. As the result of a long agitation, Congress finally appropriated a total of about $12,000,000 for an archives building — a sum sufficient to erect the best structure of its kind in the world. Ground was broken in 1931, the building was completed five years later, and, the office of Archivist of of the United States having meanwhile been created, the removal of records to this monumental home began in 1936. The stack space comprised five and a half million cubic feet. Here the papers could be kept in perfect physical condition, protected by elaborate devices from fire, burglary, dust, and sunlight; could be carefully classified; and could be made instantly available to students.

At the outset the Federal Archives were hampered by the reluctance of various departments to surrender their more interesting and valuable records, even when not needed for frequent official reference. But as this reluctance is slowly overcome, the collections promise to grow rapidly. No other government has furnished such complete facilities to historical students — catalogues, inventories, and other finding tools, aid by staff employees, and every mechanical device. As the first Archivist has written:

Filing equipment designed by government architects especially for the National Archives Building, for the purpose of facilitating the filing and handling of government archives, has been installed. Three beautiful "Search Rooms," well-lighted, air-conditioned, and furnished with comfortable desks and chairs — a feature almost unique in buildings of this kind — are provided for the use of students. Around the walls of these rooms is open shelving for approximately 50,000 books, which will place almost within arm's length of the student a carefully selected service library to supplement the archival material. . . . If he wants this material copied by other methods than pen or typewriter, reproductions can be made for him by photostating, photographing, microfilming, or multilithing processes.[1]

VI

For more than a century governmental aid to history has extended in some nations to still another field, from a literary point of view the most interesting of all. This is the publication of historical texts — chronicles, annals, collections of private or public letters, and the like — particularly for the formative periods of national life. To Germany belongs the honor of leading the way. While the Napoleonic Wars were still raging, it occurred to Von Stein that the printing of the principal sources for early German history would be a valuable contribution to patriotism and scholarship alike. His enterprise — the *Monumenta Germaniae Historica*, which by 1925 had attained its 125th volume — thus began as an expression of the new German spirit born from the Napoleonic upheaval. When peace came in 1815 a commission of the ablest German historians was named to edit the known sources, and to search out new ones. The first volume was published in 1826 under private auspices, but the German government soon took the series over and subsidized it. The first two editors were succeeded in 1886 by a board, and nearly all the distinguished medievalists of Germany for a century past have been enlisted in the undertaking. Jacob Grimm and others also initiated in 1849 the publication of a series of German translations of the chief Latin chronicles and histories of the Middle Ages, which has reached more than ninety volumes. Various German states have of course also published sets devoted to the material from their archives.

[1] R. D. W. Connor, in *Minnesota History*, XVII, No. 1, March, 1936 .

In France the historian Guizot, while minister of public instruction, planned a collection of unpublished documents on national history, of which the first volume was brought out in 1836. This was carried forward after 1881 by the Comité des Travaux Historiques et Scientifiques, with government encouragement; and not far from 300 volumes have now been published. The Comité has also issued about a hundred volumes of documents upon the economic history of the French Revolution. The French Foreign Office has meanwhile been commendably active in publishing collections of treaties, instructions to ambassadors, and other documents — though the archives of the Ministry are not open to such recent dates as those of the British Foreign Office and the American State Department. It may also be mentioned that the publication of stenographic reports of parliamentary debates began in France under Napoleon III, and is of course still carried on by the state. Meanwhile, a compilation of debates from the beginnings in 1787 down to 1860 has also long been carried forward, and is slowly approaching completion.

Other nations began to publish historical texts soon after the bodies created by Stein and Guizot did so. The work of the German and French commissions inspired King Charles Albert of Sardinia to establish a similar body in 1833; and its work for Italian history, the *Monumenta Historia Patriae*, has extended down to our own day. The Italian Historical Institute, founded a dozen years after national unification and kept under governmental control, has edited a large collection of sources for the history of Italy, as yet relating to medieval times alone, and has also carried on the publication of a valuable series of Italian chronicles, originally begun by private enterprise. Even Russia, even Spain, early fell in with the general movement. The Czar's government in 1835 created the Archeographical Commission, which in 1841 began to publish the old Muscovite chronicles, since supplemented by a wide variety of narratives and documents. In Madrid, the Royal Academy of History commenced in 1841 its *Collection of Inedited Documents for the History of Spain;* a publicly supported enterprise which, dealing chiefly with the reigns of Charles V and Philip II, had reached a total of 112 volumes before the Spanish-American War. Belgium, too, established a Royal Historical Commission in 1834, which two years later began issuing a series that has now grown to more than 180 volumes. The Dutch royal family caught the impulse, and in 1834 initiated a series of volumes drawn from the archives of the House of Orange-Nassau.

The individualistic tradition has always been strong in Britain. The state hesitated to trench upon fields which might be occupied by commercial publishers or learned societies. Yet even there, the government finally determined to publish materials upon the early history of the nation. In 1857 the Master of Rolls submitted to the Treasury a project for a series of chronicles, records, and other source works from the Roman invasion to the accession of Henry VIII, which was at once approved. Precedence was to be given to the scarcest and most valuable materials, and they were to be edited by scholars without mutilation or abridgment. Each was to be treated as a first edition, and the most accurate text possible was to be achieved by a collation of manuscripts; while each was to contain a historical and biographical introduction. The year 1858 saw the inception of the so-called Rolls Series (the full title is *Rerum Britannicorum Aevi Scriptores, or Chronicles and Memorials of Great Britain and Ireland During the Middle Ages*) with several interesting books. Among them were John Capgrave's chronicle of England to 1417, a volume of lives of Edward the Confessor by various hands, a history of the Gray Friars written in the early thirteenth century, and the only metrical history of early Scotland. These octavo volumes, beautifully printed, carefully edited, their texts superseding all previous editions, were highly useful, while their example was not lost upon individuals and historical societies. When the World War began, nearly 250 volumes of the Rolls Series had been published.

They comprised one of the fullest collections of medieval chronicles issued in any country in the world.

The American government has as yet done singularly little sustained work in publishing materials for history — materials, that is, going beyond the *Congressional Globe* and *Congressional Record* (begun in 1833 and 1873 respectively), and the annual volumes on *Foreign Affairs*. The antiquarian Peter Force, an editor and mayor of Washington, prevailed upon Congress to subsidize his compilation of documents of colonial and Revolutionary eras, called *American Archives*. Later the government supplied money for a series of American State Papers covering approximately the first half century of national activity; for a fairly complete collection of the messages and papers of the Presidents; for an admirable compilation of the military and naval records of the Civil War; for the fullest edition of Washington's writings yet made; and for some less ambitious enterprises, such as a collection of Territorial Papers. But its activity has been sporadic and has resulted in no such impressive work as the *Monumenta Germaniae Historica* or the Rolls Series. As our history lengthens, it should and doubtless will follow a more generous policy.

For more than a century the efforts of governments to promote the study of historical records have been vigorously supplemented by those of learned societies. A few of these bodies may be traced back for more than two centuries. One of the first was the Society of Antiquaries in London, which began its active career in 1717, and later won the patronage of George II. An organization of the same name later sprang up in Edinburgh. But the heyday of the British societies did not come until the nineteenth century. The Bannatyne Club, founded in Edinburgh in 1823, and the Abbotsford Club, established there in 1835, both published important sources for Scottish history. The Camden Society of London began in 1838 to issue volumes chosen from "whatever is valuable, but at present little known, amongst the materials for the civil, ecclesiastical,

or literary history of the United Kingdom." When the Rolls
Series began, the Camden Society turned to the later centuries;
but the Caxton Society Publications, commenced in 1845, pertain to the Middle Ages. Famous throughout the world are the
Hakluyt Society Publications, carried on since 1846, and consisting of rare and valuable voyages and travels by men of
divers races. The Pipe Rolls Society was founded in 1883 to
publish the Great Rolls of the Exchequer and other public documents prior to 1200 A.D.; and the Selden Society was formed in
the same decade to present materials for the history of English
law. In Ireland the Ossianic Society, established in 1853, has
brought out materials upon early Irish history.[1]

Most of the important historical societies in America bear
the names of States or cities. The first, the Massachusetts
Historical Society, was modelled upon the London Society of
Antiquaries. Founded in 1781 by Jeremy Belknap, John Pintard, and Ebenezer Hazard, it launched the next year upon its
long and distinguished work of publication. Such editors as
Charles Deane and Worthington C. Ford have given its *Proceedings* and its *Collections* — a long array of both — a value
surpassed by those of no other society in the world. Fifteen

---

[1] Similar bodies exist on the Continent. Some are of earlier date than
any in England. It is impossible here to make more than passing mention
of the work of the Bollandists, the Belgian Jesuits who began in 1643 to
publish their great collection of the lives and legends of the saints, arranged
chronologically by days. The work was interrupted late in the eighteenth
century, but was resumed with the support of the Belgian Government
in 1837. The Bollandists also began in 1882 to issue a quarterly review;
and they have published valuable catalogues and analyses of the hagio-
graphic manuscripts in the principal libraries of Belgium, France, and
Italy. Almost coeval in origin was the great work done by the Maurists,
or French Benedictines of St. Maur, who in 1645 began issuing their
scholarly series of writings of the church fathers. Their activities soon
broadened into the publication of collections of documents, works on
French ecclesiastical history, and other learned works, executed with
sound scholarship and acute critical sense. On the Continent some great
individual scholars, such as Ludovico Antonio Muratori, also carried
through remarkable enterprises in documentary publication at an early
date. Muratori died in 1750.

years after its establishment, John Pintard, with the aid of De Witt Clinton, Gouverneur Morris, and James Kent, founded the New York Historical Society, which published its first volume of *Collections* in 1811. A third prominent organization, the American Antiquarian Society, was chartered by the Massachusetts legislature in 1812; but its publications have contained less notable source material than those of the two pioneer bodies, or of the Pennsylvania Historical Society, founded in 1825. This type of enterprise was soon taken up in the West. As early as 1830 the Indiana Historical Society was organized, less than twenty years after its first president had taken part in the battle of Tippecanoe. Of all the Western societies Wisconsin's, which under Lyman Draper and Reuben G. Thwaites built up unsurpassed pioneer collections at Madison, has been the most influential. A number of historical societies in time formed close relations with neighboring universities. The work of historians at Harvard, for example, has long been facilitated by the libraries of the Massachusetts Historical and the American Antiquarian Societies; McMaster did much of his work in the Pennsylvania Society; and the Wisconsin Society greatly influenced the labors of Frederick J. Turner and other university scholars. In Minnesota and California the State universities and the State historical societies have maintained close relations.

Where the initiative of the privately-formed historical societies first blazed the way, State enterprise has followed. The Massachusetts, New York, and Pennsylvania Societies asked for no public aid. But the Wisconsin Society represents a hybrid effort, for though it is a body of private individuals, it has received liberal State grants. And in a number of States public agencies have been set up to collect manuscript materials, publish lists and abstracts, and edit volumes of sources. Among them are the State Historical Library in Illinois, the historical commissions of North Carolina and Indiana, and the departments of archives and history in Iowa, Alabama, and Mississippi. New York has an active State Historian. Four of the Canadian Provinces, Nova Scotia, Quebec, Ontario, and British Columbia, possess archival departments of real vigor, which have published valuable lists of materials and volumes of sources, and which coöperate with the extensive Dominion archives at Ottawa. Several of the Canadian Provinces also have active historical societies. The *Transactions* of the Literary and Historical Society of Quebec, for example, go back to 1829, and its important series of historical documents commenced publication in 1838. One of the younger Dominion bodies, the Champlain Society, has issued since 1907 an especially valuable series of source publications upon the period of exploration.

Throughout the world, during the past two centuries, this labor of providing source materials for historical study — of collecting official papers, manuscripts, letters, diaries, broadsides, pamphlets, newspapers, and what not; of publishing lists, calendars, and volumes of documents; of editing long series of annals and chronicles; of digesting scattered data into historical magazines and volumes of transactions — has gone on with accelerating vigor. It has of course been accompanied by a tremendous increase in the number of printed books of all kinds. At the close of the eighteenth century only a few hundred volumes were published each year in the English language; but 1935 found 16,678 volumes (not including pamphlets) issued in Great Britain, and 7,677 in the United States. What was a slender stream in 1800, a modest river in 1850, a rushing torrent in 1900, has long since swelled into a mighty sea. Where the ordinary historian in Hume's day thought of his sources as comparatively small collections of printed books, now he thinks of them as lying primarily in huge collections of papers, printed and unprinted. So vast are they that one recent historian speaks of the data on European affairs 1871–1890 as "a staggering mass . . . rapidly becoming too great for one human mind to grasp."[1] Where in even Macaulay's and Guizot's day history

[1] W. L. Langer, *European Alliances and Alignments,* 1871–90, Preface

was necessarily centered in politics and government, for three-fourths of the available materials pertained to that, now its interest has become centrifugal and diffused; history deals with a hundred facets of human life previously neglected. Whereas a century ago the talents required for writing history were primarily literary, now they are equally literary and scientific; and the historian cannot understand the evidence upon any era unless he can apply at least the elementary principles of economics, geography, sociology, and psychology to it.

It must be added that while two centuries ago the historian could blithely essay tasks on the largest scale, Hume undertaking the history of England from the earliest times to his own day, Gibbon that of ten centuries of the Western world, and Bancroft the whole American record, today the magnitude of the accumulated materials forces the historical writer to take a more modest view of his capacities. To present from the sources, in thoroughness and detail, the life of a single generation in any of the great Powers during the twentieth century, will hereafter be regarded as a staggering task.

VII

Yet it must not be thought that the progress of the written word has given historical students too much material; far from it. The gaps will remain numerous. More men become writers every decade; more books, periodicals, and documents are circulated; thanks to stenographers and typewriters, far more letters are written, mailed, and filed. Records of public and private business are preserved in ever greater detail. Yet not all departments of history have benefited equally from this increasing articulateness. Changes have come in communication which leave many transactions unrecorded. The telephone has annihilated much of the domain of the written word; railways and airplanes have made face-to-face conversation easy; the radio has created intangible newspapers and magazines which, leaving no files, vanish into thin air. Many important decisions of governments, of business, and of private individuals, are made utterly without record. Historians may learn (with or without enthusiasm) that the Federal Archives have acquired 35,000 cubic feet of records of inactive pension claims, 800 cubic feet of records of the Railway Labor Board 1920–26, and 131 cubic feet of records of the Wickersham Law-Observance Commission. But they know that many of the most important acts under Presidents Coolidge, Hoover, and Franklin D. Roosevelt were planned in unrecorded conferences of a few men or in telephone conversations. They realize that whereas in Washington's day a leader would write a long letter to explain his position, today he will catch an airplane and deliver his views orally.

Nor should we, in facing the vast stores of records accumulated by the modern world, exaggerate the importance of the written word in perpetuating the stuff of history. For history, our understanding of times past, is more than facts and ideas; it is a matter of the spirit as well. And our comprehension of the spirit of bygone ages is given us not through physical remains, inscriptions, manuscripts, and books alone; it is given us in large part through the transmission of personalities. A spiritual force runs down from generation to generation, from father to child, from teacher to teacher. The judge who welcomes a successor to the bench finds means to hand on an understanding of the spirit of the law; some undefinable force descends from Marshall to Story, from Holmes to Cardozo. Our own generation could never understand Christianity if that great moulding force of society were perpetuated only through the letter of the New Testament. It has been perpetuated far more through personalities, institutions, and successive generations of believers. An apostolic succession of saintly men, in the broadest sense, has perpetuated it; a succession of churches has perpetuated it; a Christian sentiment, traversing successive generations as a wave traverses the wide ocean, has perpetuated it. In the same way, our own generation could never fully understand the spirit of Anglo-American liberty were that written only in books, newspapers, and documents. It is written instead in the hearts and minds of more than two hundred million English-speaking people, and were every written word blotted out they would recreate its essence. A comprehension of the spirit of Christianity, the spirit of Anglo-American liberty, the spirit that animates other great social forces, is part of the data of history. It is not stored in archives or libraries, and is not cited in footnotes; but it will not be ignored by any student who realizes that the great perdurable elements of civilization have never been constructed by plumbline and yardstick — that some have not been built by human hands at all.

CHAPTER FIVE

THE CHEATING DOCUMENT

Mankind dearly loves a good story, and dearly loves to believe it true. Before any tale can greatly please the hearer thereof, it must have some degree of verisimilitude; it must conquer part of our faith. Many of the earliest masters of fiction dressed it as absolute fact, and were credited beyond their expectation. Thus multitudes have accepted Defoe's *Memoirs of a Cavalier* as a true history — Lord Chatham did so; and even astute critics, impressed by the wealth of circumstantial detail in Defoe's *Journal of the Plague Year*, have declared that it must have been based on some work by an actual observer. In daily social intercourse and in literature, an artistic lie is sooner swallowed than a clumsy truth. Indeed, many people insist through thick and thin on having the artistic lie in place of the bald and unattractive fact. Historians may explain a thousand times that Wellington never exclaimed, "Up, Guards, and at them!" and that C. C. Pinckney never blazed, "Millions for defense, but not one cent for tribute." These supposed ejaculations will nevertheless remain immortal. Sober critics have now labored for generations to show that Tacitus's portrait of Tiberius is cruelly unjust; but its vigor and artistic unity render it indestructible. Legends often become a point of faith. At one time the State of North Carolina made it *compulsory* for the public schools to teach that Mecklenburg County had adopted a Declaration of Independence on May 20, 1776 — to teach what had been clearly demonstrated an untruth.

Credulity is pleasant; we all like to be cozened a bit. We love to cover the harsh gray stone of the everyday world with the moss and ivy of fancy. And it must be added that pleasing inventions fly like gossamer before the wind. Mr. H. L. Mencken early in his career wrote an article on the bathtub, in which he asserted with plausible historical detail that it had been invented in the 1840's, that Millard Fillmore had been the first to install one in the White House, that the medical profession and public long regarded it with deep suspicion, and that laws had been passed against the perilous contraption by Virginia, Pennsylvania, and Massachusetts. He was astonished to find this *jeu d'esprit* accepted by most readers at face value. He was still more astonished to find newspapers and magazines copying these "facts" in ever-widening circles, so that they cropped up year after year in the most dignified periodicals. This naïveté of humankind has its humorous side. But to historians it is not quite so amusing. For one reason, historians prefer a critical-minded to a simple-minded public. For another, the credulity of the public pays charlatans so well in money, in applause, or in gratification of the literary instinct, that history is cursed by the constant invention of stories, letters, speeches, documents, and even whole books.

Our simple forefathers drank delightedly at many fountains on which modern scholarship long ago pinned up the harsh placard "Condemned." Take as an example that ingratiating old book called Sir John Mandeville's *Travels*. Sir John saw many wonderful matters in his Eastern journeys, and heard of more — the monarch Prester John; a haunted valley in Armenia; two-headed monsters; the dragon of Cos; the castle of the sparrow-hawks; and miracles aplenty. Long after his marvels began to be taken with large pinches of salt, men still believed him a reality and his travels a fact. But he has melted to nothingness like a ghost in sunshine. Critics now doubt whether there ever was a Mandeville, a knight, or even an Englishman connected with the book's composition. Possibly one John Burgoyne, living at Liège under the name of Jean de Bourgogne, was the author. But author is not the correct word, for the volume is an arrant jackdaw's nest. It was stolen in bits from other writings, among which may be named Brunetto Latini's *Tresor*, Albert of Aix's chronicle of the first crusade, the *Speculum* of Vincent de Beauvais, and works by Jacques de Vitry, Piano Carpini, Petrus Comestor, and Hayton the Arminian. Tracing the origins of this pastiche has furnished no little amusement to scholars.[1]

Or consider the delight with which our forefathers read Parson Weems's *Life of George Washington*, first issued in 1800 and greatly expanded by anecdotal material in successive editions. Mason Locke Weems was part clergyman, part book-agent, part schoolmaster in northern Virginia, and probably held occasional services in Pohick Church, where Washington had once worshipped. Upon this he based his title of "formerly rector of Mount Vernon Parish." In its original form the *Life* was a brief, inaccurate, and highly rhetorical record of Washington's military career. Subsequently Weems added many homely stories which, if not true, were at least *ben trovato*. Each carried an ostentatious moral. His immortal tale of George, the hatchet, and the cherry tree was introduced as "too true to be doubted," though his only authority was an "aged lady" who as a "distant relative" had sometimes visited the Washingtons. Like the book's long dialogues and set speeches, it was obviously invented. According to a grandson of Weems, it was probably suggested by the fact that one of his own children had cut down a "Pride of China" tree and frankly confessed his misdeed. But multitudes have believed it:

One day in the garden where he often amused himself hacking his mother's pea-sticks he unluckily tried the edge of his hatchet on the body of a beautiful young English cherry-tree, which he barked so terribly that I don't believe the tree ever got the better of it. The next morning the old gentleman, finding out what had befallen his

[1] See John Fiske on Mandeville in *The Discovery of America*, I, 290, 291.

tree, which by the way was a great favorite, came into the house; and with much warmth asked for the mischievous author, declaring at the same time that he would not have taken five guineas for his tree. Nobody would tell him anything about it. Presently George and his hatchet made their appearance. "*George*," said his father, "do you know who killed that beautiful little cherry-tree yonder in the garden?" This was a *tough question;* and George staggered under it for a moment, but quickly recovered himself, and, looking at his father, with the sweet face of youth brightened with the inexpressible charm of all-conquering truth, he bravely cried out: "I can't tell a lie, pa; you know I can't tell a lie. I did cut it with my hatchet."

II

Of course forgery need not ordinarily be feared by students of history working under reasonable safeguards. The contents of most historical libraries are carefully sifted and re-sifted by experts. Custodians of public archives usually take every precaution to exclude spurious documents. Dishonest books, whether forgeries or plagiarisms, are in general soon exposed. Though single letters may be forged, it is practically impossible to forge a whole file of them without detection. Newspapers almost defy forgery, for the practitioners of the art do not have the extensive apparatus required. Many a historian, many a biographer, has worked for years without being tripped by false materials. Nevertheless, the first duty of every student of the past is to make sure of the authenticity of his materials, for not a little history has been vitiated by the careless acceptance of non-authentic materials. No less a work than Lord Morley's two-volume *Rousseau*, long accepted as standard, has been shown to be profoundly mistaken in its view of Rousseau's personality because it is based largely upon Mme. d'Epinay's *Memoires*, which have been proved false.[1] Las Casas, Napoleon's faithful companion in his last years, wrote a four-volume *Memorial de Ste-Hélène* whose documents were for decades

[1] On Morley's errors see *Philosophical Review*, XXVI, 214 ff., January, 1917.

taken at face value; until it was shown that he had actually forged a number of Napoleonic letters.[1]

Forgery is in fact one of the oldest and commonest of human offenses. In ancient India grants of land made by rulers for sacerdotal purposes were often defined in inscriptions upon plates of copper. But implicit reliance cannot be placed upon these records. As early as the time of the lawgiver Manu punishments were decreed for the falsification of grants, and copper plates have been found which are barefaced forgeries. In this instance the motive was venal in the lowest sense, and the action untouched by artistry. Forgeries committed by politicians who wish to damage an opponent, such as the famous "Morey letter" falsely attributed to Garfield in 1880 — a letter approving the importation of Chinese labor — are equally devoid of dignity. Much more dangerous are those forgeries in which a skilled hand attempts to supply the market for writings by famous men. One of the first warnings the teacher of renaissance history must give students of Luther, Erasmus, and numerous other figures is to beware of the stream of manufactured documents attributed to them. The forgery of letters purporting to be by Marie Antoinette has long been a thriving industry, and still continues. In Americana, the New York Public Library maintains a large collection — a veritable museum — of false autographic material. As spurious letters of Franklin, Washington, Jefferson, Lincoln, Poe, and other famous figures come up for sale and are recognized, dealers turn many over to the library. The most notorious of American autograph forgers, Robert Spring,[2] a bookdealer in Philadelphia just before and after the Civil War, turned out hundreds of skilful forgeries to supply the market. His fictitious documents are more plentiful today than his own genuine let-

[1] Lord Rosebery, *Napoleon: The Last Phase*, 26–38, for a long discussion of the spurious letters

[2] The *New York Times*, June 18, 1936, contains an account of Spring's activities.

ters; and grandsons of his original clients are not infrequently astonished to learn that their treasured papers by early American heroes are impostures. Manufactured Lincoln letters have found their way even into printed compilations of his papers.[1]

Sometimes the motive in forgery has been a curious compound of venal and artistic instincts. No one today would censure harshly the tragic boy-genius Thomas Chatterton, whose "Rowley Papers," certain invented documents brought forward as authentic remains of medieval Bristol, were touched by an inspiration which made them valuable in their own right. Nor has anyone ever thought severely of the gay Scottish poet Allan Cunningham, who, employed to collect border ballads for an Edinburgh publisher, found it easier to invent some than to discover them in but-and-ben — and easily surpassed the ancient balladists. Sometimes a work temporarily accepted as authentic is rather a hoax than a forgery. Such was the little volume by Cleone Knox entitled *Diary of a Young Lady of Fashion*, which many accepted as a genuine document of the eighteenth century. It was of course simply a pleasant piece of fiction. Much less innocent was the impudent forgery palmed off upon the *Atlantic Monthly* in 1928 as letters exchanged between Abraham Lincoln and his sweetheart Ann Rutledge. This correspondence purported to be written by the lovers while temporarily parted, chiefly when Lincoln was living in New Salem, Illinois, and Ann attending school in Jacksonville. They deceived not only Ellery Sedgwick, perhaps then the ablest of American editors, but even Carl Sandburg and W. L. Barton, experts upon Lincoln's early career. Yet a little shrewd study by historians conversant with the details of Lincoln's life and with the period sufficed to reveal inaccuracies which proved them fraudulent. One letter spoke of Kansas before that name came into use; in another letter Lincoln was made to refer to section 40 of a township, though

[1] For example, into Emanuel Hertz's two volumes, *Abraham Lincoln: A New Portrait*

as a surveyor he knew that townships have only 36 sections. The author of this forgery was motivated in part by a desire for monetary gain — the articles based upon the letters bringing a high price — and in part by a desire for reputation.[1]

III

The most dangerous and vicious of all forgeries are those committed in behalf of a cause — the cause of a nation, of an institution, or of a leader — and intended to bring about a permanent falsification of history. Perhaps preëminent among such forgeries stands the so-called Donation of Constantine. This was a supposed grant by the Emperor Constantine to Pope Silvester and his successors. In gratitude for his conversion to Christianity, Constantine according to this document not only recognized the spiritual supremacy of the Roman pontiffs over the other patriarchates of the church in all that pertained to faith and worship, but also gave them temporal sovereignty over Rome, parts of Italy, and all provinces and places of "the western regions." This document was forged sometime between 750 and 800 A.D. During the ninth century the ecclesiastical writer now called the pseudo-Isidore included it in the collection known as the False Decretals; and in time, with the authority of Pope Nicholas, it was accepted as part of the canons of the church. Gibbon pointed out that in his own day it was still formally "enrolled among the decrees of the canon law." Throughout the Middle Ages adherents of both popes and emperors regarded it as genuine. Two early popes, Silvester II and Gregory V, used it to support important territorial claims, and in 1050 Leo IX employed it in his controversy with the Byzantines involving still larger papal pretensions. During the twelfth century and afterward it became a powerful engine of the church in its contest with the political rulers of Europe, the partisans of the Holy Roman Empire regarding it with

[1] See Paul Angle on these forgeries, *The Atlantic Monthly*, CXLIII, 516 ff., April, 1929.

dread and hatred, and the partisans of the Pope somewhat cautiously employing it. Dante regarded it as genuine, and as a good Guelph execrated Constantine for the supposed grant as a source of enormous evils. But Laurentius Valla critically assailed the Donation in 1440, and though the controversy persisted until the close of the eighteenth century, its fraudulent character was at last completely demonstrated.

In this instance the forgery, which long imposed upon chroniclers and historians as well as ecclesiastical authorities, which indeed enjoyed almost six centuries of unchallenged vitality, was at last consigned to outer darkness. Discussion has long since shifted to the question of its authorship, some Catholic writers attempting to prove that the church had no hand in it. The best evidence is that it was executed in the papal chancery about 775, partly as a defense of the papal possessions, and partly as a means of attacking Byzantine heresy. The wonder is that it had so stubborn a life. But it must be remembered that the Middle Ages were poorly equipped to deal with questions of evidence.

Another famous example of a forgery committed in behalf of great public interests is offered by the manuscripts of Kyrláové Hradec and Zelená (Koeniginhof and Gruenberg), composed early in the nineteenth century by two Czech patriots who wished to provide the world with works showing that medieval Bohemia possessed a high degree of literary culture. Many Czechs eagerly accepted these texts. They appealed to the rising nationalism of the race. But honest Slav philologists soon threw doubt upon them. When Thomas G. Masaryk founded his critical review, the *Athenaeum*, in Prague in 1883, he took up the issue of their authenticity; and while he analyzed them historically, the philologist Gebauer analyzed them linguistically. These men conclusively proved them forgeries, and this proof gave full impetus to the "realist" revolution in Czech culture and politics — an unremitting effort to apply the scientific method in these fields. A partial parallel to the work

of Hradec and Zelená is offered by the forged Ossianic poems
of the Gaelic enthusiast James Macpherson, which many ardent
Celts accepted as genuine for more than a century. But Dr.
Johnson and others denounced Macpherson's epic of *Fingal*
from the moment it was published.

In one striking instance the debate as to whether certain documents represent a political forgery still rages. Men even yet
take sides heatedly on the question of the "Casket Letters." [1]
These letters, together with a sonnet-sequence, Mary Queen of
Scots is accused of having written to her lover Bothwell in
1566–67. They have long ago disappeared. Their very disap-
pearance is a mystery, some students believing that Mary's
royal son James obtained and destroyed them. But the text
remains, and if authentic, offers incontrovertible proof that
Mary was an accomplice in the murder of her husband Darnley.
If authentic! The controversy revolves chiefly about the second
or "Glasgow letter," a long and peculiar epistle. If even the
compromising parts of it were genuine, Mary was certainly
guilty. But her accusers, the men who first produced the letters
and pushed their evidence vigorously, were completely lacking
in veracity. The Earl of Morton and the Regent Moray
cannot be believed upon oath; they lied, they contradicted
themselves, and throughout the episode they behaved most dis-
ingenuously. Nevertheless, the ablest student of the subject,
Andrew Lang, concludes that the whole "Glasgow letter" was
written by Mary. Some German writers, applying the principles of the higher criticism of Homer and the Bible, conclude
that the documents are of composite origin, being partly letters
by Mary and partly a diary, combined and edited by other
hands. Still other writers attack the letters as wholly or largely
false. As Lang writes,[2] "The topic is so perplexing, and possibilities are so delicately balanced, that inquirers may change
their views, and modify or reverse their opinions, on the ap-

[1] See, for example, T. F. Henderson, *The Casket Letters.*
[2] *Encyclopædia Britannica*, 11th Ed., V, 449–452

pearance of each fresh document that is brought to light; or even upon a new consideration of existing evidence." In this instance the problem of authenticity is of vital importance to our view of a great historical figure — and yet it is probably insoluble.

In the same way, controversy still rages over the genuineness of the Kensington Stone, though here the balance definitely inclines toward a verdict of falsity. This runic inscription was found on a stone unearthed in 1898 at Kensington, Minnesota, by Olaf Ohman, a Swedish-American farmer. It is alleged to contain a record of an expedition which had been sent from Norway to Greenland about 1354 or 1355, and whose survivors reached the present Minnesota in 1362. They had made a camp "fourteen days journey" from the sea (supposedly Hudson Bay), and carved on the stone a memorial of their heroic journey. The controversy has involved the age of the tree under which the Kensington Stone was found, the language of the inscription, the character of the runic alphabet employed, and the geographic possibilities of such a journey. Much ink has been spilled over the issue. One scholar, H. R. Holand, has written a book, *The Kensington Stone*, defending the inscription; others have entered vigorous and on the whole convincing dissent. Of course many Scandinavians would like to believe that the Norsemen reached Minnesota 130 years before Columbus sighted the West Indies. But it is a writer of Scandinavian blood who concludes that the inscription is a fabrication, and adds: "Two choices have been suggested: the forger may have wished to add strength to the belief in the Vinland narratives, which were much in debate in the seventies and eighties, or he may have intended to foist a new sort of hoax on credulous citizens for the enjoyment that the inevitable discussion would bring. The writer prefers the latter alternative as the one that produces the fewer problems." [1]

[1] L. M. Larson, "The Kensington Rune Stone," *Minnesota History*, XVII, No. 1, March, 1936, p. 14

Even when the falsity of a document has been amply proved it frequently makes so striking an impression upon the public mind that, as we have said, vestiges of belief in it linger for many years. In 1781 the Reverend Samuel A. Peters, publishing a *General History of Connecticut*, gave it a memorable bit of spice by inserting a table of "Laws made by this independent Dominion, and denominated Blue Laws by the neighboring colonies." His cloth made it seem impossible that he should prevaricate. Indeed, the laws that he quoted had a certain ring of truth, for they chimed with the popular idea of Puritan severity. Other writers began to accept them, and for decades a belief in the inhuman blue laws of The Land of Steady Habits was almost universal. But experts on colonial law and history presently began scrutinizing Peters's list with a suspicious eye. One alleged law made it criminal for a mother to kiss her infant on the Sabbath, and others had a very queer look:

No one shall run on the Sabbath day, or walk in his garden or elsewhere, except reverently to and from meeting.

No one shall travel, cook victuals, make beds, sweep house, cut hair, or shave on the Sabbath or fasting day.

No one shall read Common Prayer, keep Christmas or Saints'-days, make minced pies, dance, play cards, or play on any instrument of music, except the drum, trumpet, and jews'-harp.

Married persons must live together, or be imprisoned.

Peters had attempted to protect himself by stating that this code, which even regulated the style of the hair and the mode of crossing streams, was "never suffered to be printed." Indeed it was not, for it never really existed. Various sets of Connecticut laws were published; and while they do offer some basis for a large majority of the forty-five statutes which he cited, they fall far short of the grim picture he drew. The laws of 1650 did not even provide penalties for Sabbath-breaking. Yet a general impression that Connecticut had a frightful code of interferences with personal liberty, based upon or fortified by Peters's inventions, persists in quarters which wish to think ill of Puritanism.

Some minor forgeries, indeed, are impossible to kill. It is of course a mere misattribution which leads many people, year after year, to declare that Washington warned the country against "entangling alliances"; the truth being that Jefferson expressed that particular warning. But outright invention is responsible for a quotation which American protectionists, decade after decade, have put into the mouth of Abraham Lincoln. "I do not know much about the tariff," Lincoln is quoted as saying, "but I know this much, when we buy manufactured goods abroad, we get the goods and the manufacturer gets the money. When we buy manufactured goods at home, we get both the goods and the money. When an American paid $20 for steel rails to an English manufacturer, America had the steel and England the $20. But when he paid $20 for the steel to an American manufacturer, America had both the steel and the $20." There are three reasons for our certainty that Lincoln was not the author of this quotation: (1) Lincoln was too sagacious to make a statement containing so much economic folly. (2) The most thorough ransacking of Lincoln's speeches and writings reveals no such statement. (3) Lincoln was shot April 14, 1865, and the first steel rail was not rolled in America until May, 1865. Yet this barefaced forgery, in behalf of the high-tariff interest, was repeated as Lincoln's by no less a person than Alfred E. Smith so recently as 1934. It is of a piece with another statement not infrequently attributed to Lincoln which represents him as a prohibitionist in advance of his time.

IV

Invention, indeed, runs a strange and wonderful gamut. It may be used to cast discredit upon a whole race, as in the forgery of the so-called Protocols of the Wise Men of Zion, purporting to lay bare a Machiavellian plan for Jewish world-dominion. It may originate, on the other hand, in a trifling private jest. "This day," writes Samuel Pepys on August 28, 1661, "I counterfeited a letter to Sir W. Pen, as from the thiefe that stole his tankard lately, only to abuse and laugh at him." Or it may be employed in the Las Casas style to give verisimilitude to an otherwise bare and unconvincing narrative. Thus A. C. Buell published in 1900 a two-volume life of John Paul Jones which was praised by the *American Historical Review*, accepted as an authority in various universities, and recommended to students of the Naval Academy at Annapolis. It seemed sober history; it was actually a mixture of authentic and manufactured materials. When his sources ran thin, Mr. Buell calmly manufactured new ones. He invented a French memoir upon Jones by Adrien de Cappelle, a volume of papers by the North Carolina worthy Joseph Hewes, and a printed French collection of Jones's own papers, drawing "facts" liberally from these imagined storehouses. He invented collections of papers by Robert Morris and Gouverneur Morris in places where they had never existed, and so obtained more "facts." He invented a will by William Jones of North Carolina in order to give John Paul an estate, and had Jones deposit 900 guineas in the Bank of North America in 1776 — a wonderful feat, for the Bank was not established until 1781. In short, as Albert Bushnell Hart has written, this inventor of materials recalls Mark Twain's praise of the duckbilled platypus, so versatile and gay. "If he wanted eggs," remarked Mark Twain, "he laid them."

Invention has even been used to gain a few dollars by spurious contributions to a biographical dictionary. A long-standard and still-useful compilation, *Appleton's Cyclopaedia of American Biography*, is disfigured by not less than forty-seven sketches, and probably many more, of men who never existed. The unknown author of these sketches was paid by space, and to obtain a larger remuneration coolly created heroes out of thin air. He gave the world an explorer, Bernhard Hühne, who discovered a good part of the coast of California; a botanist, Oscar Hjorn, whose book on *Les Legumineuses Arborescentes de l'Amerique du Sud* produced a "sensation" when published; an industrialist, Penanster, who in 1755 broke up the Spanish monopoly of the cochineal dye industry; and a French scientist, Henrion, who won fame by combatting the Asiatic cholera in South America in 1783, fifty-two years before it first appeared there. It appears that the editorial work on this *Cyclopaedia* was somewhat lax; contributors were free to suggest names not included in the original lists, and their sketches were not verified, and not revised save for literary form. But the large body of excellent material in the compilation has floated the spurious articles, so that many writers have been led astray by the mis-information — the errors being repeated from book to book, even in our own day.

And not least of all, invention has been used as a ready pass-port to fame. One early volume of English impressions of the United States, Thomas Ashe's *Travels in America, Performed in 1806*, is almost as dubious a production as Mandeville's work. Written with engaging vivacity, portraying with brutal realism such backwoods scenes as a gouging rough-and-tumble fight between a Kentuckian and a Virginian, it was quoted by Henry Adams and reprinted by Reuben Gold Thwaites in his series of Early Western Travels. That it has very considerable historical value is certain. But the available evidence indicates that it was put together out of second-hand materials, and does not represent first-hand observation. It can perhaps better be classified as plagiarism than forgery. Still another famous piece of literary imposture, Father Louis Hennepin's second volume of travels, is not quite forgery and not quite plagiarism, but achieves the object of both by an unblushing piece of literary piracy. Yet as late as the time of John G. Shea, who edited an edition of Hennepin's works, this narrative was treated as trustworthy, save for large "interpolations" by another hand.

There is much in the explorer Hennepin's story to interest

students of the problems involved in authenticity.[1] He was a Recollect friar who possessed not a few virtues — an adventurous nature, genuine heroism, and powers of close observation. The church did well when it sent him out to New France. But he was spiteful and vain, a braggart, and a colossal liar. He cherished a jealous enmity toward La Salle, while he was eager to magnify his own fame as a Western explorer. Under La Salle's instructions, in 1680 he had explored the Illinois and the Upper Mississippi. In 1683, while La Salle was still alive, he published a fairly accurate account of his exploits in *La Description de la Louisiane*. But in 1697, after La Salle was dead, he issued a *Nouvelle Découverte*, in which he stated that it was at last safe to make a momentous disclosure; that having nothing to fear from La Salle's terrible enmity, he could now reveal the fact that he had explored the Mississippi as far as its mouth. He had thus anticipated the discovery which La Salle claimed as the crowning glory of his career. Of course such a claim needed proof. Hennepin realized that if he could present a journal of his pretended voyage down the Mississippi, abounding in circumstantial detail, it would be good evidence. He might have invented such a record as Dr. Cook made in 1910 of his "dash to the Pole." But he lacked a Defoesque imagination. It happened that another Recollect friar, Le Clercq, had published some years earlier a book containing the diary which a companion of La Salle's named Father Membré had kept on the authentic voyage down the Mississippi in 1680. This book had been suppressed by the Jesuits, and Hennepin, who possessed a copy, believed that all others had been destroyed. In concocting his own journal, he therefore copied whole sentences, sometimes even whole pages, from the earlier document. Of course he was undone when stray copies of Le Clercq's volume came to light. But in any event he

[1] See the discussion of Hennepin's brazen forgery in Reuben Gold Thwaites's introduction to his two-volume edition of Hennepin's *A New Discovery of a Vast Country in America* (1903). Thwaites riddles it through and through.

would have been left in Dr. Cook's predicament as soon as later generations read his weird description of the lower Mississippi:

From the mouth of the river of the Illinois this river . . . is almost a league wide. It is very deep and has no sandbanks, nothing interferes with navigation, and even the largest ships might sail into it without difficulty.

All in all, the danger that the student of history will be misled by inauthentic documents is not unreal. Any man using diplomatic collections, or perusing such "White Papers," "Blue Papers," and "Orange Papers" as the chancelleries of great Powers issue under stress of international crises, will be on his guard against possible invention or interpolation. Any man using the daily press will be on guard against inauthentic interviews, speeches, and even letters. Dickens in his picture of New York journalism about 1840 satirized the impudent mendacity of such papers as James Gordon Bennett's *Herald*. "Pray," said Martin Chuzzlewit to Colonel Diver, "may I venture to ask whether the *Popular Instructor* often deals in — I am at a loss to express it without giving you offence — often deals in forgery?" "Well, sir," replied the Colonel, "it does, now and then." Any student using even the documents published by certain early historians who held loose ideas of the editorial function will be on his guard. Jared Sparks bore an honored name, and is still rightfully esteemed as a great pioneer in American historiography. But he was capable of doctoring papers, and perhaps even of manufacturing a source when he needed one. There is strong suspicion that in his collected edition of Washington's Writings he gives a narrative of Lafayette's escape from France in 1777 to join the American army which may have been concocted by Sparks himself; so completely is it at variance with two first-hand accounts written by Lafayette himself.[1] At every point the student must be watchful.

[1] Louis Gottschalk, *Lafayette Comes to America*, p. 123

V

But just how is a suspected invention to be detected? In the vast sea of historical materials available for modern students, how shall they pick out the impostures? John Morley read 300,000 documents in writing his life of Gladstone; the principal bibliography of titles bearing upon Napoleon and his times lists more than 125,000 titles of printed works. Most of the labor of detecting fabrications and mystifications can be left to the experts, of whom a large corps is ceaselessly at work. But some general rules should be well understood by even the general reader.

A suspected document, to begin with, can often be tested by certain physical criteria. Is the paper of proper age? Sometimes it has a telltale watermark; sometimes it pretends to belong to a period in which paper was made of silk or linen fibre alone, and yet contains an admixture of cotton; sometimes it purports to be of the linen-and-cotton period, and yet is made of wood pulp. Again, is the ink really that of the supposed period? Old documents will not present any ink containing aniline hues, for such inks were not used prior to 1850. Apart from these physical criteria, does the document have a pedigree? — can it be traced back through a line of reputable, well-authenticated owners? And what, again, of the handwriting? If it is said to be the work of a well-known author, does it tally with the chirography of papers *known* to be by him? Just as paper and ink may be subjected to chemical tests, so handwriting may be measured microscopically. And since criminal bureaus and commercial agencies frequently have to deal with forgeries, experts in graphology and micrography are both numerous and extremely skilled.

If the suspected paper passes the physical tests, its contents may then be subjected to rigorous scrutiny. Does the style of the alleged writer — his use of words and phrases, his sentence structure — resemble that which he exhibits in documents of known authenticity? Do the views and opinions he expresses, if the document be of any scope, tally with those which he has expressed elsewhere? Or if this question cannot be answered, do they harmonize with his general character? Are all the facts stated or implied in the document in accord with *known* facts of the time? — can they be easily reconciled with these facts? And by no means least, are all the statements in the document harmonious with one another? Forgery of documents of any length is a very difficult matter indeed. Even the expert forger is almost certain to slip in some detail which, if his work is examined with hawk-like care, betrays him.

A rigorous examination of the Lincoln-Ann Rutledge correspondence, made by Mr. Paul Angle, now head of the Illinois State Historical Library, showed that the forgery could be detected by a number of the tests mentioned above. The paper, to be sure, was old enough, though it bore the appearance of fly-leaves torn from old books. But the ink had a greenish hue, and green ink almost invariably contains aniline dye. The alleged letters had a very weak pedigree, some of the gaps in the past ownership being glaring. The handwriting bore no resemblance to Lincoln's, and defenders of the correspondence had to explain that he had used two different hands! The stylistic differences between the letters and Lincoln's own writings were marked and painful, the letters presenting a weakly sentimental personality. At one point the contents of the letters were distinctly out of harmony with Lincoln's known views on slavery. Finally, the historical inconsistencies were numerous, and several were absolutely inexplicable. Mr. Angle, after noting that Ann Rutledge several times spoke of the New Salem schoolmaster as Newton Graham, when she certainly knew that his name was Mentor Graham, added this clinching statement:

More conclusive, however, than a mistake in a name is the following sentence from one of Ann's letters to Lincoln. "I am greatfull," the writer says, "for the Spencers copy book. I copy frum that every time I can spair." Since Ann Rutledge died on August 25, 1835 — the date is recorded in the family Bible — the letter was written prior to that time. But Spencer's first publication on penmanship, under the title of Spencer and Rice's *System of Business and Ladies' Penmanship*, was not used until 1848.

The original manuscript of Hennepin's work is no longer in existence. But in this instance internal evidence is quite sufficient to destroy its pretensions. We may put aside his flimsy excuse for not bringing out his story until years after La Salle's death, that he feared the enmity of La Salle and his followers. We may even put aside the evidence of his thefts from the Membré diary. The proof that he never saw the lower Mississippi lies fair upon the face of what he wrote concerning it. It lies in the simple fact which Reuben Gold Thwaites has pointed out in his introduction to a two-volume edition of Hennepin's *New Discovery of a Vast Country in America:*

> That it was quite impossible for him to have made the alleged trip to the lower waters of the great river, is evident from the dates given by the father himself. In *Louisiane* the party are said to have left the Illinois not earlier than the 12th of March. Upon the 11th of April his party was captured by the Sioux near Lake Pepin. This leaves a scant month for the author to have descended and ascended the Mississippi and reached the place of capture — a journey all told of some 3,260 miles. Hennepin tells us that his canoe was slow, being large and laden heavily; yet to accomplish this feat he must have ascended the river against a strong current at the rate of 60 miles a day, nearly three and a half times the speed attained two years later by La Salle, with better boats.

The cheating document seldom imposes (at least for any length of time) upon any but the ignorant or careless. A combination of scholarly knowledge and common sense can in ninety-nine instances out of a hundred expose it — but they must be reinforced by constant vigilance.

CHAPTER SIX

THE GARBLED DOCUMENT

WHILE it is sometimes troublesome to establish the authenticity of an historical source, that is usually an easy matter compared with making certain of the entire integrity of a source. The authorship of a document or book may be entirely authentic, and yet parts of it may be highly treacherous. Everywhere about the question of historical integrity, pitfalls thicken.

While the forgery is entirely false and dishonest, a far larger body of materials are only partially false, and of these many are not dishonest by intention at all — that is, do not contain any conscious dishonesty. The very fact that a document is entirely and deliberately spurious often makes its character easy to detect. But when truth and misstatements are mingled, both emanating from some writer known to be sincere, discovery becomes difficult. Many a letter, a document, a piece of autobiography, originally quite genuine and candid, all its parts possessing the same general value as evidence, has been revised, amended, or otherwise so tampered with that some parts become untrustworthy. In other words, its integrity has been destroyed. Again, students of history must deal with a large class of documents which are quite frankly composite in character, proceeding from various hands or sources. The task of discriminating among the different parts of these composite documents, and determining which are most valuable and why, requires the use of tests as searching as those which determine the integrity of a document — indeed, even more searching.

A simple and picturesque example of a problem in the integrity of documentary sources is offered by a comparison of Captain John Smith's first and second versions of his adventures in Virginia. As the whole world knows, Smith helped to obtain the charter of the London Company, arrived in Virginia with the colonists early in 1607, traded with the Indians for provisions, and when Jamestown fell into grave difficulties, took charge of the colony and by decision and resourcefulness saved it. He restored discipline, set everyone to work, and made it self-supporting. In his volume *A True Relation*, written in Virginia and published in England in 1608, he recounted his early exploits and adventures. He told how, making an excursion to the Chickahominy, he was surrounded by two hundred hostile Indians, and after bemiring himself in a swamp, was captured. They carried him before an Indian king. Smith showed this monarch his compass, and so won his favor. Thence taken before the "emperor" Powhatan, he was in danger of being killed by certain Indians whose relatives he had slain, but was saved by his guards. After he had treated Powhatan to a long discourse on the greatness of the British king, the mightiness of his navy, and "the noyes of Trumpets and terrible manner of fighting" in Europe, he was sent back to Jamestown. In this book he barely mentions Pocahontas, then a maiden of perhaps twelve. But in 1616, about the time that John Rolfe brought Pocahontas as a bride to England, he wrote a letter to King James's queen, Anne of Denmark, in which he asserted: "After some ix weeks fatting among these salvage countries, at the minute of my execution, she hazarded the beating out of her own brains to save mine." And he soon went still further.

In 1624, in his *General Historie*, Smith rewrote his early narrative of Virginia adventures. This time the two hundred hostile Indians became three hundred. This time he recalled a picturesque detail, the exhibition by the Indians of a bag of gunpowder which they proposed to plant the following spring.

Above all, he recounted in more dramatic form the tale of Pocahontas's gallantry. He described the grim and dusky Powhatan in the centre of the stage, himself in the foreground, fettered but undaunted, and the lovely Pocahontas suddenly emerging at the climactic instant:

A long consultation was held, but the conclusion was two great stones were brought before Powhatan; then as many as could layd hands on him, dragged him to them, and thereon layd his head, and being ready with their clubs, prepared to beate out his braines. Pocahontas, the King's dearest daughter, when no entreaty could prevaile, got his head in her armes, and laid her own upon his to save him from death; whereat the Emperour was contented he should live.

It is not strange that this story has inspired conflicting views among students. Edward Arber, the most careful editor of Smith's works, accepts it and other remarkable incidents; Alexander Brown, in his scholarly writings on early Virginia, discredits it. John Fiske points out that the printed text of the *True Relation* was incomplete, for Smith had written much which the editor in London omitted as "fit to be private." Perhaps he had really told the full story of Pocahontas in his manuscript of 1608. Henry Adams and Edward Channing assail the story, but Charles M. Andrews accepts it. A pretty question of the integrity of a source is involved.

If John Smith retouched his narrative to make a good story better, he did simply what many raconteurs do. Sir Walter Scott confessed a weakness for dressing up his old anecdotes with new cocked hat and walking stick. His motive was artistic. But that of many a man who renders an old tale more dramatic is vanity. In each new version, oral or printed, the teller's own rôle becomes a little more witty, heroic, or resourceful. George IV asserted so often (without impolite contradiction) that he had been at the battle of Waterloo that he at last really believed he had taken an important part there. When the first two volumes of the *Intimate Papers of Colonel House*, edited by Charles Seymour, appeared in 1926, most readers gave them the value of an autobiography buttressed by a huge variety of letters and memoranda. Mr. House had chosen his editor carefully; it was incredible that he had not read every line of the work in manuscript or proof. These volumes claimed for him a decisive part in the shaping of the Federal Reserve Act of 1913. It was not difficult for ex-Secretary Carter H. Glass, in *An Adventure in Constructive Finance*, to riddle this pretension and show that Mr. House had played no real part whatever. The claim made by him was undoubtedly an instance of self-deception. It was not essentially different from Tartarin of Tarascon's story of his heroic exploits in the repulse of Tartar raids in China; the sole basis for which was that as a young man he had been offered a clerkship in the Orient, which he had refused!

The difficulty of obtaining an accurate knowledge of what occurred in the Constitutional Convention of 1787 has been increased by examples both of the cheating document, and of the garbled document. When in 1818 Congress ordered the official journal of the Convention printed, John Quincy Adams, then Secretary of State, edited it. Undertaking to obtain material from various men, he applied among others to Charles Pinckney of South Carolina. He received what can only be described as a spurious document. Pinckney had been the youngest but one of all the delegates. Taking frequent part in the debates, he had apparently been snubbed by his elders for his boldness. At one stage of the proceedings he had drafted a scheme of government which, in view of the direction already taken by the Convention, had little chance of adoption. It was referred to the Committee on Detail, which borrowed only a few provisions. Pinckney was not even permitted to deliver a speech which he had prepared. When long afterwards Adams asked Pinckney for a copy of his scheme, the South Carolinian sent north a draft of what he "believed" was the paper he had introduced. As published by Adams, it bore a striking resemblance to the adopted Constitution — so striking that it cast great credit upon Pinckney's sagacity, and made him seem one of the most constructive members of the gathering. But it happened that in 1787 Pinckney had printed the essential parts of his scheme in pamphlet form — *Observations on the Plan of Government Submitted to the Federal Convention*! Adams was suspicious of Pinckney's later document, and justly so. It was necessary only to turn to the pamphlet of 1787 to see that the paper Pinckney "believed" he had offered was an imposture — unconscious, no doubt, but nevertheless an imposture.

The garbled document was left to the world by no less a man than Madison, "father of the Constitution." He had not only played a leading part in the deliberations of the Convention; he had jotted down full and careful notes of the proceedings. In 1840, four years after his death, *The Papers of James Madison* were published in three volumes by order of Congress. Many students supposed that this was a source entirely independent of the official *Journal* which had been published under Adams's editorship in 1819. But it was later shown that Madison had twice revised his notes before his death, using the Journals to correct his record of votes, and to supply new items upon procedure. To distinguish between the original entries and the supplied matter was a task of some nicety. Dr. Max Farrand has described the method employed:

The ink which was used at the later date has faded quite differently from that of the original notes, so that most of the later revisions stand out from the page almost as clearly as if they had been written in red ink. . . . This is not always the case, for the original manuscript has faded differently in different parts, perhaps because of different exposure or the use of more than one kind of ink. There also seem to have been at least two distinct sets of later corrections, probably made at different times. It is, therefore, sometimes difficult and sometimes impossible to determine whether or not the correction is a later one. A reference to the 'printed Journal' must of course be of later date than 1819, and the ink and writing of these words will frequently make clear all of the corrections of that date. It is also very helpful to know that it was Madison's invariable practise in his original notes to refer to himself as 'M' or 'Mr. M.' In the revision of his manuscript he filled out his own name, so that the ink and writing of 'adison' often furnish the necessary clue.[1]

II

Sometimes a published book bears frank evidence that the text belongs to two or more very different dates. David F. Houston, successively head of the Department of Agriculture and of the Treasury under President Wilson, published in 1926 his valuable *Eight Years With President Wilson's Cabinet.* This work is written in two tenses, past and present, which alternate in the most disconcerting fashion. Frequently the two tenses appear on the same page. It is obvious that matter in the present tense was lifted more or less verbatim from Mr. Houston's diary, and that in the past tense was supplied years later. But the line between them is far from clear, while nobody knows just how great were the liberties taken with the text of the diary. To the student of history it is of the utmost importance to learn whether the opinion Mr. Houston gives of Secretary Bryan, of the Federal Reserve Act, or of Wilson's neutrality policies, is his opinion of 1914, his opinion of 1926, or a nondescript combination of the two. The published volume leaves us in the dark. This medley of contemporaneous and reminiscent matter, annoying to the general reader, is maddening to the historian, who never knows whether a statement upon a man or transaction is authentically of the period, or embodies later reflections.

But while Mr. Houston made no effort to conceal his mixture of two different points of view, one during and one after the event, many a personal chronicler has tried to palm off his late-learned wisdom as early sagacity. Most diarists write consciously or subconsciously for publication. They are acutely

[1] Max Farrand, *Records of the Federal Convention of 1787*, I, Introduction, xviii; see also note 23.

alive to the impression they will make on posterity. It is difficult to resist the temptation to strike out faulty judgments, or to add new and better strokes to the old picture. The classic instance is furnished by the famous diary which Gideon Welles kept during the Lincoln and Johnson Administrations. Thirty-three years after Welles's death, John T. Morse, Jr., published it in three volumes with a prefatory assurance that the text "has been in no way mutilated or revised." It was true that the editor had not revised it; but Welles himself had done so. Examination of the manuscript, now in the Congressional Library, reveals countless changes, almost all of which have been incorporated in the printed version. Indeed, the ink shows that Welles revised it at least twice. Some changes were made for style, but even they occasionally altered the original sense. Others, made to add color, dramatic force, or picturesqueness, still more clearly distort the picture by unconsciously incorporating impressions formed at a later time, or by adding imagined details. For example, to an interview with Halleck, Welles later appended the comment that he "began to rub his elbows and without thanking me or acknowledgment of any kind said"; to the record of a tense scene with Stanton, he added the clause, "Stanton, in a suppressed voice, trembling with excitement, said." A student who has gone carefully over the manuscript lists still other ways in which the garbling of the document may easily mislead readers:

Another form of revision in which Welles indulged, notably in the cases of Seward, Stanton, and Grant, was conscious changing of the text, not to vivify but to add venom commensurate with the growth of his aversion for these men. Thus to an early interview with Halleck he added a comment of several lines: "Strange that this change of military operations should have been made without Cabinet consultation. . . . But Stanton is so absorbed in his scheme to get rid of McClellan that other and more important matters are neglected." To the entry of September 6, 1862, he added: "The War Department is bewildered, knows but little, does nothing, proposes nothing." It was in after years, too, that he injected under June 24, 1866, the comment that "Trumbull and the Senators generally thought Seward too meddlesome and presuming." . . . Similarly, to a later date belong the comment of June 30, 1866, that "Stanton has assumed frankness, but his coarse manner covers a good deal of subtle duplicity," and most of the paragraph of May 31, 1868, in derogation of Grant. Numerous cases massed together paint a picture even worse than the contemporaneous sketch of these men. . . .

Welles also revised portions of his manuscript to satisfy his pride in his powers of judgment or prophecy. One example will suffice. To the call of June 18, 1866, is added, in light of later events, the seeming prophecy: "The call, if not the Convention itself, is, I think, perverted to an intrigue in behalf of the old Whig party, on which Weed and Seward rely." [1] . . .

No memoir or autobiography should be used without an effort to make certain that judgments stated as belonging to a particular date have not actually been colored or wholly shaped by subsequent occurrences. No diary or volume of letters should be used without a watchful eye for telltale evidence that the text has been altered before publication to delete entries that have become absurd, or to insert material which will reflect credit on the writer's shrewdness and insight. The more naïveté in a diary, the better the historian likes it!

One of the most difficult of all sets of problems in the determination of textual integrity has been created by the profession of ghost-writer. It is an older profession, and has affected more books, than readers usually suppose. In recent years, as industrialists and other men of affairs unused to the pen have turned to autobiography, it has become an increasingly important department of letters. No small proportion of American memoirs are nowadays written less by the noted person whose name appears on the title page than by some journalist or scholar whose help may never be acknowledged. The practice has had its advantages as well as disadvantages. It has given

[1] Howard K. Beale, " Is the Printed Diary of Gideon Welles Reliable?" *American Historical Review*, XXX, 547 ff., April, 1925

us books which would otherwise never have been born; while a dull autobiography like Winfield Scott's makes us wish that he had been aided by a nimbler mind. But such volumes all too seldom answer the questions, Just what was the extent of the collaboration? How much does the ghost-writer put into the mouth of the autobiographer? Which man is responsible for dubious or controversial statements?

Only in recent years has it been learned that a classic of Southwestern history, Josiah Gregg's *Commerce of the Prairies* — a personal narrative of the growth of the Santa Fé trade — was to some extent ghost-written for him by John Bigelow. Poultney Bigelow, when questioned, said that his father took the field-notes of Gregg's ten years' journeys to Santa Fé and Chihuahua, and created therefrom a readable narrative. Had we known nothing more of the collaboration than this, it might have cast doubt on the authoritativeness of Gregg's volume. But fortunately an explicit letter from John Bigelow himself on the matter has been found. He records that Gregg came to New York and carefully *prepared* his notes. His statements "were so lucid, so realistic, and so unpretendingly honest that they needed little illuminating and refining from his editor." Gregg then carefully scanned every word that Bigelow wrote. He refused to tolerate any literary frills. "On the other hand, he was extremely careful about the exactness of every statement that he made, and I do not think that he allowed a word to be printed in that book that he would not have been willing to make oath to." Bigelow's statement makes it evident that historical truth suffered not the slightest loss when he held Gregg's pen. And as a matter of fact, the accuracy of the book is amply attested by much contemporaneous evidence.[1]

But much ghost-writing must be regarded with considerable misgiving. Already a large gallery of American figures, and some Europeans, are represented by ostensible self-portraits

[1] John Thomas Lee, "The Authorship of Gregg's *Commerce of the Prairies*," *Mississippi Historical Review*, XVI, 451 ff., March, 1930

really from another hand. S. S. McClure vainly tried to persuade Grover Cleveland to write his autobiography in this easy way. He did prevail upon Charles A. Dana to let Ida M. Tarbell pen his *Recollections of the Civil War.* A trusty author was found for John D. Rockefeller's *Random Recollections of Men and Events;* of course taking much of his information from talks with Rockefeller. In the same way Burton J. Hendrick wrote former-Ambassador Morgenthau's reminiscences of his World War experiences. Mr. Boyden Sparkes has ghost-written the autobiographies of Frank A. Vanderlip, Evelyn Walsh McLean, and Walter P. Chrysler, his part-authorship being confessed but its extent not defined. In weighing the value of these and like books, not a few questions almost defy answer.

For one, just how authentic is the personal note in such books? It is impossible to believe that Miss Tarbell supplied many ideas and opinions to Charles A. Dana; she would not have felt that course proper, nor would his stubbornly individualistic mind have permitted it. Nevertheless, we feel in the book a milder personality than that exhibited in Dana's capricious, witty, sardonic, disillusioned *Sun;* a softening of Dana's own acerbities. And when we are confronted with such a volume as Henry Ford's *My Life and Opinions*, in which Mr. Samuel Crowther was amanuensis and more, we are still more doubtful that this is the real Henry Ford. We find not only a literary style much above his reach, but a knowledge of economics so extensive, a set of ideas on modern industry so complex and subtle, that we cannot doubt the "opinions" are more Mr. Crowther's than Mr. Ford's. An anecdotal autobiography like Hudson Maxim's, written for him by Clifford Johnson, whose knowledge of mechanics and invention was slight, raises the question of the authority of the facts given. Does Maxim stand squarely behind every one of them? What undertones and overtones have been supplied by his collaborator? Still other questions are raised by a dashing book like Victor G. Heiser's *American Doctor's Odyssey*. Is the high, the even excessive dramatization, his own, or attributable to the skilled woman journalist who took her data from him and helped write that "autobiography"? Ghost-writing ranges from solid, carefully verified work at one extreme to mere publicity, mere presentation of some industrialist, financier, or politician in a highly favorable light, at the other. Its value ranges from that of an honest historical source to that of naked propaganda.

Certainly this dual method of composition frequently makes for irresponsibility in treating facts. Certainly it obscures or weakens the personality of the protagonist of the autobiography. He appears not as he sees himself, but as another man sees him, or as another man persuades him to pose. Reading a ghost-written autobiography, the student who wishes to know how much integrity attaches to the text — how much is really Charles A. Dana's, Henry Ford's, or Dr. Heiser's — must severely scrutinize every part. The general public assumes that the book is all Mr. Ford's or Dr. Heiser's. The publisher usually wishes it to do so. But the student must take a skeptical attitude. He may sometimes glean a few guiding facts from the preface — and reviewers and historians ought to urge that all future ghost-written autobiographies contain full prefatory explanations. He will commonly learn more from internal evidence. If he knows something of the personality of the hero, and something of that of the ghost-writer, he may disentangle the two. He may find out from the mode of narration just which facts are vouched for by the hero, and which come from his literary aide. But unless the contrary evidence is clear, he will have to regard a ghost-written memoir as lacking the perfect integrity of a book whose author can say that it is written, in Paul's phrase, "by mine own hand."

III

The document of composite authorship may be garbled in the harshest sense of that word, or it may be a frank and innocent document of strict integrity. It may represent a perversion of some original source by materials drawn from inferior sources — that is, by large interpolations. It may represent an author's honest interweaving of several sources, perhaps of equal value, into a new record stamped by his personality. Or it may represent an ordinary collaboration of two or more authors. Though usually there is nothing reprehensible in composite writings, they are often perplexing and irritating.

No composite histories are more familiar, and none more interesting, than the three Synoptic Gospels of Matthew, Mark, and Luke. None has ever been given more penetrating and exhaustive study than they. It is obvious to anyone who examines the New Testament in critical spirit that the value of its different parts to students of the past is far from uniform. It is a highly varied collection of narratives, letters, homilies, and prophecies. Some historical inconsistencies of the Gospels have been very unfairly exploited by hostile critics like Thomas Paine and Robert G. Ingersoll. Matthew and Luke, while giving accounts of the virgin birth, yet trace the genealogy of Jesus up through Joseph. Matthew declares that the Holy Family went at once into Egypt to escape Herod, while Luke states categorically that it stayed in Bethlehem forty days, then went to Jerusalem, and then to Nazareth. We are given more or less discrepant accounts of the Sermon on the Mount, the anointing of Jesus, the betrayal by Judas, the trial scene, and even in some details of the crucifixion; while at many points the narratives are vague. The attempt to wring out of the Gospels their exact historical values is full of interest. How vast an effort has been concentrated into that attempt can be understood only by those who have studied Christian Hermeneutics and what was once termed the higher criticism. It represents, in all probability, the best single illustration of what the historical method can accomplish in a difficult and obscure field. The separation of the Gospels into their component parts has been only one part of that effort.

That they have a composite origin is beyond question. Expert authorities now generally agree that no narrative of Christ's life was written for more than thirty years after his death. The gospel was first preached to people who had seen Jesus, or had heard too much about him to be curious for details of his life, while the disciples looked forward to his second advent at an early date. Since Paul's Epistles, written about 50–60 A.D., make no reference to any of the four Gospels, it is a fair inference that they did not then exist. Tradition indicates that written accounts began to be set down between 60 and 70 A.D. The first of the four was probably the so-called Gospel of St. Mark, and can apparently be dated within a decade of Paul's martyrdom. For centuries the church regarded this Gospel as less important than the others, partly because Mark was not an apostle, and partly because Matthew and Luke are much fuller. But it is now believed that a good part of Mark's narrative may have been derived directly from the lips of Simon Peter, and is not merely an earlier story than the other two synoptic Gospels, but in some respects more dependable. They are based largely upon it, or upon another narrative, now lost, which it most faithfully represents. Indeed, internal evidence suggests that Matthew and Luke lean heavily upon Mark. Some authorities believe that they lean also upon a lost Gospel, which German scholars termed the Q Gospel, and which may have run fairly parallel to Mark. The Gospel of Matthew was perhaps written last of all, and could certainly not have been penned by the Apostle Matthew, though it may have been founded in part upon some of his recollections.

Let us concentrate, for the purposes of illustration, upon Matthew. It is incontestable, in the view of modern Biblical scholars, that this Gospel is a composite work, written from two main sources which the author knew in Greek, and various minor sources. The two main sources are Mark, and an unknown work originally written in Aramaic. Scholars have accurately separated the two. For example, the matter from Matthew ix, 27, to the end of Matthew xi is taken from the

Aramaic document; then comes a long section from Mark, but with additional data from some other source; and finally we have the author's own ending. A peculiar feature of the Gospel is the way in which the author has welded together a number of discourses, or collections of sayings, by Jesus, taking part of the material from statements which other sources attribute to Christ at other times and places. Thus Matthew introduces into the Sermon on the Mount some sayings which according to Luke were uttered elsewhere. The account in Matthew x of the address to the twelve disciples contains matter which Luke x, 1–16, states was delivered to a different group, together with various other sayings of which the precise occasion is unknown. Altogether, Matthew contains eight distinct discourses or collections of sayings, put together in more or less artificial fashion from Christ's utterances on various occasions. This artifice does some violence to history, according to the strict rules of the present day, but it offers a more effective presentation of Christ's doctrine.

The Gospel of St. Mark consists of an original text studded with later interpolations, which scholars have been able to identify with fair certainty, and which stand on a lower plane of credibility than the work in general. Thus from internal evidence it is regarded as probable that the two parables in Mark iv, 26–32, are insertions made in the original, which they do not precisely fit. It is believed also that the collection of Christ's sayings in Mark ix, 41–50, is interpolated; for the author of Mark does not elsewhere make up such discourses. Moreover, some of these particular sayings are given by Luke in different contexts. Such obvious inaccuracies occur in the account of Christ's crossing of the lake after the feeding of the five thousand, inaccuracies the more striking in a book remarkable for precision of topography, that this bit may also be an interpolation. It need not be said that the historical value of St. Mark's Gospel is impaired by these interpolations, and restored when they are struck out. Similarly, the historical authority of Matthew is compromised at various points by bits which the author has apparently derived from untrustworthy traditions. Among them is the story of the setting of the Roman guards at the grave, and their presence at the resurrection; the story of the silencing of this guard by the chief priest; the story of the testimony borne by the guard and the centurion who kept watch at the cross; and the story of Pilate's effort to throw the guilt of the crucifixion upon the Jews. Competent scholars regard these episodes, to quote one of them, as "legendary additions which had arisen through the desire to commend the Gospel to the Romans," and which the very late author of Matthew inserted along with his authentic materials.

An excellent example of the kind of composite document which represents a straightforward use of several sources to make a new record — a twisting of several threads into a new cord — is offered by various books of Livy's great history. The prolific Roman, it will be recalled, was indifferent to original research. Instead, he relied heavily upon other authors. As he uses no footnote references, the identification of these authors and the parts that each contributed to the whole requires much ingenuity. Sometimes he quotes one of the Roman annalists by name; but more often he insouciantly remarks, "they say," "the story goes," or "ancient writers declare." Identification is important in order to judge the authenticity of the different parts. Patient scholarship, principally by Germans, has analyzed many of his books in satisfactory fashion. It has shown that Livy's procedure was amazingly elementary and even naïve. At rare intervals he would take several writers, and fuse their stories rather completely and carefully. More often he would follow one writer exclusively for a time, revamping his story with various embellishments; then, without warning to the reader, would suddenly turn to another annalist and follow him. Very frequently, when earlier writers differed, he would make no effort to correct one by another. The result is a mosaic, in which materials which possess different dates, different values, and different points of view, are awkwardly pieced together, often with an obvious lack of unity. Only Livy's *brio* and narrative power saved much of his history from worthlessness.

Fortunately for modern scholarship, fragments of the old annalists survive in manuscript collections and can be compared with Livy's text; while we have six complete books of Polybius, which in certain parts he followed closely. Thus it is possible in the third and fourth "decades" of Livy's work (books 31–45 inclusive) to distinguish between what he drew from Polybius, and what he drew from such inferior writers as Valerius Antias and Claudius Quadrigarius. The former contributed the materials upon Greece and the East, which here are the clearest, fullest, and most accurate parts of Livy. The latter contributed materials upon Western Europe, including Italy, some of which were highly inaccurate, and all of which were cast in a dry annalistic mould — a mould that Livy indolently followed. The volume in which a German scholar, H. Nissen, has analyzed the sources of these last surviving books of Livy (*Untersuchungen*, 1863) is a masterly work of analysis.

One of the most striking of composite works in the field of American history is John Marshall's *Life of George Washington*, published in 1804. For more than a century this biography was extravagantly admired as the product of a great mind working on a great theme. Jared Sparks thought that after this "able, accurate, and comprehensive work" it would be presumptuous for other hands to touch the subject; Justin Winsor wrote that it gave "the impress of a true historic spirit" to "the most authentic material respecting Washington's life"; and Charles A. Beard declared that it represented long and arduous study and constituted the "classic defense of Federalism." In truth, however, the biography is for the most part a mosaic of borrowings, which Marshall copied almost literally, and then hastily and carelessly pieced together. It does not represent the application of a critical method to authentic materials, for the materials were drawn from compilers and annalists who preceded Marshall. It is not a memorable Federalist interpretation of history, for there is little of Marshall or any other Federalist in it. The great jurist wrote in an age of successful plagiarism in history, when such authors as William Gordon and David Ramsay copied unblushingly from the British *Annual Register* and from any other source they could easily pilfer. When a careful analysis of Marshall's work was very belatedly made by a competent scholar, it was found that he stood on the precise level of these men.[1] A book that had been thought to possess great original value had almost none.

In his preliminary volume on the history of the colonies, Marshall levied upon such previous historians as Jeremy Belknap, Thomas Hutchinson, William Stith, George Chalmers, and Robert Beverly. Sometimes he took the matter verbatim, without acknowledgment; sometimes he condensed or skeletonized it; sometimes he paraphrased it — but throughout he was a copyist, and little more. The investigator found examples of unacknowledged copying on 268 of the 488 pages of the original edition, and could have discovered more. The whole second chapter of this volume represents simply a combination of select passages from Stith and Chalmers. In the life of Washington proper, Marshall lifted great sections unaltered or but slightly changed from William Gordon's history of the American Revolution and the *Annual Register*. A 12-page description of the battle of Camden, for example, is transcribed almost word for word from Gordon's pages. The description of the affair at Moore's Creek Bridge is a three-page appropriation from the *Annual Register*. When Paul Leicester Ford thought he was quoting Marshall's account of Washington's farewell to his officers at Fraunces's Tavern, he was actually quoting William Gordon's. Anyone who wishes to know the exact historical value of any part of Marshall's book will here-

[1] William A. Foran, "John Marshall as a Historian," *American Historical Review*, XLIII, 51–64, October, 1937

after find it necessary to make sure of the provenance of that part — a task in which Marshall's rare footnotes lend little assistance. As a composite work, it is worth just as much and as little as the brief shelf of books upon which Marshall drew.

As both internal and external evidence may be used to detect the fraudulent document, so both may be employed to analyze a garbled or composite text. Where one fails, the other may succeed. But it should be noted that one kind of internal evidence is extremely risky. Many a critic has gone astray in asserting that a passage belongs to one special author or source, basing his opinion upon character of vocabulary, tricks of style, or trend of thought. Various students of Beaumont and Fletcher have boasted that they could trace with ease the parts which each man contributed to their dramas — Beaumont being of course the more gifted writer. Yet Coleridge declared that he could find no line of demarcation whatever between them. Part of "The Two Noble Kinsmen" is supposedly Shakespeare's and part Fletcher's; yet even here, where the greatest genius of literature mated with a second-rate talent, a complete separation of the two parts seems impossible. Other kinds of internal evidence, if available, offer more certainty. When Livy refers in his text to the annalists Fabius Pictor and Aelius Tubero, the clue is clear. When the Gospels of Luke, Matthew, and Mark can be laid side by side, much can be learned from their differences and resemblances.

Yet sometimes, in dealing with a composite document, a very considerable amount of both internal and external evidence may leave students uncertain of source or authorship. One of the most famous of all composite works is the *Federalist*, written by Madison, Hamilton, and Jay. Which of the two former men deserves credit for certain papers in it will always be uncertain. Both left lists of the essays which they claimed, but as these lists conflict, and as it is impossible to say that one man is less accurate than the other, or that either lacked veracity, the question is still open. It has to be decided by the internal evidençe offered by the contents of the papers, and the external evidence supplied by Hamilton's and Madison's manuscripts. No prettier exercises in the use of such evidence can be found than the studies which Edward Gaylord Bourne, Henry Cabot Lodge, Paul Leicester Ford, and others have made of the authorship of Nos. 49–58, 62, and 63 of the *Federalist*, claimed by Madison and Hamilton alike.

Take, for example, No. 58, which refutes the objection that the House of Representatives may not be properly increased in size as the nation's population grows. Hamilton had met this very objection in New York's ratifying Convention. His argument there — that the large States will control the House, and will favor its augmentation in order to increase their influence — is repeated in No. 58; and this seems to be evidence supporting his claim to authorship of the essay. But after all this is an obvious argument. Anyone would think of it. And a quite different argument is emphasized in No. 58; the assertion that new States will advance in population with peculiar rapidity, and will therefore be interested in frequent reapportionments of representation. It happened that Madison had stated almost precisely this idea in a letter to Jefferson on Federal representation in March, 1787. No. 58 also contains one expression which was a favorite with Madison. He remarks that the history of the British Parliament shows a "humble representation of the people gradually enlarging the sphere of its activity and importance." This phrase "enlarging the sphere," occurs at least seven times in Madison's known writings upon the Constitution. It does not occur at all in Hamilton's writings on the subject, and even the metaphor (for he does once speak of "extending the sphere") occurs only twice. Finally, the last paragraph of No. 58 seems to echo the discussion in the Federal Convention on the subject of a proper quorum for the House; and while Madison was present at this discussion, Hamilton was not. On the basis of these arguments, Madison seems the better entitled to the credit of No. 58.

In conclusion, we may note the fact that problems in the cheating document and the garbled document are often wrapped up together. A classic example of the critical examination of a universally known work to weigh first its authenticity, and then its textual integrity, is the introductory chapter of Ernest Renan's *Saint Paul*. Present-day Biblical criticism differs from his conclusions at certain points, but his method remains full of illumination. He examines at great length the validity of the original sources for his study, the Epistles of St. Paul; a step the more imperative because Paul himself had spoken of false letters circulating in his name, and had frequently taken precautions against such frauds. Of course Renan had to proceed almost entirely through the use of internal evidence. The earliest surviving manuscripts of Paul's Epistles are of the third century, and it is rarely indeed that they have any evidential value; though Renan does cite the omission of the words "in Ephesus" in the early MS versions of the so-called Epistle to the Ephesians to help prove that this was not written to the Church of Ephesus at all. But by careful attention to phrasing, to ideas, to personal, geographical, and historical allusions or the lack of them, Renan arrives at ingenious and often convincing conclusions. Take, for example, what he writes of the Epistle to the Hebrews, which he regards as by another hand — an anonymous bit of apostolic writing, admitted by error into the Pauline collection. A little of his evidence is external; he notes that early churchmen hesitated over the letter, and early Latin manuscripts showed repugnance to its admission. But most of his data is internal:

Clement of Alexandria and Origen, good judges in regard to Greek style, do not discover the characteristics of St. Paul's style in this epistle. St. Jerome has the same opinion. The Fathers of the Latin Church, who are unwilling to accept it as an epistle of Paul's, give the reason of their action, *propter styli sermonisque distantiam.* This reason is excellent. The style of the epistle to the Hebrews is, in truth, different from that of Paul. It is more oratorical, fuller, the language presents particular words. The basis of the thoughts is not unlike the opinions of Paul, especially of the captive Paul; but the exposition and exegesis are entirely different. There is no personal superscription, contrary to the constant usage of the apostle. Characteristics always expected to be met with in an epistle from Paul are wanting in this. The exegesis is above all allegorical, and resembles that of Philo much more than Paul's. The author betrays Alexandrine culture; he only makes use of the so-called version of the Septuagint; his reasoning concerning the text of this version shows a complete ignorance of Hebrew; his manner of quoting and analyzing Biblical texts is not conformable to Paul's method. The author, on another side, is a Jew; he thinks to exalt the Messiah by comparing him to the Jewish high priest; Christianity is for him only a sort of Judaism fulfilled; he is far from regarding the law as abolished. The passage (ii, 3) in which the author ranks himself among those who have only known the mysteries of the life of Christ indirectly from the lips of Jesus' disciples, in no wise corresponds to one of Paul's most decided declarations. Finally, let us add that in writing to Jewish-Christians, Paul would have neglected his most inflexible resolution, which was never to perform a pastoral act upon the territory of the Jewish-Christian churches, so that the apostles of circumcision should not, on their side, encroach upon the churches of the uncircumcised.

Taking the whole question of the authenticity of the thirteen Epistles, Renan concludes that seven are of certain authorship by Paul — the two to the Corinthians, the two to the Thessalonians, and those to the Galatians, Romans, and Philippians. He holds that the Epistles to the Colossians and Philemon are probably authentic. That to the Ephesians he pronounces probably spurious, and the two to Timothy and the one to Titus certainly so.

In dealing with the *integrity* of the text of the valid Epistles, he furnishes a basis for his criticism by a severe analysis of the Epistle to the Romans, so-called. In this he arrives at what he thinks were the probable methods of the first editors of Paul's Epistles, and explains why these methods resulted in the overuse of salutatory phrases, and other repetitions. The essential part of each Epistle, he believes, was a circular letter addressed primarily to the churches of Ephesus and Thessalonica, but also to some of the Roman churches. To each copy of this general letter might be added special bits of a local or individual interest, which varied according to the destination of the copy. The rule of the editors who finally collected the Epistles, Renan believes, was to add nothing to the text; to avoid repetition as much as possible; but also to omit nothing — so that the local and individual bits have been preserved along with the main letter. They "followed a system of piecing 'or intercalation, the design of which seems to have been to save writings which otherwise would have perished." It saved these writings — but it sometimes made an Epistle a rather curious document.

IV

The integrity of written documents of all kinds has frequently been vitiated by censorships, political or religious. In many countries and in every century, texts have been mutilated, garbled, or rewritten by some tyrannical authority. No Italian, German, or Russian newspaper under the régimes of Mussolini, Hitler, and Stalin respectively could be regarded by careful students as an authentic presentation of what was originally written for its columns. Still less could it be regarded as what the journalists would have written had they been free! It would be absurd to place the *Corriere della Serra* or *Berliner Tageblatt* on the same level of integrity as the columns of the Manchester *Guardian* or New York *Times*. The same rule applies to books and magazines in censor-ridden countries. Not even the greatest of authors have been respected. A student who uses foreign sources of a type exposed to censorship will sometimes save himself from grave error by studying the conditions of bureaucratic or ecclesiastical control for his period. He will then not assume that because a periodical is conservative or obscurantist in tone, its editors and contributors were antagonistic to liberalism; that every word printed is to be taken in its literal sense.

The power of the censorship sometimes manifests itself in curious ways. Eloquent deductions may be made from a bit of reminiscence published by Maxim Gorky upon the relations of Lenin and Trotsky — and published in two forms. The first version, written in 1924 as a magazine article, runs as follows:

Yes, I have often heard him [Lenin] praise his comrades. And he knew how to do justice to the energies of even those with whom he was supposed to be personally unsympathetic.

Surprised by the flattering appreciation he showed for one of them, I remarked that a good many people might be amazed by it.

"Yes, yes, I know. They tell a lot of lies about my relations with him. Yes, they tell a lot of lies — and especially about me and Trotsky."

Pounding on the table, he declared: "Show me another man who could organize in a year an almost model army and win the respect of military experts besides. We've got that man. We've got everything, and so we'll do wonders!"

The second version, published in booklet form after Trotsky had been banished and Stalin had come into power, runs as follows:

Yes, he often praised the comrades in my hearing, even those with whom he was not personally in sympathy. Lenin knew how to appreciate their energy. I was very surprised at his high appreciation of L. D. Trotsky's organizing abilities. V. Ilyitch noticed my surprise.

"Yes, I know there are lying rumors about my attitude to him. But what is, is, and what isn't, isn't — that I know also. He was able at any rate to organize the military experts."

And after a pause, he added in a lower tone, and rather sadly: "And yet he isn't one of us. He is ambitious. There is something of Lassalle in him, something which isn't good." [1]

[1] Edmund Wilson, "Gorky on Lenin," *New Republic*, February 15, 1933

The Stalin censorship was not in effect when the first version was written, and was very effective indeed when the second appeared. It may be that Gorky voluntarily changed the passage; it may be that he changed it unwillingly and in fear of the censorship; it may be that the censor mutilated it. But it is certain that the original passage has integrity and the revision has not.

Texts may also, as every reader of general literature knows, be corrupted by bad editing; by bad translations; by careless printing; and by sheer accident. The canons applied to the editing of manuscript sources for publication have become steadily more severe. Of course these canons are not rigid. According to the nature of the text, the editor may regard his work as primarily literary, intended for the lay public, or primarily historical, intended for general readers. John Evelyn and Philip Hone wrote their diaries with a broad appeal in view; to reproduce every archaic spelling or capitalization in Evelyn, every abbreviation, misspelling, or defect in punctuation in Hone, would be to repel the general reader. It would defeat the main purpose of the diary. So with volumes of letters expected to have a broad appeal. The editor is not merely justified, but required, to spell out awkward abbreviations, make capitalization and punctuation conform to present-day usage, and otherwise, without altering the sense, to render the text readable. The editor of Grover Cleveland's letters, with this end in view, was justified in even occasional changes in paragraphing. But where a text is intended primarily for the use of historical students, it should be reproduced precisely as it stands. The *Diary* of Edward Bates, Lincoln's Attorney-General, for example, has much value to the historian and no attractions whatever to the general reader; its editor rightly reproduced every letter, every comma, verbatim.

The firm establishment of strict rules for historical editing dates in America from the controversies which attended Jared Sparks's editions of the writings of Washington (1834–37) and

Franklin (1836–40). Sparks's methods were loose and irresponsible. He treated historical documents as if they were articles submitted to the *North American Review* (which he once edited), using the blue pencil freely without any indication of his omissions. Justice Bushrod Washington enjoined upon him to avoid giving offence to writers of letters to Washington or their families, and he made editorial changes to do so. Observing that Washington in his old age completely rewrote his early letters, he felt it proper to revise the later letters, of which he had only rough drafts, not the final form, when they seemed to need it. He softened or omitted harsh criticisms of men and policies. Thus when Washington wrote of the "dirty, mercenary spirit" of the Connecticut troops, Sparks left out "dirty"; when Washington wrote of "rascally privateersmen," he deleted "rascally." He changed "Old Put" into "General Putnam," and Washington's statement that a certain sum "will be but a fleabite to our demands" into the statement that it would be "totally inadequate." In Franklin's writings he similarly paid tribute to Victorian squeamishness, and dulled the sharp edge of criticism. He declined to print the famous definition of chastity; when Franklin spoke of a beer-pitcher with "the coffee cups in its belly," Sparks omitted the belly. He changed "dung" to "manure." When Franklin spoke of the "polluted court" of England, Sparks omitted the sentence, as he omitted a reference to "George III's character for falsehood and dissimulation." A subsequent editor of Franklin's works found that Sparks had sometimes made more than thirty alterations in a single letter.

In 1851–52 Sparks was called sharply to account by Lord Mahon in England and John Bigelow in America, the latter declaring that his edition of Washington's works must be pronounced as absolutely without authority. In reply, Sparks was able to make a partial defence. He had actually performed great services to scholarship. It was his misfortune that his methods of editing were those of an older day, already being supplanted by a careful insistence upon literal accuracy. After the controversy with Mahon, it was impossible for any accredited scholar to take such liberties with a text as he and various other editors had done. But even since then — even at the present day — absolute accuracy is a goal difficult to reach. Washington's writings were reëdited by Worthington C. Ford, who was justly severe upon Sparks's work. But they have since been edited a third time by John C. Fitzpatrick, whose work has very clearly revealed Mr. Ford's many slips! John Bigelow published an edition of Franklin's *Autobiography* — a work which is almost the despair of students of textual integrity, for it was written in three main parts, separated by wide intervals of time and space (England, 1771; France, 1784; Pennsylvania, 1788), exists in two manuscripts, and was published five times in France in five separate translations, and four times in English in four separate texts, each differing from the other in almost every line. Bigelow's edition, based on the original manuscript in Franklin's hand, contained some vitriolic remarks upon all the earlier editions. But a new editor has now appeared, Dr. Max Farrand, whose careful version demonstrates that Bigelow himself committed almost countless inaccuracies!

The present-day tendency is to publish texts in ever-fuller editions, as anyone may see by comparing early versions of Boswell's *Journal of a Tour to the Hebrides* with that produced by F. A. Pottle and C. H. Bennett in 1937 from the original manuscript. But the most courageous of editors dare not and should not publish a complete text of some writings. No useful purpose is served by concessions to mere pruriency. Beyond a certain line, such concessions indeed run afoul of the law. The completest edition of Pepys still omits a small number of passages of outrageous indecency. The editor of the fullest edition of Franklin remarks: "Unfortunately, it is impossible without offence to quote many of his briefer paragraphs. . . . He out-Smolletts Smollett in his letters to young women at home and experienced matrons abroad. Among the manuscripts in the Library of Congress, and in the columns of his newspaper and the introductions to 'Poor Richard,' are productions of his pen, the printing of which would not be tolerated by the public sentiment of the present age." Such productions, generally speaking, would be valueless to history. Their omission, properly indicated, does it no violence. But indicated omission is the one allowable course; rewriting, revision, verbal softening, are not for a moment allowable.

Translations may be of all degrees of goodness or badness; as good as the authorized English translation of Mommsen's *Rome* by William P. Dickson, as bad as the current translation of Taine's *English Literature* by H. Van Laun. But it is important to remember that a translation, no matter how excellent, is always a change. It subtly alters the flavor of the original. Not a few historical works have been twice translated. Russian books, for example, have first been rendered into German or French, then into English. At least one important historical book is available to American readers only after passing through the medium of four languages. This is the autobiography of a young Chinese, Tan Shih-hua; dictated in Chinese to Professor S. Tretiakov, written by the latter in Russian, translated into German, and again translated into English! To suppose that the texture of Tan Shih-hua's thought was not transformed in these four processes is to suppose a great deal. One reason why a command of foreign tongues is valuable is that it dispenses with translation; and no man having such a command should be content with less than the original.

The garbling of texts by accident or negligence has sometimes led to grave results far outside the sphere of scholarship. A misplaced comma may cause a diplomatic crisis. In 1912 the misprinting of a single word involved a serious political issue in the United States. The official Democratic Textbook of that year published one plank of the party platform as declaring against "the Aldrich plan for a central bank" — which would have left the way open for another type of central bank. The error was multiplied by many copyings. But party leaders, referring to their records, established the fact that the plank as drafted had condemned "the Aldrich plan *or* a central bank," binding the party to a sweeping interdiction of all such banks; and President Wilson recognized this reading as valid. But the most interesting work of scholars in the correction of negligent texts lies in the field of medieval manuscripts and early printed books.

Particularly interesting, and full of lessons to the historian, is the immense labor expended upon the establishment of a correct version of Shakespeare's plays. The greatest monument ever erected to the cause of textual integrity is beyond question the New Variorum Edition of Shakespeare begun by Dr. H. H. Furness and carried on by other scholars. The lore of whole libraries, the cunning of the most ingenious minds, the sensibility of the most delicate ears, have been utilized to make straight the thousand crookednesses of the early texts. The early quarto editions of some of the plays were attacked by the printers Heming and Condell in their authorized First Folio as maimed and deformed, and they gave large assurances of the accuracy of their versions — assurances that the facts do not support. Some of their plays are less correctly printed than in the quartos they assailed. Beginning with Lewis Theobald and Alexander Pope, a long list of critics in many lands spent patient years to give the world just what Theobald entitles his book, *Shakespeare Restored.* It was Theobald who suggested the most brilliant conjectural emendation which has ever gained place in the text of an English classic. In Dame Quickly's immortal description of Falstaff's death, where the line "and a table of greenfield" had long puzzled readers, he substituted the sentence, "and a' babbled of green fields." He won equally universal acceptance for his recasting of Hermia's line, "Emptying our bosoms of their counsel swelled," into "Emptying our bosoms of their counsels sweet." He and his successors employed every possible instrument. One German scholar even spent a long period studying Elizabethan styles of chirography and ortheopy in the British Museum, and thus constructed an Elizabethan paleography which he applied to the problem. That is, he attempted to conceive what Shakespeare's long-vanished manuscripts, written like other Elizabethan scripts, must have looked like, and tried thus to puzzle out correct readings for some of the printer's misreadings. Still others have labored on the theory that the printers did not set type direct from Shakespeare's manuscript (perhaps much cut up for stage use), but had it read aloud to them.

By the use of varied instruments, Shakespeare's editors have unquestionably done marvels in turning a very corrupt text into one of fair integrity. One typical feat may be cited. By comparing the quarto of "The Midsummer Night's Dream" with the First Folio, Dr. Furness took a passage which seemed suddenly to turn four fairies into eight —

TITANIA. — And I will purge thy mortall grossnesse so,
    That thou shalt like an aerie spirit go.
Enter Pease-Blossom, Cobweb, Moth, Mustarde-Seede, and four fairies.
FAIRIES. — Ready: and I, and I, and I, where shall we go?

and converted this into the piquant and convincing fragment:

TITANIA. — And I will purge thy mortal grossness so
    That thou shalt like an airy spirit go.
    Pease-Blossom! Cobweb! Moth! Mustard-Seed!
      Enter four fairies.
FAIRIES. — Ready; and I, and I, and I. Where shall we go?

What has thus been done for great texts of literature can sometimes equally be done for important historical texts mutilated by medieval copyists or early printers. For examples the student need only turn to the Rolls Series or the *Monumenta Germaniae Historica*.

The ordinary reader of history, on learning that so many of

the materials of which it must be built are faulty, that human frailty and human malignity so often unite to undermine its fabric, may feel a momentary discouragement. But to this fact historical study owes much of its challenge and fascination. It is unfortunately sometimes not at all true of history that

> Truth, crushed to earth, shall rise again,
> The eternal years of God are hers . . .

A permanent obscuration or falsification of the past does sometimes take place. We shall never know the full truth about Aztec civilization — the Spanish conquerors destroyed much of the evidence. We shall probably never estimate certain Roman emperors correctly — there was nobody to answer Tacitus and Suetonius. But it is because so many difficulties must be conquered that historical work possesses its interest and historical achievement its frequent impressiveness. To understand these difficulties, we must now turn to the thorny subject of evidence.

CHAPTER SEVEN

PILATE ON EVIDENCE

THE DIFFICULTY which most frequently daunts the historian, in dealing with evidence, is precisely that which most often disturbs judge and jury: there is not enough of it. Rarely indeed do we encounter an historical event of importance regarding which *all* the pertinent facts are known; all too frequently we are nonplused by transactions whose most vital particulars are missing. History is frequently an attempt to find the correct answer to equations which have been half erased. And in addition to the paucity of evidence, historical students must often lament its bad quality. Even when it exists with a fair degree of technical integrity, it is not unlikely to be evidence of a type which a keen opposing attorney could riddle with holes. Quantitatively and qualitatively, students of the past frequently find their data quite inconclusive.

The present age, with its vast equipment for recording events, might be supposed capable of producing sufficient quantities of evidence on every aspect of life. But not merely do indifference, neglect, and mischance constantly do their work. In addition, a widespread and sleepless conspiracy exists against history. A host of men and not a few institutions find it important to their interests — sometimes essential — to destroy the records of their activities. Every European chancellery has its missing documents. How much German evidence on the origins of the World War might not have perished in flames but for the revolution which gave Karl Kautsky and his associates free access to the records? How many Russian documents might not have been suppressed but for the sudden rise of the Bolshevists to power? Before the United States required publicity for expenditures in Presidential campaigns, national chairmen delighted in conflagrations. Matthew Quay in 1888, for example, when bribery was openly used in New York and Indiana, consigned all the Republican records to flames. Many a dishonest official has destroyed every evidence of his activities. Tweed's associate Richard Connolly invented the watchword "Addition, division, and silence," but the idea was old long before him. Similar practices are common in business. Collis P. Huntington's order for the disposal of all papers bearing on the construction of the Central Pacific; the destruction of Standard Oil records during the anti-trust prosecutions — these are but typical of many episodes. It may be said of documents as one of Cromwell's men said of a hated opponent, "Stone dead hath no brother."

Not that the destruction of evidence is always dishonest or improper. In highly competitive businesses, corporations may well deem the utmost secrecy indispensable. Officers of the law sometimes find it wiser not to trust any records to paper, for they may easily leak out to those who will use them to defeat justice. It was a fearless prosecuting attorney, working to break up a criminal gang in Colorado, who concluded: "Better walk a thousand miles than write a letter."[1] Secretary Benjamin H. Bristow, striving to annihilate the Whiskey Ring in 1874–75, had to carry forward his labors in the dark, with as few letters as possible and most of those written in cipher. Spies in his office would otherwise have defeated all his plans. All secret services are necessarily carried on almost without record. The business of the world, in fact, will always involve a huge amount of confidential activity, public and private; and the interests of the historian are often less important than the proper dispatch of this business. Nor is this greatly to be regretted. The past is the more fascinating for its patches of

[1] Philip S. Van Cise, *Fighting the Underworld* (1936), p. 70

darkness; our imagination is sometimes better stimulated by what has disappeared into death's dateless night than by what remains in the bright light of noonday. An old letter that lacks the answer may stir the heart more than a complete file of correspondence. Plunging into a long-past period in the diaries of Pepys and Hickey, or the letters of Walpole, we find the experience all the more delightful for the surrounding twilight.

But readers of history should realize that even when the evidence of an event seems fairly satisfactory, it may actually represent no more of it than the fraction of an iceberg seen above water represents of the whole icy mass. Take, for example, a diplomatic exchange in 1938 between Great Britain and the United States. The British proposal perhaps originates at a Cabinet meeting, where only a brief minute (not any record of discussion) is entered. As it affects the Dominion of Canada, Prime Minister Chamberlain asks the Foreign Minister, Anthony Eden, to discuss it with Prime Minister Mackenzie King in Ottawa. To save time, this is done by telephone. The Canadian Prime Minister then discusses the subject with his Cabinet, this again receiving no record whatever. Meanwhile the Cabinet in London has been hearing from important financial interests, which try to reach it by other means than letters. After a final Cabinet discussion in Downing Street, the Foreign Minister communicates with his Ambassador, Sir Ronald Lindsay, in Washington. The latter deputes one of the embassy staff to call on Mr. J. P. Moffat, head of the European Division in the State Department. He and Mr. Moffat are friends, having perhaps served together in some European capital. The Englishman outlines the proposal his government has in mind, and asks for advice upon the best way to present it. Mr. Moffat requests a few days to think it over, and then talks with Secretary of State Hull. It at once comes before the American Cabinet, where no record of deliberations whatever is kept. Mr. Moffat then tells Sir Ronald Lindsay what he can. A few days later the British note arrives. It has taken shape as a result of long preliminary discussion in three capitals, and the historian is lucky if he finds a cablegram or two and a casual jotting in somebody's diary to indicate this. If unlucky, he finds nothing.

It is undeniable, however, that a deal of *needless* destruction of valuable historical material steadily goes on. Men of the utmost probity and rectitude may destroy records simply from a sense that they are confidential. Thus Senator George F. Edmunds burned his personal papers before his death, with all their intimate matter on American politics from 1860 to 1890; not because they would necessarily damage anyone, but because he thought letters from other public men a sacred trust. Still more frequently men conceal the evidence of others' misdeeds because they believe that oblivion is seemly.[1] Hamilton Fish told his daughter that he had not entered in his voluminous diary the transactions in the Grant régime most discreditable to Grant. The poet Tom Moore consented, on demand of the publisher Murray and the family of Lord Byron, to destroy the manuscript of Byron's memoirs — for Murray had been told that publication would involve the poet in infamy. We read in the autobiography of Charles Godfrey Leland how he did away with some excessively frank evidence upon various American writers collected by the waspish Rufus Wilmot Griswold:

Dr. Griswold . . . had got himself into great trouble by his remarks on Edgar A. Poe. . . . Poe's best friends told severe stories of him in those days — *me ipso teste* — and Griswold, naught extenuating, and setting down naught in malice, wrote incautiously more than he should. These are the words of another than I. But when

---

[1] Abraham Lincoln's son Robert destroyed many of his father's papers, and was estopped from destroying others only by the intervention of friends, including Dr. Nicholas Murray Butler. A. K. McClure's papers on Lincoln were deliberately destroyed; so were those of Robert Levi Todd, one of Lincoln's intimate associates. Papers and evidence on Lincoln collected by his partner Herndon were suppressed by Jesse W. Weik in writing the Herndon-Weik life, and might easily have been destroyed. See Emanuel Hertz, *The Hidden Lincoln*, pp. 17–19.

Griswold was attacked, then he became savage. One day I found in his desk, which he had committed to me, a great number of further materials collected to Poe's discredit. I burnt it all up at once, and told the doctor what I had done, and scolded him well into the bargain. He took it all very amiably. There was also much matter to other men's discredit — *ascensionem expectans* — awaiting publication, all of which I burned. It was the result of long research, and evidently formed the material for a book. Had it ever been published, it would have made Rome howl! But, as I said, I was angry, and knew that it would injure Dr. Griswold more than anybody.[1]

Tom Moore forgot, Hamilton Fish forgot, that the fame of Byron and Grant was not the only interest to be considered, but that posterity also had its rights — a right to the full truth. After a certain lapse of time, letters such as Senator Edmunds doubtless received from various American statesmen cease to be private property and become affected with a public interest; to destroy them is to injure the public. But historians have learned to take philosophically the inevitable loss of much of the raw material of their calling. Libraries, learned societies, governmental archives, and individual scholars will strive to save what they can. The business of the historical student is to make the most of what evidence he has, not to repine that it is not fuller. But it should be added that more systematic effort to stimulate the writing of contemporaneous records — such a work as H. H. Bancroft did when he sent stenographers to take down the dictated narratives of California pioneers — is much needed.[2]

What the honest historian will never do is to use conjecture in piecing out the imperfect evidence of the past; save, of

[1] Charles Godfrey Leland, *Memoirs*, pp. 201, 202

[2] It is interesting to note how narrowly the Robert Morris Papers escaped destruction. Jared Sparks had access to them; they disappeared; they were discovered by George Meredith Read in a French country town just as they were about to be consigned to a paper mill; he guarded them like a dragon, letting nobody see them; but they finally went to the Library of Congress.

course, as he frankly confesses that it is a guess at truth. It is extraordinary how far pseudo-historians will go in substituting conjecture for fact when symmetry and completeness of narrative are otherwise unobtainable. Hilaire Belloc, in his life of Marie Antoinette, is certain that the friendship of the beautiful queen for Comte de Fersen never passed platonic bounds, for Mr. Belloc had a Catholic's conception of what his heroine must never allow herself to do. Arnold Zweig, however, in his biography of the queen, is certain that she and De Fersen loved one another with romantic unconstraint; for Herr Zweig's code expected that of a woman in Marie Antoinette's position. The fact is that no evidence exists for a positive statement. Wisdom would have dictated the course which Froude recommends, absolute avoidance of guesses. One of the *obiter dicta* of his stimulating *Short Studies* runs:

> In perusing modern histories, the present writer has been struck dumb with wonder at the facility with which men will fill in chasms in their information with conjecture; will guess at the motives which have prompted actions; will pass their censures, as if all the secrets of the past lay an open scroll before them. He is obliged to say for himself that, whenever he has been fortunate enough to discover authentic explanations of English historical difficulties, it is rare indeed that he has found any conjecture, either of his own or of any other modern writer, confirmed. The true motive has almost invariably been of a kind which no modern experience could have suggested.[1]

But let us turn to the quality of what evidence historians do possess.

II

Those acquainted with legal procedure are aware that jurists use the term evidence in a variety of senses, and direct much of their effort to determining the degree of falsity or truth in

---

[1] "Dissolution of the Monasteries," *Short Studies on Great Subjects*, First Series, World Classics Ed., p. 286

any fragment of it. The courts draw an emphatic distinction between direct evidence, and circumstantial evidence; that is, between the evidence of witnesses, documents, and material facts, and the evidence of environing circumstance. The latter kind of evidence may be termed presumptive evidence; certain facts are proved from which the existence of a fact vital to the case may logically be inferred. The courts distinguish, again, between original evidence and hearsay evidence. The former means the sworn statements of competent witnesses standing before the judge; the latter refers to a statement by some witness of what he heard another say outside of court. In dealing with documents, the law distinguishes between primary and secondary evidence. The original of a disputed contract is primary evidence, while a sworn copy of that contract is secondary evidence.

Beyond certain obvious limits, no hard and fast rules exist by which courts can distinguish between good and bad evidence. It is clear that except in the most bizarre cases, original evidence is better than hearsay evidence; indeed, the latter is usually excluded altogether. It is equally clear that when some question of documents arises, the originals are better than copies. But there is no sure touchstone for distinguishing between a veracious and an unveracious witness. Some men perjure themselves more plausibly than others tell the truth. And contrary to the popular view, direct evidence is frequently inferior to circumstantial evidence. This is because human beings lie, while material circumstances (if properly observed) do not. Judge Alton B. Parker used to tell jurymen who evinced undue suspicion of circumstantial evidence the story of his first murder case — a case which showed that such evidence may be absolutely conclusive. A man was tried for killing a woman at Coshocton, Sullivan County, New York. Nobody had seen the killing. But it was proved that the defendant had bought powder and shot in the village; had borrowed a shotgun from a resident there; had torn a page from a copy of the *Deaf Mutes'*

Institute, a magazine received by this resident, and using one-half for wadding, had put the other half in his pocket; had been seen approaching and returning from the murdered woman's house on the night of the murder; and had tried to spend a $5 bill which was well known in the village to be the property of the murdered woman's husband because it had been identified as counterfeit. The wadding had been found near the body. The other half of the page was in the defendant's pocket. The $5 bill was also in his pocket, though he tried to throw it away when the constable arrested him. On this circumstantial evidence the defendant was convicted and executed.

Similarly, no fixed rules exist by which historians can discriminate offhand between good and poor evidence. Historical writers are commonly not so rigid in examining evidence, or at least so bound by rules and precedents, as judges and juries are compelled to be; they should be equally severe in essentials, but their procedure may be marked by greater flexibility. This is because the issues at stake seldom affect life or property, because the verdict can always be reversed, and because the conditions under which evidence is taken are looser, broader, and less obedient to close control. But the best historians try to make their evidence meet ultimate tests as severe as those of the courts, and to reach many verdicts that are as compelling and trustworthy. Their regard for the veracity of witnesses and documents must be as close. And in several respects their practice runs precisely parallel with that of the courts. For example, if an accusation is involved, if one character in history denies a charge while others press it, in most instances guilt cannot be held conclusively established save by corroborative evidence from at least one independent source.

Even this parallel, however, must not be pushed too far. One obvious difference between courts and historians in handling evidence is that the former must, at least in all criminal cases, establish substantial certainty; while the latter can be satisfied with establishing probability. When there is a direct conflict of testimony, the historian can give more weight than the court to the inherent evidence of the situation. A court of law might not have held Mary Stuart guilty of connivance in the murder of Darnley, or might at least have brought in the Scots verdict of "Not proved"; but the historian Andrew Lang could pronounce her probably guilty. No public official can be held guilty in court of taking a bribe simply on the oath of a single witness that he has paid one to the official; cancelled checks, marked money, the testimony of independent witness, or some other distinct and clinching evidence, is required. A Federal Court in St. Louis, lacking such evidence, declared Orville E. Babcock guiltless of complicity in the Whiskey Ring. But several historians, after careful scrutiny of the collateral and inherent evidence, have unhesitatingly declared the probability of Babcock's guilt to be so great as to be conclusive. A neat problem of disputed evidence has been presented by the famous interview which James G. Blaine arranged in Washington with Jacob Mulligan in May, 1876, just before Mulligan was to appear before a House investigating committee with letters highly damaging to Blaine. The two men met alone in a hotel room. According to Mulligan, Blaine begged on his knees for the letters, saying that they would blast his career forever and ruin his six children. Finally he borrowed the letters, and stubbornly kept them. Blaine, who admitted getting the letters by this trick, denied the remainder of this story. No other evidence as to his pleas for pity was available. A court of law could not have accepted Mulligan's statement. The historian, however, accepts it because Mulligan bore a good reputation, had no incentive whatever to lie, and told a circumstantial tale which bore many inherent marks of truth. Blaine had every motive for lying, and his reputation for veracity was bad.

In short, the tests of evidence, in history as in courts, are principally *ad hoc* tests. They must vary with the witness, the problem, and the circumstances. Students of history may to some extent profit, in developing a method of weighing evidence, by reading such legal works as Thayer's *Preliminary Treatise on Evidence*, or Dean Wigmore's *System of Evidence*. But in the end such students have to devise their own methods to meet each problem, and the success of every historian depends upon his judgment, ingenuity, and honesty. It is possible to give only a few general words of advice. The chief of these must always be the old maxim, "Be skeptical — regard every assertion with doubt."

III

The best evidence is that in which no element of self-interest, no element of ignorance, and no element of bias appears. Among written materials, ordinary government documents in highly civilized lands meet the tests here implied more perfectly than anything else. When we use the report of debates in the *Congressional Record*, in the British or Canadian *Hansard*, or in the official journal of the Chamber of Deputies; when we refer to a law in the officially-printed Federal Statutes at Large, or official volumes of State statutes; when we read the text of a Presidential message in one of the executive documents, we may be certain we are using almost absolutely dependable material. This reliability holds true of court records, treaties, proclamations, and such official correspondence as that published in the annual volumes of *Foreign Relations* and in the British Blue-Books. In so far as this material states matters of record, not of opinion or supposition, it is as authentic as human productions can be. This is because the honor of nations, States, and cities is bound up in the accuracy of their records, and proportionate care is taken to prevent error. It is because while at rare intervals the interest of an individual might be promoted by falsification, in general such vast and overwhelming interests are served by accuracy that unreliability would be regarded as intolerable. It is because governments are able to hire corps of experts animated by strict discipline, and this discipline demands the rigid elimination of ignorance or bias — the instant correction of even the slightest error.

Thus in history, as in courts of law, complete credence is usually to be given records of fact from official government sources. Of course this record must not be used naïvely. A student of the *Congressional Globe* or *Record* is expected to know that, as its pages plainly show, not all speeches printed there have been delivered on the floor of Congress. "Leave to print" accounts for extensions of spoken discourses, and for long discourses of which not a word was ever spoken. Such a student is also expected to know that important speeches delivered in executive sessions of the Senate do not appear in print at all for many years, and perhaps never. He is expected to know that the speeches published in the *Record* are frequently revised by the author, sometimes drastically, while at times rude or profane language is expurgated by the clerk; so that press reports of Congressional speeches may be quite accurate, and yet differ materially from the official report.

Students of diplomacy are supposed to know that some foreign nations make treaties with secret clauses, as even the United States once in its early history did; so that the published version may be incomplete. Everyone should know that proclamations are frequently used for propagandist purposes only, and are not always to be taken at their face value. And everyone should be constantly alive to the fact that while an officially published statute proves the passage of a law, it may prove nothing whatever as to its vitality. Many statutes, Federal, State, and local, have been dead letters from the moment of their enactment. Many more, like the Fugitive Slave Law of 1850, have been effective in some areas while a nullity in others. Many men who realize that this is true in our own day forget that it has always been true in the past. They are aware that the Eighteenth Amendment and Volstead Act were inoperative for great urban communities before their repeal, but they assume that the European laws which once punished trifling offences with death, or the colonial laws which seemed to bear harshly upon religious minorities, were enforced to the letter. As a matter of fact, the old criminal laws were in practise mitigated by an extraordinary number of expedients. So were the old laws against debtors; King Charles II even took poor folk into his nominal employ as royal servants to save them from debtors' prisons. Though various American colonies had harsh laws against Catholics, the general colonial practice was mild. A careful work written by a Catholic

offers exhaustive evidence that in the general history of religious intolerance the Puritans and other Protestants of the colonies were far from being the worst offenders. After all, no blood was shed; no martyrs were burned at the stake; no confessors were made to suffer and die in dark prisons. . . . Extreme *violence* against the Catholics was more oratorical exercise and display of verbal fireworks than actual practice. It had no counterpart in the use of violent means of repression or bloody persecutions. Even when laws were enacted which, if strictly applied, would have prevented any Catholic from taking up residence in a colony, very seldom do we find a very rigorous enforcement of them. In most cases Catholics, though deprived of special rights, could live in peace.[1]

IV

The newspaper as a form of evidence merits consideration immediately after the official document. For one reason, to students of modern history it is second in importance only to official sources — if not actually equal; for another reason, parts of the modern newspaper have a quasi-official character. It is obvious that the extraordinary expansion of press activities has made the historical value of the newspaper a complex and somewhat baffling subject, on which easy generalizations are impossible. The accuracy of newspapers varies greatly from land to land. In the same country, their reliability and fullness varies greatly from city to city. A newspaper may

[1] Review of Sister Mary Augustina Ray's *American Opinion of Roman Catholicism in the Eighteenth Century, New England Quarterly*, X, 143–146, March, 1937

utterly change its character within a few years, sometimes almost overnight. The Washington *National Intelligencer* was a valuable repository of historical material in the 1840's, less valuable in the 1850's, almost worthless after 1860; the New York *Times* was of mediocre value in 1890, but of steadily increasing usefulness after 1895.

One generalization, however, may be ventured. Journalism has reached its highest development in English-speaking lands, and the evidential value of the average newspaper in English is distinctly higher than in most other languages. Many journals in Continental Europe and Hispanic-America must be used with extreme caution. The press of France, as we know from the pages of Balzac, from the Panama and Dreyfus scandals, and from more recent revelations, has in great part been shamelessly venal. Before the World War, the press of Czarist Russia was rigidly and that of Imperial Germany somewhat less strictly controlled. The rise in post-war years of Hitler in Germany, Mussolini in Italy, and other dictators elsewhere was accompanied by the stifling of all independence in the presentation of both press news and opinion. In contrast, the best American, British, Canadian, and Australian newspapers have long occupied a high plane of independence, enterprise, and accuracy in gathering news and in editorial comment. The largest of these dailies are invaluable to students of nineteenth and twentieth century history, and in the broad view have become steadily more useful. At various times and places famous Continental journals — the *Journal des Debats*, the *Berliner Tageblatt*, the *Frankfurter Zeitung*, the *Corriere della Sera* — and a few such South American dailies as *Il Prensa* of Buenos Aires, have had great importance. But the significance of their files to the modern historian does not equal that of the London *Times*, founded in 1785, the Manchester *Guardian*, founded in 1821, the New York *Evening Post*, founded in 1801, the New York *Tribune*, founded in 1841, and the New York *Times*, founded in 1851.

Another generalization may be ventured as to the departments of the press. The modern newspaper is a curious mixture of official, semi-official, and unofficial information. Its weather reports are strictly official; barring misprints, they may be trusted with confidence. The reports of stock markets, produce markets, and merchandise markets are semi-official. They are presented without bias, without self-interest, and by experts working under carefully guarded conditions. Behind their accuracy stands the honor of the newspaper, and the knowledge of its managers that error would mean angry protests, loss of confidence, and a ruinous drop in circulation. News of the results of all kinds of games and contests is likewise semi-official, its accuracy guaranteed by precisely the same considerations. So with news of ship-movements, announcements of radio programs, and lists of deaths, births, marriages, bankruptcies, and probated estates. But this almost closes the list. The remainder of the newspaper — and "all the world is in the newspaper," said Thackeray— is a mixture of the reliable and unreliable, the impartial and the tendencious, the shrewd and the naïve, the superficial and the well-informed. Useful as the news-columns and editorials are, their best values can be extracted only by patient winnnowing.

Since all newspapers are produced by men working under extreme pressure of time, a small percentage of outright inaccuracy is inevitable. Reporters and correspondents gather facts in a hurry and write with eyes on the clock; copyreaders revise this material hurriedly; headline writers fit it with hurried captions; the proofroom corrects it hurriedly. On such newspapers as the London *Times*, Manchester *Guardian*, and New York *Times*, gross inaccuracies are infrequent. Substantial errors are punishable by discharge; they are publicly corrected. But inadequacy of news is much more common, and sometimes amounts to inaccuracy. All newspapermen, from editors to reporters, feel a despairing sense that they write from a half-knowledge of affairs. With their limited time and sources of information they simply cannot gain a full knowledge. Samuel Bowles once remarked that no journalist could wait to get his work precisely right, and then publish it just as the last trump sounded. While aiming at the whole truth, good newspapermen must frequently content themselves with half or three quarters of it. Men engaged in any complicated transaction, political, economic, or cultural, often waver, as they read press reports of this transaction, between admiration that the reporter has learned so much and irritation that he has not learned more. They realize that the story is accurate so far as it goes, and yet without challengeable misstatement or conscious dishonesty, sometimes subtly misrepresents a situation. Readers of press files must bear this in mind. Those who can gauge newspaper reports by intimate sources of information, such as letters or diaries, are not likely to forget it.

Nor will any careful student forget that bias enters the news columns of even the best journals. Such journals sometimes go to extreme lengths to prevent any coloring of the news. Thus the New York *Times*, itself antipathetic to Bolshevism, maintained for years in Moscow a correspondent (Mr. Walter Duranty) who was distinctly sympathetic to the Soviet régime; thus the New York *Herald Tribune*, sternly opposing Franklin D. Roosevelt in 1936, chose as its correspondent with his Republican opponent a biographer and warm admirer of Roosevelt's. The best English-language journals the world over try to exclude from their news all trace of overt editorializing. But coloration nevertheless insidiously creeps in. Reporters and correspondents of the Manchester *Guardian* simply cannot forget that its general attitude in labor questions, colonial questions, and issues of international relations is that of the left-wing Liberals; this fact unconsciously affects their observation of events and their mental composition of a news-story before it is written down. A writer for the *Guardian*, however honest, will not be so quick to see an outrage by labor as one by capital — because he is looking for the latter; not so quick to see the benefits of imperialist rule overseas as its defects. He has a subconscious sensitiveness to one, a subconscious insensitiveness to the other. This general principle applies still more clearly to American newspapers. Every great journal has its *tone*, and it is remarkable how men of the most salient abilities lose all individuality on such journals, merging with it their own personality. The point at which it ceases to be legitimate for a managing editor to play up that news which supports the editorial attitude, and play down that news which runs counter to it, is a difficult question. Crusading journals like the New York *Tribune* under Greeley in the fifties, and the New York *World* under Pulitzer in the nineties, tended to weld the news and editorials together in a seamless fabric. The editors fought these newspapers as a captain fought his battleship. They did good service for one side of the truth, but they were often very one-sided indeed.

During the first three quarters of the nineteenth century the bias in American newspapers was primarily political, and could easily be detected. Any reader could see that the news favored Whigs, Democrats, or Republicans, and also favored certain sectional interests allied with parties. But as the nation became an industrial giant the newspaper bias grew more and more largely economic. As such, it was better concealed and more dangerous. Democrats and Republicans long divided the press with some evenness; but by 1890 belief in the *status quo* of the economic system almost monopolized it. The historian finds it difficult to obtain a fair statement of the Free Silver cause in 1896 in the Eastern press; difficult to obtain a balanced treatment of labor upheavals like the Colorado Coal & Iron strike, the Paterson and Lawrence strikes, and the steel strike of 1919; and difficult to obtain a fairminded treatment of some aspects of the New Deal 1933–38. Issues between business and government in recent years have been widely misrepresented by the daily press, which, since even small-city newspapers now require a large investment, has become distinctly an organ of business. Of course those newspapers in which bias is most obvious present the fewest dangers to students of history. Such students will be on their guard in using Bennett's sensational *Herald* in the 1840's, or the still more sensational Hearst press in the period 1895–1920. They will see that the Chicago *Tribune* has been decidedly partisan on economic issues from the time when it assailed the Pullman strikers of 1894 until its latest criticisms of organized labor. It is the journal of but mild and occasional news-coloration that is likely to mislead later students.

Managers of the New York *Herald Tribune*, one of the most respected newspapers in the world, in 1935–36 circularized schools and colleges, urging its use in the classroom. "Its news columns are impartial and open to news of all parties and sections," they declared. Again, "For fairness and accuracy, the *Herald Tribune* has gained a wide reputation." The owner, Mr. Ogden Mills Reid, said publicly on October 17, 1935: "My conception of the news columns of a great newspaper is that they should first find out the news and then tell the facts just as they happen or as they are about to happen. Also, in cases of controversial subjects, we naturally get all the parties to the disagreement to state their versions. We want to get the very best evidence we can on every side of the question. When it comes to a matter of opinion . . . we reserve that for the editorial page . . ." The sincerity of these statements need not be impugned. Yet it is impossible for a highly partisan journal, the *Herald Tribune* being staunchly Republican and on economic questions rather conservative, to keep its news absolutely objective. A brief examination of the *Herald Tribune* news columns in 1934–35 yields such natural examples as these:

I. — Omission

A. — On May 18, 1935, Howard Davis, business manager of the *Herald Tribune*, speaking at Colby College, asserted that radio broadcasting had suffered from political interference by the Roosevelt

Administration. Full text of this address was published in the *Herald Tribune* next day. This was followed by a detailed denial by A. J. McCosker, president of the Bamberger Broadcasting Service, and a recognized expert in the field, who said: "Such an accusation is entirely unjustified." The *Times* published this denial (May 28, 1935); the *Herald Tribune* did not.

B. — On April 13, 1935, Mr. Norman Thomas and Mrs. Elinore Herrick discussed the New Deal at an important luncheon meeting in New York. Mrs. Herrick warmly praised the New Deal. Mr. Thomas approved its intent, though he regarded it as inadequate to meet the current economic crisis, holding more radical measures necessary. The *Times* published an account of this meeting, April 14; the *Herald Tribune* published nothing on it.

II. — Special Emphasis

A. — The *Herald Tribune* was hostile to the experts (largely drawn from universities) who served the Roosevelt Administration. In April, 1935, the Carnegie Foundation for the Advancement of Learning published its annual review of legal education in the United States. Discussing the place of educators in public life, this report concluded that specialists in any field — soldiers, bankers, educators, to cite only outstanding groups — can perform a great service by supplying ideas and plans; but that administration should be entrusted to persons not too closely devoted to any one specialty. "Soldiers, bankers, educators, cannot safely be left to themselves," although they may possess "infinitely greater knowledge and capacity than a mere layman can hope to acquire."

The *Herald Tribune* published a summary of this report. It made no mention of the conclusion that it was the specialist in general, whatever his field, who was pronounced ill-fitted for public administration. The news account mentioned only the educator. And the sub-head placed over it read: "Carnegie Education Review Holds Pedagogues Likely to Blunder as Leaders."

B. — At the annual meeting of the American Civil Liberties Union on May 24, 1935, reports were read on activities of the year. Mr. Roger Baldwin expressed fear that a serious threat to personal liberties was involved in demands made by "the forces of reaction." Specifically, the Union assailed "the program of legislation proposed by the United

States Chamber of Commerce, the American Legion, the Order of Elks, and the Hearst and McFadden press." The *Herald Tribune* headline omitted all mention of these groups, and stated instead: "Civil Liberties Body Links 'Gag Bill' to New Deal."

III. — Partiality in Reporting

A. — The Chemical Industry in New York celebrated its tercentenary April 24, 1935, at a meeting in New York of about 5,000 members of the American Chemical Society. Mr. L. du Pont spoke of the advances in chemistry which had helped make the United States more secure in the event of war. Mr. W. B. Bell criticized certain New Deal policies which affected the chemical industry. The *Times* headline next day mentioned both speakers; the *Herald Tribune* headline mentioned only Mr. Bell. The *Times* news account devoted eleven paragraphs to Mr. du Pont's summary of the advances in chemistry, and four paragraphs to Mr. Bell's attack on the New Deal, thus reflecting the true ratio of interest. The *Herald Tribune* devoted its first eleven paragraphs to Mr. Bell's attack on the New Deal, and only four to the gains in chemistry, one alone of which contained any direct quotation from Mr. du Pont.

B. — In June, 1934, the *Literary Digest* published early returns from a nation-wide poll on the popularity of the New Deal. Morning papers on the 30th carried reports from 20 communities, 18 of which favored the New Deal while 2 opposed it. The *Times* captioned its account, "Eighteen Cities Back New Deal. Ossining and Red Bank Give Adverse Vote in Digest Poll." The *Herald Tribune* headline ran: "Red Bank Against New Deal. New Jersey Town Joins Protestors in Literary Digest Poll."

When partiality creeps into the careful columns of the *Herald Tribune*, one of the very best of American journals, we may be sure that it is present in much greater degree in a long list of less conscientious newspapers of the present day, and in most newspaper files belonging to earlier and less scrupulous decades.

Many files may also mislead uncritical readers by habitual and natural magnification of the news. Reporters usually desire to give their accounts an air of importance, and to do this resort to various formulas, the principal being the substitution of general for particular statements. Thus several policemen are ordered to search for a certain criminal. Newspapers next day may report, "Police were ordered today to begin a dragnet hunt for so-and-so," the implication being that most of the city force is so engaged. We even see, "Police of three states were hunting today," etc., the truth being that half a dozen detectives were at work. So when a flood threatens a city, a reporter interviews several barge-captains or fishermen, with the resulting statement, "Fears of rivermen were increasing today," or even, "River experts agreed today in predicting . . ." A factory superintendent makes a statement to a reporter, and next day the public reads, "Officials of the Blup Manufacturing Corporation declare . . ." Or a correspondent goes downtown in New York and sees a half dozen brokers and bankers. Next day: "Wall Street circles viewed with apprehension the news that the Administration . . ." This is shortly countered by a dispatch from the Washington correspondent, who has seen several bureau heads and Congressmen: "Circles close to the President today met with grave resentment the Wall Street view . . ." Of course the more reputable journals avoid this exaggeration.

Students of bound newspaper volumes should be suspicious of vague and general statements. "Informed Washington quarters" may be only a minor civil service employee; "medical experts" may mean a young doctor; "Pennsylvania authorities" may cloak the identity of a few justices of the peace. Particularly in the foreign news is this tendency toward a vague magnification often given absurd rein. A London correspondent sees an under-secretary at the Foreign Office, and cables home: "Downing Street evinced great irritation when told today of news from Tokyo that . . ." In certain journals the hurried headline-writer plays this up as "British Suspicion of Japan Grows," and the reader is left to picture 45,000,000 Britons and 60,000,000 Japanese glowering angrily at one another.

Still another danger to history lurks in the steady and often successful efforts of press agents and propagandists to reach the columns of the press; efforts against which editors wage a sleepless but not always successful warfare. One or two generations ago not a few newspapers still published the paid reading-notice — a puff or advertisement indistinguishable or barely distinguishable from ordinary news. That is dead. But no little part of the news for many years from Washington and State capitals has originated in press releases by government departments or bureaus ("handouts"), often decidedly biassed in character. Recent years have witnessed an alarming increase in the use of press agents by different branches of the Federal government. Washington correspondents formerly obtained their information by hard work, but now the less efficient may collect news — of a sort — without material effort. Corporations and individuals offer press releases of the same kind, and go to ingenious lengths to gain a place in the news.

Thus any intensive use of the files of a given newspaper for historical purposes should be preceded or accompanied by an effort to determine its *tone*, and how much that counts in its treatment of events; the degree to which its editors permit coloration of the news; its canons of accuracy; and its special sources of information. Important staff members should as far as possible be identified. It may be of value to know that the Washington correspondent whom Theodore Roosevelt most trusted for years was Francis E. Leupp of the New York *Evening Post*, and that President Hoover made a similar confidant of Mark Sullivan of the New York *Herald Tribune*.

V

Beyond the field of the government document, beyond the field of the newspaper, lies that vaster field presented by personal source materials — letters, diaries, memoirs, and autobiographies. A government is largely impersonal and a newspaper often tries to be; but when we come to records made by individuals in their private capacity, new difficulties appear.

Each personal witness must be regarded by the student much as judge and jury regard witnesses on the stand. Testimony must be evaluated as first-hand or hearsay, fresh or stale, prejudiced or unprejudiced, corroborated or uncorroborated, vague or definite. All this should be obvious, but to many students and writers it is not. Theodore Roosevelt includes in his *Winning of the West* a number of amusing paragraphs on the difficulty of educating American writers to treat personal narratives of the frontier critically. He found it necessary to point out "the very obvious truths that with the best intentions in the world the average backwoodsman often has difficulty in describing a confused chain of events exactly as they took place; that when the events are described after a long lapse of years many errors are apt to creep in; and that when they are reported from tradition it is the rarest thing imaginable for the report to be correct."

We can best illustrate the means of testing personal evidence by examples. Take as one a letter that has become famous for its direct bearing on disputed questions in the career of Joan of Arc. It was written July 21, 1429, when Joan had raised the siege of Orléans and set out for Rheims to attend the coronation of Charles. Its author, Perceval de Boulainvilliers, chamberlain to Charles, addressed it to the Duke of Milan. After some preliminary words, he thus took the witness stand:

Already, I am sure, news has reached your ears of a certain Maid, sent to us, as we devoutly believe, by God, and in order that I may briefly set forth her life, deeds, station, and character, [I] shall first tell of her origin. She was born in the small village of Domrémy, in the country of Bar, within the confines of Kingdom of France, on the river Meuse, near Lorraine, of upright and simple parents. During the night of the Epiphany of our Lord, when the nations are wont most joyfully to recall the acts of Christ, she entered upon mortal life, and all the people of the place were wondrously moved by a great rejoicing, and though ignorant of the birth of the Maid, they rushed hither and thither in search of what might be the new event.

The hearts of some were conscious of a new gladness. More: the cocks as heralds of a new joy, against their wont, burst forth in songs not heard before, and with flapping wings for more than two hours appeared to foretell the coming of a new thing.

The child is reared, and when she had reached the age of seven years, after the custom of peasants she was placed by her parents in charge of the lambs, during which time no lamb is known to have died, nor was anyone killed by wild beasts, and while she was under her father's roof so great was the security she afforded the whole household that they suffered not the least injury from enemy, deceit of barbarians, or other ill. Finally when she had reached the age of twelve years, the first revelation was made to her in the following manner:

When she and other maidens were guarding the sheep of their parents, they were wandering about the field. Those round about approached, and they asked her whether she would like to enter a race for a handful of flowers, or the like. She consented, and the conditions being agreed upon, she moved during the second and third circuits with such speed that they did not think she touched the ground at all, so that one of the children cried out:

"Joan," for that was her name, "I see you flying close to the ground." [1]

Thus far the witness is not in the least credible. He is giving us hearsay, and a poor quality of hearsay at that — the popular fables of the time. It is probable enough that the villagers of Domrémy rushed gaily about the streets on Twelfth Night, perhaps causing the cocks to crow, but the rest of this farrago is worthless. But the letter-writer continues, more soberly:

The Maid is of a satisfying grace, of a manly bearing, and in her conversation displays wondrous good sense. Her voice has wondrous charm. She eats little, partakes even more sparingly of wine. She delights in beautiful horses and armor and greatly admires armed and noble men; avoids contacts and converse with the many, sheds tears freely, her expression is cheerful, and she has great capacity for work. Of such endurance is she in the handling and bearing of arms that she remained for six days and nights in full armor.

[1] Albert Bigelow Paine, *Joan of Arc*, I, 352–358

She declared that the English have no rights in France, and that she herself was sent by God to overcome them, and that God had so declared to her. For the King she has the greatest reverence. She declares that he was chosen by God, and was and will continue to be under her special protection. She further declares that the Duke of Orleans, your grandson, will be set free by a miracle, a warning having first been given to the English who are holding him in custody, to set him free.

Here the witness plainly begins to be of value, for he is no longer writing hearsay, but giving facts on his own authority. As he was chamberlain of the French monarch and constantly at court, he had ample opportunity to observe Joan; he was certainly at Chinon during part of the time she was there. His portrait thus carries conviction. At one point he drops into hearsay again, writing that Joan remained six days and nights in her armor. This is doubtless a wild exaggeration, for she was never six days and nights in the field at one time. But when he says that her voice is charming, that she is cheerful of mien, and that she is emotional of temperament, he is speaking from his own knowledge. Moreover, corroborative testimony exists. Another contemporary, Gui de Laval, speaks of her pleasing voice, and still another, Louis de Contes, of her sparing appetite, while her whole career proves her emotional warmth. Altogether, the letter of Perceval de Boulainvilliers offers a perfect illustration of the weakness of hearsay evidence, the strength of original evidence.

It is equally easy to demonstrate the general superiority of direct evidence over circumstantial evidence. American historical literature presents a singularly striking instance of a blunder, committed through reliance upon circumstantial evidence alone, by one who was both a practiced scholar and a highly experienced man of the world. Charles Francis Adams, Civil War minister to England, and the biographer of his grandfather John Adams, published soon after the Civil War (1873) a brochure on William H. Seward. He made therein the rash assertion that the success of Lincoln's Administration was traceable primarily to the keenness and wisdom of Seward. For this statement he marshalled a variety of circumstantial evidence. Lincoln was uneducated, Seward a graduate of Union College, deeply read and widely travelled. Lincoln possessed little experience of public office when chosen President, having been merely an inconspicuous Congressman for two years; Seward's public experience had begun with his election as Governor of New York, and in 1861 included twelve years of leadership in the Senate. Lincoln had been reared in a frontier State, Seward trained in the richest and most populous part of the nation. Lincoln had never taken that determined stand on questions of the day which Seward had long taken and which had led him in 1850 to refer to "a higher law than the Constitution." Lincoln had made Seward his Secretary of State, obviously meaning to lean heavily upon him — to make him Prime Minister. Lincoln had been given the benefit of Seward's advice at every step, consulting him not only in the Cabinet but in frequent private meetings. It was clear, declared Adams, that the enduring work of the administration had been done by Seward.

"It is the duty of history," he wrote, "in dealing with all human events, to do strict justice in discriminating between persons, and by no means to award to one honors that clearly belong to another. I must then affirm, without hesitation, that in the history of our government, no experiment so rash has ever been made as that of elevating to the head of affairs a man with so little previous preparation for his task as Mr. Lincoln. . . . Mr. Lincoln could not fail soon to perceive that whatever estimate he might put on his own natural judgment, he had to deal with a superior in native intellectual power, in extent of acquirement, in breadth of philosophic experience, and in the force of moral discipline. On the other hand, Mr. Seward could not have been long blind to the deficiencies of his chief in these respects." In brief, all the circumstances rendered it inevitable that Seward should lead, Lincoln follow. Mr.

Adams pointed to circumstantial evidence that he had done so. Seward wished the emancipation of the slaves treated cautiously; and emancipation was effected at just the time and in just the way that Seward would have wished it done. Seward wished the Administration to defy the more radical and impetuous leaders of Congress; and Lincoln had defied Thaddeus Stevens and Zachariah Chandler. The evidence seemed overwhelming.

But one blow at the weakest point of that circumstantial evidence which is founded on the mere outward aspect of affairs, and it comes toppling down. So it was with Adams's impressive array of arguments. Gideon Welles, Secretary of the Navy under Lincoln, stepped forward with a small volume called *Lincoln and Seward* which proved conclusively that Lincoln had always been master of his Administration — that he had led and others had followed. By direct evidence drawn from his own unpublished diary, and buttressed by other data, he showed that as between the two groups in his Cabinet, the radicals headed by Chase and the moderates by Seward, Lincoln had acted with masterly independence. He proved that all of the President's decisive acts had been stamped with his own sagacity. Sixteen years later Nicolay and Hay, in their ten-volume life of Lincoln based on the Lincoln papers, demonstrated just how fatal any reliance upon Seward would have been. They staggered the admirers of the great New Yorker by showing that on April 1, 1861, he had proposed that the United States should provoke a war with France and Spain as a means of reuniting the American people, suggesting that he be permitted to carry out this and other policies. They showed how magnanimously Lincoln, while rejecting this folly and putting Seward into his proper place, had suppressed all public notice of the proposal, and how quickly he had brought Seward to recognize his superior wisdom and firmness. Later research has revealed so much evidence of Lincoln's complete control of his Administration, including at times the State Department, that it seems almost incredible that C. F. Adams should ever have made his reckless statements. His circumstantial evidence was worthless.

The most difficult form of evidence to test is that given by the single witness, who may be affected by a hundred forms of personal bias, self-interest, or party, national, or other feeling. The varieties and complexities of bias are almost endless, and they are frequently compatible with the utmost sincerity. Of course the simpler types of prejudice are easy to detect — but how seldom we meet the simpler types! The primary rule, in historical study as in the courts, is to cross-examine the witness in an effort to ascertain how many varieties of bias he expresses, and to what degree; for it is a safe rule that everyone has some bias, conscious or unconscious. Suppose, for example, the student of Jefferson turns to the well-known passage in John Quincy Adams's *Memoirs* in which that shrewd observer expresses his conclusions upon the Virginian:

Washington, January 11, 1831. — I read about fifty pages of the first volume of Jefferson's *Memoirs*. [J.Q.A. means the *Anas*.] He states that he began his autobiography on the 6th of January, 1821. . . . He tells nothing but what redounds to his own credit. He is like the French lady who told her sister she did not know how it happened, "but I am the only person in the world who is always right." Jefferson, by his own narrative, is always in the right. That is not uncommon to writers of their own lives. Dr. Franklin was more candid. Mr. Jefferson names the teachers from whom he learnt Greek, Latin, and French, and speaks gratefully of William Small, a Scotchman, professor of mathematics at William and Mary College, who became attached to him and probably fixed the destinies of his life. . . . Loose morals necessarily followed. If not an absolute atheist, he had no belief in a future existence. All his ideas of obligation or retribution were bounded by the present life. His duties to his neighbor were under no stronger guarantee than the laws of the land and the opinions of the world. The tendency of this condition upon a mind of great compass and powerful resources is to produce insincerity and duplicity, which were his besetting sins through life. . .

[From 1790 to 1809] all the good and all the evil parts of his character were brought into action. His ardent passion for liberty and the rights of man; his patriotism; the depth and compass of his understanding; ... the perpetual watchfulness of public opinion, and the pliability of principle and temper with which he accommodated it to his own designs and opinions: — all these were in ceaseless operation during these twenty years; and with them were combined a rare mixture of infidel philosophy and epicurean morals, of burning ambition and of stoical self-control, of deep duplicity and of generous sensibility, between which two qualities, and a treacherous and inventive memory, his conduct toward his rivals and opponents appears one tissue of inconsistency. His treatment of Washington, of Knox, of my father, of Hamilton, of Bayard, who made him President of the United States, and lastly of me, is marked with features of perfidy worthy of Tiberius Caesar or Louis XI of France. This double-dealing character was often imputed to him during his life and was sometimes exposed. His letter to Mazzei and the agonizing efforts which he afterwards made to explain it away; his most insidious attack upon my father with his never-ceasing professions of respect and affection for his person and character; and his letter to Giles concerning me, in which there is scarcely a single word of truth — indicate a memory so pandering to the will that in deceiving others he seems to have begun by deceiving himself.

Here we find Jefferson accused by one who knew him well of loose morals; of being a freethinker, irreligious and probably atheistic; of having no principle; and of displaying utter selfishness in trying to gratify an inordinate ambition. We find him accused of duplicity, of treachery to superiors and friends, and of deliberate falsehood. It is a staggering indictment, drawn by a statesman famous for both astuteness and probity. But if we summon Adams for cross-examination, what do we find? We learn that he is now sixty-three, with a memory not always accurate. We learn that Jefferson defeated his father for the presidency, and that this event terminated J. Q. Adams's service as Minister to Prussia, a comfortable post — for John Adams recalled him, in order not to embarrass Jefferson. We learn that during Jefferson's Administration Adams was a political independent, distrusted by both parties, and frequently piqued because neither was friendly toward him. We learn that as a Massachusetts man he was constitutionally incapable of liking Virginians. As he mentions religion, by a little inquiry we find that he is one of the devoutest of Congregationalists, distrusting Episcopalianism and detesting Deism; and that his ideas of what constitutes irreligion are narrow and dogmatic. As he mentions morals, a little inquiry elicits the fact that he regards card-playing, horse-racing, and any waste of time on mere amusement as immoral. And finally, we learn that a multitude of witnesses will testify that Adams, however great and good, was the most censorious and cantankerous of mortals, whose diary has been called "a graveyard of slaughtered reputations."

In this instance bias stands revealed at a glance; but usually it is far better concealed. Adams and Jefferson spent much of their lives in opposing political parties, while they usually held antagonistic sectional views. But take an equally well-known passage, that in which President James K. Polk in his diary excoriates John C. Calhoun; and is any such obvious bias present? Polk and Calhoun were both staunch Democrats. Both were Southerners, reared in neighboring States. Both were slaveholders. Yet Polk writes under date of April 6, 1847, that he has no use for either Martin Van Buren or Calhoun:

The people of the United States, I hope, will cast off all such intriguers, and make their own selection for the Presidency, and this if they are wise they will do. I now entertain a worse opinion of Mr. Calhoun than I have ever done before. He is wholly selfish, and I am satisfied has no patriotism. A few years ago he was the author of Nullification and threatened to dissolve the Union on account of the tariff. During my administration the reduction of duties which he desired has been obtained, and he can no longer complain. No sooner is this done than he selects slavery upon which to agitate the country, and blindly mounts that topic as a hobby. . . . I am utterly disgusted at such intriguing of men in high place, and hope they will be rebuked by the people.

Here is another withering indictment of one of our most eminent statesmen. Calhoun is accused of utter selfishness, base intriguing, and an entire lack of patriotism and party spirit. But a cross-examination of Polk reveals that two years earlier, when he was pressing for hostilities against Mexico, Calhoun spoke and voted against war to the last. It reveals that one year earlier, when Polk was reluctant to settle the Oregon boundary on the 49th parallel, Calhoun vigorously advocated that compromise. It reveals the fact that Polk in 1847 wished to annex a large part of present-day Mexico to the United States — indeed, he ultimately favored annexing it all; but that Calhoun strongly opposed unlimited annexation, and wished to carry the line no farther south than it now stands. In brief, the men had been in constant collision ever since Polk took office, and Polk, smarting under Calhoun's blows, was far from a good witness as to his character and motives. On the stand in open court, an opposing attorney could have riddled his prejudiced testimony.

But the commonest form of bias in memoirs, autobiographies, letters, and travels is that which requires only a slight discount; and determination of the proper degree of reserve is often a nice task. Take a passage from the graphic memoirs of Henry Villard — part of his description of how, as a journalist, he reported the Lincoln-Douglas debates of 1858. He writes:

I was introduced to Lincoln at Freeport, and met him frequently afterwards in the course of the campaign. I must say frankly that, although I found him most approachable, good-natured, and full of wit and humor, I could not take a real personal liking to the man, owing to an inborn weakness for which he was even then notorious, and so remained during his great public career. He was inordinately fond of jokes, anecdotes, and stories. He loved to hear them, and still more to tell them himself out of the inexhaustible supply provided by his good memory and his fertile fancy. There would have been no harm in this but for the fact that the coarser the joke, the lower the anecdote, and the more risky the story, the more he enjoyed them, especially when they were of his own invention. He possessed, more-over, a singular ingenuity in bringing about occasions in conversation for indulgences of this kind.[1]

How much weight is to be attached to this decidedly un-favorable judgment of Lincoln? Unquestionably it offers valid evidence of one of Lincoln's small weaknesses. It is sufficient in itself to destroy Mrs. Honoré Willsie Morrow's statement that Lincoln's stories, while somewhat broad, never held an evil suggestiveness. (Mrs. Morrow asserts that she is sure Lincoln never repeated bawdy anecdotes because she asked various men, experts on Lincoln's humor, to tell her the worst, and they never told her one that was really offensive!) But is the con-demnation of Lincoln's vulgarity to be taken at full face value? An examination of Villard discloses some significant facts. Was he a man of mature judgment in 1858? He was twenty-three, when rash estimates are often founded upon surface im-pressions. Was he well acquainted with America and its robust Western life? He was a Bavarian who had spent but five years in the United States, chiefly in the East. Had his surroundings made him tolerant of the broad if not ribald humor of Boc-caccio or Ben Jonson? Reared in the home of an eminent German jurist, he had moved in the most refined circles of Speyer, Munich, New York, and Boston, and had known few but cultivated gentlefolk. He was of a literary and artistic bent. Moreover, he was hostile to Lincoln's politics and wished to see Douglas reëlected Senator. In all, Villard's evidence is insufficient to convict Lincoln of innate vulgarity — to dis-prove Lord Charnwood's judgment that what delighted him in a rough anecdote was the wit and not the roughness. Villard's paragraph showed a natural bias.

The varieties of bias growing out of a general subjective state of the witness, like that given to John Quincy Adams by his Yankee-Congregationalist-Federalist training, that given to Polk by Expansionist Democracy, and that given to Villard by

[1] Henry Villard, *Memoirs*, I, 93, 94

nurture in a refined Bavarian home, are obviously endless. No greater error can be made in historical study than to regard man as primarily a rational being; he is primarily an emotional being, and even when he is most rational his thinking processes are insensibly colored by subjective feeling. Everyone recognizes the five or six principal sentiments which dominate men: racial feeling, national feeling, local feeling, political feeling, religious or sectarian feeling, class feeling, professional or vocational feeling, and the feeling of attachment to particular codes of morals. These are universally recognized because everyone responds to one or more of them, and because everyone perceives that their intensity frequently amounts to passion. But less prominent emotions, less important sources of bias, must also be considered. The ordinary person who looks critically into his own tenets, or scrutinizes closely those of his associates, will find that they arise not so much from a cold examination of facts as from aggregates of sympathy and antipathy. Few men even try systematically to prevent the growth of irrational likes or dislikes of certain doctrines, institutions, ideas, and organizations, while those who do try never quite succeed. A set of convictions, which many will even call principles, is gradually evolved in harmony with these sympathies and antagonisms; and almost every man who looks into his own bosom must admit that his attitude toward every new public and private issue is determined by the mass of these convictions. It is the resultant, that is, of an immense number of forces, some rational, some emotional, but as a whole shot through with bias. It is because of the multitudinous biases of environment that men vary so widely — that

> . . . the wildest dreams of Kew
> Are the facts of far Peru
> And the crimes of Clapham chaste in Martaban.

The ablest treatment of bias in relation to historical evidence is still that given in Herbert Spencer's *Study of Sociology.* He shows how profound a bias is imparted to all civilized mankind by education; an education, he remarks, still curiously divided between those who teach doctrines of amity as exemplified by the New Testament, and doctrines of enmity as illustrated by the Greek and Latin epics and the nationalistic histories. It is the bias given by this latter education which makes men overestimate belligerency, "pluck," and "personal honor," a bias evident in a thousand bits of historical material. He shows just how deep is the bias inculcated also by patriotic teachings, leading even to such silly extremes as the American assertion, "Our country, right or wrong." This bias is obviously a form of egoism; and though emancipation from personal and national interests is essential to a balanced judgment of current transactions and events, it is almost impossible to attain. There exists also an anti-patriotic bias. This may originate in an honest reaction against chauvinism and exaggerated patriotism, or it may spring from a desire to be thought original and emancipated. The man who is sure that all our American wars were just and noble, and the man who is certain that our dominant motives for entering the Mexican, Spanish, and World Wars were mean, selfish, and materialistic, are equally guilty of bias — or, if the element of insincerity enters, of cant. As a super-patriotic bias informs much of whatever evidence the Hearst papers and the Chicago *Tribune* may present on recent American history, an anti-nationalistic bias equally informs much of the evidence presented by the *New Republic* and *Nation*. It is valuable as a corrective, but it is bias none the less.[1]

Class bias and professional bias are also far more pervasive than their victims like to admit. They too are essentially a reflex egoism; they possess their uses as well as abuses, but they must be allowed for in any judicial estimate of historical

[1] For an interesting analysis of national bias in history, see Hugh Miller's *Macaulay on Scotland, a Critique*. This tracks Macaulay through old newspapers and pamphlets, and attempts to prove him anti-Scottish from the very sources he used.

evidence. The economist David A. Wells, who in the generation after the Civil War was employed by great corporations
and died worth $600,000, held that the income tax was beautiful
in theory but would never work in practise in the United States.
Was his testimony on the subject unconsciously biassed? The
great majority of American business men from 1870 to 1933 held
that no abuses existed which really demanded Federal regula-
tion of business; while large bodies of American farmers and
workingmen held during this period that grave and widespread
abuses required firm intervention, and even such drastic
measures as government acquisition of railroads and telegraphs.
Again, in Herbert Hoover's record of his own Administration,
what allowance would have to be made for the professional
bias given him by his long career as engineer? Since that training had made him definitely hostile to governmental action in
the field of industry, a large allowance would be imperative.
Still again, the class bias, almost a caste bias, evident in Henry
Adams's autobiography and Emma Goldman's memoirs, no
one could mistake; but there is a definite bias also in much
middle-class writing which cannot be weighed save with delicate
balances.

The racial bias is equally evident and is familiar to all Americans. No one can examine the various eulogistic histories of
what the Germans, Irish, Scandinavians, Italians, Czechs, and
other races have contributed to American life without feeling
that the sum of the parts far exceeds the whole. No student
would accept Cole Blease's estimate of Negro achievement, or
W. E. B. DuBois's estimate of poor-white achievement. Theological bias is even more conspicuously an ingredient of everyday life and its records; while almost equally potent is the
anti-theological bias of many individuals — their reaction
against extreme religious dogmatism. The bias of a Catholic,
fostering ideas hostile to Protestant doctrines, has often led to
thoroughly false estimates of Protestant morality and Protestant
institutions. An equal injustice characterizes many Protestant

records bearing upon Catholic institutions and practises; while there are many written records which illustrate the tendency of agnostics and Marxians to depreciate the service done by all creeds and churches to society.

In dealing with all the innumerable kinds of biassed evidence, the student must discipline himself to a scientific attitude. To do this he must not merely be on his guard against crass misstatements, obvious prejudices, and witnesses of the any-stigma-to-beat-a-dogma school. He must above all form an analytical habit of mind. He must realize that the causation of social phenomena in past history, as in present-day affairs, is not simple but complex, and is not merely complex but marked by continuity and contingency. Realizing this, he will be prepared to discard or discount all partial views of causation. The clearest mark of the biassed witness is his desire to over-simplify historical events; to distort them by giving excessive emphasis to some single factor. The Pennsylvania protectionists long shouted that the agitation for a low tariff was financed by British interests eager to sell their goods, and that Cobden Club gold flowed steadily into the United States. The Populists declared that Cleveland defended the gold standard because he was controlled by Wall Street. A host of young radicals have proclaimed that the United States went to war in 1917 to save its munitions trade, its loans to the Allies, and the commissions paid to J. P. Morgan & Co. — though the munitions trade had flourished under neutrality, though practically all the Anglo-French borrowings were secured by American and other neutral securities with a market value one-fifth greater than the loans, and though one of the first results of American entry into the war was Morgan's withdrawal from the Allied agency. Herbert Spencer writes, with some force, that nothing conduces more clearly to a comprehension of the fact that causation in this world has almost never been simple, but multiple and complex, than a study of the natural sciences:

Every organism, if we read the lesson it gives, shows us continuity of causation and complexity of causation. The ordinary facts of inheritance illustrate continuity of causation — very conspicuously where varieties so distinct as the Negro and white are united, and where traces of the Negro come out generation after generation; and still better among domestic animals, where traits of remote ancestry show the persistent working of causes which date far back. Organic phenomena make us familiar with complexity of causation, both by showing the cooperation of many antecedents to one consequent, and by showing the multiplicity of results which each influence works out. If we observe how a given weight of a given drug produces on no two persons exactly like effects, and produces even on the same person different effects in different constitutional states, we see at once how involved is the combination of factors by which the changes in an organism are brought about, and how extremely contingent, therefore, is each particular change.[1]

VI

In short, the scrutiny of all types of historical evidence should be conducted as critically and searchingly as the scrutiny of evidence in the best courts; with these vital differences, that not being bound by legal rules, we may search much more widely for relevant facts, and our combination of analysis and synthesis in weighing them can be more scientific in temper than the deliberations of most judges and juries. A few general maxims may be laid down. All the witnesses available must be summoned. Mere hearsay testimony must be given a low valuation — the word of one observer who was on the spot is worth that of ten who talked with somebody who was there. The freshness of evidence should always be considered; a witness who testifies at seventy-seven to what happened when he was twenty, as Jefferson did in his *Anas*, must be heard with doubt. All witnesses should be cross-examined for evidence of bias, and even the most honest witnesses must often be heard with reservations on this score. Circumstantial evidence of a

[1] *The Study of Sociology*, pp. 294, 295

purely superficial character must be counted inferior to direct evidence, and its deceptive possibilities explored — for it is only in very limited situations that circumstantial evidence can be conclusive.

Above all, the student of historical evidence will find an ark of safety in the collection of all possible scraps of relevant testimony. He should hunt in every nook and cranny for corroboration — or, what is equally valuable, contradiction. He should lay documents side by side in an effort to find discrepancies and disparities. It is amazing how often the whole truth can be disengaged only from two half-truths. In any complicated transaction, one witness is likely to see but one side of the event, another witness the opposite side. A brief reading of Congressional or Parliamentary debates will impress upon the student the fact that the half-truth may be extremely plausible. The Conservative will present an argument, involving a long train of facts, which seems utterly convincing. A moment later the Liberal will rise, and treating precisely the same facts, present them in an entirely different light which nevertheless also seems momentarily convincing. It is frequently only by a direct conflict that the truth can be established. Even in simple historical events, where observation as distinguished from interpretation is alone important, it is often vital to find corroboration. If a witness testifies that General Joseph Hooker was drunk at Chancellorsville, and Hooker denies it, asserting that he was merely stunned by a cannonball which struck the house-pillar against which he was leaning, judgment must be suspended until fuller evidence is found. (In this instance Hooker has been exonerated.) A few documents, a few extracts from memoirs, letters, and newspapers knitted adroitly together do not constitute history; history is the measure of sound grain sifted by rigorous criticism from the straw and chaff of good, bad, and indifferent testimony.

CHAPTER EIGHT

PROBLEMS IN HISTORY

THE AMATEUR fashion of looking at history is to regard it as a simple array of generally undisputed facts. Many readers do not understand why an historical expert, who presumably has the means of ascertaining these facts, cannot present them in a treatise which defies criticism. The ordinary inquirer wishes an absolutely impregnable account of the causes of the Crimean War, for example, or the character of Bismarck, or the battle of Jutland, and expects the historian to furnish it much as industry will furnish five pounds of sugar on demand. In this spirit naïve people are constantly demanding of librarians: "Give me a book that contains the precise truth about Henry VIII's struggle with the Pope," or "Find me a volume that explains just why we got into the Mexican War." In their opinion, the whole truth about Henry VIII and the dissolution of the monasteries, or about Polk and the declaration of war upon Mexico, are substances which the historian may search out, put up in neat packages, and sell to the public. The history of any definite part of the past is a bundle of scientific facts which can be packed into a standard volume or set of volumes.

Of course many historical facts are sufficiently indisputable to be the property of standard works of reference; but amateurs are usually shocked when told that these are merely the skeleton of history. Any reader satisfied with them is satisfied with a valley of dry bones. The entire vitality and interest of history depend upon the fact that universally acceptable summaries are impossible. The naïve soul who jauntily inquires, "What were the real causes of the American Revolution?" must be told that apart from certain obvious factors, students have not yet agreed upon the subject, that great doubt envelops it, and that historians can only present a number of varying theories, each supported by more or less plausible evidence. If the amateur persists, he learns that it is only on the most limited and precise topics that a "definitive" history is possible. Someone may produce a standard history of the land-system of medieval Yorkshire, or the tax-budgets of Chicago. But any subject of genuine scope and complexity, interwoven with the growth of society, defies final treatment. When readers ask for the definitive history of the French Revolution, they find that such a work is impossible; that we shall never have anything but a violently controversial literature upon that upheaval. They may be told by a Democratic free-trader that Dr. F. W. Taussig's history of the tariff is a standard treatise; but a Republican protectionist will immediately declare that it is a bundle of lies and that Edward Stanwood's tariff history is alone dependable. They will learn that it is almost impossible to write a thorough history of the Protestant Reformation, the Italian struggle for national unity, or the origins of the World War, which does not make half of its readers boil while it pleases the other half.

Hereupon the disgusted amateur may commit either of two errors; he may give up history in chagrin, declaring that historians are a band of charlatans and liars, or he may conclude that since it is useless to try to ascertain the final truth, he will read only the type of history that pleases him. It would be as reasonable to give up the study of current affairs because men disagree violently upon the truth of important issues. In this sense Freeman was perfectly right in asserting an identity between past history and present politics. As for reading only what history pleases our prejudices, it is the surest means of confirming ourselves in error. Catholics should read Protestant history, and Protestants read Cathlic history; radicals would do well to read conservative history, and vice versa. But it is best of all to read writers who are sufficiently objective to point out errors by every historical group, Catholic or Protestant, conservative or radical.

II

The most important part of history is really a series of problems, and more than half of the historian's work is to make a statement of attempted solutions. Obviously a great part of these problems can never be settled. Some are insoluble because they are too vast and complex — the problem of the causes of the fall of the Roman Empire, for example. Others are insoluble because of the loss or suppression of historical evidence. We shall never know whether the visit of the high Jesuit official Francis Borgia to the French court just before St. Bartholomew's had any connection with the massacre; the evidence has been destroyed. We shall never penetrate many another secret for the same reason. Still other problems are insoluble because they involve psychological motives of extreme difficulty. What was the nature of Burr's conspiracy? — was it a conspiracy against the United States or against Spain? Claude G. Bowers declares that it was treason; but Walter F. McCaleb has written a powerful monograph to prove that it was not. In the last analysis, the answer rests upon what was in Burr's mind in 1805–06. How much real danger existed in August, 1863, that the British Ministry would recognize the Confederacy? In the last analysis, the answer rests upon what was in Palmerston's mind. And perhaps Burr and Palmerston never quite knew their own minds! Still more completely insoluble are those problems which involve the psychology of whole peoples. Why did the people of the Lower South determine upon secession in 1861? It is always difficult to say what public opinion is, and it is certainly impossible to produce any clear determinant of social psychology — to say what was dominant in the mind of millions of people at a given hour.

The array of unsolved if not insoluble problems is innumerable; and indeed it is their endless variety, their constant challenge to fresh research, their changing aspects as time throws them into new perspective, which makes history so fascinating. There are problems of time: What are the true dates for those of semi-mythical character in the Anglo-Saxon calendar? — When did the desire for independence take firm root in the American colonies? There are problems of identity: Are present-day Armenians the descendants of the ancient Hittites? — Who was the Man in the Iron Mask? There are problems of character, like that met by Paul Van Dyke's searching study of Catherine de Medici, or Nathaniel Stephenson's analysis of Lincoln's personality and its "springs of action as revealed and deepened by the ordeal of war." There are problems of motive: for example, the analysis by George Otto Trevelyan of General Howe's reasons for not going to the aid of Burgoyne, or the sifting by M. Coquelle of Napoleon's reasons for breaking up the Peace of Amiens. There are problems in the origin of ideas — such as Charles A. Beard's exposition of the economic roots of many ideas written into the American Constitution, and John N. Figgis's discussion of the Divine Right of Kings. There are problems of place: Where is the battlefield of Bannockburn? — Just how far east did Alexander the Great penetrate toward India? There are problems of specific cause: compare Mr. Tenney Frank's view of the reasons why Carthage entered upon the First Punic War with Ferrero's view. There are problems as minute as the still unanswered question whether Swift married Stella; and as broad as the inquiry into what was the effect of the frontier upon the American people.

The solution of highly limited problems is usually assigned to monographs or articles. Historical periodicals specialize in them; anyone who examines the reviews now devoted to history in most important countries will see that they are largely devoted not to portraits, descriptions, or narratives, but to resolving old problems. They publish fresh material to furnish a new solution, or fresh interpretations of old material. A student of history cannot better learn how single problems are attacked, elucidated, and at least provisionally solved than by reading those reviews which most interest him. He can choose from the *American Historical Review*, the *Journal of Modern History*, *Speculum*, the *Mississippi Valley Historical Review*, *Southern History*, the *English Historical Review*, *History*, the *Scottish Historical Review*, the *Canadian Historical Review*, the *Revue Historique*, the *Historische Zeitschrift*, and many more. In *History*, the organ of the English Historical Association, there long appeared a series called "Historical Revisions," dealing with topics which demanded a fresh attack. It must be said that most monographic literature, whether in periodical or book form, is needlessly pedantic and lacking in literary quality. Nevertheless, brilliant exceptions can be found. No less striking a work than Parkman's *Conspiracy of Pontiac* is a monograph written to solve a single problem of American history.

In very extended histories the solution of problems is necessarily, and properly, combined with much general and non-controversial matter; with descriptions of places, miniatures of persons, and accounts of occurrences accepted by all. A flowing narrative like Macaulay's or Froude's thus merges the solution of successive problems, almost imperceptively, with the whole graphic tale. Yet some comprehensive histories resolve themselves, upon close examination, into a clear succession of problems freshly restated, freshly attacked, and freshly resettled. Conspicuous in the list is Edward Channing's six-volume history of the United States, written largely as a product of his seminars. If we examine his sixth volume, covering the years 1850–65, we perceive that, making no attempt at a full narrative, it omits much that ordinary readers expect to find in a history of these crowded fifteen years; but that what it

does contain is very largely novel.   Leaving out the old
familiar story of Congressional battles, foreign difficulties, and
Civil War campaigns, it attacks a series of distinct questions as
if no historian had ever dealt with them before.   Was slavery a
profitable institution? — What was its real strength, its real
weakness?   Was it true that the South had no manufacturing
and no immigration?   What effect had the low price of cotton
in 1848–50 upon the Compromise of 1850?   How many advocates of that Compromise saw that if secession could be postponed, the North would soon outstrip the South in manpower
and material resources and so attain control of the situation?
How many fugitive slaves actually crossed the border?   What
were the true reasons of the South for secession?   How many
Northerners wished to resist secession by force of arms?   During the war, what was the relative importance of Southern cotton and Northern wheat to Great Britain?   What changes were
effected in Northern commerce by the closing of the Mississippi
and the Southern railways?   Why did the Confederacy gain
such a start on the North in organizing and equipping its
armies?   How did conscription actually work at the South?

It is plain that in writing his history, Channing put to himself one searching interrogation after another.   He avoided a
rehearsal of the firing on Fort Sumter, the Trent affair, Pickett's
charge at Gettysburg, and other oft-told tales; he was searching for new light, and found it by treating the period as a
series of great new problems.   No good critic would call Channing's history an ideal work.   It is addressed too much to the
specialist and too little to the lay reader; it lacks continuity,
symmetry, and completeness; and the succession of problems
gives it a jerkiness that is inimical to literary finish.   At the
same time, it admirably illustrates the means by which the best
historians attain penetration and originality.   The ability of
the writer to ask himself the most important and revealing
questions, and to ask them constantly, is indispensable to the
attainment of reach or depth in his work.

We have previously stated that the spirit of doubt, of scientific criticism, is the beginning of wisdom in historical study. Nothing must be taken for granted; everything must be subjected to strict rules of evidence. It is a simple further step to say that in the practical study of history, the primary requirement is that it be dealt with as a set of problems. If it is treated merely as an entertaining story, a theme for picturesque narrative or well-colored description, the student slips over its surface. The way to penetrate beneath the pretty superficialities and come to grips with historical realities is to propound one incisive question after another, until the past ceases to look like a smooth record and becomes instead a rough and puzzling set of difficulties. It would be too much to say that a good course of historical study is a series of headaches, but that element certainly enters into all true history. When the puzzling problems have been identified and correctly stated, then and then only can profitable study be begun. Obviously, the march of historical writing thus becomes more and more a march of specialization. In the more recent period of history, as yet little treated, a broad narrative can have freshness and originality; in the more hackneyed epochs of the past, originality can be attained only by bold new generalizations, or by the minute reëxamination of monographic topics. It was possible for Frederick Allen to write *Only Yesterday* on the history of the preceding decade (1920–30) without taking up a single problem. But he who wishes to produce a fresh work on the Civil War period will have to write such a work as *King Cotton Diplomacy* or *Salt as a Factor in the Confederacy*, addressed to a very special problem indeed.

III

But once a problem is isolated and stated, what is the best method of bringing evidence to bear upon it? Suppose a historian to have set himself the task of writing upon the Franco-Prussian War. He intends to make it something more than a mere exciting narrative of what everyone already knows about the Spanish succession, the Ems telegram, Gravelotte, Sedan, and the siege of Paris; he means to bring out fresh ideas, and novel facts marshalled from original points of view. At the outset he may attack the problem: Was Napoleon III really afraid of a revolutionary movement in France, and convinced he must reëstablish his prestige by a successful war? Or the problem: How much did Eugénie and her religious advisers have to do with precipitating the conflict? Or the problem: Was French unpreparedness due to defective administration, to over-confidence, or to corruption? The method of dealing with such problems involves distinct rules. These, broadly stated, are three. The writer must collect all the evidence that he can find; he must make sure that he has every pertinent fact available, not merely part of the pertinent facts. He must then classify this evidence and examine it according to the inductive method — which is of course the only method open to the historian, and was indeed called by John Stuart Mill the historical method. In other words, as men would say in looser terms, he must analyze it. Next, in this process of inductive scrutiny the writer will often find that the facts point to one or several hypotheses as likely to explain the problem and afford a solution. He should then formulate the most satisfactory hypothesis; examine all the evidence anew in the light it offers; and test it carefully. Thus he should proceed until he finds an hypothesis, or a combination of several hypotheses, which fits the facts and explains the historical result. Finally, having established his grand cause (or, as in nine instances out of ten the problem will demand, his multiple causation), he should state his proof in the strongest manner possible; or if he is unwilling to load his pages with proofs, at least indicate where they may be found.[1]

The importance of assembling *all* the pertinent facts upon a given situation is not often fully realized by the amateur student

[1] See the chapter on "Plurality of Causes" in John Stuart Mill's *Logic*.

of history. It means a tiresome multiplication of details, he will say; some process of selection is necessary anyhow; why not be content with enough facts to support a previously-determined formula? We decide by a rapid preliminary survey that Roosevelt broke with Taft in 1911 because he wanted a third term in 1912; how much easier just to pick out enough facts to prove it! A vast deal of so-called history is indeed written in that fashion. It is always easier to write, is usually easier to read, and is open to only one objection — that it generally misses the truth. By a one-sided choice of details almost anything can be proved. But the true historian is not content to prove almost anything; he wishes to establish a conclusion by logic as nearly inexorable as his own human fallibility, and the state of the evidence, will permit. The dangers of a one-sided selection of facts have been forcibly stated by Froude in his essay on the dissolution of the English monasteries:

We can conceive a description of England during the year which has just passed over us (1856), true in all its details, containing no one statement which can be challenged, no single exaggeration which can be proved; and this description, if given without the correcting traits, shall make ages to come marvel why the Cities of the Plain were destroyed, and England was allowed to survive. The frauds of trusted men, high in power and high in supposed religion; the wholesale poisonings; the robberies; the adulteration of foods — nay, of almost everything exposed for sale; the cruel usage of women; children murdered for the burial fees; life and property insecure in open day in the open streets; splendor such as the world never saw before upon earth, with vice and squalor crouching under its walls; — let all this be written down by an enemy, or let it be ascertained hereafter by the investigation of a posterity which desires to judge us as we generally have judged our forefathers, and few years will show darker in the English annals than the year which we have just left behind us. Yet we know, in the honesty of our hearts, how unjust such a picture would be. Our future advocate, if we are so happy as to find one, may not be able to disprove a single article in the indictment; and yet we know that, as the world goes, he will be right if he marks the year with a white stone — as one in which, on the whole, the moral harvest was better than the average.[1]

To go into the technicalities of logic — of induction and deduction — in reference to history would be a barren labor. It is sufficient to say that historians generally accept the statement that the cause of any occurrence lies in one or more preceding events without which the occurrence would not have taken place. Both causes and effects in history are always events; not brute static things, but things in action. To find the complete cause of a given event we should have to ascertain all the indispensable previous events, running back to prehistory. But since human inquiry has to be confined with limits to be of any practical value, it is sufficient to attempt to catalogue all those events which may have a clearly demonstrable and significant connection with the occurrence under discussion. The net should be cast wide to catch *all* these events — the careful historian will never be satisfied with a partial group. Having made a comprehensive enumeration of what seem to be the significant causes, the writer must choose between those which are important and those which are unimportant; must select some and reject others. He is in the position, to use a very rough analogy, of a mathematician who is given the number 15 and told that it is the sum of four other numbers, of which one is 3. By assembling his data the mathematician knows that the other three may be 1, 7, and 4; or 2, 5, and 5; or 3, 5, and 4; or various other combinations. But if he can find proof somewhere that the second number is 6, that at once limits the number of unknown elements. If he can find additional proof that the third number is 2, then he can at once state what is the fourth number.

For the purposes of history, the laws of induction as long ago formulated by John Stuart Mill really have some utility. Sup-

[1] *Short Studies on Great Subjects*, First Series, World Classics Ed., pp. 284, 285

pose the problem is the cause of the extreme savagery of the Reign of Terror in France. Suppose the writer has collected all the data bearing on the rôle of violence in the English, American, French, and Russian Revolutions. It is not difficult then to discover the value of Mill's five rules for scientific inferences by induction. The first canon reads: "If two or more instances of the phenomenon under investigation have only one circumstance in common, the circumstance in which alone all the instances agree is the cause of the given phenomenon." The second asserts: "If an instance in which the phenomenon under investigation occurs, and an instance in which it does not occur, have every circumstance in common save one, that one occurring only in the former, the circumstance in which alone the two instances differ is the cause, or an indispensable part of the cause, of the phenomenon." The third canon continues: "If two or more instances in which the phenomenon occurs have only one circumstance in common, while two or more instances in which it does not occur have nothing in common save the absence of that circumstance, the circumstance in which alone the two sets of instances differ is the cause, or an indispensable part of the cause, of the phenomenon." We proceed to the fourth canon, the most useful of all to historians: "Subduct from any phenomenon such part as is known by previous inductions to be the effect of certain antecedents, and the residue of the phenomenon is the effect of the remaining antecedents." But the fifth canon is almost as important: "Whatever phenomenon varies in any manner wherever another phenomenon varies in some particular manner is . . . connected with that phenomenon through some fact of causation."

Many brilliant examples of inductive reasoning have been furnished by the exact sciences. We may take, for example, Leverrier's memorable discovery of the planet Neptune without a telescope. Certain perturbations had been observed in the orbit of the planet Uranus, constituting an effect which puzzled astronomers. All the facts bearing on the subject — that is, all the actions of the other known bodies upon Uranus — were collected and weighed. They left it certain that some additional cause was required to explain Uranus's eccentricities. Leverrier made the inference that this was some hitherto-unobserved planet, and mathematically determined its position and pull. Other astronomers, turning their telescopes to the quarter indicated, then found Neptune within one degree of the spot indicated. Just so, in history, many a brilliant surmise — an inductive inference — from known facts which seem only partially to account for a cause, has been proved valid by fuller investigation. The surmise that Cleveland's rash action in the Pullman strike of 1894, so unlike his usual deliberation and balance, was due to Olney's misrepresentation of the situation, has been amply proved from Cleveland's and Olney's papers.

IV

But historical problems never present themselves as neat logical exercises. Almost every historical puzzle has to be solved in part, and often wholly, by *ad hoc* methods peculiar to itself. In determining antecedence and consequence, most historians proceed by plain common sense, not by the rules of logic. However, one general method, the use of the working hypothesis to select what is pertinent and reject what is irrelevant in explaining an historical event, is so important that all readers of history should understand its utility. The hypothesis is a key that *may* fit a complicated lock; a pattern that *may* assemble in their just relations the scattered parts of a jigsaw puzzle. No sound historical work has ever been written which does not employ hypothesis liberally to arrive at the explanation of complex occurrences. Ordinarily this use is carefully concealed; but sometimes it is exhibited to impress the reader, or to cut off objections.

An illuminating illustration is afforded by some pages late in

Channing's treatment of the Civil War. In his sixth volume he attacks the question, Why did the Confederacy collapse in April, 1865? — a problem particularly interesting in its analogy with the German collapse in 1918. The Southern organization broke down, he remarks, with a speed and completeness that were entirely unexpected, and that are not easy to understand. Having assembled all the available evidence upon this collapse, he has subjected it to inductive examination to reach the proper inference. His method, having classified his evidence, was to formulate various hypotheses and test each one exhaustively. Did the breakdown result from the military defeat of the Confederacy? This hypothesis was long accepted as satisfactory, but he rejects it as untrue. The Confederacy in April, 1865, was not yet beaten in the field. Lee still had some 30,000 men, Joseph E. Johnston nearly 30,000, and Kirby Smith west of the Mississippi about 25,000; while scattered throughout the lower South were smaller commands. All in all, when Lee evacuated Richmond between 150,000 and 200,000 Confederate soldiers were still under arms and ready to fight. Such a force, says Channing, might have kept up a guerrilla warfare for years. Breaking into small detachments like the Revolutionary partisans under Marion and Sumter, or like the Boers in 1900, they might have fought on until the North was worn out; Texas alone might have resisted indefinitely. President Jefferson Davis held this opinion. At a conference with Breckinridge and Johnston at Greensboro, N. C., in April, 1865, he urged them to keep up the struggle, as a little later he urged Breckinridge and Bragg at Abbeville, S. C. "Judging from the history of other wars and other revolutions," writes Channing, "the end had not come and was not even in sight had the Southern people, or the mass of the people of the seceded States, wished to continue the fight for Southern independence."

A second hypothesis is that the collapse was caused by a dearth of military supplies. According to this view, the blockade so completely stopped imports, and invasion so completely paralyzed various centres of supply, that the Southern armies were without essential equipment and fighting became hopeless. Until the end of 1863 the Confederacy had relied almost wholly upon French and British arms, and now these were cut off. But after examining this hypothesis, Channing asserts that it is empty. The Southern ordnance service, directed by General Josiah Gorgas, had established a number of effective manufactories of war material. Large arsenals had been organized, a superb powder mill had been built at Augusta, Ga., lead-smelting works had been established, a cannon foundry had been set up at Macon, and other works were scattered throughout the South. Many English mechanics of ability had been imported. Gorgas wrote in 1864 that he had succeeded beyond his brightest expectations in accelerating the production of powder and arms. "If anyone has doubts," writes Dr. Channing, "as to the capacity of the South to continue warfare in April, 1865, so far as war materials are concerned, he has only to read Gorgas's accounts to satisfy himself that it was not any dearth of material that brought about the ending in the spring of 1865."

A third and even more familiar hypothesis would explain the defeat of the Confederacy by the starving condition of the Confederate soldiers and people in April, 1865. "Those twin monsters, hunger and malnutrition," many Southerners have said, "forced our gates." But Dr. Channing attempts to show that the high prices which people in Richmond and other cities seemed to pay for provisions in the spring of 1865 were not really high; that measured in gold instead of the superabundant paper, flour was actually cheaper in Richmond than in New York. The Southern food crops of 1863 and 1864 had been excellent, cereals being abundant, while bacon was run through the blockade in quantity until the latter part of 1864. Official reports on April 1, 1865, showed in Richmond 300,000 rations of bread and meat; at Danville, Va., 500,000 rations of bread and 1,500,000 of meat; at Lynchburg, Va., and Greensboro, N. C., 1,680,000 more rations of bread and meat. In February, 1865, Joseph E. Johnston held stored between Weldon and Danville sufficient rations to supply 60,000 men for more than four months. A well-known Confederate leader, J. L. M. Curry, states that at the close of the war enough corn was available along the transportation routes between Jackson, Miss., and Montgomery, Ala., to furnish the Confederate forces with breadstuffs for a year or more.

There remains another obvious hypothesis to account for the Confederate collapse: the disintegration of Southern morale, the seizure of the people by a despair which sapped their energies. Dr. Channing, after weighing all the evidence, adopts this hypothesis as that which best fits the facts. "It is evident to the under-surface seeker," he writes, "that by the summer of 1864, and even more so by December of that year, the will to fight had gone from large sections of the Southern people." What is his evidence? He quotes from the diaries or letters of such representative Southerners as Howell Cobb, Benjamin H. Hill, and Secretary of War Seddon. He points to the alarming number of resignations of officers from Lee's own army, indicating a loss of hope; on January 18, 1865, and again on March 9, the Confederate Adjutant-General issued a list of 1,200 officers whose resignations had been accepted by President Davis. As additional evidence, he notes the enormous amount of absenteeism and desertion from the ranks. In September, 1864, President Davis wrote despondently that two-thirds of the troops were absent; some sick, some wounded, some on leave, but most of them gone without leave. On December 31, 1864, field-records for Hagood's brigade of South Carolinians showed 1,592 present for duty, and 2,011 absent. General Hardee had marched out of Charleston in 1864 with more than 10,000 troops, and had reached the North Carolina line with only 4,000, straggling and desertion accounting for the remainder. Many Southern communities were filled with deserters and fugitives. The Confederate authorities in the winter of 1864–65 complained that they were intercepting many letters from families urging soldiers to desert. Finally, as very telling evidence indeed, Channing notes the way in which the South recoiled from its terrible losses at the Wilderness and other battles late in 1864. The conclusion Channing reaches is not satisfactory; it evades the question, Why did morale collapse? But the method is interesting.

Channing's treatment of this problem differs from most historical expositions in that he places his rejected hypotheses as well as his accepted explanations upon paper. In general, the historian is content, having found what he believes the correct key to an historical event, to state it and assemble his facts in support of it. History would become intolerably prolix and confusing if the rejected planks, shavings, and splinters of the historian's workshop were not carted out of sight, leaving only the finished product. The more literary polish, in general, the greater the economy, and the less the evidence of labor. E. P. Cheyney, in his long scholarly account of the relations of Queen Elizabeth, the Earl of Essex, and Francis Bacon, includes hypotheses, arguments, and details of a kind which Lytton Strachey in his classic work on *Elizabeth and Essex* thought it wisest to omit; with the result that Strachey's account, while nearly as good history as Cheyney's, is immeasurably superior as literature. But though concealed, in all ambitious historical works hypotheses have been used; they have been fully examined, all but one or several rejected, and the latter alone presented to the reader.

V

The principal dangers in the use of hypothesis are three. The first and most frequent is the temptation to let bias, prejudice, or what we fondly call "conviction" supply a ready hypothesis which we abstain from testing rigorously. Such is the "devil theory" of war. War is made by militarists and autocrats — so millions of Americans believed in 1914. War is made by wicked munitions interests allied with greedy bankers — so a group of radical writers upon America's entry into the World War would more recently have us believe. The hypothesis that American prosperity had been caused by a high protective tariff was asserted by innumerable Republican historians in the eighties and nineties, and Senator Watson declared just before the Smoot-Hawley Tariff passed in 1930 that this law would restore our impaired prosperity within a month. The cold fact was that the Smoot-Hawley Tariff signalized (no true historian would say it caused) the most complete collapse of prosperity in American annals. For these biassed hypotheses it is always possible to supply some evidence, though never enough to satisfy impartial and scientific minds. Herbert Spencer touches on this common misuse of hypothesis. He writes that a striking example of the effect of a too-cherished hypothesis in vitiating evidence was once unconsciously yielded to him by an enthusiast for sanitary laws:

Producing his papers, he pointed out the great contrast between the number of deaths per annum in the small town near London where he lived, and the number of deaths per annum in a low district of London — Bermondsey, or Lambeth, or some region on the Surrey side. On this great contrast he triumphantly dilated, as proving how much could be done by good drainage, ventilation, and so on. On the one hand, he passed over the fact that his suburban place was, in large measure, inhabited by a picked population — people of means, well fed and clothed, able to secure all appliances for comfort, leading regular lives, free from overwork and anxiety. On the other hand, he passed over the fact that this low region of London was, by virtue of its lowness, one out of which all citizens pecuniarily able to take care of themselves escaped if they could, and into which were thrust great numbers whose poverty excluded them from better regions — the ill-fed, the drunken, the dissolute, and others on the highway to death. Though, in the first place, the healthiness of the locality obviously drew to it an excess of persons likely to live long; and though, in the second case, the unhealthiness of the locality made it one in which an excess of those not likely to live long were left to dwell, or hid themselves to die; yet the whole difference was put down to direct effects of pure air and impure air respectively.[1]

A second danger in the use of hypothesis lies in the temptation toward over-simplification. Channing's explanation of the sudden collapse of the Confederacy as attributable to loss of morale is beyond question an over-simplification. He overlooks the fact that it may have been, and probably was, a conjunction of all the elements he has named — dispersion and defeat of armies; scarcity of munitions; shortage of food; and weariness of the long butchery — which brought about the surrender. He overlooks the fact, so cogently pointed out by Charles Francis Adams in *Lee at Appomattox and Other Essays*, that the alternative of prolonged guerrilla warfare, which he thinks was not considered because of the breakdown of morale, was weighed by the Confederate high command and rejected for humanitarian and patriotic reasons. He entirely overlooks one highly important element, the collapse of transportation. Altogether, Channing attributes too much to a single factor in a complex situation.

Various writers who are more fertile in brilliant ideas than inclined to the drudgery of testing them thoroughly offer many examples of this over-simplification. Thus James Truslow Adams's stimulating volume, *The Epic of America*, which states many problems admirably, and gives many penetrating answers, sometimes falls short of the *entire* truth. What was the central motive of European emigration to America? asks Mr. Adams. It was not religious, not political, but economic and social — to establish better homes, and gain a better living. But was this all? What was the origin of American lawlessness? he asks again. It was the fact that the colonists had to obey laws made 3,000 miles away; that the regulations of a distant overseas power governed their use of land, forest, minerals, the development of their manufactures, trade, and marine, and even their church relations. Once more, was this

[1] Herbert Spencer, *The Study of Sociology*, p. 73

all? Were they not lawless as to the statutes of their own Assemblies, and even the sentiment of their own communities? Did the Scotch-Irish of the Pennsylvania frontier obey the Quaker legislature? Again, Mr. Adams asks why Americans are so self-confident and optimistic. He explains their attitude by two hypotheses. It was because the simplicity of life on the frontier, without complications, bred an unworried outlook; and because success in the new American environment demanded optimism and courage, so that the quality naturally developed. But, we may ask, were there not other factors? Selection by emigration? Wealth of natural resources? Absence of chilling traditions? Even the influence of climate? Mr. Adams deals with the problem of the inferiority of post-Revolutionary culture to pre-Revolutionary culture. He offers two hypotheses: the cultivated Loyalists fled elsewhere, and America moved over the mountains. But this neglects the immense war-wastage, while the second part of the answer is properly no answer at all.

As an absurdly extreme example of the assertion of a single cause against a multitude of suggested causes, we may take the statement of two collaborators, Drs. Warren and Pearson, upon the origin of the great depression of 1929–37:

> The present depression is not an act of God for the purification of men's souls. It is not a business cycle. It is not due to extravagant living. It is not due to unsound business practices. It is not due to overproduction. It is not due to too great efficiency. It is not due to lack of confidence, but it is the cause of lack of confidence.
> It is due to a high demand for gold following a period of low demand for gold. It teaches the devastating effect of deflation, but teaches no other lesson that is good for society.[1]

This is obviously an overstatement; to ascribe the panic and depression to the one factor of the automatic fall of the price level is as erroneous as President Roosevelt's ascription

[1] George E. Warren and Frank A. Pearson, *Prices* (1933)

of it to the stubbornness and incompetence of "the rulers of the exchange of mankind's goods." (And Mr. Roosevelt was prudent enough to insert the word "primarily.") Presumably the paragraph written by Drs. Warren and Pearson was not meant to be taken literally, but was rather a rhetorical over-statement, designed to point out the cardinal importance of that factor.

The third danger is the tendency of excessively clever writers to reject the obvious hypothesis merely because it is obvious, and to present instead some wire-drawn explanation which will give them a reputation for independence, ingenuity, and sub-tlety. Highly original minds dislike the obvious. They realize that history which merely states the obvious is dull and un-stimulating. Hence some men continually fly to the bizarre. They explain the heroes of history by hypotheses drawn from Freudian psychology. Harvey J. O'Higgins, for example, sug-gested that Lincoln's place as a great humanitarian and emanci-pator was due in large part to the inferiority complex which he formed in early life, to his sense of belonging to a humble stratum of society. Other men explain social phenomena by recourse to the hypothesis of obscure economic motives. Some-times the bizarre hypothesis, as opposed to the obvious and logical, gains an extraordinary foothold.

It is perhaps illuminating to take, as an extreme instance, the treatment of one of the great facts in cultural history, the appearance of Shakespeare's plays — plays which indeed con-stitute the greatest single event in the literary history of man-kind. The old hypothesis which accounted for them was simple: William Shakespeare of Stratford and London wrote them. Most people in Shakespeare's time believed that. Ben Jonson, next in eminence among the Elizabethan dramatists, a man for whom Shakespeare obtained a first stage hearing in 1598, believed it. Edmund Spenser believed it, as his references to Shakespeare in "Colin Clout's Come Home Again" prove. The next generation in England universally believed it. John

Milton, who was eight years old when Shakespeare died, did
so. Indeed, for two hundred years the whole world accepted
this hypothesis. Then arose Delia Bacon, a friend of Hawthorne and a woman of brilliant but eccentric parts — who
finally died mad — and she found the hypothesis too obvious.
She hit upon a rival explanation, that the plays had been written
by a coterie numbering Lord Bacon, Sir Walter Raleigh, and
one or two other distinguished men. Various students took up
this preposterous hypothesis, and a whole school has arisen,
numbering such sane men as Mark Twain and Carter Glass,
which ascribes the plays not to Shakespeare but to Bacon, or
to Edward de Vere, seventeenth Earl of Oxford, or someone
else.

Just so, it is a bizarre hypothesis which attributes the fall of
the Roman Empire to the spread of malaria in Italy; but it is
an explanation that has been seriously advanced. It is a bizarre
hypothesis which would explain Lincoln's assassination as the
result of a plot by Secretary of War Stanton, acting to ensure
drastic treatment of the conquered South; but it has been
seriously advanced. (As a matter of fact, the assassins had
plotted the murder of the supposedly radical Johnson as well
as Lincoln.) It is a misleading hypothesis for the Protestant
Reformation that it was fundamentally economic in motive;
but various commentators have defended that thesis. And so
the list of strange theories might be extended to great length.

VI

In nine instances out of ten, as we have said, any important
historical transaction should be treated as of multiple causation, its roots as numerous and far-ramifying as its consequences. The office of the historian is not to select one or two
explanations, excluding or minimizing all others, but to ascertain *all* the factors and assign to each its proportionate weight.
Channing's explanation of the collapse of the Confederacy
would have been stronger had he done that. An ingenious

magazine writer has offered a monistic explanation of Mc-
Kinley's action in deciding early in 1898 upon war with Spain.
Mr. Louis M. Hacker suggests three possible hypotheses to
explain the war message of April 11. (1) McKinley had no
faith in the sincerity of the Spanish Government's offer of an
armistice pending negotiations for greater Cuban autonomy,
for he was familiar with its previous evasions and procrastina-
tions. (2) He saw an opportunity for imperialistic aggrandize-
ment in the seizure of Spanish-owned islands. (3) He expected
a short and successful war to ensure Republican domination in
home politics, and to augment his authority as head of the
party. Rejecting the first two hypotheses, Mr. Hacker fixes
upon the third alone as offering a satisfactory explanation of
the message.[1]

But this monistic interpretation is misleading. While we
may set aside the second hypothesis (for McKinley was certainly not at this date eager to annex Spanish-speaking islands),
the first cannot be rejected as unimportant. McKinley might
well have distrusted the ability of the Spanish Government to
make the indispensable concessions to Cuba in the face of a
public opinion not prepared for surrender; Minister Woodford
had just informed him that it did not possess that ability.
Moreover, the Cubans distrusted Spain too completely to accept an armistice. And Mr. Hacker overlooks two other
factors, or hypotheses for McKinley's course. (1) The last
Spanish note did not, as he assumes, meet the essential American stipulations. In its latest communications, the State Department had demanded an armistice as a preliminary to
Cuban independence (not autonomy), and had stipulated that
if Cuban-Spanish negotiations during the armistice failed, Mr.
McKinley should be made arbiter. Spain neither promised
independence, nor accepted the condition as to McKinley's
arbitership. (2) Many evidences existed that public sentiment

[1] Louis M. Hacker, "The Holy War of 1898," *American Mercury*, July,
1930

in America was heavily against further temporizing and for immediate liberation of Cuba. McKinley sincerely believed in the principle of government by popular will. Altogether, his course in submitting the question of peace or war to Congress had a more complex causation and a larger justification than Mr. Hacker would have us believe.

Sometimes the enthusiastic students of social and economic history tend to harden a single hypothesis of broad scope into a deterministic theory that approaches the character of a law. For generations historians have disputed upon the causes of the rise of the medieval town in Western Europe. Various theories have been advanced. Some men have taken the view that the medieval town developed out of the free village community of the Germans. Some hold that it emerged from the manor by the conversion of manorial institutions into town institutions — that it was of servile rather than free origin. The "market law" theory suggests that the "peace" of the markets created a protected area which was detached from local feudal tribunals, and inhabited chiefly by merchants and artisans; the administration of the town gradually growing out of the administration of the market. The "immunity theory," applying principally to episcopal towns, holds that the immunity of the bishops over neighboring territory created boroughs which finally grew strong enough to establish self-government. The "garrison theory" is based on the view that a population grew up in proximity to fortified military posts which brought trade and industry in its wake and became the nucleus of the future town. Some students have traced the growth of the civil magistracy of the towns back to supposed origins in Carolingian civil administration; others regard the German guilds or fellowships as offering a possible origin for the towns. But in late years a large group of scholars, represented in Europe by Henri Pirenne and in the United States by Dr. Carl Stephenson, have adopted the "mercatorial" or "faubourg" hypothesis. They believe that in the ninth and tenth centuries new burghs or faubourgs came into existence outside the feudal castles or the abbeys, and especially at crossroads, river fords, or other commercially advantageous places. This new burgh was essentially different from the old burghs or seats of important officials. Beyond question, the weight of opinion among recent scholars upon this important question of town origins has favored the "mercatorial" theory. But some of its adherents have erected it into a sweeping dogma, and overlook the fact that no absolute proof exists that the other theories are not also sound, at least for certain areas and times.

Multiple causation is obviously less dramatic than monistic causation. It is always arresting to point the finger at one cause and say, "This did it!" Moreover, when a multiplicity of causes are admitted, it is often difficult to assign the correct weight to each, and the labors of the historian are thus enhanced. (Of course not all the complexities need be stated — some should be merely hinted. The best history is like a painting by Rembrandt, casting a brilliant light upon certain select causes, and leaving others in semi-darkness.) Henry Adams in his *Education* has described some of the difficulties of dealing with the tangled web of causation. He writes that he published a dozen volumes of history to ascertain whether, by the severest process of stating, with the least possible comment, such facts as seemed sure in such order as seemed strictly consequent, he could fix a necessary sequence of human movement during a brief period. The result disillusioned him. "Where he saw sequence, other men saw something different, and no one saw the same unit of measure." Nevertheless, it will be observed that the more scientific the historian is, the more he will lean to a multiple explanation of events; the deeper he goes into the subject, the surer he will find such a course imperative. Parkman does not give a monistic explanation of the French failure in North America, nor does James G. Randall confine himself to even a few causes for the Civil War. Since much history has recently been rewritten by the use of new economic interpretations, perhaps the most common fault of present-day historians is an excessive emphasis upon economic hypotheses, and insufficient emphasis on emotion, sentiment, and other imponderables as factors in events.

It is of course evident that many historical problems are too simple in form to require use of the working hypothesis. Their answer is sometimes a flat yes or no; if not that, it is at any rate supplied directly by research. Take the problem: Were American labor trends in the nineteenth century affected by any considerable participation of wage-earners, especially during periods of discontent, in the westward movement to free lands? It is a very pretty problem. Frederick J. Turner, without thoroughly investigating the facts, assumed that the answer was "yes." He wrote in his essay on "The Significance of the Frontier": "Whenever social conditions tended to crystallize in the East, whenever capital tended to press upon labor . . . there was this gate of escape to the free conditions of the frontier. These free lands promoted individualism, economic equality, freedom to rise, democracy. Men would not accept inferior wages and a permanent position of social subordination when this promised land of freedom and equality was theirs for the taking." But two recent students, after careful investigation, tentatively assert that the answer is "no" — that actual wage-earners made little use of the frontier as a safety-gate.[1] They qualify this conclusion by adding that so many *potential* wage-earners settled upon western land that the movement did tend "to hold up the level of industrial wages." Whichever view is right, the answer will clearly be found simply by getting at a sufficient body of facts. Indeed, a multitude of problems have to be stated in terms which show that but one of two or at most three alternatives is possible. Was it Justice Shiras, Justice Gray, or Justice Brewer who changed his vote in the

[1] Carter Goodrich and Sol Davison, "The Wage-Earner in the Westward Movement," *Political Science Quarterly*, June, 1935, vol. 50, pp. 161 ff.

unfortunate income tax decision of 1895? We know that it could not have been another Justice. And a multitude of problems are stated in terms, again, which call simply for an assignment of special weight to one of several factors, all being recognized as present. Was the German submarine defeated in 1917 chiefly by the new British convoy system, by the depth charge and other anti-submarine devices, or by American aid in warships and merchant tonnage? The historian, having decided that the convoy system was easily the most important factor, can then give the other two whatever credit seems due.

But the fact remains that just as the ability to ask the right questions, thereby raising problems, is the mark of the original historian, so the ability to suggest new hypotheses in answering them is often the mark of penetration and insight. Indeed, it is evident that the qualities chiefly required in solving historical problems are (1) industry, (2) penetration or ingenuity, (3) sound judgment, and (4) intellectual honesty. Industry is needed to assemble all the evidence, to dig out the multitude of significant facts bearing upon the problem. Penetration or ingenuity is needed to supply all the possible interpretations of the material. A commonplace mind will make but an obvious, commonplace combination of facts; a subtle and original mind, full of ideas, will make new and stimulating combinations of facts. Sound judgment is required to bar out eccentric or spurious hypotheses. And intellectual honesty is more frequently needed to enable a scholar to face the facts unflinchingly than the novice would suppose. Nothing is easier than to become enamored of a particular answer, a cherished hypothesis, for an historical problem. But if in the end the student finds that the facts run counter to it, what then? The only honest course is to confess error, no matter how publicly he may have committed himself to his pet theory, and bend to the evidence. But that is often more easily said than done. We need only think of the reputable American writer on the origins of the World War who once placed himself in an untenable position by stubbornly cleaving to the story of the Potsdam conference of German leaders in July, 1914, to plot the conflict, long after it was exploded. We need only think of the writer on John Reed who, glorifying him as a staunch revolutionist, was informed before publishing his book of the existence of letters that John Reed had written from Russia shortly before his death expressing a keen disillusionment with the Bolshevist Revolution. To include them would have injured the portrait of Reed as a Revolutionary hero, and they were ignored.

VII

It remains for us to mention one special difficulty in using historical evidence and solving historical problems — the difficulty of evaluating events and figures of the far-distant past by the standards and atmosphere of their own time, not of ours. The very essence of truth often depends upon giving the correct setting, material and more especially moral, to an occurrence. Yet the *nunc pro tunc* fallacy crops up repeatedly in even the best writers. Though it is probably impossible for us ever to see events of a past age precisely as men living in that age regarded them, we can at least avoid the grosser errors of perspective.

Winston Churchill has pointed out in *The Aftermath* how natural it is to misjudge Britain's policy toward Ireland in the time of William Pitt by applying to it the canons of a later day. At present Great Britain is one of the two greatest Powers of the globe, flanked by a firm ally in the French Republic; Ireland is a weak island of four million people divided into two states. Looking at powerful Britain and helpless Ireland, we pronounce Pitt's policy in 1798 brutal. But we forget that in 1798 England was a country of only 12,000,000 people; that on one side lay a hostile France of 20,000,000 people, and on the other a half-hostile Ireland of 6,000,000; that sandwiched between them, Britain felt her very existence menaced. If we recall this, the harsh repressive measures adopted by Pitt become more understandable and excusable. Again, it is usual and beyond doubt just to condemn the Inquisition in scathing terms, for no one defends its many excesses. But critics should measure its cruelties against the practises of the Middle Ages, not of the twentieth century. As a Protestant, Williston Walker, remarks in his work on *The Reformation:* "There is some reason to believe that the methods of the Inquisition, cruel as they seem from a modern standpoint, were milder than those of contemporaneous civil law." That is certainly true of its more moderate phases.

It is particularly hard to recapture past modes of thought; and frequently the *nunc pro tunc* fallacy throws an entirely false atmosphere about some event that involves them. John Fiske, in his *Discovery of America*, notes that Washington Irving (whose work he greatly admires) was guilty of amusing lapses of this kind in his life of Columbus. Irving, in describing Columbus's second voyage, relates that while coasting along Cuba the explorer encountered evidences (as he supposed) that he was coasting India or China. As Fiske comments:

Mr. Irving . . . could not quite rid himself of the feeling that there was something strange or peculiar in the Admiral's method of interpreting such information. "Animated by one of the pleasing illusions of his ardent imagination, Columbus pursued his voyage, with a prosperous breeze, along the supposed continent of Asia." This lends a false color to the picture, which the general reader is pretty sure to make still falser. To suppose the southern coast of Cuba to be the southern coast of Toscanelli's Mangi required no illusion of an "ardent imagination." It was simply a plain common-sense conclusion reached by sober reasoning from such data as were then accessible (i.e., the Toscanelli map, amended by information such as was understood to be given by the natives); it was more probable than any other theory of the situation likely to be devised from these data; and it seems fanciful to us today only because knowledge acquired since the time of Columbus has shown us how far from correct it was. Modern historians abound in unconscious turns of expression

— as in this quotation from Irving — which project modern knowledge back into the past, and thus destroy the historical perspective.[1]

Time is not the only distorting element, for sometimes distance in space, and alien standards and conventions, play precisely the same rôle. No one could properly write the history of present-day Tibetans by applying to them the psychology of the Western World. No one should judge of Japanese music, which has qualities all its own, by the conventions of European music, which simply do not apply. And sometimes alien times and alien conventions combine to test very severely the ability of the historian to get outside his own skin. A good example is afforded by the scornful way in which many modern writers have written of Egyptian pictorial art, which at first glance seems somewhat naïve and ludicrous because it totally lacks perspective. The fact is that Egyptian artists responded to a set of rules which to the Egyptian mind seemed just as admirable as the rules of Rembrandt and Turner seem to us. Twenty centuries from now the world of art may have passed under a totally new set of rules, which will make the classical painters of today appear incredibly quaint and absurd; and indeed, the art of the modernists or surrealists is already poles apart from that of the classicists. Thus we find an acute critic very properly defending Egyptian art from one of the historians who committed this *nunc pro tunc* error:

Vigorous exception must be taken to Mr. Hall's opinion that Egyptian art is "absurd" in its convention of drawing, which disregards perspective and shows different parts of the human body now in profile, now in full front view. The conventions of drawing familiar to the modern world are still merely conventions, and not necessarily the best that might be devised. Ancient Egyptian artists used a different idiom of expression, no more illogical than our own. As realists they sought to give both plan and elevation in the same drawing, to "see around" the figure represented. When we understand their aim and have taught our eyes to apprehend their unfamiliar

[1] John Fiske, *The Discovery of America*, I, 472 note

vocabulary, we shall unhesitatingly accord to the great artists of ancient Egypt the supreme credit which is their due as masters of line, of composition and design, and of surpassing technique in the manipulation of materials.[1]

Because of the rapid material progress of the past few generations, the most frequent present-day form of this fallacy is a tendency to underrate the difficulties which men of recent periods faced. People who take the sleeper-plane from New York to Los Angeles find it difficult to comprehend the perils and obstacles that the predecessors and companions of Daniel Boone met in blazing the Wilderness Trail. From the deck of the *Queen Mary* the most timid man thinks of the fears of Columbus's sailors with a condescending smile. Only in recent years has history been able to show that Braddock, long assumed to be a blunderer, was an intelligent and efficient as well as brave officer, who took due precautions, and whose difficulties had not been clearly understood.

Sometimes this underestimation of difficulties is carried over from the material to the intellectual sphere. It is easy for historical students to be wise after the event; it is a besetting temptation to clever writers to prove their superior sagacity by demonstrating that the statesmen of grandfather's time were simple-minded, and grandfather rather silly for believing in them. Lytton Strachey exhibited great brilliancy in setting a dunce-cap on the head of Arnold of Rugby; by emphasizing his "slightly puzzled look" as a key to his career, he made him seem decidedly stupid. The truth is that there was never anything puzzled about Thomas Arnold's look or mind. He was a manly, resolute leader, decisive in action and untiring in industry; a great progressive force in nineteenth century education; an historian of acuteness and diligence; and altogether a man whose numerous activities deserved his son's poetical wreath, and the more recent prose tribute of H. A. L. Fisher. Mr.

---

[1] Ashton Sanborn, *Saturday Review of Literature*, June 27, 1931, reviewing Sir E. D. Ross, *The Art of Egypt Through the Ages*

Walter Millis, using the Lyttonian irony, has pilloried William McKinley as a shallow politician, and Woodrow Wilson as a naïvely idealistic egotist, greatly understating the difficulties and perplexities of both; and in both portraits adroitly suggesting how much better the nation would have fared had its heads in 1898 and 1917 possessed an intellect as profound and a vision as infallible as Mr. Millis's. Similar in character is the stereotyped denunciation of the "old diplomacy" of pre-World War days. One of the most thorough students of that diplomacy calls this denunciation cheap and ignorant, and adds that as his researches progressed "I have become less and less willing to believe that men in that day were more wicked, more unscrupulous, and more evil-minded than in our own or any other day."[1]

But one clear distinction should be made in urging students of history to judge the past by the conditions of the past. A few fundamental moral standards ought to be held absolute, and applied equally to all modern ages. Murder cannot be excused on the ground that all Turks were cruel, or most Italians of medieval times violent, or many nineteenth century Texans ready to look lightly on the bowie-knife and six-shooter. The historian should have certain fixed moral canons, and be as ready as Calvin Coolidge's pastor to denounce sin — at least by implication. Lord Acton remarked that one current tendency against which his moral sense revolted grew out of the laudable desire of historians to be sympathetic to men of distant ages and alien modes of thought — a desire that was pushed into an indiscriminate tolerance of past abuses. He saw with dismay that "the general growth of historical methods of thinking supplied a sense of the relativity of moral principles, and led to a desire to condone if not to commend the crimes of other ages.[2] It became almost a trick of style to talk of judging

---

[1] W. L. Langer, *European Alliances and Alignments, 1871–90*, Preface
[2] See J. N. Figgis and R. V. Laurence, Introduction to Lord Acton's *History of Freedom and Other Essays*.

men by the standard of their day and to allege the spirit of the age in excuse for the Albigensian Crusade or the burning of Huss." Acton felt that this was to destroy the very bases of moral judgment and to open the way to a boundless skepticism. Anxious as he was to uphold the doctrine of growth in theology, he allowed nothing for it in the realm of morals, at any rate in the Christian nations, since the thirteenth century. He demanded a code of moral judgment independent of time and place, and not merely relative to a particular civilization. Within limits, he was right. In complex situations, social or political, moral judgments are usually risky and confusing, and often puerile; witness the easy condemnation of the Southern cause 1861–65 as immoral by a long generation of Northern historians. But murder is always murder, robbery always robbery, cruelty always cruelty. The historian should never debase the moral currency; he should never suffer any man to escape the undying penalty that history inflicts upon wrong.

VIII

Great art is the product of inspiration and not of rules of thumb — though the inspiration must usually be combined with great labor; great skill is the product of long experience. A Macaulay or Thierry masters the principles of evidence partly by intuition, and partly by long practice. In his mature work he will apply them as unconsciously as the artist of genius applies the rules of drawing and composition. It is this subconscious mastery that the student of history should try to attain. He will then detect instantly a dubious piece of evidence; he will classify and analyze his historical data without much thought of first principles; he will think out his various hypotheses without troubling to set them down on paper. By long practice in examining masses of historical material, his judgment and inference may be developed to a high degree of proficiency. He enters the same realm that the expert in any art or profession rules and enjoys — the realm that William James has described. "Saturated with experience of a particular class of materials, an expert intuitively knows whether a newly-reported fact is probable or not, whether a proposed hypothesis is worthless or the reverse. He instinctively knows that, in a novel case, this and not that will be the promising course of action. The well-known story of the old judge advising the new one never to give reasons for his decisions, 'the decisions will probably be right, the reasons will surely be wrong,' illustrates this. The doctor will feel that the patient is doomed, the dentist will have a premonition that the tooth will break, though neither can articulate a reason for his foreboding. The reason lies imbedded, but not yet laid bare, in all the countless previous cases dimly suggested by the actual one, all calling up the same conclusions, which the adept thus finds himself swept on to, he knows not how or why." [1]

[1] William James, *Principles of Psychology*, II, 365

CHAPTER NINE

IDEAS IN HISTORY

I T HAS often been remarked that the world is ruled by ideas, or as Napoleon put it with the same meaning, by imagination. The ideas that so frequently control society may be divided into two groups, the practical and the philosophical. By the former we mean those concepts which, expressing immediate mundane aims, can actually be realized by an expression of the human will. As we scan the dark backward and abysm of time we can descry a long list of such ideas which have exercised the most powerful sway over human affairs. Among them are the idea of the ecclesiastical or papal supremacy over temporal powers; the idea of the divine right of kings; the idea of nationalism; the idea of toleration; the idea of self-determination, which ruled events so potently during and after the World War; the idea of rugged individualism; the idea of State Socialism; and the idea of collectivism or the abolition of private property. These are practical ideas because they depend primarily upon man's will; because they can usually be made to work if most men agree to promote them; and because they are tested by the question whether they are useful or useless, not true or false. Mussolini's idea of the totalitarian state depends for its validity on the readiness of most Italians to employ it, and that readiness will endure just so long as most Italians believe that its advantages offset its disadvantages.

But mankind is also powerfully swayed at times by philosophical ideas. They are theoretical rather than practical, and are judged not by pragmatic tests but by men's conviction of what is valid and invalid. Society accepts or rejects them not as beneficial or injurious, but as true or false. Such is the idea of personal immortality — and few people realize how profoundly human institutions would be altered if that concept were abandoned by mankind. Such also is the Greek idea of fate, or the Calvinist idea of predestination, with other religious ideas. Such is the idea of Progress, in modern times probably the most important of all human concepts of a philosophical nature.

All historical work which pretends to any elevation or importance is written under the influence of ideas. Much of the historical work, though by no means all of it, is important by virtue of its ideas; that is, its interpretation. Consciously or unconsciously, all significant historians are affected by their intellectual environment, whether they evince hostility to some phase of the prevalent thought of the time, or espouse and defend it. And if the historian is a man of intellectual vigor, he assuredly views his task not as the mere recital of a series of facts and events, but as their arrangement in a pattern which illustrates some underlying truth. The effect of this impulse upon the history of ideas has been very great; but we are here concerned primarily with its effect upon the course of historical writing.

While the analysis of historical evidence is an important process in the study or writing of history, it is not the most important. In the highest type of history the synthesis or interpretation is a much more vital element. The task of analysis involves the discovery of the truth about various episodes or events by a combination of industry, ingenuity, judgment, and honesty. The writer collects all the authentic and relevant facts, he assorts and classifies them, he finds the best possible explanation for them, and he rigorously tests this explanation of their significance. This is a minute process. It is essentially a bit of anatomical work. But to arrive at an interpretation, the historian takes a considerable body of problems and events, and so arranges them as to illustrate some dominant idea. That is, he synthesizes his material about some concept which governs the whole of it; he utilizes a series of analyses, which at first may have seemed chaotic and jumbled, and produces a general conclusion which throws them into perspective. This is not anatomy; it is physiology. It breathes the spark of life into dead materials and makes them move as living bodies. Or to change the figure, it lifts the reader above the immediate thicket he is exploring, and shows him the trend of the terrain — the significance of the valley, or the mountain range, of which the thickets are a part.

Thus the *Cambridge Modern History*, or the *Histoire Générale* of Lavisse, offers a huge body of facts upon human events since 1500, caught together merely in a long series of highly factual — and rather badly related — monographs. But Oswald Spengler, in *The Decline of the West*, offers an interpretation of this long period. Discarding the old simple and optimistic view of linear evolution or endless progress, he substituted — as a number of others have done — an interpretation of history as a recurring cycle, a Foucault pendulum swing, placing our own unhappy time in the bleakest part of a spring-summer-autumn-winter succession. To take a more limited example, Channing's book on the Civil War offers a score of analyses of problems, but declines to draw them together upon any interpretive thread. But in *The Rise of American Civilization* Charles and Mary Beard synthesize the Civil War according to an economic pattern. They view it as essentially a conflict between the old rural culture and the new industrial culture of America. Discarding the old concepts of the slavery and State Rights issues as dominating the Civil War period, the Beards make their concept of a sharp collision between a business civilization and an agrarian civilization the vehicle of a fresh and stimulating interpretation of the events of 1860–69.

II

At the outset it is important to enforce a firm distinction between a general philosophy of history, and a specific interpretation of historical materials. The distinction is mainly one of scope. But it is also related to the distinction which we have just drawn between philosophical ideas, tested by our faith in what is true, and practical ideas, tested by our experience of their workability. General philosophical concepts of history will not bend to pragmatic tests. The dominant idea of Spengler's book is obviously of this nature. No one will ever know — at least for hundreds of centuries to come — whether history does move in regular cycles or not; to read and write history in that way is simply an act of faith. So is the philosophy of history built on the doctrine of evolutionary progress, a creed so popular in the nineteenth century. So is the philosophy, toward which Pareto leans, of history as a pendulum alternating between liberty and authority. But an interpretation like that which the Beards give the Civil War can be subjected to practical tests; the facts within a limited domain either sustain or destroy it — when we learn them. The interpretation may provoke a discussion which drags on through decades, but each student will decide upon its merits by consulting the facts. A philosophy of history springs from a writer's whole view of human destiny, and thus embodies his philosophy of life; an interpretation of historical material is merely a writer's explanation of the significance of a series of events, an epoch, or a movement. The one usually bears a close relation to the thought of the age; the other is usually more personal in origin.

All the principal philosophies of history save two have originated within the past three centuries — a fact which speaks volumes for the close alliance between rationalism and modern history. Greek and Roman writers of history knew but one philosophy, that of Fate. To them the word held a far richer theological significance than it has to us, and from Thucydides to Appian it sufficed to cover their view of human destiny. They made varying allowances for the interposition of the gods, but they never formulated any view of a grand final goal, some far-off, divine event, toward which the gods guided mankind.

But early in the Christian era there naturally arose a very different philosophy of history, stamped by the fervors of the new faith; and it held almost undisputed sway for more than thirteen centuries. First enunciated by St. Augustine in *The City of God*, it asserted that the whole record of the world turned upon the overwhelming fact of divine concern for mankind. The decisive event of history was the life of Christ, before which all mankind had been doomed, and after which all of the elect were saved. St. Augustine, donning the mantle of seer, described the birth, growth, and destiny of two cities, one of this world and one of God, culminating in the triumph of the latter. His followers continued to regard the earth simply as the footstool of history; the story of humankind as simply part of the divine comedy. That view, which often had Neo-Platonist elements and which could be given a compelling grandeur, swayed medieval chroniclers no less than Dante and Milton.[1]

This Christian philosophy of history indeed continued to possess the field down to the time of Bossuet's eloquent book, the *Histoire Universelle*, which largely summed it up. His volume, written from the standpoint of dogmatic theology and the official Catholic hierarchy, was imbued with a belief that the pivotal event of time was the crucifixion, and that the one all-powerful force in human affairs was God's benevolent interposition. He conceived of the changes in history as all slowly tending toward the progress and universality of the true religion — not merely Christianity, but the papal form of Christianity. The book naturally passed Moslem civilization by; it treated Greece and Rome only as part of the *Preparatio Evangelicum*. Voltaire, remarking caustically that "It seems to have been written solely to suggest that everything in the world was made for the Jews," was stung by it and similar

---

[1] For a much more thorough account of the philosophy of history than is here possible, see the articles by Vladimir G. Simkhovitch on "Approaches to History" in the *Political Science Quarterly*, Vols. XLIV, XLV, XLVII, and XLVIII. See also Appendix III of this volume.

productions into an angry reply. His *Essai sur les Moeurs* a generation later wholly rejected the miraculous interposition of Providence in history, asserting instead a rationalistic interpretation of the past. In Voltaire's opinion, the events of history were attributable not to design but to chance or fortuity. His brilliant though vague exposition helped to open the way for other rationalistic philosophies. But the Christian synthesis long persisted, and even in America had its followers. Benjamin Trumbull's *General History of the United States*, of which only one of three proposed volumes appeared (1810), attempted to point out the special interposition of Providence in behalf of the American people.

Since the time of Hegel, whose brilliant *Philosophy of History* appeared in 1830–31, metaphysical analyses of the whole range of human events have become oppressively numerous. They may now be found on every counter, for it is a poor sociologist, economist, or philosopher — not to mention historian — who does not present one. Hegel, whose doctrines have inspired a whole school, attempted to show that every epoch in history was inspired and dominated by some specific idea; for example, he regarded Napoleon, the new Caesar, as "die Weltseele" of his time. He taught that each idea, affirmed as truth, brings with it the idea that is its negation; they do battle, and a new idea emerges. Then the cycle repeats itself. Such recent historians as Kuno Fischer likewise lay emphasis on the "Einheitstendenz" of every period, which permeates all aspects of its life, and by which alone it is to be understood. A quarter century after Hegel's great book the Darwinian theory of natural selection as a key of evolution seized all history in its powerful grasp, which has not yet greatly relaxed; for most historians of the non-esoteric schools still believe in progress, and believe it is attained by evolutionary processes. Indeed, evolutionary ideas long preceded Darwin, who gave them simply a special form and force. Such writers as Lecky, Freeman, Parkman, and McMaster were unconsciously pervaded by the evolutionary philosophy, and such writers as Froude, Bagehot, John Fiske, and Rhodes were very consciously pervaded by it. Challenged by few save the Marxian group, the evolutionary writers for decades ruled history with autocratic sway, and even yet dominate the field. But an increasing band of dissenters, a vigorous group of advanced intellectuals, today assert that simple evolution is nearly as absurd as the old theological view of history.

Two of the ablest statements of the evolutionary philosophy of history are to be found in Walter Bagehot's stimulating *Physics and Politics* and John Fiske's *Outlines of Cosmic Philosophy;* both the more typical for having been written in the very heart of the Victorian era. Of Fiske's views we shall say something later. Bagehot significantly gave his work the subtitle, "Thoughts on the application of the principles of natural selection and inheritance to political science." His book did more than state a theory of history; for in its deep influence upon such future leaders as Woodrow Wilson it made history. Essentially, it was an attempt to show that in social institutions as well as in the animal kingdom the rule of the survival of the fittest applies; and that as an acquired faculty of the parent animal is sometimes distinctly transmitted to its progeny (or so Bagehot believed), so acquired characteristics of society are inherited by succeeding generations. "The continuous force which binds age to age," writes Bagehot, "enables each to begin with some improvement on the last, if the last did not itself improve." This implies a general, though of course not uninterrupted, continuity of progress in the world, under which weak and erroneous institutions are gradually eliminated. Upon this view, if it is valid, a grand systematization of history can be built, and Bagehot asserts as much. "We thus perceive that a science of history is possible — a science to teach the law of tendencies, created by the mind and transmitted by the body — which act upon and incline the mind of man from age to age."

In developing his thesis, Bagehot begins with a "Preliminary Stage" of civilization in which progress was achieved by the triumph of the strong over the weak. Powerful tribes, nations, or peoples always tend to prevail over the feeble, and while Bagehot does not believe that might makes right, he does assert that "in certain marked peculiarities, the strongest tend to be the best." In his section on "Nation Making" he accounts by evolutionary theory for the development of national traits. It has been an innate propensity of man to imitate what is before him; thus the primitive savages imitated their leaders and copied their most striking characteristics, "preserving them as they did their favorite animals." These traits gradually tinged the whole community. "Ages are required, but at last a national character is formed." National character is but the name for a collection of habits, more or less universal, which in the course of long generations have produced vast mental and physical effects. Bagehot then continues his evolutionary exposition by showing how primitive and simple nations have given way to modern and complex nations. In the former "fixity was the invariable ingredient," and the cake of custom held peoples in a mould that was sometimes as viciously static as the old-time framework of Chinese society. But as the Middle Ages ended, various tendencies broke the cake of fixed custom and ushered in the "age of discussion," which is progressive inasmuch as it gives a premium to intelligence. Though Bagehot saw certain dangers in even the modern age of discussion, notably in a tendency toward hasty political action which he calls "a hereditary barbaric impulse," and though like Malthus he feared "a diminished reserve for race maintenance," his outlook upon the future was fundamentally hopeful. All evolutionists are meliorists if not optimists. While the conclusions which flow from his evolutionary concept appear somewhat naïve to many present-day students, even they must admit that in the course of his argument he elucidates many secondary truths with memorable eloquence and force.

The "Marxian interpretation" of history is of course really a Marxian philosophy, as imposing in scope, despite its materialistic temper, as any other philosophy. It has to be carefully distinguished from the writings of many of Marx's followers, who in his own lifetime so perverted some of his doctrines that he mordantly remarked, "Je ne suis pas un Marxiste." Briefly stated, his thesis is that the mode of production in economic life primarily determines the general character of the social, political, and cultural processes of life. With every change in the economic foundation brought about by changes in relationship between man and productive forces, the entire superstructure is more or less rapidly transformed. Marx thus became the first to formulate, in explicit fashion, the economic interpretation of history. Unlike some of his disciples, he and Engels never gave this interpretation so narrow a form as to exclude all non-economic factors as contributing causes of events; they merely declared the mode of production to be the dominant factor. Indeed, Marx clearly perceived that society is moulded by spirit and thought as well as material environment, and did not believe that history could be explained by a monistic materialism. Rather, he regarded society as an interacting whole of environment and thought, of objective and subjective conditions, and of activity and its practical goals, in which mode of production was the most important single element. It should also be noted that Marx's general conception of history does not have, for students of historical writing, any connection with his belief that society would be remade by passing through a dictatorship of the proletariat into a classless world. As Dr. E. R. A. Seligman says, "there is nothing in common between the economic interpretation of history and the doctrine of Socialism, except the accidental fact that the originator of both theories happened to be the same man."

This philosophy has been under intensive fire ever since Marx very briefly presented it in his *Critique of Political Economy* — for he never gave it an elaborate statement. The attack upon those of his followers who take an extremely narrow and dogmatic view of the economic interpretation has of course been more effective than the attack upon Marx himself. German Socialists like Kautsky and Hilferding compressed the Marxian theory of history into preposterously strict limits, making human thought and action not so much derivatives as by-products of economic processes. The Russian Communists have gone to equal extremes in their treatment of history. Lenin's reductive materialism in his *Materialism and Empirio-Criticism*, Bukharin's emphasis upon a technological interpretation of history, which he falsely ascribed to Marx, and Pokrovsky's monistic materialism, which completely excluded either chance or great men as real determinants of events, were all vulnerable. But the true Marxian philosophy in no way excludes ethical or spiritual forces from history. It simply asserts that the concept of morality is a social product, varying with the state of civilization or with the social class, and as such largely determined, in the last analysis, by economic forces. It does not deny that great men have sometimes exercised a controlling influence upon history. It simply asserts that in general they would never have been great had it not been for certain social conditions which made their rise possible, and that these conditions are in turn governed chiefly by economic factors. But it must be added that Marx's own brevity and partial obscurity in stating his philosophy left some of its implications vague, and opened the way for such assaults upon it as those of Dr. M. M. Bober and F. R. Salter.

The vast convulsion of the World War and its aftermath, which convinced tens of millions of men that social progress is but an empty word, and that an "evolution" which marched whole nations to death or ruin offered no hope to mankind, could not but have a profound effect upon the philosophy of history. Certain new scientific theories of the universe formulated during the same period exercised an almost equal influence. The universe, which Newton had conceived as infinite in extent and subject to fixed physical laws, was transformed by Einstein into a finite universe governed by relative laws. It was perhaps a universe, as Jeans, Eddington, and others suggested, in which a ceaseless process of destruction and construction went on without assignable object; energy being dissipated into remote space, and there gradually reconstructing new galaxies to dissipate themselves again. The fashion in historical philosophies swung abruptly to exercise in cosmic rhythm. H. G. Wells still believed in evolution, and his *Outline of History* pointed the way to a grand perfection of society through science and education. But a dozen post-war writers, most of whom dipped their pens in earthquake and gloom, explained . that history was a series of pulsations; was a swing and counterswing of the pendulum; was a cycle of summer-fall-winterspring seasons endlessly repeating themselves; was in fact anything except the magnificent upward climb toward a higher and better life which Bossuet had believed to be directed by God, and the Victorians to be directed by Evolution (which after all, in Tennyson's if not in Huxley's view, was little else than another name for God).

Upon the principal recent treatises offering one or another rhythm-philosophy of history — Spengler's *Decline of the West*, Pareto's *Mind and Society*, Arnold Toynbee's *A Study of History*, and most pretentious of all, Pitirim Sorokin's *Culture and Cultural Dynamics* — it is happily unnecessary to speak at any length. Their own length is not a little oppressive: Spengler's two volumes, Pareto's and Sorokin's four, and Toynbee's projected thirteen. These men all differ violently as to the precise form of the rhythmic alternation, just as they differ as to the precise position of the present-day world in the grand repetitive movement. Spengler, with his four seasonal phases of the cycle, and his certainty that Western civilization has been entering a long winter of decay, plainly represents the pessimism of a defeated Germany. Pareto is less willing to assume the rôle of a prophet, and more inclined to present sociological evidence for his generalizations. To him history represents past sociology just as surely as to Freeman it represented retrospective politics. He sees in history a repetitive alternation of liberty and authority — the foxes and the lions — and he believes that our own post-bellum period has clearly represented the swing toward authority. Professor Sorokin presents history as a fairly complex cycle which carries it from the Ideational at one extreme to the Sensate at the other, and then back again. These terms can be roughly translated into collectivism and individualism, and Mr. Sorokin believes that Western society is just completing a Sensate (individualist) and beginning an Ideational (collectivist) period. Mr. Toynbee's general ideas are as yet only partially adumbrated; though they postulate a challenge-and-response rhythm, he seems still to cling to a modicum of faith in evolution.[1]

In direct application, these newer philosophies are not at all helpful to practitioners of history. The Hegelian idea of history has been fruitfully applied by students and writers. So also with the evolutionary concept of history, which stimulated many writers to arrange their data in more interesting and significant patterns. But while Spengler and Pareto offer many stimulating suggestions and present many flashes of insight into detailed historical problems (as does Toynbee), their grandiose concepts of human cycles or curves seem of no practical use. The value of these ambitious philosophies is indirect. They foster a healthy discontent with existing approaches to history, which leads to an effort to obtain a deeper understanding of it. They predispose students to utilize new formulae and new scientific apparatus in an experimental search for truth. They lead to an impatience with the shallower forms of history, a demand for more profound treatments of it. Scornful as we

[1] Dr. Simkhovitch, in the fourth article of his "Approaches to History," *Political Science Quarterly*, XLVIII, 23 ff., names and describes still other exponents of a rhythmical philosophy — Scherer, Karl Joel, O. Lorenz, and others.

may be of the flatulence and vagueness of some of these philosophies, or pseudo-philosophies, we must agree with Henry Adams — who himself tentatively entered the field — that the impulse behind them is natural:

> You may be sure that four out of five serious students of history who are living today have, in the course of their work, felt that they stood on the brink of a great generalization that would reduce history under a law as clear as the laws which govern the material world. As the great writers of our time have touched one by one the separate fragments of admitted law by which society betrays its character as a subject for science, not one of them can have failed to feel an instant's hope that he might find the secret which would transform these odds and ends of philosophy into one self-evident, harmonious, and complete system. He has seemed to have it, as the Spanish say, in his inkstand. Scores of times he must have dropped his pen to think how one short step, one sudden inspiration, would show all human knowledge; how, in these thickset forests of history, one corner turned, one faint trail struck would bring him on the highroad of science.[1]

Yet it should be added that general agreement upon any philosophy of history is as undesirable as it is impossible. The great unifying law of which Henry Adams speaks will never be found. If men assented to any such law, it would bind history in fetters as adamantine as the old theological formula of Bossuet, and would ultimately render historical scholarship as monotonous and sterile as the work of the monkish chroniclers.

III

But the ordinary reader of history needs to have little concern with the grandiose conceptions of philosophy. His interest in the application of ideas to history will be confined to the more modest, more practical, more personal form which we term the historical interpretation. One of the distinguishing hallmarks of modern historical writing is its powerful inter-

[1] Henry Adams, *Degradation of the Democratic Dogma*, p. 127

pretive tendency. While the best ancient and medieval historians had a distinct point of view, only a few of them — among the ancients, Thucydides, Polybius, and their disciples — were possessed by that intense desire to revise history ever nearer the truth by arranging it in ever subtler patterns which masters most present-day historians. The element of intellectual *originality* in historical work has become steadily larger since 1750. While the forces which brought this interpretive tendency to its modern vigor are numerous, four may be singled out as particularly important.

The growth of rationalism was of course as indispensable to the unfettered use of ideas in history as it was to their unfettered use in science. It was no accident that the Age of Enlightenment coincided with the first great flowering of modern history. Originally in France, and later in England, the eighteenth century produced a special and extraordinary activity in historical work. And it is significant that this activity was promoted by the very men who were doing most in other spheres to emancipate humanity from the trammels of authority. Montesquieu's *Spirit of the Laws*, one of the most important books ever written, perhaps the greatest book of eighteenth century France, is largely historical in content, as the subtitle indicates: "du Rapport que les Lois doivent avoir avec la Constitution du Chaque Gouvernement, les Moeurs, le Climat, la Religion, du Commerce, etc." Its third part, consisting of six books which treat at length of the dependence of manners and customs upon climatic conditions, has been especially interesting to historical students. Montesquieu was the first writer to emphasize this relationship as it deserved. But the work should be considered as a whole; so taken, it is one of the foundation-stones of comparative politics, and its novel and brilliant generalizations in this field at once suggested a number of new ways of interpreting history. With it should be considered the work of Voltaire. He realized that when he and other rationalists loosed the grip of the old supernatural versions of history, when they proved that men really made their own world, a new significance instantly enveloped the past. Historians must make use of these thousand new *aperçus*. Casting aside the murky lanterns of the religious chroniclers and churchly recorders, they must reconstruct the past under the brilliant light of reason. The same conviction animated Hume and Gibbon, two mighty assailants of the reigning superstitions, across the Channel. It was no accident that the best secular histories of the period were written by the greatest of the rationalists.

Voltaire has left an exceptionally full record of the circumstances under which he embarked upon his own rationalist interpretations of history. His active-minded friend, Mme. du Chatelet, whose special talent was for mathematics and philosophy, disliked history.[1] "What does it matter to me," she asked, "a Frenchwoman living on my estate, that Egil succeeded Haquin in Sweden, and that Ottoman was the son of Ortogrul? I read with pleasure Greek and Roman history, which offers great pictures which attract me. But I have never yet been able to finish any long history of our modern nations. There seems nothing in them but confusion, a host of minute events without connection or sequence, a thousand battles which settled nothing. I renounced a study which overwhelmed my mind without illuminating it." Voltaire replied that what was needed was simply a rational interpretation of history, utilizing the ideas forbidden to previous generations. If all the tedious and untrustworthy details of wars, all the pointless negotiations of diplomacy, all the minute incidents which obscured the grand tendencies of history, were shorn away, then a general and well-arranged picture could be made of the significant factors. It would be worth Mme. du Chatelet's time to read *that*. The history of the human mind, remarked Voltaire, was the truly important part of the human record. His word mind, of course, embraced a great deal — law, arts, manners, literature, ideas — which he would make the chief concern of

[1] Voltaire, *Essai sur les Moeurs*, pp. 1, 2

history. But every fact that the historian recorded should lead to something else. "Details which lead to nothing are in history what baggage is to an army, impedimenta, for we must look at things in the large, for the simple reason that the human mind is limited and sinks under the weight of minutiae."[1] Unconnected minutiae he would leave to annalists and encyclopaedia-makers. These conceptions Voltaire illustrated in his *Charles XII* and *Age of Louis XIV*.

The new scientific attitude toward history was strikingly exhibited by Voltaire in his flat refusal to accept Tacitus at face value. He did not have the evidence which later scholars have found for believing Tacitus prejudiced and inaccurate. But relying on internal evidence, he pointed out the improbability of much that Tacitus had written upon Tiberius, Nero, Caligula, and other emperors. How could we accept the word of a man born long after Tiberius's death for the sensational story of how the emperor, after living to nearly eighty with unblemished name and a reputation for austerity, thereafter passed his time in monstrous debaucheries? Voltaire applied this same scientific incredulity to other fables of so-called history, demanding more sensible interpretations. Still another new principle which he helped bring into history was his insistence that persons and personal interests are of secondary importance; that it is the community, not the individual, which counts for most. This in itself was a basis for many new interpretations of the past. As Lord Morley says in his essay on Voltaire:

Voltaire was always conscious, though not so clearly as writers are now, of the great historical principle that besides the prominent men of a generation there is something at work underneath, a moving current on whose flood they are borne. He never fixed this current by any of the names which now fall so glibly from our lips, — tendency of the times, tenor of public opinion, spirit of the age, and the like, by which we give a collective name to groups of sentiments and forces,

[1] Voltaire, *Ibid.*, p. 9

all making in what seems to be a single direction. But although un-named, this singular and invisible concurrence of circumstances was yet a reality to him. The age was something besides its heroes, and something besides its noisiest and most resounding occurrences. His divisions of the great epochs of humanity are undoubtedly open to much criticism, because the principles on which he drew the dividing line have lost their force in new generations. . . . Nevertheless, we are bound to recognize that a new way of regarding human action, as well as a new way of composing history, was being introduced by a writer whose first paragraph declared that he proposed to himself a greater object than an account of the life of Louis XIV; that he designed to paint for the instruction of posterity, not the actions of a single man, but the spirit of men; and that while all periods must be alike to one who only desires to fill his memory with facts, discrimi-nation among them cannot be dispensed with for one who thinks.[1]

The temper of the Enlightenment appears quite as clearly in David Hume's *Essays, Moral, Political, and Literary*, as in Voltaire's works. His famous disquisition upon miracles, a masterpiece of irony, was a blow at the very padlock of the old fetters upon history. His essay upon the population of ancient cities, highly skeptical in temper, was one of the first sugges-tions of the importance of statistics in interpreting history. His views on money, trade, and government, marked by intellectual impartiality and critical acuteness in points of detail, carried many historical illustrations and had a clear applicability to history. Despite his allegiance to the Tory party, they pointed a clear road forward to what in the next century was called Liberalism. They had a profound influence in England and France, and it has been said that but for the conservative re-action following the French Revolution they might even have resulted in the parliamentary adoption of free trade and elec-toral reform before 1800. But Hume's *History of England*, which followed the *Essays*, was his greatest work. He was the first eminent Briton, as Voltaire was the first eminent Frenchman, to see clearly that history should not be a mere record of war

[1] Lord Morley, *Collected Works*, VII, 249, 250

and political intrigue, but should concern itself primarily with the mode of life, the morals, the manners, and the mind of the people. Far more than any previous writer, he had an insight into the complex social forces of history. After his six-volume work (1754–61), no Englishman could write history as it had been written before.

In Gibbon's *Decline and Fall* the Age of Enlightenment produced its principal historical monument. That work still seems, to many acute judges, the greatest piece of interpretive history yet written. To be sure, the interpretation is simple; it is largely summed up in Gibbon's famous sentence, "I have traced the triumph of Christianity and of barbarism." He was animated by a glowing admiration for the empire of Augustus and Trajan as embodying a "solid fabric of human greatness" unmatchable elsewhere; an empire which to him came nearer giving the earth its golden age than had any other régime. Imbued with this admiration, he felt little but distaste for the Christian religion which had done so much to help overthrow the Roman civilization — which had given to him in the eighteenth century the sight of barefooted and superstitious friars chanting vespers in the temple of Jupiter beside the ruins of the Capitol. That so great a work should be written upon a a theme so antagonistic to all the tenets of theological historiography was, whatever we think of the validity of his interpretation, the blow of an irresistible battering ram against the old narrow citadels. Their walls collapsed in utter ruin.

The second great constructive influence upon historical interpretation came with the rise of economic science, and was ushered in by Adam Smith's *Wealth of Nations* in the same year that witnessed the Declaration of Independence and the publication of Gibbon's first volume. Smith had taken not a few of his views from the *Political Discourses* of his close friend Hume. His classic book, usually regarded as the main foundation of economics, was also one of the foundation-stones of modern historical writing. The Rationalists had dealt a shattering blow at the theory that history revolved exclusively about the facts of Christianity; Adam Smith now dealt a shattering blow at the whole aristocratic theory of history. Up to that time nearly all chroniclers of the past had held to a hierarchal conception of history, regarding the upper ranks of society as those alone worthy of a large place in the record. The king, noble, soldier, priest, and statesman had been the personalities with whom history was concerned; battles, dynastic changes, treaties, and other elements of the contest for power had been the salient events of history. But Adam Smith's ideas let in a new blaze of light. He and other writers showed that the great central currents in the life of any modern nation were economic; that the principal forces which governed that life were those of production, markets, transportation, labor-supply, prices, and raw materials. These, like an irresistible current, bore national affairs forward while kings, priests, and soldiers — with some few exceptions — were tossed like flotsam and jetsam on the surface. Important though wars and battles were, they held their importance, in general, because they grew out of economic forces or interrupted these forces; much as treaties often counted, it was usually because they were the visible outcome of greater factors beneath the surface. It was impossible for well-read men, after *The Wealth of Nations*, to write of nations without proper attention to all that built up wealth. A great new interpretive highway had been driven into the wilderness that bordered the old-fashioned history, and colonists were soon making that wilderness rich with fruitful crops.

One of the first and most influential of these explorers was Arnold H. L. Heeren, long professor at Göttingen, who was sixteen when Adam Smith's book appeared, and who lived until 1842, becoming George Bancroft's master and inspirer in the art of history. Heeren's unforgettable service was that he first fully applied the new interpretive apparatus to the ancient field. In his *Ideen über Politik, den Verkehr und den Handel der vornehmsten Völker der alten Welt,* and in other works, he presented an altogether fresh point of view. He examined ancient agriculture, manufactures, commerce, finance, and in short, the whole economic system of the early world, together with its politics, laws, and constitutions, and was thus enabled to throw a flood of light on the development of the civilizations of antiquity. His vast and varied learning, calm impartiality, and insight helped to make his works notable. Unfortunately Bancroft, while learning much from Heeren in scholarly method and zeal, never acquired his peculiar interest in the economic aspects of history. In England the Benthamite or utilitarian school of historians, like Jeremy Bentham himself, were originally inspired by Adam Smith.

As a third vivifying influence, novel political ideas also contributed to the transformation of history by supplying a number of fresh interpretations; and it need not be said that the most striking of these ideas came with the French Revolution. That event was to half of mankind as the rising of a golden sun. "Bliss was it in that dawn to be alive" — to be a young historian, no less than poet, very heaven. Through the lurid flame and smoke of the overwhelming convulsion, the masses of the people came into view. These masses, unknown to the old-time chroniclers of royalty, military glory, and the church, had been neglected as unimportant, but they now made history with unforgettable vigor. They lifted to power one of their own number, and Napoleon took charge of the destinies of Europe for fifteen years. Thenceforth no historian could slight them. And when the era of the Napoleonic wars ended, it was also seen that history must henceforth be interpreted not merely in terms of the common man, but in terms of a rampant nationalism. Once the monarch had been thought more important than the state — often, as Louis XIV boasted of himself, he *was* the state. But now the people were the state; and the force of national sentiment diffused throughout the people brought a new Germany, a new Spain, in one sense a new Russia, into existence.   In the course of another·long generation, the growth of nationalism among the masses gave birth to a new Italy and a newer Germany, while still further triumphs lay before it.

Altogether, by 1830 the age of multiform historical inter-pretations of the past had fully opened.   The presentation of the human record had been broadened in a fashion that would have been inconceivable to pious readers of Bossuet.   It no longer took account of divine providence at all — or at least not in the ablest writers.   Instead, it took account of all that the ration-alism of that era had to suggest, for Montesquieu's enlistment of geography had been only one of various utilizations of scientific knowledge; it took account of the cultural and moral history which Voltaire had pointed out to Mme. du Chatelet as central to all understanding of man's past; it took account of economic factors; of democratic factors; and of nationalistic and patriotic factors.   A series of radically new outlooks, within seventy-five years, had come in.   Every student was at liberty to use one or several of them in his synthesis, his interpretation.

Yet although much had been done, fertile fields of speculation remained to be entered.   The fourth great element in the modern growth of history lay in its acquisition of the new scientific tendencies of the nineteenth century.   In such writers as Macaulay, Guizot, and Prescott the interpretation is what we nowadays term, with due respect, old-fashioned.   Why?   Be-cause while they reflected the ideas which had been imported into history by Montesquieu and Voltaire, Hume and Gibbon, Adam Smith and Heeren, the Industrial Revolution and the French Revolution, still other ideas arose during and after their lifetimes which have profoundly impressed all subsequent his-torians.   History had in particular to keep up with the march of the various sciences, and some were marching fast.   In addition to the development of geography, economics, and biology, wholly new sciences were born — first sociology, and later psy-chology, both extremely useful in historical interpretation.

Professional historians are justly suspicious of sweeping sociological theories as likely to be unsound and useless. But the more exact sciences are of indubitable value.

One important book which partly revealed a shift in the trend of historical interpretation, and which partly caused it, was H. T. Buckle's unfinished *History of Civilization in England*, published in 1857. As everyone knows, this huge fragment — broken off by his untimely death — is part of an introduction in which he intended, first, to state the general laws governing human progress, and second, to exemplify these laws by the history of certain strongly-individualized nations — Spain, Scotland, the United States, and Germany. It is unnecessary to list all of the ten or twelve main principles, some of them largely fallacious, which he laid down. His most important contentions are as follows: (1) Inasmuch as historians have been shortsighted and unreflective, and as the social phenomena of the modern world are extremely complex, little has yet been done to establish a science of history. (2) It is nevertheless proved by scientific inquiry, and particularly by sociological statistics, that human action is controlled by fixed and predictable rules. (3) It is a basic fact of history that the chief causes of intellectual progress are climate, soil, and food, which govern it indirectly by determining the accumulation and distribution of wealth, and the aspect of nature, which touches intellectual development directly by influencing the cast and vigor of thought — for peoples reared in sublime scenery are more imaginative than their fellows, people reared in harsh surroundings are tougher-minded, and so on. (4) The huge distinction between European and non-European civilization rests primarily upon the fact that in Europe man has been stronger than nature, subduing it to his objects, while outside Europe nature has been stronger than man and has largely subdued him. (5) The advance of European civilization is characterized by a steady growth in the importance of intellectual laws, and a steady diminution in the influence of physical laws.

Though some of his ideas have never convinced others, and perhaps none of them is wholly true, Buckle's work was nevertheless extremely influential everywhere from Russia to the United States. Particularly was one central thesis of his work important. He taught that written history had been too much a record of individuals or select groups, and not enough of whole societies or nations; he believed that the action of great human masses ought to be traced, especially with the aid of statistical law. He also held that in the natural surroundings of every people — its command of necessary raw materials and luxuries, its conditions of soil and climate — lie the chief moulding influences of its career, and that parliaments have nearly as little as kings and heroes to do with that moulding. In short, Buckle was one of the forerunners of a history built upon sociology, social statistics, and economic geography. His emphasis upon the life of the whole people appears in transmuted form in John Richard Green's *Short History of the English People*, and in John Bach McMaster's *History of the People of the United States*. Both these writers attempt to trace the life of a whole nation, and to deal with the people as an organic body; the people as they lived, worked, prospered, suffered, as they developed moral codes, manners, and arts in city and country. Both writers had to fall back upon description much more heavily than Buckle would have approved, for tables of statistics and other sociological data did not exist in any volume. But both were obviously influenced by his doctrines, while he had helped to prepare a reading public for them. The deep impression made by his insistence upon laws of progress was of course heightened by the publication of Darwin's *Origin of Species* only two years after his book.

Only less important than the scientific contribution made to historical interpretation by Buckle and the great evolutionists — Darwin, Lyell, Huxley, Wallace, Hooker — was the quasi-scientific contribution made by the founders of sociology. One such founder, August Comte, preceded these men; another,

Herbert Spencer, followed them. Neither wrote at any length upon history in itself, but the works of both contain much incidental material upon history. Spencer was of course one of the chief apostles of evolution, who attempted to make universal the principle of evolutionary development and to formulate its law. Comte, whose *Positive Philosophy* was completed in 1843, seventeen years before Darwin's *Origin of Species*, had no connection with evolutionary theory. Nor had he the least sympathy with the desire of Buckle and others to study history by discovering the scientific laws governing society. On the contrary, he maintained that no such laws exist; that while human knowledge has as its objects phenomena in their reciprocal relations, nothing absolute lies at the base of these phenomena. With one exception stated below, the only absolute law is, All is relative. His views represented a development of the rationalistic and skeptical doctrines of Hume and Condillac.

For the purposes of the interpretive historian, the part of Comte's encyclopaedic system which holds the richest interest is the Law of the Three States laid down at the beginning of his Positive Philosophy, and always treated by both disciples and opponents as the key to it. He declared that each branch of human knowledge passes successively through three phases, or three modes in which men explain the phenomena they observe. The first phase is the Theological, in which credulous observers refer phenomena to a supernatural principle, the immediate volition of the object itself or of some supernatural being. The second phase is the Metaphysical, the phenomena being viewed not as an act of volition, but as due to an abstract force residing in, yet apart from, the object. The third is the Positive phase, when phenomena are referred by way of succession or resemblance to some other fact, and so studied. All this has been aptly illustrated by an English follower of Comte: "Take the phenomenon of the sleep produced by opium. The Arabs are content to attribute it to the 'will of God.' Molière's medical student accounts for it by a *soporific principle* contained in the opium. The modern physiologist knows that he cannot account for it at all. He can simply observe, analyze, and experiment upon the phenomena attending the action of the drug, and classify it with other agents analogous in character." The principal object of Comte's Positivistic teachings was to carry the study of social phenomena into the third stage — to remove them from the sphere of theology and metaphysics, and to see that they be given the same scientific examination of their relations and classifications as had already been given to physical and chemical phenomena. To use John Morley's summary:

While men's minds were in the theological state, political events, for example, were explained by the will of the gods, and political authority based on divine right. In the metaphysical state of mind . . . political authority was based on the will of the people, and social facts were explained by the figment of the falling away from a state of nature. When the positive method has been fully extended to society, as it has been to chemistry and physiology, these social facts will be resolved, as their ultimate analysis, into relations with one another, and instead of seeking causes in the old sense of the word, men will only examine the conditions of social existence. When that stage has been reached . . . the whole of our knowledge will be impressed with one character, the character, namely, of positivity or scientificalness; and all our conceptions in every part of knowledge will be thoroughly homogeneous. The gains of such a change are enormous.[1]

In addition to this emphasis upon the necessity for a science of society, an emphasis which could not but affect historical work in proportion as Comte's views were accepted and diffused, the Positive Philosophy had another important object. This was to show that the sciences are all branches from a single trunk, parts of one great whole. Comte's special aim was the promotion of sociology, a science never formulated until his ad-

[1] *Encyclopædia Britannica*, Ninth Ed., VI, 234

vent; but while promoting it he tried to assign it a clear relation to other branches of knowledge. He arranged a hierarchy of sciences, each in his view more specialized than the member just before it, and dependent upon all the preceding sciences: (1) mathematics, (2) astronomy, (3) physics, (4) chemistry, (5) biology, and (6) sociology. Of course he held sociology the greatest of all. If we remember that not a few writers now view history as retrospective sociology, it is at once plain that this doctrine also has had its effect upon historical interpretation.

We have spoken of evolution as giving the world a new philosophy of history; but it also supplied various new interpretations of it, practical and immediate in nature. Until the doctrine was fully introduced to the world by Darwin, Spencer, and others, historians had talked of development rather than evolution. During the Age of Enlightenment advanced thinkers had taken a keen interest in the origin and development of language, of philology, of law, of pictorial art, of legendary and written literature. It was natural that this should be enlarged to include an inquiry into the origin and development of animal life. This investigation, in the hands of men like Darwin, Spencer, and Huxley, soon included an inquiry into the source and means of progress of humankind; and it soon also brought forth a revolutionary conception of development. In the eighteenth century the animal world had been looked upon as a series of species or types, but it had never been supposed that the types evolved into one another; each was thought of as independent. Now it was demonstrated by careful investigation that species or types did change into others. In short, development had become evolution. Though Darwin was by far the greatest scientist to investigate the supposed laws of evolution, Herbert Spencer made the most ambitious effort to apply evolution as a universal interpretive principle, using it to explain the development of human society as well as of the animal kingdom. His doctrine of integration followed by differentiation remains highly suggestive to the historian even today.

The old view of the factors involved in the development of organic life had been childishly naïve, falling back upon a series of cosmic cataclysms to explain what was otherwise inexplicable. Darwin declared that the true factors were increasing complexity, infinite differentiation, adaptation to environment, natural selection by the survival of the fittest, and the transmission of acquired characteristics. Previously an apparently unbridgeable gap had existed between men and dumb animals; now this chasm was filled. Previously no clear alternative had been offered to the theological doctrine of creation; now one was formulated. Previously a huge body of historical facts had seemed trivial and without sequence or relationship; now relationships could be suggested and the significance of nearly all facts demonstrated. A large number of biological analogies suggested themselves to students of history. It is hardly too much to say that most departments of human thought reoriented themselves after the publication of *The Origin of Species*, and history was one.

Within a single generation the range of evolutionary interpretations became extremely wide. It ran from Freeman's work on the evolution of the English Constitution, and Sir Henry Maine's on the evolution of law, both highly scientific in character, to such a book as Winwood Reade's summary of world history called *The Martyrdom of Man* — a book which, first published in 1872, has gone through fully a score of British and American editions. Reade pictures the past of mankind in colors of repellent darkness, and hints at a future of dazzling brightness; finding the bridge between the two in the process of evolutionary betterment. In America the Spencerian interpretation was best applied to history by John Fiske. He interpreted the rise of democracy in this country by analogy from biological evolution, and explained it as analogous to the growth of British democracy from the ancient Teutonic folk moot. The word evolution soon crept into book-titles, and has become so firmly established there that no conceivable force could dislodge it; men write on the Evolution of Congress, the Evolution of Fashions, the Evolution of the Novel, the evolution of every force or social element that has a history. The biological analogy is seldom encountered, and even when met is seldom pushed far. But it is safe to assert that more than half the historians now writing bring insensibly to their interpretation of the facts at least a few fragmentary ideas of the mutation of species or types, of adaptation to environment, and of natural selection by survival of the fittest. Their minds have consciously or unconsciously taken much of the Darwinian mould.

IV

It is impossible to pursue further the various interpretations brought in by new scientific knowledge or theories. Psychology has resulted in the rewriting of a vast deal of history; not merely by furnishing new concepts of great leaders, but by throwing fresh light on mass-emotion, mass-thinking, the behavior of special groups, and the growth and decay of certain states of mind. The newer medical knowledge, as everyone can see by reading Dr. Hans Zinsser's *Rats, Lice, and History* or Dr. C. MacLaurin's works on the pathological record of eminent men and women, has affected the treatment of the past.[1] The progress of economic geography has made possible brilliant new interpretations of history. And this scientific advance goes on along an ever-widening front. Many old views are slowly discarded; few present-day historians would think of citing Buckle or Comte to buttress an interpretation — many do not even know what they taught. But even the exploded and

[1] In *Post Mortem* Dr. MacLaurin deals with the medical history of Joan of Arc, Charles V, Anne Boleyn, Napoleon I, and Cellini; in *Mere Mortals* with the medical record of Ivan the Terrible, Henry VIII, Frederick the Great, James I, and others. He thinks that the true reason for Charles V's retirement lay in arteriosclerosis.

outmoded theories have helped to generate a spirit of unfettered inquiry and discussion, to stimulate men to use new tools fearlessly, and to give historical study a pervading atmosphere of alertness and energy. Believers in history realize that it must be kept in touch with other branches of knowledge, and abreast of them. As a result of the successive injections of new ideas, today we have numerous large schools of historical interpretation, and a great many minor schools or sub-schools.

The oldest of the schools is the still-surviving group of religious-minded historians. While the theological philosophy of history has decayed in the sense that few men would think of making Christianity the central pattern of world-history, nevertheless many writers believe that certain phases of history illuminate God's workings in the world. Sometimes the belief is explicit, more often sub-conscious. Thomas Carlyle wrote of the French Revolution as a gigantic object-lesson in the penalty that quackery, greed, and evil bring upon themselves, a tremendous illustration of God's determination to make crooked ways straight. With theological dogmas Carlyle had no patience whatever; he condemned them as "Hebrew old-clothes," talked of priests as apes chattering by the banks of the Dead Sea, and remarked that Newman had the brains of a moderate-sized rabbit. But he was highly religious in a deeper, more mystical sense, and his histories are the utterances of a religious prophet preaching by pictures of the past — flaming and unforgettable pictures. Often accused of holding that Might makes Right, he protested sternly that he believed the precise opposite; that Right and Might are in the long run identical because Right alone is ultimately enduring. His belief that Right is the expression of the divine will he wrought into every texture of his histories. It was of course a very different type of religious history that John Henry Newman wrote, but it had more force than Carlyle believed. And many later historians have had theological preconceptions. The shallower kind of religious history receives — and de-

serves — general disregard. We have little patience today
with George Bancroft remarking in his eulogy of Lincoln:
"That God rules in the affairs of men is as certain as any truth
of physical science . . . Kings are lifted up and thrown down,
nations come and go . . . but nothing is by chance, though
men, in their ignorance of causes, may think so. The deeds of
time are governed, as well as judged, by the decrees of eternity."
We have little patience with Hilaire Belloc's twaddle about the
figure of an Ultramontane and very Bellocian God in all human
affairs.[1] But history that discloses a deep pervasive under-
current of religious conviction may often merit the utmost respect. As Woodrow Wilson declared, the record of nations
possesses a spiritual quality, and is fundamentally a product
"not of institutions, but of the heart."

An almost equally venerable school of writers still interprets
history largely by the lamp of political science. They hold
that the most significant aspect of the human past lies in the
effort of men to give objective form to the principles of governmental theory. Of this school Von Ranke remains the great
exemplar, for even his studies in church history were essentially
studies in statecraft and state-organization. To it belong such
English historians as Gardiner and Froude; such French historians as Guizot and Michelet; such American historians as
Schouler and Rhodes. It remains strong despite all the inroads of the "new" history. So young a scholar as Mr. Crane
Brinton can write: "Not so very long ago, most of us knew
what to expect when we encountered the word history. We
could count on an orderly narrative of the doings of kings and

[1] A famous passage in Newman's *Apologia Pro Vita Sua* (Chapter V)
shows that even he sometimes lost faith in a divine pattern. He speaks of
the unhappy lot of mankind — "their aimless courses, their random
achievements and acquirements, the impotent conclusions of long-standing
facts, the tokens so faint and broken of a superintending design, the blind
evolution of what turn out to be great powers or truths, the progress of
things as if from unreasoning elements, not towards final causes . . . all
this . . . inflicts upon the mind the sense of a profound mystery, which is
utterly beyond human solution."

statesmen, soldiers and priests . . ." [1] It will continue to persist and to show strength. In the hands of this group history is a definite and dignified entity, explaining much that is undeniably of first importance in the past, and offering a fixed and solid discipline to the mind. Its history is narrow and at times a bit arid, but it possesses form and significance. While the record of mankind has become much more than the history of states, state-history remains no mean part of it.

One of the most vigorous schools of all, the school which expounds one form or another of the economic interpretation of history, now boasts of so many departments that it has become difficult to treat it under a single rubric. It has been an extremely fertile school, producing within a century a vast sea of historical literature. For example, Labriola calls the Reformation an economic rebellion of the German nation, and R. H. Tawney has placed the whole Reformative movement on an economic basis. Émile Durkheim (a sociologist rather than historian) asserts that history is essentially the progress of the principle of division of labor.[2] Marxian or pseudo-Marxian historians have interpreted the record of many communities and nations as primarily a history of the division and antagonism of classes — the class conflict. Some historians of the economic school, like Guglielmo Ferrero, have taken a highly pessimistic view of the course of the human race. Some, like H. G. Wells, who has also been greatly influenced by evolutionary doctrine and Marxian ideas, are highly optimistic; they look forward to the rise of society from level to level until it attains a millennial state. The ablest of all the compendious histories of the American people, Charles and Mary Beard's *Rise of American Civilization*, is primarily an economic interpretation. Anyone who looks at a critical bibliography of American history must be struck by the sweeping extent of the present-day movement for rewriting the history of American colonization, American

---

[1] *Saturday Review of Literature*, August 14, 1937
[2] Cf. Émile Durkheim's *De la Division de la Travail Social* (1893)

expansion, the Revolutionary and Civil Wars, and the party conflicts, in terms of their economic springs. But this tendency toward economic reinterpretation has gained equal vigor in almost all Western lands.

The school which presents a geographical interpretation of history is by no means a mere subdivision of the preceding school, but maintains a place of its own. It holds that the degree of a people's civilization is determined primarily by its physical surroundings and by climatic influences. One of the most important living exponents of this theory, Ellsworth Huntington, has made particularly notable studies of the influence of climate upon history. To the stimulating effect of certain climates, conjoined with the possession of rich natural resources and other factors, he attributes the rise of great civilizations in a few favored lands — the western part of the European continent, the British Isles, eastern North America. To the lack of such stimulation he attributes the cultural barrenness of other lands, and to changes in the climate he would trace much of the decay of earlier civilizations in Western Asia and the Mediterranean basin. More modest and conventional uses of geography are to be found in the writings of such Americans as Ellen C. Semple and R. H. Brigham. But the whole relation of geography and history must be reserved for fuller treatment later in this volume.

Social history, cultural history, intellectual history — these names are applied to the work of various interpretive groups between which it is hard to draw clear boundary lines; groups which all unite, however, in giving history a wide and loose significance. Cultural history can perhaps be set in a special category. In the strictest sense it is a history of cultural institutions related to underlying currents of national or community life. Leslie Stephen in his *English Literature and Society in the Eighteenth Century* (1904), an admirable example, not merely furnishes a systematic and satisfactory history of English letters from Addison to Walter Scott. He goes further and shows how the *content* of this literature arose from the social conditions of the time. Not only this, but he goes still further and demonstrates that literary form itself has a vital unity with these social conditions. That is, the lines along which this form — the drama, the epic, the essay, the novel — will develop, depend upon the character, origin, and tastes of the literary class which uses it as a vehicle for its ideas and impulses; upon the constitution of the reading class which offers a market for these ideas; and upon the correspondence between these ideas and the most powerful intellectual tendencies of the time. W. J. Courthope's comprehensive *History of English Poetry* places the development of prosody upon a solid foundation in the developing social conditions of English history. Such a striking little masterpiece of interpretation as Taine's *Art of the Netherlands* does the same. So, also, do the learned, vivid, and beautifully written (though occasionally inaccurate) volumes of John Addington Symonds on the Renaissance, and Burckhardt's single volume on the subject; Georg Brandes's *Main Currents in Nineteenth Century Literature;* and Parrington's work. Samuel Eliot Morison's history of Harvard in the seventeenth and eighteenth centuries presents a highly satisfactory cultural history of all early New England.

Sociological and social history of course constitute a much larger and vaguer department of scholarship and letters. At the one extreme we find a group which would base history upon the dictum of Franklin H. Giddings: "Sociology is an attempt to account for the origin, growth, structure, and activities of society by the operation of physical, vital, and psychological causes working together in the process of evolution." This group has given us books like Kidd's *Social Evolution*, which is a brilliant interpretation of the function of religion in history, and J. Donald Forrest's *Development of Western Society.* At the other extreme we find a group devoted to what the Germans long ago called *kulturgeschichte* — that is, writers who attempt to describe the life of a people during a certain period in all its phases. An early example is offered by Karl Biedermann's *Germany in the 18th Century*. Excellent recent examples are offered by the best volumes of *The History of American Life*, edited by Arthur M. Schlesinger and Dixon Ryan Fox, and inspired in part by H. D. Traill's coöperative work, *Social England*. The principal weakness of this type of history is that in undisciplined hands it easily grows into an encyclopaedia of unrelated details, a mountain of petty facts piled loosely together. These facts may be departmentalized by labelling one part of them The Changing Church, another part The Educational Revival, another Home Life, another The Deepening of Culture, another Professions and Business. But an encyclopaedia is not converted into history by departmentalizing it. Carefully pondered principles of selection — principles of high and permanent significance — are necessary before the facts of social history can be properly assayed; and even when this is done, effective presentation of the facts requires an insight that approaches genius. The best specimens of social history in English remain the third chapter of Macaulay's *History of England*, and the first six chapters of Henry Adams's *History of the United States Under Jefferson and Madison*.[1]

V

As from philosophy we descend to interpretation, so from the latter we descend to thesis or synthesis. Perhaps few works of history are directly touched by philosophy. Many of the best are also quite untouched by any special interpretation; Macaulay and Parkman, for example, rather wrote history according to their individual bent than according to any school of thought, though accepting to some extent the idea of the superior significance of the state. But few histories of any distinction lack a thesis, or if that word is too strong, at least a definite principle of synthesis; the author wishing to demonstrate some view. It may be a commonplace and obvious view.

[1] Two political historians!

It may be marked by great originality and insight, and in the most brilliant histories it is. But history which lacks a thesis is a body lacking a skeleton — it is invertebrate. It may contain exhaustive research, may be striking in detail, may throw new light into dark places, but its total effect will be limp. Channing's volumes on the colonial period contain no thesis worth mentioning, while those of George Louis Beer contain a sharp-cut, novel, and emphatic thesis. The result is that while nobody ever speaks of Channing's ideas, Beer's ideas have been a staple of discussion ever since they were propounded; while we try to remember Channing's facts, we very distinctly remember Beer's views.

More than once a volume enforcing a thesis has changed the views of millions and itself made history. Thus it was with Treitschke's insistence upon the importance of national unity and a powerful central government; his histories altered the attitude of a multitude of Germans toward their national destiny. Some have traced Germany's plunge into the World War to his works, as a generation earlier some students ascribed the War of 1870 to the histories of Thiers. Frederick J. Turner's thesis of the effect of the frontier upon American life and character has colored not only all historical thought in this country, but all literary thought, all social thought, and all political thought. Alfred T. Mahan, by the vigorous thesis of his *Influence of Seapower upon History, 1660–1783,* followed by his *Influence of Seapower upon the French Revolution, 1783–1812,* affected the governmental policy of all the great maritime powers. His interpretation threw an entirely new light upon one department of the past, and read from it arresting and convincing lessons for the future. Japan, Germany, Great Britain, and the United States applied these lessons to their naval programs and strategy.

Sometimes a historical thesis may be non-controversial. Students could hardly quarrel over the central thesis of Parkman's *Jesuits in North America,* for example; which is simply that the Jesuits failed because they built their hopes of an American empire on the Hurons and their kindred tribes, and these were ultimately conquered by the hostile Iroquois. Parkman himself spoke of this thesis as "obvious," and drew from it only an elementary inference: "Liberty may thank the Iroquois that, by their insensate fury, the plans of her adversary were brought to nought and a peril and a woe averted from her future." More commonly, however, the thesis is avowedly controversial. Take, for example, any one of the half dozen principal works upon the authorship of Homer. After Friedrich A. Wolf's epochal *Prolegomena to Homer* (an astonishing piece of work for its early date, 1795), which contended that the Iliad and Odyssey in their present-day form have been materially changed from the originals, and are made up of separate poems composed at different times by various authors, it was impossible to write on that subject without some highly argumentative thesis. Andrew Lang in *Homer and His Age* sounded a counterblast to the disintegrationists. He held that the Iliad, far from being the work of four or five centuries, a score of bards, and a medley of old and new ideas, was the product of a single age and a single state of culture, the poet describing his own environment. It was an age which had given up burial and adopted cremation, substituted iron tools for bronze while still retaining bronze weapons, and learned the art of writing, so that it preserved Homer's work on palm leaves, papyrus, or parchment, now perished. Or as examples of controversy, take the innumerable theses applied to the French Revolution. That great event is still current politics as well as past history. Pierre Saro writes of it with a Royalist thesis, and his idealization of the Ancien Régime has gone through some seventy-five editions in France; Prince Kropotkin writes of it with an Anarchist thesis; Albert Mathiez writes with a Radical Socialist, even a Communist, thesis, idealizing the Terror.

Sometimes a thesis rests upon striking new evidence which

really puts an entirely different face upon an old problem. Thus several books have now been written, based upon fresh documentary material, to show that the soul of Abolitionism in the years 1835–60 was not found in William Lloyd Garrison and his Boston group, as men long supposed, but in the Tappan brothers of New York, the Grimkés, and Theodore D. Weld, that Garrison was rather an encumbrance than an aid to the progress of Abolition, and gained his prominence partly by accident, partly by rashness, and partly by an insatiable appetite for the spotlight. Sometimes the thesis represents rather a stimulating new study of old material. Henry Osborn Taylor's *The Medieval Mind* affords an example. Most of the evidence he examined was familiar to everybody. But he took the unusual view that the true key to the medieval mind lay not in the vernacular writings, English, French, Spanish, and so on, but in the Latin writings of the period, which he held incomparably more valuable for the study of medieval thought — even Dante being in a sense but a byroad from the main highway of medieval culture. He amplified this thesis by stating that the supreme medieval achievement in thought was the "vital appropriation and emotional humanizing of patristic Christianity," represented by such thinkers as Albertus Magnus and Thomas Aquinas. Or a thesis may combine interesting new material with a novel reworking of old material; see Henri Pirenne's view, in his *Economic and Social History of Medieval Europe*, that it was not the collapse of the Roman Empire but the swift rise of the Moslem empire which in the eighth century cut off Western Europe from its Eastern economic connections.

Sometimes the thesis of a book may carry almost instant conviction. Julius W. Pratt's *Expansionists of 1812*, for example, made so clear the rôle of land-hunger in provoking the second war against Great Britain that at once every student stood ready to accord that factor much greater emphasis than before. Sometimes the thesis may be regarded dubiously. A good example is presented by Owsley's *King Cotton Diplomacy*.

Its argument that the blockade of the South was totally ineffective until late in the Civil War — an argument based on figures of captures rather than comparative trade figures — seems worse than dubious to experts on the diplomacy of the period. And sometimes the extravagance of an argument soon puts its maker out of court. Take, for example, the various forms of overstatement in Sydney George Fisher's interesting and provocative *Struggle for American Independence*. He asserts, quite correctly, that the struggle did not arise from British misrule, but from an effort by the British to reorganize their colonial system, and by using the sovereignty recognized as belonging to their government, to modernize it. He goes on to say that this assertion of sovereignty was an absolute necessity after the expulsion of the French from North America — that it was imperative that it be carried through if Great Britain were to retain her control. It was not, he further argued, a policy begun carelessly and stupidly by a corrupt government and arrogant king; it was launched after long deliberation and investigation by capable statesmen who were asserting the only principles upon which, at that time, colonies could be retained and governed. On the part of the Americans, independence was the object in view from the opening hour of the quarrel, and with many even before sharp friction began. The way for it had been paved by economic interests and political ideas which had long made an attempt at independence inevitable. These last assertions all contain some truth — but they also contain a great deal of error.

VI

It is the special glory of history that it touches the realm of ideas at more points than almost any other study. Regarded by many as singularly arid in original thought (and with some reason in view of the multitude of mere factual compilations miscalled history), its greatest productions are actually shot through with intellectual elements. Written history is in the deepest sense the world of our epistomological construction of reality; as such it draws from and contributes to the profoundest metaphysical thought of the ages. In a more prosaic sense, it responds to every great new current of ideas that flows through the Western World; it has so responded from the time of St. Augustine to that of Darwin, Bergson, and Einstein, and it will continue to respond. In still more practical fashion, it has vital connections with every other social science — economics, sociology, public law, jurisprudence, social psychology, human geography — and relations of importance with the chief physical sciences, from biology to geophysics. As they grow and change, the content and outlook of history, the range of its ideas, grow and change also. Finally, history challenges its disciples to arrange the ever-growing mass of facts in ever-better patterns, and thus offers scope for the keenest insight and the most subtle ingenuity. All in all, success in history is proportioned as exactly to intellectual power as success in pure literature or in pure science. Behind every really great history stands a great man:

> Not from a vein of shallow thought
> His awful Jove young Phidias brought.

With the special glory of its many-sided relation to ideas, history has also a special responsibility. The intellectual element is but one part of history, and its ideas must never be given too loose a rein. As the bounds of history widen, as its outer territories become vague and shadowy, the importance of maintaining precise standards of factual accuracy and a high level of significance increases. History pushed too far toward sociology, like sociology pushed too far toward history, falls into a limbo in which it lacks form and value. Interpretation should be the leaven of the lump; but the result of applying a pound of interpretation to an ounce of fact is disappointing. A balance must be maintained between history as a body of facts, based solidly upon research, and history as an exercise in analysis, interpretation, and generalization.

CHAPTER TEN

MAN'S HOME AND HIS HISTORY

BEYOND QUESTION, the first science which men perceived to have a helpful or auxiliary relation to History was Geography. The connection between them is so intimate that it could not escape the most elementary observers. At least as early as the time of the Greek philosopher Parmenides, whose ideas were later elaborated by Aristotle, thinkers conceived of both physical geography and climate as having an influence upon human action. Parmenides, like Aristotle after him, believed that the earth was a sphere; and he described it as containing a torrid zone in which man could not act effectively because of heat, two frigid zones in which they could not act effectively because of cold, and two temperate zones placed intermediately in which they could live with comfort and progress successfully. The Greek writer Strabo, who came much later, in the time of Julius Caesar, was both geographer and historian, and indeed combined the two equipments in a study of historical geography. To be sure, his conception of the relation between the two branches of knowledge was rudimentary; but he at least knew that a relation existed, and his great work on geography was so planned as to include mathematical geography, physical geography, political geography, and geography in relation to human history. He, like Parmenides, accepted the theory of a spherical earth, and of its division into five zones, whose conditions of life largely controlled human action. His descriptive writings contain numerous historical notices, often of high value.

When the Age of Exploration fully dawned in the fifteenth century, and men's ideas of the earth were first broadened to attain general accuracy, scholars began to perceive with greater force than ever before the truth which the Greeks had merely adumbrated. They gradually realized that however striking are man's conquests over nature, nevertheless the physical environment of man largely inspires and limits his activities. They perceived that the entire process of life upon the planet is a process of adaptation — that this principle applies as fundamentally to the civilized German or Englishman as to bird, beast, or fish. Hakluyt, in introducing his *Voyages*, declared: "Geography and Chronology I may call the sun and the moon, the right eye and the left, of all history" — thus assigning geography a higher rank than chronology. Another early British writer on geography, Peter Heylyn, declared in his *Microcosmus* in 1625 that while geography could possess a certain vitality without history, the converse was not true. "History without geography, like a dead carcass, hath neither life nor motion at all, but moves at best but slowly on the understanding." Francis Bacon also showed that the Elizabethan Age possessed some very modern notions of the interrelation of history and geography. As knowledge in both domains grew, men of course became able to demonstrate this relationship more completely. By the last decades of the eighteenth century, the greater part of the world had been roughly mapped, while Voltaire, Hume, Gibbon, and other writers had introduced the critical age in historical writing. In fine, the scientific temper had been applied to both subjects; myth and tradition were being fast eradicated from cartography and historiography alike. It is not surprising, therefore, to find the philosopher Kant by this time giving a broad and systematic statement of the interdependence of history and geography.

A genuine understanding of this many-sided interdependence, indeed, was perhaps first exhibited in Kant's lectures on geography at the University of Königsberg beginning in 1765. He taught that history and geography were two parts of a whole: one being a description of the world and its inhabitants in the order of time, the other a description of them in the order of space. He taught also that physical geography was the primary basis of history, for it was the great determinant of various branches of geography which obviously affected and controlled history. That is, it was the determinant of (1) moral geography, which has reference to the different characters and customs of peoples, varying according to the lands they occupy; (2) of political geography, which has reference to the governmental divisions of mankind; (3) of mercantile geography, or as we should now say, economic geography, which refers to the various occupations of mankind; and (4) of theological geography, which has reference to the distribution of religions. It is clear that an epochal forward step had been taken in relating the human past to the human environment when students began to be taught, for example, that the history of religions has been largely determined by soil, climate, natural resources, physical communications, and like factors. That teaching effectively began with Kant. Some of his ideas were peculiar; he believed, for instance, that the vertical relief of the land was of particular importance to human development. But he set men thinking, and even his more bizarre doctrines inspired other students to inquiry. There were broad hints of the evolutionary theory itself in Kant's writings upon physical geography.

Alexander von Humboldt was strictly a geographer; a geographer who, beginning with his voyage to South America in 1799, and ending with his trip to the Urals and Yenisei in 1829, travelled over almost the whole known world to make his observations, and gathered and classified a huge body of facts upon physical geography. His *Cosmos* was published between 1845 and 1858. He was not greatly interested in history, for what absorbed most of his attention was simply the forms of the land's surface. But he had an encyclopaedic range of observation; he made interesting studies of the languages, architecture, and customs of ancient peoples in Central and South America; and he demonstrated that land forms exercise a determining influence not only upon climate, plant life, and animal life, but upon man himself. For this great principle he offered a multutide of interesting illustrations. His eminent contemporary Carl Ritter (1779–1859), who was less strictly a geographer, expanded and disseminated the same views. He became far more interested than Humboldt was in the influence of climate and terrestrial relief upon human history. He was thus led deeper and deeper into a study of archaeology and history; and his voluminous work on geography, *Die Erdkunde*, an encyclopaedia of geographical lore as to Asia and Africa, gives great space to the effect of the earth's surface upon man, and is thus largely historical in content. He asserts that certain parts of the world were predestined for the historical rôle which they actually played. It has been complained that some of his followers look upon geography rather as an auxiliary of history than an independent study.

II

By the time of Ritter's and Humboldt's deaths, the relationship between geography and history was occupying numerous other able pens. Buckle, in the first volume of his *History of Civilization in England*, laid down the great geographical laws which he believed contributed so powerfully to the governance of history. He agreed with John Stuart Mill that the most crude, vulgar, and irritating of all means of evading the effect of physical and social influences upon the human mind was "that of attributing the diversities of conduct and character to inherent natural differences." He classified under four heads the physical agencies exerting the most powerful influence upon the human race — climate; food; soil; and the general aspect of nature. The first three, as he explained, must be studied together, for each is largely dependent on the others. These three influence mankind, he declared, primarily because they govern the accumulation of wealth, and the amount of wealth in turn governs the culture of peoples. Under the rubric of soils, he called attention to the roving Tartars who forsook the barren steppes of Asia, and betook themselves to the fertile plains and valleys of China, Asia, and Russia, there developing great empires and civilizations; to the Arabs who left their stony deserts, and developed brilliant civilizations at Bagdad and Cordova.

Buckle also pointed out that physical causes governed not only the accumulation but the *distribution of* wealth. In dealing with this topic, he presents some suggestive pages upon the relation of cheap foods to the growth, standards, and general culture of different populations — rice to India; the date to Egypt; the potato to Ireland; and maize and potatoes to the natives of Peru — showing how such cheap food for the laboring masses may be a national handicap rather than a benefit. In this connection, he hints at the familiar fact that temperate climates, with alternating seasons of plenty and scarcity, develop provident characteristics in a nation. Turning to the general aspects of nature, Buckle attempts to show that it does much in different lands (1) to stir the imagination (2) to affect the understanding. He ascribes to scenery, for example, much of the difference between the ancient civilizations of India, where nature shows itself in forms of "startling magnitude," and of Greece, where it manifests itself in forms more suave, beautiful, and "less threatening to man." Buckle's geographic interpretation of history is impressive not so much by reason of any novelty — for his general ideas are not new — as through its systematic, closely reasoned character, and its many pregnant and thought-provoking observations.

Beyond question Buckle exaggerated the effect of environment on human societies and its rôle in history. Nevertheless, there was much truth in what he wrote; and his influence was enormous, for he was read all over the world with immense enthusiasm — and unlike Humboldt and Ritter, is still read.

His contemporary Michelet, in the second volume of his *History of France*, showed the influence of the general ideas of the times by giving much space to a treatment of the physical geography of the country. "History is first of all geography," he wrote, and added: "Without a geographical basis, the people, the actors of history, seem to be walking in air, as in Chinese paintings. . . . Ground or soil is not only the theatre of the action. Through food, climate, etc., its influence is felt in a hundred ways. As the nest, so the bird, and as the country, so the man." Indeed, few European historians writing on a broad scale after 1850 failed to take note of geographic factors. We may instance, as a not untypical figure, John Richard Green. Geography is sketched in, briefly to be sure, at every stage of his *Short History of the English People*. And in another book, *The Making of England* (1882), geography is almost the chief actor in the drama. Green of course introduces us to Roman and Dane, Jute and Saxon. But the physical state of the country — with the fens, the downs, the forests, the chalk areas, the mountain fastnesses — is shown on almost every page as determining the conduct of the piratical raiders, the defenders, and the new colonists. Note, for example, the passage in which he describes why London became London:

The commercial greatness of London has made men forget its military importance, but from the first moment of history until late in the Middle Ages London was one of the strongest of our fortresses. Its site, indeed, must have been dictated, like that of most early cities, by the advantages which it presented as well for defence as for trade. It stood at the one point at which either merchant or invader could penetrate from the estuary into the valley of the Thames; and in its earlier days, before the great changes wrought by the embankment of the Romans, this was also the first point at which any rising ground for the site of such a town presented itself on either shore of the river. Nowhere has the hand of man moulded ground into shapes more strangely contrasted with its natural form than on the site of London. Even as late as the time of Caesar, the soil which a large part of it covers can have been little but a vast morass. Below Fulham the river stretched at high tide over the ground that lies on either side of its present channel from the rises of Kensington and Hyde Park to the opposite shores of Peckham and Camberwell. All Pimlico and Westminster to the north, to the south all Battersea and Lambeth, all Newington and Kennington, all Bermondsey and Rotherhithe, formed a vast lagoon, broken only by little rises which became the "eyes" and "hithes," the "islands" and "landing-rises," of later settlements. Still lower down to the eastward the swamp widened as the Lea poured its waters into the Thames in an estuary of its own — an estuary which ran far to the north over as wide an expanse of marsh and fen, while at its mouth it stretched its tidal waters over the mud flats. . . . Near the point where the two rivers meet, a traveller who was mounting the Thames from the sea saw the first dry land to which his bark could steer. The spot was, in fact, the extremity of the low line of rising ground which was thrown out from the heights of Hampstead that border the river-valley to the north, and which passed over the sites of our Hyde Park and Holborn to thrust itself on the east into the great morass. This eastern portion of it, however, was severed from the rest of the rise by the deep gorge of a stream which fell from the northern hills, the stream of the Fleet, whose waters, long since lost in the London sewers, ran in earlier days between steep banks to the Thames at Blackfriars.

The rise or "dun" that stretched from this tidal channel of the Fleet to the spot now marked by the Tower, and which was destined to become the site of London, rose at its highest some fifty feet above the level of the tide. . . . Such a position was admirably adapted for defence. It was, indeed, almost impregnable. Sheltered to east and south by the lagoons of the Lea and the Thames, guarded to westward by the deep cleft of the Fleet, it saw stretching along its northern border the broad fen whose name has survived in our modern Moorgate. Nor, as the first point at which merchants could land from the great river, was the spot less adapted for trade. But it was long before the trader found dwelling on its soil. Old as it is, London is far from being one of the oldest of English cities; till the coming of the Romans, indeed, the loneliness of its site seems to have been unbroken by any settlement whatever. The "dun" was in fact the centre of a great wilderness. Beyond the marshes to the east lay the forest track of Southern Essex. Across the lagoon to the south rose . . . woodlands.

. . . To the north the heights of Highgate and Hampstead were crowned with forest masses through which the boar and the wild ox wandered without fear of man down to the days of the Plantagenets.

With the coming of the Romans, however, this solitude passed away. We know nothing of the settlement of the town; but its advantages as the first landing-place along the Thames secured for it at once the command of all trading intercourse with Gaul, and through Gaul with the empire at large.[1]

III

But much as had been done by 1880 to relate geography and history, a more advanced set of principles remained to be discovered. In the latter part of the nineteenth century arose the eminent founder of human geography, or anthropogeography, as Friedrich Ratzel himself called it. The first volume of his *Anthropo-Geographie* appeared in 1882, and the second in 1891. It is not unfair to say that Ratzel, with such enthusiastic pupils as the Frenchman Jean Brunhes, have attempted to reverse the concept held by Carl Ritter, that geography is an appanage of history, and substitute a concept in which no true historian will acquiesce — that history is an appanage of geography. Anthropogeography has been defined as the science of the expansion and distribution of mankind over the earth. To Brunhes we owe the best brief and adequate explanation of the objects which Ratzel sought in his published works. "He considers the human race and human peoples in a constant state of displacement, ferment, expansion, and retreat, and from his point of view history is merely the sum of population-movements. But he also treats of peoples and societies as developing in natural domains, occupying a definite area and requiring a certain amount of territory for subsistence and growth. He attaches great importance not only to immediate environment, but to the relation of peoples to the position of the continents, the seas, and the islands, to the zones, to vegeta-

[1] John Richard Green, *The Making of England*, pp. 95, 96

tion-belts, to accidents of relief, and to the great pathways of land and sea commerce."

One of Ratzel's principal doctrines is that the relation between man and his environment is not that of two hostile and contending forces, but is a process in which man develops himself as part of the earth's equipment. Man has been changed by terrestrial transformations — by glacial ages, warm ages, changes in plant and animal life, changes in rivers, lakes, and seas; man today is a product not only of social development, but of the planet's development, and is inseparably linked with his mother-earth. A second of Ratzel's doctrines, and a very weak one, is that nations and societies are actual *organisms* responding to nature as an animal does to its physical environment. He emphasizes the distribution of population (which depends upon geographical factors) as one of the key-elements in all history. Civilization and political superiority, he maintains, have always flourished in the thickly populated districts; and the whole of human development has been a progression from small populations dwelling in extensive regions to large populations concentrated in more limited areas.

Among the principal followers of Ratzel have been Ellen C. Semple in America, Elisée Réclus in France, and Halford J. Mackinder in England — though they of course do not accept all of Ratzel's teachings. They agree upon the fundamental postulate that a great part of history must be treated as the result of geographical factors; that looking back of every historical event, we will nearly always find a geographical fact expressed in it. "Back of Massachusetts's passionate abolition movement," writes Miss Semple, "it [human geography] sees the granite soil and boulder-strewn fields of New England; back of the South's long fight for the maintenance of slavery, it sees the rich plantations of tidewater Virginia and the teeming fertility of the Mississippi bottomlands. This is the geographical significance of Herder's saying that 'history is geography set in motion.' What is today a fact of geography becomes tomorrow a factor of history." Miss Semple's theories are set forth in her book on *The Influence of Geographical Environment*. She differentiates four great classes of geographical influence: (1) direct physical effect; (2) psychical effects; (3) economic and social effects; and (4) effects on the movements of populations. Like Réclus, she emphasizes the necessity of distinguishing between the static aspects of the geographic environment, and the dynamic aspects, changed oftenest by man's own inventions. Seas, oceans, rivers, were once great barriers; but later man's hand made them the avenues of civilization. Miss Semple's ideas are to some extent applied in her earlier volume on *American History and its Geographic Conditions* — a book which describes first the effect of the geography of Western Europe upon American history; then the part played by the great coastal rivers; then that of the Appalachian mountain barrier; and then that of the interior rivers and plains. She explains, for example, precisely why it was that Kentucky was settled by a trail that led across the headwaters of the Tennessee.

The effort to formulate novel laws regarding the influence of geography upon history, and to strike out fertile new generalizations, has by no means ceased and will not do so. The most daring recent theorem has been the attempt of Dr. Ellsworth Huntington to establish a direct and invariable connection between a stimulating climate and a high degree of civilization. "Whatever the motive power of history may be," he writes, "one of the chief factors in determining its course has been geography; and among geographical forces, changes of climate have been the most potent for good or bad." A stimulating climate, in his opinion, is one which, though generally temperate — neither excessively hot nor excessively cold for long periods — nevertheless fluctuates constantly in temperature and humidity, so that the body is kept in a perpetual state of readjustment. Such a climate exists today in the Eastern United States, in the British Isles, in Northern Europe, in Argentina, and in New Zealand; it does not exist in India, Brazil, or Southern California. He believes that it existed not only in ancient Greece and Rome, but in ancient Egypt, Assyria, and Babylonia; that is, he attacks the conventional notion that civilization first developed in warm climates, and later was transferred to the temperate zone. Instead, he contends that all the successive centres of civilization had about the same climate at the time their cultures reached an apex — the inference being that the climate north of the equator has been slowly growing warmer. But while asserting that "prolonged study of past and present climatic variations suggests that the location of some of the most stimulating conditions varies from century to century, and that when the great centres of antiquity rose to eminence they enjoyed a climatic stimulus comparable with that existing today where the leading nations now dwell," he carefully safeguards the implied generalization:

Today a certain type of climate prevails wherever civilization is high. In the past, the same type seems to have prevailed wherever a great civilization arose. Therefore, such a climate seems to be a necessary *condition* for great progress. This is not the cause of civilization, for that lies infinitely deeper. Nor is it the only, or the most important, condition. It is merely one of several, just as an abundant supply of pure water is one of the primary conditions of health. Good water will not make people healthy, nor will a favorable climate cause a stupid and degenerate race to rise to a high level.

Many of Dr. Huntington's conclusions seem open to question. We may well hesitate over his attempted correlation of periods of Roman expansion with eras of stimulating climate, periods of Roman decline with depressing climatic conditions; did the Italian climate change when Mussolini came in? He explains Germany's remarkable World War effort as due to the fact that "no other nation in the world has so many people who live under a highly stimulating climate"; but why did Germany remain politically and economically backward during two thousand years of substantially the same climate? Some observers believe that admirable civilizations may hereafter flourish in lands of heat and of uniform climate. The Australians hope that they may develop energetic and cultured communities in their equatorial zone, and are trying the experiment under almost ideal conditions. The human stock is one of the best in the world; natural resources are great; nothing need be feared from the native races; tropical diseases are few and science can control them; the Australian government is as good as any on the globe, and better than most. North Queensland, as Dr. Huntington admits in his book *West of the Pacific*, may yet disprove his generalization that a stimulating climate is a necessary condition for a splendid civilization.

One reason for a skeptical attitude toward Dr. Huntington's generalization lies in the fact that bad climates — i.e., climates bad for civilization — have so often been disease-ridden climates; and that the fall of some civilizations, the retardation of others, have been with little doubt traceable in part to epidemic or endemic ailments. Malaria has been a powerful factor in all recorded human history. It is quite possible that the decline of civilization in the Tigris-Euphrates basin has been due much more largely to the conquest of that area by malaria than to changes in climate. For centuries malaria affected a great part of Greece; for centuries it made the Roman Campagna one of the notorious fever-holes of the world. Students have seriously argued that, brought in from conquered lands, it was an important factor in the decline of Greek and Roman civilization. The effect of the hookworm upon the cultural level of society in our Southern States has undeniably been heavy; but Dr. Charles Stiles showed how it could be combated, and that brake upon progress is fast being removed. In recent times bilharzia — a disease rife in Egypt for thousands of years, for the examination of mummies has shown its ancient prevalence — has also been brought under control. Transmitted by a fast-breeding micro-organism, it penetrates the skin of any person who touches infected water, and causes debility, inanition, and death. It may well have cost civilization in Egypt much more than did any changes in the climate; for we possess no real evidence that the climate altered substantially in the centuries in which civilization was sinking from a high to a low level. During the World War competent pathologists accompanied the British troops to Egypt, set to work to discover why so many English soldiers died of bilharzia, isolated the micro-organism, and perfected preventive measures. Here again a brake upon progress is being fast removed.

IV

But while the influence of geography (including climate) upon history may be overstated — while it would be unfortunate if a rabid mania for geographical interpretation sprang up akin to the frenzy of many economic interpreters — beyond question the influence is great. Beyond question, also, its principal lines can be defined, though this is a complex matter. The dominion exercised over mankind by geography has not only taken exceedingly numerous forms, but has also varied in the most complicated fashion from age to age, according to the amount and kind of knowledge which man has been able to accumulate. The geographical controls effective in the dawn of history, when civilization first arose in the basins of the Nile, the Tigris, and the Euphrates, were very different from the controls effective some centuries later, when the Egyptians and Cretans, later followed by the Phoenicians and Greeks, learned what the Babylonians never did — to master the inland seas. China until recent times has remained in the Babylonian stage of mastery over its physical surroundings; that is, it has been a river nation instead of a maritime nation. But the Egyptians, Phoenicians, and Greeks learned to convert the Mediterranean from its ancient troublesome status of a barrier into the highly serviceable status of a highway.

Another revolution in man's relation to geography occurred

some centuries later, when the Romans perfected the art of road-building, and erected an empire which was held together partly by the old sea-roads, and partly by the new land-roads. Later still man's mastery of environment was enlarged by the discovery of improvements in shipbuilding and the art of navigation, which enabled him to convert the great oceans as well as the inland seas into highways. A new road to India was discovered; the new world of the Americas; Australia and the new world of the South. Thus a novel set of geographical controls was brought into existence, while the old set sank into desuetude. The seat of empire rapidly shifted from the Mediterranean to northwestern Europe, because this now became as much the centre of the new planet as Italy had been of the old *orbis terrarum*. Most of the geographical factors in this shift are familiar, but one of them may escape everybody save the specialist. This lies in the fact that northwestern Europe, and especially Great Britain, is a region of heavy tidal energy. These tides prevent the rivers from silting up; rising, they carry vessels far inland, against river currents and adverse winds; ebbing, they carry ships out to sea and around difficult headlands. Still later, when man's knowledge extended to the use of coal and steam, and the Industrial Revolution was born, yet another set of geographical controls achieved prominence. The lands endowed with a great deposit of stored energy in the form of coal were those which physical geography now favored. It is evident to everyone that the growing mastery of the air by mankind is doing away with certain former geographical controls, and substituting fresh and until recently unforeseen factors.

Thus man and environment act and react upon one another, and every advance in science, invention, and technology affects the force and pattern of the interaction. The subtle and often arresting ways in which geographical controls are established, broken down, and reshifted by man's capacity to seek out many inventions, present a challenge to the imagination and penetra-

tion of the historian. An admirable example of this form of
study is to be found in Walter P. Webb's *The Great Plains*.
The author of this volume shows how the broad section of the
United States between the Missouri and the Rockies was too
refractory for hand tools, and could be conquered only when
the Industrial Revolution had attained full maturity, and had
been brought into the heart of the area by railroad-building.
The plains country was level, windy, arid, hot in summer, cold
in winter, and practically devoid of timber; it was roamed by
especially vigorous and warlike Indian tribes, mounted on
horses that had descended from the stock of the Spanish explorers, and well armed with bows and arrows. The natural
resources of the region could not be exploited until special tools
were invented and used to overcome the obstacles. The introduction of the Colt revolver gave the mounted Westerner
superiority over the mounted Indian; fixed ammunition as-
sisted in the extermination of the buffalo. The cattle kingdom
sprang up as railways spread fanwise to an increasing number
of "cow-towns." Then the invention of barbed wire just after
the Civil War sharply reduced the costs of stock-growing and
crop protection in an area where no wood existed for fences.
The windmill gave the stockman and farmer a means of reaching water. Power machinery, culminating in the wheat-com-
bine, made low-cost grain crops possible; while after disastrous
experiences in periods of drought, methods of dry-farming were
introduced to aid settlers in the semi-arid belt. Altogether,
there are few sections in which human invention and industry
have altered the old geographical controls with more striking
results within a half century than in the Great Plains.

One broad generalization may thus be laid down regarding
the effect of geography upon history. "On the material side,"
as James Fairgrieve expresses it, "history is the story of man's
increasing ability to control energy." The progress of humanity
in practical fields may fairly be summed up as the history of its
endeavor to acquire and use as much energy as possible, and to

waste as little of it as could be avoided. While man's knowledge remained small, available energy was most abundant in warm fertile lands like Egypt and Mesopotamia, where life was sustained easily. At the same time, seasonal changes there required a provision against the future, and so inculcated forethought and the advantages of accumulation; people lived for the year, and not, as in Central Africa with its unfailing plenty, for the day. Another advantage was that, since desert and sea protected the community, no costly expenditure of energy for defence was needed. Step by step we may follow the pursuit of energy throughout world history to the present day, when the great coal, iron, and petroleum nations dominate the world. Whenever man learns a practical method of utilizing the energy of the tides, the radiation of the sun, or atomic forces, the geographic controls will again be revolutionized. This single generalization permits the student of history to take reasoned account of all the complex conditions of climate, communications, natural resources, and salubrity which govern the physical use of energy; it likewise permits us to take account of the jerky but irresistible increase in human knowledge which governs the use of energy on the technological side. It presents us with the two halves of that whole which constitutes the material element in history. But beyond this single broad generalization it is hardly profitable for students of history to go.

The applications and elaborations of this law, however, are endlessly instructive, and may of course be studied in various ways. For example, the complementary rôles of the plain, the mountain range, the desert, and the sea in the history of various nations is a subject full of illumination. Some students of geology assert that it was a subsidence of the flat Baltic plain early in the Christian era which caused the first large migration of Goths to the Black Sea area and the Danubian basin. Beyond question, the great invasions of the Roman Empire by the Huns and Goths in the fourth, fifth, and sixth centuries were made possible by the flatness of the Russian plain and the central European plain. An epigrammatist has remarked that Rome fell because the Chinese built a wall to keep out the Tartars. The statement is as unsatisfactory as most such sweeping dicta; but it is true that when the nomadic peoples of central Asia could no longer prey successfully upon the wide Chinese plain, they turned hungrily westward to the wide European plain. "Had Europe been ruled off from Asia by a great mountain range, there would have been no need for Constantine to build another capital on the Bosporus, nor perhaps for Gibbon to write his history." On the southwestern sector, fortunately, the central European plains did have protection by a mountain wall. When the Saracens poured northward through Spain and crossed the Pyrenees, their numbers diminishing in the process, Charles Martel smashed them at Tours; and they did not dare to repeat the experiment.

We may see the importance of the relation of mountain to plain in the sharp contrast between the happy history of Switzerland as a nation and the tragic history of Poland. The political explanation of the downfall of Poland in the eighteenth century emphasizes her vicious constitution, and the want of character in her governing class. But the geographical explanation emphasizes the fact that Poland was a flat country with no natural barriers to defend her, and so offered an irresistible temptation to the three great military powers surrounding her. They could thrust armies into Poland with ease. But Switzerland, though smaller and weaker, is protected by tremendous mountain ramparts. They have enabled a people of three races, three languages, and two religions to maintain their national unity and independence. One good reason for doubting the stability of the Czechoslovak Republic is that a glance at the map shows that its indefinite continuance in its present form is well-nigh a geographical impossibility. China is of course a great plain, but it is well protected on two sides by the Tibetan mountains and Gobi Desert. The broader aspects of its history have been well summed up by James Fairgrieve in a passage which indicates its complete dependence upon geographical factors. He writes that —

owing to the existence of three rivers, themselves the product of the more remote geographical conditions of relief and climate, China has produced a homogeneous people, whose essential unity has been strengthened by the existence on the west of a plateau of enormous breadth [Tibet]. These two sets of features, the river system and the plateau, are the chief controls of Chinese history.

Other geographical conditions have had a like result; the position of China fronting the open ocean, on the road to nowhere by sea, and the absence of any Mediterranean Sea, are great, silent, negative controls, which have to an incalculable degree tended to confirm the Chinese in their habits as landsmen, and to prevent their becoming seamen. Nor were the Chinese forced to take to the sea, as were the Norsemen, by the poverty of a cold, sterile land. There was no effective pressure behind, as was the case with the Saxon. China is vast enough to allow such pressures as did come from the plateau or Manchuria to dissipate themselves ere the seaboard was reached, and there was always the southern land where these pressures were less felt. No way reached the sea, as was the case with the Phoenicians. The coast of China is a great round curve with no peninsulas to tempt men seawards, as was the case with the Greeks. China has never been a seapower, because nothing has ever induced her peoples to be otherwise than landsmen, and landsmen dependent on agriculture, with the same habits and ways of thinking drilled into them through forty centuries; so that even when tribes from the plateau have broken in and seized the reins of power, even when millions of inhabitants have been massacred, China has not broken up into numberless units, as did the Roman Empire. The homogeneity of her people, the result to a very large extent of geographical conditions, has always asserted itself.

Some students have attempted, with no little success, to trace the influence of landscape upon national character. Various theories as to this influence have etched themselves upon literature: "When Freedom from her mountain height —"

Buckle, as we have seen, tried to lay down generalizations on the subject, and his principles may well possess more validity than the offhand student of the subject would think. Lord Bryce, in his *Memories of Travel*, remarks that he had once intended to give some account of the effect of North American scenery upon the American people, "finding in it a feature of the country which will continue through all the ages to affect the minds of its inhabitants." Beyond doubt this is true, though our country is too young and our population has been too mobile for this influence yet to exhibit itself strongly. But visitors to Southern California have already discerned there a regional character which exhibits a gay Mediterranean tinge, and which differs decidedly from the old-time Puritanism of rocky New England, or the dogged and somewhat unimaginative industriousness of the Middle West.[1] Ruskin believed that the scenery of the gray-sandstone country between Fribourg and Berne in Switzerland was ideal for the development of character and mind. André Siegfried, in a stimulating essay in human geography, maintains that the whole history of France since 1789 proves that the parts of the nation where limestone predominates have had a radical culture, while the portions where granite rocks have been predominant have had a conservative character! Moreover, he has furnished elaborate maps to help sustain this contention.

An interesting but more detailed and less significant part of

[1] Cf. Clarence Cason, *90° in the Shade*, pp. 45, 46: "I once was led to believe that I could interpret the Middle Western peoples in terms of my own impressions of their prairie lands. It seemed to me that my personal emotional reactions had given me the key to the restless urge of the Middle Western pioneers: the pent-up nervousness of their bodies, their determination to push their acres farther and farther toward the horizon. . . . As the mariner of the sea — so I reasoned with perhaps some injustice to such characters as those portrayed by Joseph Conrad and John Masefield — has but one ultimate pattern, which he constantly repeats from voyage to voyage, that of working with all his strength to pass beyond the monotony of the waves, so the prairie-dweller of the Middle West toiled single-mindedly at his plough, work being his only recourse, his only means of accomplishment."

the application of geography to history lies in the study of the effects of weather upon events. In its month-to-month aspects, weather must of course be rated among the accidents of history. If there had not been a thick fog on the night when Washington withdrew his defeated army from Long Island to Manhattan, the American Revolution might easily have been crushed in its incipient stages. The battle of Valmy was won not alone by the strategy of Dumoriez, but in part also by the weather. The Prussian troops, marching through the heavy clay mud of the Argonne, were exhausted when they reached the French positions, and had to plow up steep and muddy hillsides under the French fire. The great British offensive on the Somme in the World War, which might have succeeded had fair weather continued, was bemired by heavy and constant rains. And when we try to rise above details and take a larger view, we can only say that weather is so constant and important a factor in history that both statesman and student must always take account of its haphazard possibilities. In England weather played a part in the momentous repudiation of protection and acceptance of free trade in the middle forties. Sir Robert Peel and Cobden still faced the prospect of heavy fighting in their endeavor to repeal the Corn Laws, when the rains of 1845, the wettest English summer in memory, ruined the harvest; and Lord Morley trenchantly remarks in his biography of Cobden that "it was the rain that rained away the Corn Laws." In America the work of the AAA in restoring farm prices during the first Administration of Franklin D. Roosevelt was enormously aided by two droughts, and the rapidity of the restoration was a large factor in Roosevelt's reëlection. A writer has attempted an interesting study of "Rainfall and the Populist Party in Nebraska":

To suggest that the farmer held the politician responsible for the shortage of rainfall would be an unwarranted exaggeration of the thoughtlessness of the voters. But it is quite another matter to suggest that the drought in Nebraska made a bad set of agricultural conditions worse, and that the politicians were held responsible for some of the conditions. Perhaps some held them responsible for most of them. The situation of many farmers forced them to think about the things that had brought about that situation. This contemplation resulted in a determination to remedy such matters as lay within their power. They could not make it rain, but they thought they could lower railroad rates. . . . Altogether, in estimating the factors which produced Populism the item of rainfall must not be omitted.[1]

In conclusion, we may point out that geography is valuable for the historian only if it is studied in its most comprehensive aspects. If we are to evaluate it properly as an element in history, we must scrutinize not merely physical geography, not merely climate, but the entire situation of a community or a nation — strategic, industrial, commercial, climatic, and in terms of its natural resources. Any geographical study that is narrower than this is likely to be misleading. We may also point out that even when used in this inclusive way, geography is of much more use in helping to elucidate the broad outlines of history than its narrow episodes or phases. It throws a bright illumination on the career of China, or Great Britain, or the United States from the beginnings to the present day; but it does not help much to explain the Administration of Martin Van Buren. And finally, we may note that it is often dangerous to try to explain very much of even the sweeping lines of history by this single science. Those who have mastered one key to the past tend to ignore the fact that it has many doors, and that other keys are of equal importance. After all, viewing man not merely as a biological phenomenon but as a thinking entity, geography explains only part of his accomplishments. Highly important factors of a psychological and sociological nature are also involved. An example of geographical history at its best is supplied by Rupert B. Vance's compendious *Human Geography of the South*, which relates geog-

---

[1] John D. Barnhart, "Rainfall and the Populist Party in Nebraska," *American Political Science Review*, August, 1925, XIX, 527 ff.

raphy, economics, and history in well-balanced fashion. He asserts that the climate is not responsible for Southern indolence; he holds that the so-called poor whites possess no inherent defects; and he shows just what factors have made for Southern backwardness and Southern progress. The pages on the Southern diet and its historical consequences, for example, are illuminating.

An animated debate which bears upon this subject was presented more than fifty years ago in two thoughtful papers written by William James and John Fiske. The essay of the former, "Great Men, Great Thoughts, and the Environment," appeared in the *Atlantic Monthly* for October, 1880; that by Fiske, "Sociology and Hero Worship," may be found in his volume *Excursions of an Evolutionist*. Both writers fell afoul of the extravagant statements of such geographical theorists as Grant Allen, who had said that if the people who went to Hamburg had migrated instead to Timbuctoo they would now be indistinguishable from the semi-barbaric Negroes of Central Africa, while if the race which went to Timbuctoo had migrated to Hamburg they would now be white-skinned merchants maintaining a great commercial city. To this rash assertion James replied by asking the question, What was it that made the England of Queen Anne so different from the England of Queen Elizabeth? The difference was not due to environment — that had remained constant. It was due chiefly to "the accumulated influences of individuals, of their examples, their initiatives, and their decisions." But while William James and Fiske agreed in rejecting the exaggerated statements of the geographer, they came into violent collision upon the value to be attached to other elements operative in man's past. And this brings us to the extremely important question of the relation between sociology and history.

CHAPTER ELEVEN

SOCIETY AND HISTORY

OLD-STYLE HISTORY, the history of the great masters writing a century ago, dealt for the most part with the grand pageantry of human action. Its authors were concerned chiefly with political affairs, and found their synthesis in the fortunes or misfortunes of the state. Von Ranke and Mommsen, Freeman and Macaulay, Prescott and Motley, wrote primarily of royal courts and parliamentary chambers, of diplomatic duels and tented fields. Such history lent itself to a dramatic emphasis upon the achievements of powerful individuals. It became a stage on which picturesque figures could strut and fret their little hour. "Universal history," wrote Carlyle in rationalizing this approach, "is at bottom the history of the great men who have worked here." And in another connection he asserted: "Yes, from Norse Odin to English Samuel Johnson, from the divine founder of Christianity to the withered Pontiff of Encyclopaedism, in all times and places the Hero has been worshipped. It will ever be so. We all love great men, love, venerate, and bow down submissive before great men; nay, can we honestly bow down before anything else?" Carlyle eloquently illustrated his belief in his own writings. His longest work is a record of the hero (for so he thought him) Frederick the Great; perhaps his most effective single work historically was his *Cromwell*, wherein he forever overthrew the widespread view that the Great Protector had been a canting, insincere, and sly usurper, and demonstrated instead his true stature.

But in one of his books, *The French Revolution*, even Carlyle

significantly failed to demonstrate his thesis that the great man
dominates all history. That volume contains admirable portraits of the more arresting personalities of the time — Voltaire
with face shrivelled to nothing and eyes glittering like car-
buncles; the "swart, burly-headed Mirabeau," with Samson-
locks; the sea-green, incorruptible Robespierre; Marat with
his cruel soul looking out from his "bleared, dull-acrid, woe-
stricken face." But until the last paragraphs of the long
volume no dominating Hero emerges. The reason is unescapable. The French Revolution was a vast social movement,
tumultuous and mutable as a stormy tide; it represented a
multitudinous complex of emotions, economic forces, social
aspirations, ideas, and philosophies. All the people of France
were the actors, and if any central figure existed, it was an
abstraction — the Spirit of Revolution. Indeed, in one of his
most memorable pages Carlyle pictures the era as a conflict between the Spirit of Imposture and the Spirit of Reformation.
The movement comprised a sequence of revolutions, rather
than a single convulsive overturn; it had a hundred facets,
and only a few of its phases can be attributed to any single
leader. If Carlyle had attempted to sum up the French
Revolution in the career of one or a few Heroes, he would
have given his readers an entirely false perspective; he was
too wise and honest to try. Instead, he described it as a
tremendous social conflagration:

Higher, higher yet flames the Fire-Sea; crackling with new dis-
located timber; hissing with leather and prunella. The metal Images
are molten; the marble Images become mortar-lime; the stone Mountains sulkily explode. RESPECTABILITY, with all her collected Gigs
inflamed for funeral pyre, wailing, leaves the Earth: not to return
save under new Avatar. Imposture how it burns, through generations: how it is burnt up; for a time. The World is black ashes; —
which, ah, when will they grow green? The Images all run into amorphous Corinthian brass; all Dwellings of men destroyed; the very
mountains peeled and riven, the valleys black and dead: it is an

empty World! Woe to them that shall be born then! — a King, a Queen (ah me!) were hurled in; did rustle once; flew aloft, crackling, like a paper scroll. Iscariot Égalité was hurled in; thou grim De Launay, with thy grim Bastile; whole kindreds and peoples; five millions of mutually destroying Men.

As democratic institutions advanced during the nineteenth century and their spirit pervaded historical writing, the individual was more and more frequently left for biography to celebrate, while history concerned itself with the People. Moreover, as we have seen, when a new world was created by the spread of the Industrial Revolution, the growth of dense populations, the advance of science and technology, and the rise of a myriad of interrelated corporations and associations, it became impossible to write history in the old terms. They were too obviously superficial. The most striking characteristic of society in the Western world became its complexity; and the modern historian was expected to deal with the multiform aspects of this ever-richer complex. By the middle of the nineteenth century political history was seen to represent but one of the many departments which made up history in its entirety. It became the duty of historians to concern themselves with numerous forces quite apart from politics — economic forces, constitutional forces, cultural forces, educational forces, moral forces, religious forces, artistic forces, and so on. At first writers tended to deal with these facets of history in serial fashion. Neat water-tight compartments were built, and to some extent still exist. One writer gave us the economic history of a nation or of a period. Another gave us the ecclesiastical history. Still another gave us the literary history. The result was decidedly burdensome, and not a little confusing. Taken together, all these works showed that human history had been the resultant of many factors operating simultaneously, and that none could be neglected if a complete picture were desired. But it did not explain how these factors collaborated with one another, or just what their interrelations were. The student who read a constitutional history of the United States, then a literary history, and then economic and political histories, had felt the trunk, the legs, the ears, and the sides of the elephant, without quite realizing how they were all combined in one animal. Men began to ask whether there was not, after all, some way of integrating all these separate departments of history?

From one quarter came a firm and confident "Yes" to this question — the quarter occupied by the sociologists. Sociology was one of the youngest of the sciences; it is roughly accurate to say that it originated with Comte and came of age with the volumes of Herbert Spencer, not earlier than 1860. In the generation after 1875 various sociologists began declaring that their so-called science offered the only true means of integrating the diverse aspects of human society in either the past or the present. Given time, they asserted, they could measure, analyze, and define the exact nature of the social processes which produced historical results; but much time would be necessary to permit them to collect sufficient data in a scientific fashion. Human history, the bolder sociologists argued, is primarily a record of social evolution. Certain laws which govern this evolution could gradually be established. These laws would reduce to order the chaos of political history, cultural history, economic history, and so on. Dr. Franklin H. Giddings in 1903 set forth to the American Historical Association his doctrine that human development might thus be synthesized, entitling his paper "A Theory of Social Causation." Much later, in a volume called *The Scientific Study of Human Society*, Dr. Giddings went on to describe part of the scientific technique — the methods of social measurement — that would be necessary to create a sociological explanation of history.

Still other writers, such as Benjamin Kidd, Karl Pearson, and Albion W. Small, have similarly asserted the possibility of finding a sociological key to history. The first-named writer made bold in *Social Evolution* (1894) to state what he regarded as the central feature of human history. This was the inherent and irreconcilable conflict between the interests of the individual, and those of the social organism; a conflict that has existed since men first formed communities, and that has steadily grown more intense. On the one hand the self-assertive reason of the individual is more and more developed by evolutionary forces. On the other hand, the immensely wider interests of the social organism demand an absolute subordination of this ever-increasing self-assertiveness of the individual. "In the conflict which results, we have the seat of a vast series of phenomena constituting the absolutely characteristic feature of our social evolution. It is impossible to fully understand the spectacle presented by human history in the past, or the main features of the social phenomena now presenting themselves throughout our Western civilization, without getting to the heart of this conflict. It is the pivot upon which the whole drama of human history and human development turns." Kidd devotes about a hundred pages to a brief survey of human history from the days of the Roman Republic to our own time as illuminated by this general idea.

Carlyle would beyond doubt have been horrified by the way in which sociologists attempted to sweep away the theory that great men offer the best key to history. Not that they swept away the great men — for sociology frankly admitted that they constantly appeared, and that their work had high significance. But even the Hero was reduced to a unit obeying immutable sociological law. William James, for example, pointed out in the before-mentioned essay on "Great Men, Great Thoughts, and the Environment" that there is a striking analogy between geniuses in human history, and "spontaneous variations" or "sports" in the animal kingdom. Darwin had described the immense importance of the "spontaneous variation" in bringing about progress in the biological world. Just so, James believed that geniuses were "sports" who produced a kindred

result in the human world. Both represented a marked devia-
tion from the average or norm. If we take a million specimens
of a particular species of moth, we shall find that the proboscis
of the great majority varies in but the slightest degree from the
average length. But perhaps ten or a dozen moths out of the
million may each possess a proboscis that is a half-inch longer,
or a half-inch shorter; they are extreme instances of the
"spontaneous variation." So with man's intellectual capacity.
Among the six million people in New York City, five million
nine hundred thousand come somewhere near the average in
intellect. Most of the remaining hundred thousand fall decidedly below the average. But a few may rise far above it —
there may be a Byron, a Pasteur, a Newton, even a Beethoven
or Shakespeare, among them. He is the impressive *sociological
variation;* and every age produces a few such variations.

Of course nobody can explain their appearance. All the
teachings of Mendel and his fellow biologists cannot tell us
precisely why a moth suddenly appears with a proboscis twice
the usual length; still less can anyone tell us whence comes a
genius like Shakespeare or Goethe. William James very justly
remarks that "the causes of production of great men lie in a
sphere wholly inaccessible to the social philosopher. He must
simply accept geniuses as data, just as Darwin accepts his
spontaneous variations." But does it follow that the sociologist, attempting to subordinate parts of the historical process
to a law, is daunted by this fact? Not in the least.

For William James at once lays down a sociological law upon
the way in which great men affect the pattern of history; a law
which makes society as important to the hero as the latter is to
society. The relation of the social environment to the genius,
he declares, is strictly parallel to the relation of the physical
environment to the variation in biology. "It chiefly adapts or
rejects, preserves or destroys, in short *selects* him." In the
insect world, if the environment is such as to make an additional half-inch of proboscis advantageous to moths, then the

moths with more than an average length will tend to survive; moths with less than an average length will tend to die out; and the miraculous moth with an extra half-inch may found an entirely new breed. Those moths which have varied in the right direction have changed the character of all moth society. So, according to James, the great man acts as a powerful releaser of energy, a ferment; he unlocks huge reservoirs of force, and sets in motion powerful new social currents. He alters the constitution of society much as the advent of a new biological species changes the balance of animal and vegetable life in the region in which it suddenly appears. Most people are familiar with Darwin's remark as to the influence of cats upon the growth of clover. We introduce some cats near a large field; they kill the field-mice; the field-mice cease their destruction of bumble-bee nests; and clover then flourishes in that field. We introduce a great man named Robert Clive into India; and for generations afterward, the hundreds of millions of people in India lead lives that are transformed or at least perceptibly altered.

In short, the stimulating influence of geniuses, whose advent is incalculable, upon social evolution, is strictly comparable to the stimulating influence of spontaneous variation, whose advent is also incalculable, upon biological evolution. But sociologists like Herbert Spencer emphasize even more strongly than William James the thesis that the great man is largely dependent upon his environment. They would insist upon the importance of the following passage from James's essay:

Not every "man" fits every "hour." Some incompatibilities there are. A given genius may come either too early or too late. Peter the Hermit would now be sent to an insane asylum. John Mill in the tenth century would have lived and died unknown. Cromwell and Napoleon need their revolutions, Grant his Civil War. An Ajax gets no fame in the day of telescopic sighted rifles; and to express differently an instance which Spencer uses, what could a Watt have effected in a tribe which no precursive genius had taught to smelt iron or turn a lathe?

The important thing to notice is that what makes a certain genius now incompatible with his surroundings is usually the fact that some previous genius of a different strain has warped the community from the sphere of his possible effectiveness. After Voltaire, no Peter the Hermit; after Charles IX and Louis XIV, no general protestantization of France; after a Manchester school, a Disraeli's success is transient; after a Philip II, a Caesar makes little headway; and so on. Each bifurcation cuts off certain sides of the field altogether, and limits the future possible angles of deflection.

Thus social evolution is a resultant of the action of two wholly distinct factors: the individual, deriving his peculiar gifts from the play of physiological and infra-social forces, but bearing all the powers of initiative and origination in his hands; and second, the social environment, with its power of adopting or rejecting both him and his gifts. Both factors are essential to change. The community stagnates without the impulse of the individual. The impulse dies away without the sympathy of the community.

Carlyle had seen little besides the great man; William James saw both the great man and his social environment; and, with greater emphasis upon the latter, so did Herbert Spencer, John Fiske, and all the sociologists who have followed them. All these writers have agreed upon one point: that the influence of geography or physical environment upon the history of mankind may readily be exaggerated. All would scoff at Grant Allen's rash statement about the Negroes of Timbuctoo and the white merchants of Hamburg. A geographical environment cannot produce a given type of mind, but can only foster and further certain types, thwart and frustrate still others. John Fiske even declared, in his *Outlines of Cosmic Philosophy*, that the ecclesiastical reforms of Gregory VII had (of course in their remote results) wielded more influence upon American history than the direction of the Rocky Mountains or the position of the Great Lakes. Rebutting Buckle's theory that the difference in Arabic civilization before and after Mohammed was due to the difference between the physical geography of Arabia and that of Spain, Persia, and India, he had remarked that the utter superficiality of this explanation could be demonstrated by asking two questions: First, if the Arabs had become highly civilized only because they gave up their native deserts for Spain, India, and Persia, why did not the Turks become equally civilized when they exchanged their barren plateau for the rich empire of Constantinople? And second, what was the impulse which led the Arabs to leave their ancestral deserts and conquer the vast region from the Ganges to the Pyrenees? The answer to these queries would have seemed equally clear to the historian Carlyle, the psychologist James, and the sociologist Herbert Spencer. They would have replied that the principal explanation of the Arabian transformation was psychological, not] psychical. Carlyle would have ascribed it to the genius of Mohammed; modern sociologists would ascribe it to Mohammed and the social conditions which made Mohammed's work possible.

But while the sociologists admit the striking rôle of the genius, they unanimously believe that for the general development of society, the social environment, the general human milieu, is more important than the commanding individual. They hold that the slow progress of this average society should hold the primary attention of historians. "If it be true," writes Fiske (here echoing Spencer), "that a genius of a given kind can appear under certain social conditions, and not under others, as a Newton among civilized Englishmen but ·not among Hottentots; or if it be true that a given genius can work out its results under certain social conditions, and not under others, as a Mill in the nineteenth century but not in the tenth; then it follows that in order to understand the course of history from age to age the mere study of the personal characteristics and achievements of great men is not sufficient. Carlyle's method of dealing with history, making it a mere series of prose epics, has many merits; but . . . it does not *explain* the course of events. History is something more than biography . . . One might learn all of Plutarch's lives by

heart, and still have made very little progress toward compre-
hending why the Greek states were never able to form a coherent aggregate, or why the establishment of despotism at
Rome was involved in the conquest of the Mediterranean
world. The true way to appreciate such historical problems
as these . . . is to consider the popular assemblies of the
Greeks and Romans in their points of likeness and unlikeness
to the folkmoots and parliaments of England and the town
meetings of Massachusetts." In short, Fiske would place his
emphasis upon comparative history, resting upon a sociological foundation.

And it must be admitted that, due as largely to sociology as
to economics and geography, an impressive revolution overtook
historical writing in the century which followed Gibbon and
Von Ranke. The difference in method between Macaulay and
his grandnephew George Macaulay Trevelyan or Élie Halévy
was hardly less than the differences which separate a scientist
of 1830 from a scientist of 1930. The new auxiliary sciences,
of which sociology was one of the chief, had done most to produce this change. A simple illustration of the change in emphasis, cited by more than one writer, is offered by the books of
Froude and Mommsen upon Julius Caesar. Both treat Caesar
as one of the greatest heroes of all history. But Froude, who
came to maturity before he could profit by the new scientific
analysis of social phenomena, lifted Caesar out of his social
environment and presented the latter only as a shadowy background. Mommsen, on the other hand, thoroughly schooled in
sociological ideas, the comparative method, and the study of
institutions, gave careful attention to Caesar in relation to
his complex social environment. He thus did better justice not
only to Roman history, but to Caesar himself, than Froude.
We cannot really understand Caesar's rise to power without
the rich social history included in the chapter on "The Joint
Rule of Pompeius and Caesar"; we cannot fully understand
the use he made of this power without the profound examina-

tion of Roman institutions in the subsequent chapter on "The Old Republic and the New Monarchy." [1]

Yet most historians have always been intensely hostile to the claim that sociology can offer any master key to the historical past; and rightly so. Even if fuller and more scientifically exact data were available on the social aspects of past ages — even if trained sociologists had been collecting statistics according to Dr. Giddings's formula in the midst of the Renaissance, the Reformation, the Wars of Religion, and the French Revolution — it would be impossible for the sociologist to fix an indisputable pattern upon any part of history. The reasons for this belief are numerous. The tremendous and overwhelming complexity of the facts of history stands in grimly majestic contrast to the puny weapons of the sociologist for measuring and classifying these facts; a Himalaya of iron and granite defying a few feeble pickaxes. Then too, as no less a sociologist than Pareto recognizes, the irrational element in all human activity is so enormous, and the unpredictable or fortuitous elements are so much vaster still, that no conceivable formulae can ever deal with past or present in any spirit of certainty. Historian and sociologist alike, despairing of any demonstrable relationship between cause and effect in many phases of life, must turn to such ideas as that of the interdependence of variables for a vague clue — and that conception has little practical helpfulness. The true historian is still suspicious of any but elementary laws, though he admits that the area of law has grown and is still growing. Finally, many historians insist that their special field of interest must always lie quite apart from the special field of the sociologist; indeed, that it lies in an entirely different direction.

Summed up in a single sentence, the distinction which such men would make is this: Sociology is concerned with the con-

---

[1] Mommsen, writing in the Bismarckian period of blood and iron, undoubtedly overemphasized the genius of Caesar; his interest in Roman society is all the more remarkable.

stant and repetitive element in human affairs, past and present, while history is concerned not only with the constant element, but still more largely with the unique and individual element; with the elements which can never repeat themselves or be arranged in a neat pattern. When Dr. Giddings read his paper on "A Theory of Social Causation" to the American Historical Association, three historical writers, Ephraim Emerton, George L. Burr, and Willis M. West, replied to it. All three struck the same note. They asserted that history is rather a branch of literature than of science, though it has relations with both. While the historian, they declared, may busy himself in part with repetitive patterns in social evolution —patterns traceable for him by sociology — he must be concerned much more largely with fortuitous, individual, and unique elements in the record of the past. It is true that certain elements are common to the Puritan, American, French, and Russian revolutions, and that historians should touch upon them. But what is of paramount interest to the historian, and what chiefly makes history worth reading, are the elements peculiar to each of these revolutions. When we study the Russian Revolution, we wish first and foremost to learn in what ways it differed from the French Revolution, and why; the differences are innumerable, the reasons for them complex, and the exposition of them may be fascinating. We cannot appreciate its significance without understanding its unique elements.

From this point of view, sociology may even be envisaged as inimical to history. Certain writers have asserted that, with its flair for all-comprehending syntheses and its demand for generalization on a broad scale, it is merely that age-old siren, the philosophy of history. This philosophy of history, they add, is always a will-of-the-wisp, which changes with every period and simply leads to a distortion of facts. In Fred Morrow Fling's *The Writing of History* we find an extreme statement of this view that sociology and history are *au fond* antagonistic:

. . . The historian is concerned with tracing the unique evolution of man in his activities as a social being, the unique life-record of humanity. If this be history, then history cannot repeat itself; there cannot be historical laws, for law is a generalization and generalization assumes repetition. . . .

History deals with past social facts, but it is important to note that all social facts are not necessarily historical facts. A past social fact becomes an historical fact when it has been made part of an historical synthesis. . . . When our attention is directed toward the *uniqueness*, the *individuality*, or past social facts, when they interest because of their importance for the *unique evolution of man in his activities as a social being*, in selecting the facts and in grouping them into a complex, evolving whole, we employ the historical method; the result of our work is history.

If, on the contrary, we are interested in *what past social facts have in common*, in the way in which *social facts repeat themselves*, if our purpose is to form *generalizations or laws* concerning human activities, we employ another logical method, the method of the social sciences. We select our facts not for their individuality or for the importance of their individuality for a complex whole, but for what each fact has in common with others, and *the synthesis is not a complex unique whole, but a generalization in which no trace of the individuality of the past social fact remains*. The result of our work is sociology, not history. Thus the work of the historian supplements that of the sociologist. The historian is interested in quality, individuality, uniqueness; the sociologist in quantity, in generalization, in repetition.

Within limits and properly qualified, the distinction made by Dr. Fling is sound. Indeed, sociologists admit its validity; admit that they are interested chiefly in the repetitive elements of the human past, while the historian must be interested principally in the non-repetitive elements. But Dr. Fling goes too far and throws out the baby with the bath. While it is true that historians must be occupied primarily with the unique and individual features of any historical situation, Dr. Fling writes that he must be *exclusively* interested in them. Why? Why should historians not be interested also in the elements common to different situations, different societies, and different periods? Can a historian of the Russian Revolution exclude those parts of it which run parallel with the French Revolution? Comparative history may be made an exceedingly stimulating and fruitful study, even if it does come close to sociology. The examiner of slavery in the United States will gain much from an inquiry into slavery in ancient Greece and Rome, in Russia and the Barbary States, and in South America; the student of our own Western frontier will find a great deal of illumination in a scrutiny of the history of the Canadian frontier, the South African frontier, and the Siberian frontier.

It is fairly obvious, in fact, that in some branches of history the constant or repetitive element offers by far the largest part of the subject matter. The study of comparative history is possible only because so much human action is repetitive. Dealing even with peoples far removed from one another, we can study comparative folklore, comparative religions, comparative literature, comparative jurisprudence, and comparative politics with a certainty of discovering some fairly clear patterns. In these comparative studies, the sociologist may be of distinct use to the historian. He will not offer any all-inclusive synthesis or master key, but he can furnish a number of minor keys. The fact that the two studies are at many points complementary to one another has been vigorously pointed out by C. A. Ellwood in his book *Sociology in its Psychological Aspects:*

Although written history furnishes but a part of the facts with which the sociologist deals, nevertheless the coöperation between the sociologist and the scientific historian . . . should be of the closest sort. They are working in the same field and to a large extent have the same aim. The sociologist needs scientific history. He cannot complete his inventory of the social world without its aid. Moreover, sociology cannot content itself, as one author has well remarked, with being merely illustrated psychology; it must also be, at least in its final development, analyzed and compared history. . . .

On the other hand, the scientific historian has need of sociology. Without some knowledge of the principles of social organization and evolution he can scarcely obtain a proper perspective of his facts;

nor can he rightly interpret his facts or explain the causes of social change without reference to such principles. The scientific historian could do his work more scientifically if he had a critical knowledge of sociological laws and principles. We conclude, then, both that scientific history is necessary to the sociologist, and that sociology is equally necessary to the scientific historian.

Necessary in just what way? The question is not difficult to answer. It is possible to discern, after reading a dozen pages of any modern writer who treats of non-political subjects, whether he knows anything of sociological thought or not. If he has really steeped himself in the knowledge which sociology has accumulated since Spencer, and the generalizations which it has based upon this knowledge, his work will have a richness of texture, a depth of penetration, and a sureness of touch exceeding that of any historian of equivalent talents who knows nothing about sociology. How could a writer on American civilization since 1890 neglect the two books on Middletown by Robert and Helen Lynd, not merely for their facts but still more for their interpretation — a purely sociological interpretation? Glance into Élie Halévy's *History of the English People in 1815*, and we find three sentences in the introduction which fix the key for the whole book. "Divided one from another by strong passions," Halévy writes of the European nations, "they are nevertheless in many respects internationalized by common interests, by a common outlook on life, and by a common literary and scientific culture. The institutions or ideas which one nation has neither borrowed from nor imparted to their neighbours will be found on analysis to be few indeed. The difference between the nations of Europe consists after all not so much in the elements which compose their national character, as in the different proportions in which are combined, in each nation, elements common to most or all." These three sentences strike the sociological keynote; they show that an interest in comparative institutions will dominate the book. It would be possible to quote passages from the historical work of Henry

Adams showing that he had familiarized himself with numerous sociological writers; it would be equally easy to quote passages from Macaulay betraying that he knew as little about sociology as about radio-activity.

Speaking concretely, it can be said — despite James Harvey Robinson's denials — that sociology is of the greatest usefulness to students of intellectual and cultural history. Burckhardt approached history through art; Taine approached history through literature — both regarding these as expressions of social consciousness. Vernon L. Parrington could never have written his *Main Currents in American Thought* without a grounding in sociology, and especially in social psychology. From period to period, his work shows how American ideas, sentiments, and convictions grew out of the social and economic conditions in various sections. In writing each part of his work, he first devotes great labor to the social background; and then he takes up each writer or school of writers, and demonstrates how he or they naturally flowered from this milieu. Thus the first chapter of all is entitled "English Backgrounds." The reader will have no difficulty in discovering how deftly Parrington applies certain sociological principles to the English scene from which the first colonists migrated. The first chapter of Book II, again, is called "Colonial Backgrounds," and is an equally deft analysis of the society of America in the first half of the eighteenth century. Thus the social currents of our history, as the chief forces shaping the American mind, are traced down to the decades after the Civil War, when the author opens his study of the literature of the Golden Age by a chapter on "The American Scene" in 1870. Parrington's method owes much to Taine, who in his sparkling volumes on the history of English literature likewise tried to depict the social background of each period, and to explain the literature as an outgrowth of social life.

Perhaps the greatest of all intellectual historians, the German Karl Lamprecht, whom J. B. Bury calls "the ablest product of the sociological school of historians," issued his *Deutsche Geschichte* in the years 1891–1909. Far transcending the bounds of intellectual history, it treats comprehensively all German activities, cultural, economic, political, constitutional, and literary. But Lamprecht, anxious to give his work integration and symmetry, avoided an encyclopaedic range of details, and tried instead to present a highly analytical study of society in each epoch of German life. He did this by attempting to disengage from the movements and events of a given period the soul of society, the social psyche or *geistleben*. Dividing German history into five great periods, he attempted to show that each of them had its social intellectual character, its spirit of the age or social mind. His method in taking up each period was to dissect its social life with care; then to list the psychological traits or forces generated by these social conditions; and finally to explain a thousand definite events or special activities as the product of these socio-psychological impulses. Thus, treating of the early Middle Ages, he finds an underlying connection between the early Gothic architecture, the form of the popular ballad, the design of furniture, the Donations of Charlemagne, the crude heraldic designs, and the weapons of the soldiers. Burckhardt, from whom Lamprecht had learned a great deal, had tried in similar fashion to describe the social psyche or *geistleben* of the Italian Renaissance. But Lamprecht's task was far more difficult; for he dealt with a succession of epochs, not merely one, and he had to explain how the social psyche of one period was gradually transformed into the psyche of the next. His work is really a study of the evolution of the social mind of Germany. It is a tribute to its quality that both historians and sociologists regard it with high admiration, and both — since it lies on the frontiers of the two studies — would be glad to claim it.

If carried too far, or used without careful judgment, Lamprecht's method of course gives absurd results. The historian, abandoning the objective world of history and plunging into a subjective sphere, gropes at moonlight and cobwebs. He takes the vast, dynamic complexity of events and forces that make up history, and interprets them in terms of a few simple and static categories — usually quite arbitrary, often eccentric. The so-called *Volks*-psyche which he coolly presents may not have any real substratum of fact at all and may never have existed. But when the method is applied by a powerful, practical, and rigidly honest mind it may produce a convincing result. As Carl Becker writes: "It is quite possible to deal with the various sets of particular activities in any period — the political, economic, religious, and intellectual activities — as illustrating or as related to certain mental or psychic characteristics common to the social group or nation. These common characteristics thus become a unifying principle around which facts or events, political or other, may be grouped." But the hand of a master is required to do this effectively.

Anyone who reads the social history so enthusiastically written by Americans in recent years must be impressed by the extent to which it is merely descriptive. The writings of McMaster and E. P. Oberholtzer, like some of the volumes of the excellent series called "A History of American Life," are deficient in integration and unification. They present a serial description of economic phenomena, cultural phenomena, religious phenomena, and legal phenomena; a mass of facts upon dress, foods, important books, colleges, theatres, popular songs, railroads, manufacturing plants, amusements, inventions, and so on; a good deal of information upon popular ideas and prejudices — all with but an elementary amount of system and arrangement. Lamprecht, holding up his hands at such books, would have demanded, Where is the *geistleben*, the social psyche? Historians of the future will hardly go as far as he did in trying to find a unifying state of mind for each period, for that leads to oversimplification. Nevertheless, such historians will undoubtedly turn to sociology for aid in analyzing the immense mass of facts upon the life and mind of the people more acutely. By applying the principles of sociology, they will be able to understand a little better the morphology of peoples, the workings of the mass mind, and the ways in which society has changed and developed; they will be able to achieve a more valid synthesis of social factors.

But in all this, caution is requisite. Sociology no more holds the principal key to history than does geography, or economics, or psychology. It can help the historical student at some points, as philology, archaeology, anthropology, and political science help him; but it is only one of many servants, and must never be made a master. No worse fate could overtake history than for a multitude of men, with nothing like Lamprecht's erudition, analytical power, or calm sanity, to begin rewriting all history in terms of the social psyche; it could have no worse fate than to be turned over to sociologists to be laid out in artificial and dogmatic patterns. But it is in no danger. History has a broad torrential power which will always set at naught those who try to crib and confine it within one department.

CHAPTER TWELVE

BIOGRAPHY AND HISTORY

THE BIOGRAPHER appeared on the stage of letters hand in hand with the historian; hand in hand they walk there still. Biography may be termed a form of history — a form applied not to nations or groups of people, but to the single man or woman; history is certainly from one point of view a compound of innumerable biographies. All study of the past, whether for pleasure, instruction, or moral growth, must be based upon a reading of both history and biography, and it is a poor literary prescription which demands one at the expense of the other. While some men have a preference for life in general, and some for *the* life of the individual, each so illustrates the other that neither can be put aside. The commemorative instinct of mankind found expression in biography as early as in history, and very nearly as vigorously. In the Bible, the story of Noah, the story of Abraham, the story of Isaac, and above all the story of Joseph (its length considered, almost a model biography), belong to the category of lives rather than history. Xenophon's *Memoirs of Socrates* is not in strict form a biography, being a defence of the philosopher against his defamers, but in its effect it is a brief biographical masterpiece. During the first century of the Christian era Plutarch produced a book which has ever since been "a pasturage of great minds," his parallel lives of forty-six Greek and Roman heroes; and in the second century Suetonius wrote his untrustworthy but unforgettable *Lives of the Twelve Caesars.* Since the birth of modern memoir-writing in France and Britain, since Rohan and De Retz,

Walton's *Lives* and Fuller's *Worthies*, biography has been an even more fecund mother of books than history, and has yielded as many masterpieces.

Like history, biography has its overtones and undertones. It is more than a literary recreation, more than a portrait-gallery of striking faces, more than a study which makes the past vivid with personalities. As H. H. Asquith said: "It brings comfort, it enlarges sympathy, it expels selfishness, it quickens aspiration." But the principal reason for its fascination to many readers may be stated in a sentence: It humanizes the past, while at the same time it enriches the present by showing us life with a vividness and completeness that few men experience in life itself. Particularly in recent decades the biographical approach to history has become the principal highroad in that field. For every man who reads a history of the Civil War, there are probably ten who read lives of Lincoln, Jefferson Davis, Grant, or Lee; for every man who reads a history of the Tudors, there are probably ten who read lives of Queen Elizabeth or Henry VIII. In English and American literature the greatest publishing successes of the first third of the twentieth century, apart from fiction, lay in biography and autobiography. Now and then a volume of history, such as H. G. Wells's *Outline*, rose to a mass-circulation, but far more frequently the vogue lay with a work like Strachey's *Queen Victoria*, Beveridge's life of John Marshall, Emil Ludwig's *Napoleon*, the autobiography of Henry Adams, the memoirs of Lloyd George. Many of the historical works which did attain a wide circulation had been cast in a form closely akin to biography, one or two personalities dominating such books as Maurois's *The Edwardian Era* and Claude G. Bowers's *Jefferson and Hamilton*. To men who lack imagination, history is difficult to visualize, while biography brings them the past in concrete, real, and vivid terms. To men who have known little of life or dwelt in narrow environments, history is often a meaningless confusion, while the reading of a series of biographies holds out all the richness that human existence can present.

Because biography humanizes the past and enriches personal experience of the present in a way that history can seldom do, its continued popularity is certain. It is perfectly valid to argue that the personal element in the past is less important than the communal element; that the cultural tendencies of any period, its great economic forces, its governmental forms and traditions, its social fabric, are in general more potent than the actions of any single man or coterie. The ordinary reader will readily admit this. But he will assert that what he most readily understands, and what interests him most strongly, is the play of personality in history; that he likes to view the past as a swift drama, with the principal figures of the dramatis personae strongly lighted up. Those economic forces, those governmental institutions, those cultural traditions and ideas, he will say, are interesting to me chiefly as elements against which the figures of the drama contend or which they use to achieve their victories. I prefer to select some eminent person as protagonist, and observe how he wrestles with these elements; to learn whether his talents and energy are more than a match for them, or whether he allows himself to be conquered by rival men and adverse social forces. Having said this, the lay reader (not, we hope, the student) respectfully lays aside the history of England in the nineteenth century, and opens Morley's life of Gladstone.

It is a defensible position for the general reader; and, in answering the chief objections to it, three arguments may be offered for biography as an approach to history. It may be objected that biography tends to oversimplify the past; that it invites us to scrutinize the Reformation, the Napoleonic era, or the American Civil War with reference to the ideas and acts of a single man. But the lay student of history will reply that, since the full history of the Reformation, the Napoleonic era, or the Civil War is too vast and complex to be comprehended without great effort — since it overloads the memory and fatigues the attention — a certain amount of simplification is a virtue. It is better to take a well-laid road through a rough and diversified country than to explore every square mile. Again, it may be objected that the biographical approach to history is always subjective and frequently biassed; that instead of trying to view events impartially, the biographer of necessity presents them as colored by the ideas, emotions, and interests of his hero. But the reader may reply that biography at its best is hardly more biassed than history at its best; that he can make allowance for any natural sympathy with the subject of the biography; and that he is more than compensated for any bias by the increased vividness of the personal view. Impersonal history, he will declare, is too often history robbed of all color and immediacy. When I read a general description of Waterloo I am not particularly thrilled. But when, approaching the climax of Philip Guedalla's *Wellington*, I sit with the Duke on his hill while the tall bearskins of the Guard follow Ney to break against the British squares, my heart is sick with suspense, and I rise from watching the pursuit roll away with a new sense of the reality of history. When I read Pepys's account of the great fire in London — how he lay in a boat on the Thames, shedding tears as he watched the deep red flames destroy the wealth and pride of the city — I feel that spectacle far more keenly than any general record. I would rather have less impartiality and more personal emotion.

The third objection to the biographical approach to history is that it offers no understanding of mass action or social law. The objection is of course irrefutable, and presents a firm basis for our contention that history should always be combined with biography. But, assuming such a combination, defenders of biography can point out that it supplies its unique element no less than history. It furnishes a knowledge of individual psychology just as history furnishes a knowledge of social motives and actions. As history invites us to study the race or mass, biography invites us to explore the mind and heart of man; it, and still more autobiography, lays bare the will and emotions in relation to events and environment. "Personality was Plutarch's quarry" — and has since been the goal of every good biographer. How can we understand the past without understanding in detail the psychology of its principal agents? What is the Reformation without Luther, Calvin, and Knox? How can we comprehend these three without listening to their table talk, reading their letters, hearing the anecdotes which illustrate their character? It would be going too far to take the advice of Disraeli, who made the father of Contarini Fleming counsel his son: "Read the memoirs of Cardinal de Retz, the life of Richelieu, everything about Napoleon; read works of that kind. Read no history, nothing but biography, for that is life without theory." But, says the general reader, good biography, recreating the individual, does give us one set of psychological truths for which history has not the time or space. The two are complementary; each is essential.

Even the sociologist, who deprecates emphasis on the individual and calls for ever-greater attention to social and economic elements, must admit the force of these arguments. Herbert Spencer presents a balanced view in his *Principles of Ethics*. After registering his objections to the great-man theory of history, "tacitly held by the ignorant in all ages," and declaring that the impersonal elements of the past should chiefly occupy our attention, he goes on to say that some study should be given to personal elements. "While no information concerning kings and popes, and ministers and generals, even when joined to exhaustive acquaintance with intrigues and treaties, battles and sieges, gives any insight into the laws of social evolution — while the single fact that division of labor has been progressing in all advancing nations regardless of the wills of lawmakers, and unobserved by them, suffices to show that the forces which mould society work out their results apart from, and often in spite of, the aims of leading men; yet a certain moderate number of leading men and their actions may properly be contemplated. The past stages in human progress, which everyone should know something about, would be conceived in too shadowy a form if wholly divested of ideas of the persons and events associated with them. Moreover, some amount of such knowledge is requisite to enlarge adequately the conception of human nature in general — to show the extremes, occasionally good but mostly bad, which it is capable of reaching." If this statement can be questioned, it is only because it is too grudging and allows too little to biography.

For Spencer does not state adequately the historical values of biography — quite apart from its literary and moral values. Biography is useful, as we have said, as a means of breaking down the complexity of wide movements and crowded periods into parts sufficiently simple to be readily grasped and long retained. It is useful as a means of gaining a vivid insight into past conditions of life; still more useful in drenching past events with some poignancy of personal emotion. It is valuable as a gallery of portraits, a presentation of character in history. It is generally agreed that biography in the English tongue is richer and has reached greater heights than in other languages; that Boswell's *Johnson*, Lockhart's *Scott*, Froude's *Carlyle*, Morley's *Gladstone*, Albert Bigelow Paine's *Mark Twain*, and Beveridge's *John Marshall* have hardly been equalled by French and German biographers. The reason beyond question lies in the deep-rooted individualism of the English-speaking peoples, a race especially rich in character. Biography is valuable, again, as a means of understanding the psychology of past generations of men. Its best examples lay bare the man's inner soul and explain the motives back of human actions with a finesse that the pen of history, drawing bolder, cruder strokes, cannot match. Particularly instructive in this respect are those great autobiographies which give us authentic human documents, divested of all self-consciousness; books like Cellini's, Rousseau's, Benjamin Franklin's, Aksakov's, John Stuart Mill's, and Anthony Trollope's. Finally, biography is valuable as a study of one important form of historical force — for we cannot question the fact that some historic personages have been sufficiently power-ful to constitute each a great force in himself. Caesar was a force; Mohammed was a force; Luther was a force; Napoleon was a force. Mussolini, remarking that "I am not a man but an event," would have us believe that he is a force. Still other men, by no means so powerful, have at least been typical of an age and worth studying because they embody so many of its characteristics. Cobden was not in himself a great force, but was admirably representative of the force called Manchester Liberalism. Mazzini, though not a great force, was typical of one entire side of European nationalism.

II

But if biography is well worth studying, only the best biog-raphy deserves any sustained attention; and what is the best? Boswell remarked: "Biography occasions a degree of trouble far beyond that of any other species of literary composition" — and it is true that a world of pains must go to the making of any really excellent life of a man. Biography in the modern sense did not appear in the English language until Izaak Walton, beginning in 1640, produced that collection of works known as *The Lives of Dr. John Donne, Sir Henry Wotton, Mr. Richard Hooker, Mr. George Herbert, and Dr. Robert Sanderson.* Even this was not strictly modern biography; he wished to edify a little, to amuse a little, above all to collect and present enough of the acts and virtues of departed friends to save them from obliv-ion, and he was more eulogist than biographer. Nevertheless, he showed simplicity, genuineness, and vividness, while his use of letters and anecdotes (as in the tale of Donne and the ap-parition of his wife and dead child) to illustrate character was admirable. Fuller's *Worthies* and John Aubrey's *Minutes of Lives* also evinced an understanding of the personal element essential to good biography. The same element is likewise prominent in Mrs. Lucy Hutchinson's *Memoirs of the Life of Colonel Hutchinson*, written about 1670; a book interesting to historians for its light on the Roundhead side of the English Civil War, but more interesting to general readers for the vividness of its courtship scenes, the pungency of its dialogue, and the pathos of its detailed description of the colonel's imprisonment and death. We all know how highly Charles Lamb thought of the Duchess of Newcastle's intimate biography of her husband — "No casket is rich enough . . . to honour . . . such a jewel."

But as the first great archetypes of modern history appeared in the eighteenth century, so did those of modernized biography. It is customary, after due obeisance to Dr. Johnson's *Life of Richard Savage*, to point to William Mason's *Life and Letters of Thomas Gray* (1774) as breaking the old moulds and bringing in a freer, fuller, more truthful form. Mason had the happy idea, never before really used by any writer, of telling the story of Gray's life by means of his letters, with a ribbon of editorial narrative. Unfortunately, he used but a small part of the letters and papers he collected, while he grossly tampered with the correspondence, altering, transposing, omitting, and redating at his own sweet will. Boswell enormously improved upon Mason's example when he published his life of Dr. Samuel Johnson in 1791. With justice he boasted that he had shown Johnson as no man had ever been shown in a book before, and had "Johnsonized the land." This prince of all biographers was, if not a great man, at least a natural artist, with a quick and sure instinct for obtaining the best materials and making the best use of them. To live, talk, and breathe with his subject, "to become strongly impregnated with the Johnsonian aether," to treasure every detail which added to the completeness and truth of the portrait, in the conviction that "every little spark adds something to the general blaze" — this was his method. For the first time the world found in a biography a photographic — nay, a cinematic — delineation of an arresting personality by a minute observer who used dialogue, letters, anecdotes, and a thousand trifles as well as great acts and events to fill out his portrait. After Boswell, the recipe was open to all. Southey's lives of Nelson and Wesley struck the true note again; Lockhart's magnificent life of Scott (1837–38) came near equalling the performance of Bozzy; Stanhope's four-volume life of Pitt brought in the long series of distinguished political biographies.

The chief requirement of a really good biography is that it recreate an individual, convincing the reader that he lived, moved, spoke, and enjoyed a certain set of human attributes. We must not merely be shown what he did, but what he was, and why he was that kind of man. In other words, his inner soul, or at least his personality, must be revealed. The task is obviously more difficult with well-balanced, self-contained, and reticent personalities than with those which present deeply-stamped traits and picturesque eccentricities. Irving, who in his life of George Washington produced the first great American biography, faced a far more baffling undertaking than Boswell; the first President was notable for the harmony of his traits, the iron restraint of his will, and the smooth dignity of his private and public appearances. Nevertheless, some of Irving's successors, notably Paul Leicester Ford in *The True George Washington*, succeeded in penetrating to the inner springs of Washington's personality. In general, the portraiture of personality is easier in dealing with literary men than with political, military, or business leaders, because the former usually have richer minds, and almost always have been more articulate, more self-expressive; they have written more letters and more autobiographical passages, have figured in more anecdotes. It is no accident that the best English biographies are of writers: Boswell's *Johnson*, Lockhart's *Scott*, Froude's *Carlyle*, Trevelyan's *Macaulay*, Forster's *Dickens*. It is no accident that the richest American biography is Albert Bigelow Paine's *Mark Twain*. But even when a character has lineaments as strongly marked as those of Walter Savage Landor, Andrew Jackson, or Bismarck, even when a wealth of personalia exists, to seize upon the main elements of character is a task demanding the highest talents — a task that can be executed with perfection only by something like genius.

For personality is an elusive matter, and the best indications of character are often so subtle that they escape all but the keenest observers. What is a man's soul? How can his motives be disentangled? How can his acts be generalized? Perhaps personality, whether developing, static, or deliquescent, is primarily the sum of a man's habits. A kindly man has the habit of doing kindly acts, an avaricious man the habit of avaricious acts, an arrogant man the habit of arrogant acts. But the biographer must realize that cruel men may occasionally do benevolent deeds, a kindly man may once or twice commit a cruel action; that the rogue may meet some compelling crisis with an honest act, like Sidney Carton walking to the guillotine, while the honest man may wreck himself, as Lord Jim did, by a single base deed. An American who gave long years to searching men's hearts, Gamaliel Bradford, has written: "The most minute study, the widest experience in the investigation of human actions and their motives, only make us feel more and more the shifting, terrible uncertainty of the ground under our feet." The keenest perception must be allied with the most rigorous honesty in using the scalpel. Not merely must no significant detail be overlooked, in the spirit of Plutarch's remark that "an act of small note, a short saying, a jest, will distinguish the real character better than the greatest sieges and most decisive battles." Insight must be applied to these details. It was Bradford who observed how much the taciturn Robert E. Lee had revealed of his character in his pregnant remark at Fredericksburg: "It is well that war is so terrible, or else we should grow too fond of it."

Yet biography must do a great deal more than recreate a personality. Essayists, like Sainte-Beuve in his *Monday Chats*, Gamaliel Bradford in his psychographs, and Lord Bryce in *Studies in Contemporary Biography*, can sometimes vividly evoke a character. They can limn a rapid, arresting portrait which reveals essential traits like a miniature by Isabey. But this is far from sufficient. Dr. Johnson wisely remarked that "a character is not a life"; that "a character furnishes so little detail, that scarcely anything is distinctly known, but all is shown confused and enlarged through a mist."

A good biography must also present as complete, accurate, and unbiassed an account of the deeds and experiences of its subject as can be executed; provided, of course, that the completeness does not extend to impertinent and tiresome detail. Most great biographies have been planned on full, copious lines. In Lockhart's *Scott*, Froude's *Carlyle*, Morley's *Gladstone*, Monypenny and Buckle's *Disraeli*, Nicolay and Hay's *Lincoln*, Beveridge's *Marshall*, and Baker's *Woodrow Wilson*, exhaustive research was applied to establish and record every useful fact. Douglas Freeman gave twenty years to his *Robert E. Lee* to make every part of the four volumes as nearly definitive as possible. Men of lesser stature than the heroes just named can of course be dismissed more briefly; four volumes on Martin Van Buren or Calvin Coolidge would be ridiculous, as would even two volumes on a career so devoid of external incident as Edward Fitzgerald's or Emily Dickinson's. But in steering the middle course between meagreness and redundancy, the biographer has most to fear from the former. The lives of important men are often so eventful and rich that justice cannot be done them in narrow compass; details are essential to *vitality;* and traits must be illustrated again and again before their force can be grasped. The hurried or indolent reader may think an outline life of Walter Scott or John Marshall — such as John Buchan and E. S. Corwin have ably provided — quite adequate; but the impression made by such brief volumes rapidly fades, while that left by immersion in the full stream of narrative, anecdote, letters, utterances, and comment provided by Lockhart and Beveridge is permanent. A great biography is a creation on the symphonic or operatic order, not a lyric.

To make a biography factually accurate is materially easier,

especially in dealing with recent figures, than to make it unbiassed. Voltaire was quite just in saying, "We owe consideration to the living; to the dead we owe truth alone." But in
addition to all the forms of bias which may injure history, biographical work is subject to some cankerworms peculiarly its
own. The most frequent and striking is the family bias. The
papers of great men are usually held after death by widows,
children, or other close relatives. Not a few important biographies have been written by sons (Alfred Tennyson, Nathaniel
Hawthorne); by widows (Charles Kingsley); by widowers
(George Eliot); by daughters (Julia Ward Howe); by sons-
in-law (Scott, William Cullen Bryant); by daughters-in-law
(Joel Chandler Harris); by brothers (Longfellow); by nephews
(Washington Irving); and by assorted relatives (William Lloyd
Garrison). It is unnecessary to say that all the figures just
named were presented as faultless — some as archangels. Pierre
M. Irving, to draw a portrait of his uncle as faithful to the
memory of Matilda Hoffman until death, suppressed the evidence of his courtship of other women. Of course it is more
frequent for the family to consign its papers to some literary
man for the preparation of a life, but this is too often done
with express or implied conditions. Mr. Burton J. Hendrick's
Carnegie barely hints that the ironmaster had one small fault,
vanity; many "authorized" biographies are of necessity equally
eulogistic. The obstacles which widows in particular throw
before honest biography sometimes inspire a wish for the revival
of *suttee*. One of the last acts of Robert Louis Stevenson's
widow was to suppress a book which revealed certain facts about
the novelist which a few years later were far more frankly related by others.

Closely allied with this impediment is the bias of official or
social decorum. The "authorized" biographer of a man of
high station is frequently moved by a false sense of propriety to
suppress or color his evidence. He shows his figure in the most
dignified light; he omits matter which would reflect on living

men. A more sensible attitude was taken by Carlyle when Froude, preparing Mrs. Carlyle's letters for publication, asked whether he had not better exclude some sharp criticisms of a public man still living. Carlyle rejoined that it "would do the public personage no harm to know what a sensible woman thought of him." But some Americans would think it highly improper to publish an incident, however authentic, which reflected discredit on George Washington; many Southerners would think it treason to print anything which derogated from Robert E. Lee's merit. Still another distortion common in biography is what Sir Leslie Stephen called the ethical or edificatory bias — the desire to use a life as an improving example. Nearly all ecclesiastical biographies fall under this disability. When Archdeacon Hare wrote the life of his one-time curate, John Sterling, he treated it as a tragedy of spiritual torment, a spectacle of the misery caused by religious doubt. Carlyle, who knew that Sterling's life was not tragic and who honored his honest skepticism, retorted by a biography which has become classic. The biographer's business is to tell the truth about Lincoln and Poe, not to use them respectively to illustrate the glories of patriotism and the woes of intemperance.

Finally, one indispensable requirement of a good biography is that it carefully relate the man it treats to history — that it define his position and significance in the broad stream of events. Obviously this is a requirement which historians will most of all emphasize. They know full well that much of their material first reaches them through biographical and autobiographical channels. American history from 1910 to 1920, for example, could not be written with any approach to completeness until the papers of Taft, Theodore Roosevelt, Woodrow Wilson, Bryan, Lansing, Baker, and numerous others had become available. In no instance were these papers released to general historians until biographic use had been made of them, while in several instances they were withheld even after the biographies appeared. It was therefore important to history that the biographies be full; but it was also important to biography. Critics who take a purely literary view sometimes deplore the tendency to write books which treat the "lives and times" of eminent men; the times, they declare, should be omitted, the writer confining himself to the depiction of personality and the recital of acts and thoughts. But to this the historian could never consent, and the biographer never should. Every life is to a great extent a reflection of — a response to, or a reaction against — the conditions of its time, whether political, economic, literary, or artistic. And no biography succeeds unless it brings out the import of every life to its own generation and those which follow. A memoir of Howells, Meredith, or Anatole France must relate him accurately and expertly to American, English, or French literature — and to the social life of his own land; a biography of Cleveland, Peel, or Gambetta must relate him to every contemporaneous turn of national politics. This cannot be done by a few brief allusions.

The demand for spare and stripped lives would deprive us of the great panoramic biographies like Morley's *Gladstone*, Monypenny and Buckle's *Disraeli*, J. L. Garvin's *Chamberlain*, Gardiner's *Harcourt*, Spender's *Campbell-Bannerman*, Ronaldshay's *Curzon;* of the six volumes of David Alec Wilson's *Carlyle*, the three of W. L. Cross's *Fielding;* of Freeman's *Lee*, Nicolay and Hay's *Lincoln*, and Baker's *Woodrow Wilson*. Some of these neither biography nor history could well spare. It may be true that a certain amount of repetition is involved in long biographies; that readers of the lives of Gladstone, Disraeli, Harcourt, and Chamberlain get the Home Rule quarrel four times over, and readers of biographies of Cleveland, Blaine, McKinley, and Aldrich four treatments of the tariff. But the repetition in good biography is slight. What is a common denominator of knowledge can be very briefly summarized; for the rest, the reader studies Home Rule or the tariff under four lights, from four points of view, each with its own novelty. None of the multitude of intelligent users of Morley's *Gladstone* and

Buckle's *Disraeli* has ever complained of irksome duplication; rather, they have been surprised to find how unlike the same issues appear when seen from opposed sides. To be sure, in treating the "times" of a hero all that is irrelevant to his career should be omitted. This Nicolay and Hay's old-fashioned biography, essentially a history of the Civil War, does not do; but the younger biographers named above commit no such error. The day that the "life and times" expires and all biographies are reduced to one volume, that day the full-bodied, vigorous, convincing presentation of distinguished men, so depicted that we can walk all around them and see them in their natural surroundings, will be dealt a fatal blow.

III

The mistaken demand for briefer, sketchier lives is connected with the emergence of a so-called New Biography, which André Maurois tells us first originated about 1910. From one point of view, there was less novelty in the short biography fixing its attention upon character alone and presenting personality by a few sharp strokes than its practitioners supposed. Gamaliel Bradford had been anticipated in general fashion by Plutarch, and much more directly by Sainte-Beuve, who was great less as a literary critic than as an exquisitely finished painter of the chief intellectual figures of France. In England a "new biography" had been born soon after 1850, when the scientific spirit was gaining ground fast and Darwin, Huxley, and Spencer had affected all thought. Realism was coming into fiction; sculptors, ceasing to drape their statesmen in togas, were putting them into honest trousers. In biography the result of the new spirit was seen in such books as John Morley's *Voltaire*, his *Burke*, his *Rousseau*, and his *Cobden*, works of a type not previously known in English. He abandoned chronological outlines, fixed his attention upon the inner man, and adopted oblique methods of portraiture. A rigidly critical attitude, avoiding all attempt at panegyric, permitted a keener insight.

Froude in several brief biographies, notably his *Erasmus* and *Caesar*, used a similarly incisive approach and drew a sharply-outlined portrait with great economy. These works were realistic without being irreverent or iconoclastic.

Yet a still newer biography was unquestionably born from the travail of the World War years, and was closely connected with changes in the spirit of the age.[1] The principal agent in introducing it to the world was Lytton Strachey, who scored so brilliant a success in 1918 with *Eminent Victorians*. The date was significant. In that quietly caustic work he registered his protest against the idealization of the past, against the hero-worship which still characterized so much biography and history. His attack on the Victorian era was the voice of a great disillusion, and fell upon the world in the bitterest year of disillusion in modern history. Mr. Strachey directed his readers' gaze at four heroic pieces of statuary — General Gordon, Arnold of Rugby, Florence Nightingale, Cardinal Manning — and by a deft twirl of the pedestal showed the seamed and pitted brass, the hollow artificiality of the image. With artistic skill he demonstrated that much of seeming greatness is after all mere pomposity; that the Carlylean heroes who pretended to compel the clouds and direct the lightning were after all mere puppets jerked by the great social and economic forces, by fate, or by their own passions. He was happy in his moment. A world looking at Clemenceau, Lloyd George, and Sonnino was quite willing to admit the hollowness of the great. A world helpless under the bludgeonings of circumstance was quite aware that events are greater than men. Even had Strachey's irony been less deft, witty, and entertaining than it was, it would have struck the mood of the age, and have found many imitators.

But Strachey's method no less than his message had a compelling novelty. He carried a long step further the art of Sainte-

---

[1] Be it noted that Georg Brandes's incisive works on Goethe, Nietzsche, Voltaire, Caesar, Michelangelo, and Heine all followed 1910.

Beuve in his brief portraits, of Morley in his *Voltaire* and
Rousseau, of Frederic Harrison's *Cromwell*, of Rosebery's *Pitt*
and *Lord Randolph Churchill*. Abandoning chronology, substituting a dexterous, keen-sighted, and highly allusive exposition
for narrative, using high-lights and shadows as effectively as
Velasquez, wringing a world of meaning from a single incident
or quotation, and employing a mordant satire where older writers would have sacrificed truth to sympathy, he obtained striking effects by the most delightful means. He was, in fact, a
consummate literary artist. Behind the rapid brushwork was a
memory packed with learning, and a brain of very exceptional
acuteness and power. Unfortunately, just as his ironic attitude
could be imitated by anybody, so the superficial quality of his
brushwork could be — and was — copied by a host of men who
had none of his erudition or insight.

The result was that the newer biography which followed the
World War in a veritable spate of books did much to lower the
standards of this branch of literature, and brought in a larger
and more unabashed body of charlatans than were produced in
the same years by the New Poetry, New Novel, and New History (which also flourished) all combined. Honest, painstaking
craftsmanship was for a time shouldered rudely aside; an
inexperienced writer would gather a half-dozen books about
some great figure of the past, reshuffle the facts, add a strong
dash of contempt, lard with epigrams, and turn out a new
portrait. Critics appeared who sneered at the dull men who
went to the trouble to investigate sources and write thorough,
well-documented lives. It is not difficult to understand why,
although the New Biography of Froude and Morley in 1870 had
produced a restricted and creditable list of imitators, the Newer
Biography of Strachey in 1918 loosed such a huge and in part
disreputable stream of works. Morley and Froude had offered
no easy formula. Their scientific, thoughtful, and learned
method obviously required high gifts, prolonged study, and intense intellectual exertion. Strachey, on the contrary, offered

a formula which *appeared* easy of imitation. A passable copy, indeed, such as Maurois's *Ariel: The Life of Shelley*, could be achieved by merely superficial study of the subject and by substituting cleverness for profundity. This statement does not imply that Strachey was a lesser writer than Morley; Rembrandt and Raphael are possibly of equal stature, but Rembrandt defies easy imitation, while Raphael offered a formula which gave birth to a large school. Readers of *Eminent Victorians* saw what effects Strachey had achieved by his ironic detachment — by turning the hero into an unheroic mediocrity — and many writers rushed to choose subjects, and treat them with condescending disrespect. Moreover, Strachey had with enviable skill suppressed all evidence of the more wearisome labors of the historian and biographer. The labor had really been expended, but by delightful anecdote, amusing epigram, unerring selection of facts, and expert interpretation, he concealed it. His imitators leaped at the conclusion that because the labor had been suppressed it was unnecessary; that they could just dispense with it. Biography was becoming a form which cost neither the writer nor the reader any real effort.

To realize just what harm this facile doctrine did we must recur to our definition of the three principal objects of biography. A good biography must vividly recreate a character; it must present a full, careful, and unbiassed record of his acts and experiences; and it must indicate the place of the hero in history. Strachey himself, in the light of these tests, was rather an essayist and interpreter than biographer; and his more reckless followers achieved something like a perversion of biography. Theirs has well been called "plastic biography."

In presenting a personality, the ironic approach has its advantages — especially in depicting a villain or imposter, as Fielding long ago showed in *Jonathan Wild*. But in general, it is much easier for the writer to succeed with his presentation if he happens to be in sympathy with his subject. Boswell was rather unblushingly in sympathy with Dr. Johnson, Lockhart with Walter Scott, Morley with Gladstone, Dr. Harvey Cushing with William Osler — and all the resulting books we count major successes. Indeed, of the principal biographies in English, it would be hard to mention a successful depiction of personality which is malicious rather than sympathetic. Even Lytton Strachey, when he came to Queen Victoria, hauled down his flag, surrendered to the Victorian glamour, and closed in a burst of commemorative eloquence; he had been ironic in spots, but the final effect was of admiration. Even Philip Guedalla, after doing his worst with Napoleon III, made a true hero out of Wellington. It is impossible to present a personality merely by showering it with brickbats, while the attempt to make Longfellow and Washington more real by patting them affably on the back and calling them "Henry" and "George" on every page (as Mr. Herbert Gorman and Mr. W. E. Woodward did) is indescribably feeble. Satire and irony are not biography, and their uses in biography are after all singularly limited. We all know nowadays that Wordsworth had an illegitimate daughter and that Washington fell in love with a neighbor's wife, but these facts tell us more about personality when stated with dignity and sympathy than when offered with a sly jeer. Even Ben Butler and Warren G. Harding can be better understood if approached with an effort to comprehend them than if gibbetted for ridicule.

But the failure in inexpert hands of this part of the Stracheyan formula — the ironic or satiric detachment — was nothing compared with the failure of another supposed part: the rule that the biographer must be entertaining at all hazards, and that the less labor he gives himself or the reader the better. This rule (to which Strachey himself would have been the last to subscribe) made it impossible to meet the second and third tests of good biography. A distinguished biography, which traces fully a man's career and defines expertly his historical station, is never all entertainment. It demands not merely enormous toil from the author, but a wholesome mental exertion from the reader. It cannot compete with the detective story, the current film, or other forms of intellectual anaesthesia. The books of M. Maurois, assuredly among the ablest of Strachey's successors, are delightful. They give us for a time the virtuous feeling that we are combining instruction and pleasure without baser alloy; but in the end they are hardly more nourishing than ginger ale, for they hopelessly over-simplify their subjects. We are offered a stream of anecdote about Shelley, Byron, and Disraeli, an engrossing adventure-story based upon their careers, and some amusing thumbnail portraits of collateral figures. But we do not attain any par-ticular understanding of the complexities and depths of char-acter, we get a sadly incomplete record of the subject's acts and ideas — many of the most important being omitted — and we miss a thorough appraisal of the hero's position in history. We are told nothing about Byron's standing and influence as a poet, about Shelley's special rôle in the romantic movement, or about Disraeli's final achievements and failures as a statesman. A Southern professor of philosophy, when his class raised some particularly intricate question, was wont to say, "That is a bit difficult just now; we will come to it later on." M. Maurois never comes to it, and at length, much as we admire his art-istry, the fact breeds in us a certain suspicion. From his *Disraeli* we turn back, with a not unhappy sigh, to the six volumes of Monypenny and Buckle, sure of finding there the real man in his complete setting.

Some of the defects of another post-Stracheyan author, Emil Ludwig, may be due to a slight tendency toward overproduc-tion. Philip Guedalla once caustically referred to the German school of biography, "the day shift of which compiles the life of Napoleon while the night shift is pumping the life out of Lin-coln." But the deeper and more vital defects would remain if Ludwig had written no more volumes than Morley. His volume on Napoleon had every ingredient for a popular suc-cess. With all the blood and fire, all the charges and retreats, all the amours, all the backstairs gossip, all the horrors of the Moscow debacle, told in a style that now reminded the reader of a George Arliss movie and now of a Bernard Shaw lecture, it was precisely suited to those who had never before opened a book on Napoleon. As history, it was excellent melodrama. Perhaps no deeper meaning inheres in Napoleon's career than such a Sunday-supplement chronicle of his life would indicate, but those who believe that it does would never send amateurs to Emil Ludwig. When Francis Hackett's life of Henry VIII appeared, it was observed that the enthusiasm of the critics was in inverse proportion to their knowledge of Tudor England. When the book was finally reviewed by Wallace Notestein of Yale University, though due tribute was paid to its fine literary qualities, the general verdict upon it was cool. The idea that exact and patient scholarship, the scholarship matured through years of study, can be dispensed with in biography is analogous to the belief that an architect or engineer can raise magnificent structures without long years of training and apprenticeship.

The radical leaders in the newer biography might be regarded with more tolerance had not some of them added critical insults to the injury that was done by meretricious books. Mr. Lewis Mumford in 1932 reviewed a sheaf of biographies in the *Atlantic*. Two kinds of biography existed, he remarked: the good, which was post-Stracheyan in character, and the bad, which was pre-Stracheyan. Pointing to Van Wyck Brooks's *Emerson* as an admirable example of the former, he condemned with an indignant gesture Burton J. Hendrick's *Carnegie* and Claude G. Bowers's *Beveridge* as deplorable illustrations of the latter — stuffy, pedantic, uncritical, excessively long. It seems not to have occurred to the critic that he was regarding two wholly different types of work. Mr. Brooks's *Emerson*, though possessing numerous excellences, is for whole chapters a close paraphrase of Emerson's journals, letters, and the works of previous biographers. Parts of it are founded so largely upon these previous works that they raise a rather nice question of literary method. It has hardly more originality, so far as its factual content goes, than Mr. Mumford's own *Herman Melville*, whose reliable materials (for a great deal of unreliable guessing at psychology was added) were nearly all borrowed from Raymond Weaver's scholarly biography. Mr. Hendrick's *Carnegie* and Mr. Bowers's *Beveridge*, on the contrary, were primary works. Each author, writing the life of his subject for the first time, had to be reasonably exhaustive, thoroughly attentive to scholarship, and ready to take the prosaic along with the dramatic. Each was unfortunate, from one point of view, that he could not sack some previous biographer, appropriate his materials, and write a book which played up all the succulent, sparkling parts of the story. Had he done this, with a curt, contemptuous acknowledgment of his debts in the preface, Mr. Mumford would have praised him. Each was fortunate, from another and better point of view, that he could write a book which is likely to remain standard while ephemeral snapshots of the subject appear and fade away.

The fact is, of course, that a distinction must be drawn between three literary types: the source biography, the popular biography, and the critical interpretation of a life. Nothing should be allowed to diminish the respect paid to the original biographer who spends toilsome years in poring over old letter-books and manuscripts, hunting through crackling newspaper files, interviewing ancient survivors — by myriad labors slowly bringing to light the essential facts of a great man's life; particularly if he shows literary art in shaping his results. Every such biographer is a true servant of history. Even greater respect may sometimes be due to the learned and profound interpreter, who takes the salient facts gathered by another and pours a flood of new light through them. But such an interpreter must have both a great mind and a solid foundation of knowledge; he must be a Sainte-Beuve or John Morley. Commanding interpretive studies like W. C. Brownell's volume on six *Victorian Prose Masters*, like Goldwin Smith's *Three English*

Statesmen, no more come from hasty amateurs than figs from thistles. The popularizer deserves the least respect, and if he is slipshod and dishonest, the very opposite of respect. He often tends to bring the whole art of biography into disrepute, and to convince lay readers that it and history are without standards or enduring values. It is important to keep in the foreground the trustworthy source biography, and the trustworthy interpretation; important, since neither can be dispensed with, to avoid invidious comparisons between them. Van Wyck Brooks's *Mark Twain* is a stimulating interpretation, though Mr. Bernard De Voto tells us in *Mark Twain's America* that it is ill-informed and ridden by an erroneous interpretation. Critics like Mr. Mumford would doubtless assert that it is shapelier, more artistic, and more acute than the work on which it so largely draws, Albert Bigelow Paine's solid volumes on Mark Twain; but they would go too far when they would contemptuously brush Paine from the earth. No Albert Bigelow Paine, no Van Wyck Brooks!

The ideal in biography is the patient investigator who can write lives which combine scholarship, interpretive power, and literary charm; which are thorough, expert, and yet full of popular interest. In the past this ideal has repeatedly been attained. It better than anything else puts the charlatans to shame and deprives the biographical popularizers of their chief excuse for being. Dogmatism as to form and content in this field is as dangerous as in history. A great biography may be as long as Lockhart's ten volumes on Scott, or as short as Edmund Gosse's *Father and Son*, J. E. Neale's *Queen Elizabeth*, or Arthur Bryant's *Pepys;* it may be as acidly critical as Froude's *Carlyle* or as sympathetic as Lord David Cecil's *The Stricken Deer* (William Cowper); it may be as full of interpretation as Lounsbury's admirable life of Fenimore Cooper, or as devoid of it as Thomas Beer's highly objective life of Stephen Crane. But it is seldom difficult to discriminate between pure gold and base metal. And when found, the distinguished life is always an indispensable ally and supporter of history. Not seldom is biography the best means of gaining an introduction to a historical period; almost invariably it is the best means of filling out the *human* meaning of any era.

CHAPTER THIRTEEN

LITERARY ASPECTS OF HISTORY

THERE ARE twenty different ways, says Kipling, of writing tribal lays, and every single one of them is right. The same assertion may happily be made of history, which is one of the most variegated departments of literature. Yet certain elements do give a common stamp to the work of the greatest historians, certain touchstones make the reader aware when he is in the presence of a master. Perhaps the chief is suggested by Thackeray in his well-known comment on the genius of Lord Macaulay. He praises Macaulay for his enormous erudition — but also for a much rarer quality than erudition.

"Take at hazard," writes Thackeray, "any three pages of his Essays or History; and, glimmering below the stream of the narrative, you, an average reader, see one, two, three, a half score of allusions to other historic facts, characters, literature, poetry, with which you are acquainted. Your neighbor, who has *his* reading and *his* little stock of literature stored away in his mind, shall detect more points, allusions, happy touches, indicating, not only the prodigious memory and learnings of this master, but the wonderful industry, the honest, humble, previous toil of this great scholar. He reads twenty books to write a sentence, he travels a hundred miles to make a line of description."

Be it noted that it was not merely Macaulay's vast learning and toil of research which stirred Thackeray's admiration; it was his ability to distil this learning and toil into tiny compass, and his readiness to present it without ostentation. "He reads twenty books to write a sentence; he travels a hundred miles to make a line of description." It was literally true that Macaulay did this. He expended endless pains to ascertain a fact, and then set it down with the simplest brevity. For example, in the third chapter of his history, the famous description of the state of England in 1685, he had occasion to state the population of Leeds. His biographer Trevelyan publishes some of the numerous letters which he wrote in an effort to obtain this single figure. He consulted all the books and pamphlets that might throw light on the question. Through the City Recorder he had the municipal archives searched; through church officials he had ecclesiastical records ransacked. One letter reveals that he was scrutinizing the data given him by a churchman, who reported a number of burials in 1685 which Macaulay found twice as great as the burials of Manchester, supposedly a town of equal population. By using the ordinary percentage of urban mortality in 1685, Macaulay found that the vicar's figures indicated a population of about 16,000 — which from other circumstances he knew to be excessive. He therefore discarded the statistics, declaring that either some error had been committed, or there had been an extraordinary mortality in Leeds in 1685. By continued research he finally found a list of all the houses in Leeds in 1663, numbering just fourteen hundred. This argued a population of about 6,000, which various computations and tests led him to believe had increased by 1685 to about 8,000. And having spent all this effort in learning the number of houses and people that Leeds possessed, how much space did Macaulay use in stating his discoveries? Five lines.

Macaulay wrote on February 8, 1849, after publishing his first two volumes: "I have made up my mind to change my plan about my history. I will first set myself to know about my whole subject; to get, by reading and travelling, a full acquaintance with William's reign. I reckon that it will take me eighteen months to do this. I must visit Holland, Belgium,

Scotland, Ireland, France. The Dutch archives and French archives must be ransacked. I will see whether anything is to be got from other diplomatic collections. I must see Londonderry, the Boyne, Aghrim, Kinsale, Namur again, Landen, Steinkirk. I must turn over hundreds, thousands of pamphlets. Lambeth, the Bodleian and the other Oxford libraries, the Devonshire Papers, the British Museum, must be explored and notes made; and then I shall go to work. When the materials are ready, and the History mapped out in my mind, I ought easily to write on an average two of my pages daily." He added that when the next section of his history had been finished, then "I reckon a year for polishing, retouching, and printing." This arduous programme Macaulay duly carried out. When he studied the disrepute into which the English clergy had fallen under Charles II, he steeped his mind in the ecclesiastical literature of that reign to pen a few pages. When he wrote of the battle of Killiecrankie he paid the field two visits, and employed much of one in a long walk over the pass to write a single sentence upon the time spent by the English army in mounting it.

It is true, as Macaulay's biographer remarks, that few who read such a brief statement in the *History of England* as that upon the population of Leeds can "form a conception of the pains which these clear and flowing periods must have cost an author who expended on the pointing of a phrase as much conscientious research as would have provided some writers, who speak of Macaulay as showy or shallow, with at least half a dozen pages of ostentatious statistics." Macaulay is delightful to read not merely for his full, rich mind, not merely for his carefully cultivated style, but because he took extraordinary pains to digest his materials. His method of composition was to fill his capacious memory with his subject, until he had completely mastered every part of it. Then, with few notes or books of reference, he would sit down and write off the whole story at a steady pace, securing in black and white each idea, epithet, and turn of phrase as previously thought out. Every part of the exposition had passed through the alchemy of his brain before it was committed to paper, and the dross had been refined away. An inferior writer, yielding to the temptation of showing on the printed page the extent of his labors, would have given his readers a neat dispute on the population of Leeds, peppered with footnotes. But Macaulay was content to thrust the non-essentials out of sight. He was interested in the finished structure, and did not bother his readers with a view of the scaffolding used to put it up, or the shavings and litter discarded in the process.

The same characteristic stamps the work of such literary historians as Parkman and Prescott. The fact that both men were for long periods almost blind and could not refer constantly to notes and printed works made it indispensable for them to master their materials completely before beginning composition. Parkman during most of his active career had to hire an assistant to read every book and document aloud. First came the labor of ferreting out, buying, or copying materials, in which he showed remarkable keenness. Then he had his assistant read the principal materials to him with care, that he might delineate the chief features of his subject—might plan it in his mind. Later came a much more detailed reading, during which he took notes of the details of the story and of background or accessory materials. Finally, a still minuter scrutiny of the most difficult parts of his mass of documents would follow, Parkman trying to fix the whole in his memory. "By this slow method," writes his biographer, G. H. Farnham, "he acquired perfect possession of the materials needed for a volume. He then set to work at composition, always finishing one volume before touching another. His inability to compose rapidly, as we have already seen, offered some very valuable compensations for difficulties and delays. It forced him to consider well his plan, *to digest his materials thoroughly;* and by keeping him living for some time in each part of his subject as he went along, secured freedom and leisure for the exercise of both imagination and judgment." And emphasizing the fact of Parkman's patient pre-mastery of his materials, Farnham adds:

> In the long hours of enforced solitude and illness in the subdued light of his study, or during his sleepless nights, his subject pressed upon him with the insistence of an absorbing interest. It is easy to understand that his hardest effort was to keep his mind at rest. Few men could have sustained their interest and power under such tedious delays; but he had precisely the faculties needed to meet the situation — breadth and firmness of grasp for details and general lines, a retentive memory, great constructive skill, and a vivid imagination — the whole driven by supernormal energy. When it came to writing or dictating the book, he had each day's production already arranged, probably some of it composed and memorized. He dictated at a moderate pace — sometimes holding a few notes in his hand — without hesitation, and with a degree of finish seldom requiring any correction.

Prescott also, with the sight of one eye destroyed and that of the other impaired, had to have most of his historical materials read to him. His subjects, especially in Spanish history, being more complex than Parkman's, he took more detailed notes. If his eyes happened to be sufficiently strong, he studied these notes himself; if not, he had them read aloud repeatedly — rarely less than six times; some, he says, "a dozen times." They were thus stamped upon a memory which he cultivated to very remarkable retentiveness. Having mastered his data, he began the task of mental composition, a difficult process because of the exactness to be observed as he progressed. But he became able to rely upon this faculty more and more heavily, until at last he attained extraordinary power in the application of his richly stored memory. It was never such an astonishing memory as that of Macaulay, who once said that if all copies of Milton's *Paradise Lost* and Bunyan's *Pilgrim's Progress* were destroyed, he would undertake to reproduce these works intact; but training and use had made it a remarkable instrument. George Ticknor writes of Prescott's method of fusing his materials — of Bessemerizing them — mentally:

It was really desirable to write, not almost, but altogether, from memory. He labored, therefore, long for it, and succeeded, by great and continuous efforts, in obtaining the much-coveted power. "Think concentratedly," he says, "when I think at all." And again, "Think closely, gradually concentrating the circle of thought." At last, in 1841, when he was employed on the *Mexico*, he records, after many previous memoranda on the subject: "My way has lately been to go over a large mass — over and over, till ready to throw it on paper." And the next year, 1842, he says: "Concentrate more resolutely my thoughts the first day of meditation — going over and over — thinking once before going to bed, or in bed, or before rising — prefer the latter. And after one day of chewing the cud should be (i.e. ought to be) ready to write. It was three days for this chapter." (*Conquest of Mexico*, Book V, Chapter II.) Sometimes it was longer, but in general a single whole day, or two or three evenings, with the hours of his exercise in riding or walking, were found to be sufficient for such careful meditation.

The result was remarkable — almost incredible — as to the masses he could thus hold in a sort of abeyance in his mind, and as to the length of time he could keep them there, and consider and reconsider them without confusion or weariness. Thus, he says that he carried in his memory the first and second chapters of the fifth book of the *Conquest of Peru*, and ran over the whole ground several times before beginning to write, although these two chapters fill fifty-six pages of printed text; and he records the same thing of chapters fifth, sixth, and seventh, in the second book of *Philip II*, which make together seventy-two pages, and on which he was employed sixty-two days.

He frequently kept about sixty pages in his memory for several days, and went over the whole mass five or six times, moulding and remoulding the sentences at each successive return.

II

Three principal reasons exist why the inexperienced writer fails, and the inferior writer refuses, to digest his materials after this fashion. He may be the victim of a false kind of vanity. Having gone to immense pains to ascertain all the facts, he wishes to impress his public with the scope and thoroughness of his work; he gives his page not merely the results of his labor, but the labor itself — discarded data, rejected hypotheses, long citations of authority. This may be exhaustive — it is certainly exhausting. Instances of this tiresome vanity lie thick in the works of the more pedantic historians. A second reason, however, arises from the very converse of vanity — timidity. The amateur is likely to feel distrustful of his ability to take a step unless bolstered on the crutch of a citation of fact. Instead of saying in ten words that Leeds in 1685 had a population of about 8,000, he summarizes all the data because it makes him feel *safe;* for he fears that some critic will accuse him of snap judgments, of haste and superficiality. He lugs in his raw material as an entrenchment against attack. The silly reviewing common in some historical periodicals — pedants writing for pedants — encourages this timidity. Such amateurs should pluck up courage; Macaulay also was accused of superficiality, but Macaulay is still read by tens of millions.

A third explanation for the failure to digest historical material lies in sheer clumsiness, or more exactly, in lack of literary discernment. Many persons deficient in literary instinct think that a patchwork of quotations and citations, or such crude summaries of original material as strew the chapters of John Bach McMaster, are almost as good history as a fused and digested narrative. They speak of the flavor which raw materials, such as quotations from an antique document, give. It is true that in biography copious quotations from letters, diaries, and conversations are almost essential to any lifelike presentation of personality; the difference between Boswell's life of Johnson, and Macaulay's essay on Johnson, is simply the difference between authentic biography and an authentic chapter of literary history. Even in history a limited number of quotations do help give the color of a varied and lively background, the flavor of the more salient personalities. Henry Adams uses them more frequently than Macaulay, Parkman and Froude more generously than Adams. The point at which to draw the line is a matter of taste. But it is always best to err on the side of parsimony in using unsmelted ore.

The ideal in history is a work on which infinite labor has first been expended to obtain and utilize the materials, and infinite pains have then been expended to hide the labor. An effort to attain the ideal is important for two reasons. Not merely does the complete smelting of the ore, the absorption of the inchoate mass of original fact into the mind of the author and its conversion there into a unified and harmonious whole, make history far more attractive to the reader. It holds another great benefit. It releases the imagination and the reflective power of the author. The mind ceases to be tied to mere minutiae. So long as the author plods, fettering himself at every step to his rough materials, his higher faculties must remain in abeyance. When he lifts himself above his materials, seeing them as a whole, fresh significances occur to him; new associations and generalizations become possible; he can act much more effectively in applying ideas to history.

III

But the amateur of history who intends to write a paper, a monograph, or a book is carried only a short distance by the advice that he should digest his information thoroughly before he sets pen to paper. For one consideration, few men can ever trust half so much to memory as Macaulay or Prescott; many cannot compose more than a page or two mentally. For another, what is to be done after gaining a fairly vigorous grasp of the material to be used? How arrange it, how proportion it, how make it truly interesting? The answer to these questions involves study, discipline, and practice.

There is of course no real conflict between literary and scientific history, and if terms are properly defined, there never has been. The most vehement exponent of scientific method admits that literary grace is desirable, and the most ardent apostle of style in history confesses that exact research is also requisite. A spirited quarrel over the relative emphasis to be given these qualities did rage during much of the nineteenth century. The scientific school held that overwhelming weight should be given to the unvarnished record of the precise facts; that matter and substance were all-important, manner and form were but pleasing trifles. This school believed that it was the chief business of history to clear up dark areas and settle disputed points, and that being artistic was unimportant. Von Ranke's idea of history was fairly summed up in his oft-quoted statement that it should describe the past *wie es eigentlich gewesen* — as it actually happened. But literary historians treated this school with contempt as mere fact-grubbers; Carlyle had Von Ranke in mind when he excoriated Professor Dryasdust, while Frederic Harrison wrote scornfully of Stubbs's dulness. The controversy was carried on with an animosity which became theatrical and unreal.

One truth is indubitable: it is possible to be scientific and exact, and also to write with high literary charm. Thucydides, who was scientific in temper, is not less effective as a literary artist than Plutarch, who was unscientific. No man of sense ever esteemed Tacitus inferior in style to the far less accurate Livy. In modern times, such writers as Clarendon, Guizot, Michelet, Lecky, Mommsen, Villari, John Addington Symonds, Parkman, Prescott, and J. R. Greene in varying degrees illustrated the fact that men can be distinguished in research, in insight, and in expression at the same time. Here and there a historian has so sacrificed substance to literary effect that he has become discredited and is little read; some parts of Froude's work fall into this category. At the other extreme are historians like S. R. Gardiner, who writes clearly but with absolute lack of color, or Herbert L. Osgood, whose style is exasperatingly clumsy. Both extremes are to be avoided; the combination of literary polish and sparkle with scientific adequacy is the true object.

Another truth is almost as indubitable as the first: the world at large will sooner forgive lack of scientific solidity than lack of literary charm. The great preservative in history, as in all else, is style. A book of consummate literary art may abound in passages of bad history, but nevertheless carry generation after generation before it. It is almost useless to protest that Tacitus was hideously unjust to several Roman Emperors; his portraits are marked by sufficient literary genius to make them forever pass current. It is useless to protest that Lord Clarendon was far too biassed on the English Civil War; he will be read for centuries by all who savor a close-packed, pithy, eloquent style, full of graphic sketches] of men and events. Motley is unscientific in his treatment of Spanish misrule in the Netherlands, but the world will continue to read Motley. If a historian were compelled to take his choice, fame might urge him to select the winged pen rather than the Aristotelian mind, to choose Apollo against Minerva. But he may choose both.

It is not absolutely necessary, remarked Bishop Mandell Creighton, to be dull in order to prove that you can write history. Indeed, we may add that the converse is true. Usually it is the luminous-minded author, whose work satisfies exacting scientific tests, who also writes with color, point, and ease; it is the muddle-headed author, who goes wrong on facts and evidence, who also makes the inferior literary statement.

The first step for the historical amateur is precisely that which the author of any other piece of extended exposition must take. He should resort to the mechanical device by which all writers obtain unity; he should make a written outline. His attempts at mental digestion of his material will have carried him a long way in this direction. But in most tasks it is important to draft the first outline before note-taking has been carried far, so that subsequent notes can be arranged under headings of the outline. Thereafter, as material accumulates, as digestion keeps pace with it, the outline should be drastically revised. It is seldom that even experienced writers are willing to give as much time to outlining their essays or books as they should; however important, it is a piece of drudgery, and it is easy to make a thousand excuses for sidestepping it. It involves slow, careful thought, and thought is always painful. Emerson once remarked that he had trained himself to *think*, with utter absorption, as much as fifteen minutes a day; and that the man who could train himself to think for half an hour daily might rule the world. A good outline for a historical essay or chapter requires fully fifteen minutes of concentrated, laborious thinking.

Impatience often conspires with laziness, for to think any considerable subject through, and then to prepare an analysis as good as the brief of a careful lawyer, may actually require weeks of time. It is much pleasanter to leaf through books, to jot down notes, to gather materials in all possible nooks — for the hunt after materials may be as exciting as a detective story. The amateur does this work in the vague hope that when his files are packed with citations and references, the monograph will somehow emerge without any trouble. Yet this is to make trouble for himself, and ten times as much trouble for the poor reader. If he begins collecting a large body of materials without a careful plan, in the end his helter-skelter, amorphous accumulation of facts is likely to overpower him; they master the author, who should at all times master them.

The amateur who believes that he is above the drudgery of a preliminary outline believes his mind better than Macaulay's; for the clearest evidence exists that Macaulay, retentive as was his memory and lucid as was his brain, carefully outlined his best historical work in advance. His letters speak of his plans and outlines. He tells how he discarded one subject, the early history of George III's reign, because on making a preliminary sketch he found the subject unmanageable. His essay on Machiavelli may be taken as an example of admirably proportioned and arranged historical argument. It is essentially an attempt to vindicate the Italian thinker from the opprobrium in which he has been held — an opprobrium which had converted his last name into a synonym for trickery, and his first into the nickname for the devil, "Old Nick." In a monograph of about 16,000 words, Macaulay develops the thesis that the characteristics which have rendered Machiavelli hateful belonged rather to the age than to the man. He begins with an introduction upon Machiavelli's disrepute, admitting that *The Prince* is indeed a shocking book. He then propounds the historical problem offered by this and other writings: How did Machiavelli come to present such immoral doctrines? He states several hypotheses, only to reject them — the hypothesis that Machiavelli's private character was hypocritical and grasping, and so warped his judgment of right and wrong; the hypothesis that his public conduct lacked integrity, and he therefore laid down the principles of his book to excuse his official behavior. Macaulay then introduces the true explanation of the unethical tone of *The Prince*. It lies in "the state of moral feeling among the Italians of those times," and in the desperate disorders of the country, racked by the wars of petty despots and the devastations of mercenary bands, which required a desperate remedy. That remedy, which he was ready to see achieved by fair means or foul, was to solidify the small Italian states under a powerful central ruler upheld by a national army. To the elaboration and proof of his main thesis Macaulay properly devotes most of his essay, about 9,000 words. He then adds a vigorous conclusion of perhaps 1,000 words. The construction of the essay is so good that Arlo Bates gave it a special scrutiny in his *Talks on Writing English*.

An historian whose plan is always lucid and often impressive (sometimes, alas, its most impressive feature) is John Fiske. Since each of his books contains a detailed table of contents, summarizing nearly every page, it is as easy as it is profitable for students to take his best volumes and study the outlines for each chapter. His strongest book by far is the two-volume *Discovery of America*, while next in value stands the graphic history of *Old Virginia and Her Neighbours*. These works are marked by symmetry of structure, unity of design, strong narrative interest, and concentration of effect; they sing like Quentin Durward's arrow to the white bullseye of the target. But even so inferior a book as the *Critical Period of American History* maintains a certain place by virtue of its effective architecture and charm of style. It is doubtless still more widely read than the far richer volume on the period by Andrew C. McLaughlin, the far acuter volume by Charles A. Beard — and the ordinary rapid reader will perhaps carry away more from its perusal than from the other two, for it is so arranged that all its values can be seized.

In *The Critical Period*, Fiske begins both dramatically and logically with the surrender at Yorktown and the treaty of peace. He follows this by a chapter on the thirteen States at the end of the Revolution, showing how strongly the people were attached to their own commonwealths, how well most of the new State governments had operated, and how much they had done for liberty, equality, and progress. He then turns by a natural transition to the contrasting clumsiness, inefficiency, and disrepute of the national government under the Articles of Confederation. This requires two chapters, his narrative rising to a climax as he describes the quarrels of the various States, the paper-money craze, and Shays's Rebellion. Then he takes up "The Germs of National Sovereignty" — the national domain steadily built up by State cessions of land beyond the Alleghenies; Washington's interest in the West and in interstate navigation; and the calling of a commercial convention at Annapolis in 1786. This brings him to the Federal Convention which met at Philadelphia in May, 1787, and to which he properly devotes his longest chapter, nearly a hundred pages. Then comes a final chapter called "Crowning the Work," which describes the ratification of the Constitution by the

States, and the placing of the new Federal Government in operation. As a piece of exposition, without reference to questions of scholarly completeness or depth, the volume could hardly be better done.

Nearly all writers who have attempted any sustained piece of historical composition will agree upon the principal difficulty they have encountered in planning their books. It lies in the necessity of somehow reconciling the temporal order with the topical order of treatment. In most comprehensive histories a number of topics, let us say politics, religion, education, literature, and art, have to be discussed; with perhaps a war thrown into the beginning of the study, an important Parliamentary election into the middle, and a financial panic near the close. Since such a history extends over a number of years, it is imperative that it give the reader a sense of progression, and highly desirable that it stimulate his interest by employing suspense and climax at various points. Yet if it is given a purely topical pattern, nearly all sense of continuity in the book as a whole will be sacrificed. The writer will carry politics, let us say, from 1789 to 1803; he will then go back and carry the record of education down from 1789 to 1803; and then go back again to 1789 for art. If on the contrary, he attempts to give a broad temporal sweep to his narrative, relating first what was done in all fields from 1789 to 1793, then what was done from 1793 to 1797, and finally from 1797 to 1803, his topical elements must be mingled together in hopeless confusion. Obviously, in nearly all large histories a compromise must be effected. While the nature of the compromise must depend entirely upon the materials, we may assert that one characteristic it should always have — it should be adroit, smooth, and persuasive. Sometimes, however, so difficult is the task that the best historians fail; even Parkman, most of whose books are sharply unified, did not solve the problem in his sprawling *Half-Century of Conflict.*

Still another difficulty in planning many historical books lies

in the unevenness of materials. It may seem easy to construct
an *ideal* outline for the Administration of James Monroe; so
much space will go to the decay of Federalism, so much to internal improvements, so much to the defence of the Atlantic
seaboard, so much to the purchase of Florida and the Seminole
War, so much to Lafayette's tour, so much to South American
relations, and so much to the Monroe Doctrine. But what if
the writer finds a perfect gold mine of unexploited material
upon several topics, say the Monroe Doctrine, internal improvements, and the Seminole War, while he discovers almost
nothing new on the others? Shall he sacrifice his materials, or
mar the symmetry of his book? The unescapable answer is
that he must sacrifice some part of the symmetry of his volume.
Nevertheless, he is gravely at fault if he does not try to attain
as much symmetry as is possible in view of the capriciousness
of his data, and if he does not give an adequate view of the
Administration as a whole. A writer in whom the literary instinct is powerful will go to great lengths to keep each part of
his work in due proportion to the whole, rigidly compressing
and even rejecting rich materials. Mr. Harold Nicolson tells
us a significant anecdote of his admirably arranged book
Byron: The Last Journey:

In my researches . . . in the last year of Byron's life I came across
certain documents which threw a wholly new light, not only upon
Byron's character, but even upon the problem of his separation and
departure from England. To have divulged this information would
have created a sensation and have destroyed for many romantic people
the picture they had formed of Byron's character. I decided that I
should make no use of this material except in so far as it colored and
confirmed my own estimate of Byron's strangely complicated temperament. I think I was right in so doing, and I should justify myself
upon the following biographical principle, listed under the heading of
"Truth and the Whole Truth." My principle is as follows: "If a
biographer discovers material which is so shocking and sensational that
it will disturb, not only the average reader, but the whole proportion
of his own work, then he is justified in suppressing the actual facts.

He is not justified, however, in suppressing the conclusions which he draws from those facts, and he must alter his portrait so that it conforms to those facts." That is what I did in my treatment of Byron. Should some future research-worker come upon that same material he will recognize from my book that I also was in possession of that material, that it colored my interpretation of Byron's temperament, but that I suppressed the material itself for perfectly legitimate reasons.

An excessively mechanical arrangement of materials is of course as deadly as a purely mechanical piece of writing. A political history of England arranged according to prime ministries, or of America according to presidential administrations, would be a poor history for any but those elementary readers who like to get their dates straight. A book which totally lacks plan may sometimes, on the other hand, achieve a curiously high degree of interest, for variety, novelty, and the spice of the unexpected are important elements in interest; but such a book will utterly fail to achieve the effect of an organic whole. Theodore Roosevelt once wrote his friend Lodge: "If all of McMaster's chapters were changed round promiscuously it would not, I am confident, injure the thread of his narrative in the least. He has put much novel matter in a brilliant, attractive way; but his work is utterly disconnected." The successive volumes of Mark Sullivan's *Our Times* are likewise almost totally without plan. A chapter on Republican politics lies cheek by jowl with one on Walter Reed and the conquest of yellow fever, which in turn is followed — with no connection or transition — by a chapter on the early development of the automobile; while at the end of the book a veritable cartload of unrelated facts upon popular songs, successful books, changing fashions, foods, furniture, crime, and passing sensations is lumped together in a hundred pages of potpourri. All this, enlivened by some vivid writing, bountifully illustrated, and dealing with so recent a period that it awakened the adult public's memory, proved highly entertaining. But it left the reflective reader convinced that while Mr. Sullivan had collected many valuable materials for history, he had fallen decidedly short of writing history itself.

IV

If symmetry and clarity of design are the first essential of good history, progression is the second. The narrative (for all sustained history presupposes a narrative) should move from point to point; the writer must beware of merely marking time. While description, static analysis, and pure exposition have their place in history, they do not suffice, taken alone or together, to make good historical work. Any account of more than a microscopic segment of the past involves time, and time involves movement. In other words, history is dynamic: it deals with mankind in action, and it should trace changes or at least explain the lack of changes resulting from this action. One writer has gone so far as to say that history must make clear three elements: first, the original condition; second, the action; and third, the condition which results, emphasizing the essentially novel features in this resultant condition. While generally sound, this is perhaps too mechanical a rule to be entirely serviceable. It fits some history badly, and a little not at all. For example, an action may end in utter failure and abortion, changing nothing, and yet be well worth recounting. It is simpler and truer to say that any important piece of historical writing must have progression, and that this progression must consist in demonstrating some relation between cause and effect. In other words, we return to the familiar principle that the facts of a piece of history must be synthesized — must be given coherence and significance by some theory of causation.

This is a simple principle, and the theory of causation may be both simple and obvious. A man may be writing a history of Sag Harbor, L. I., let us say, and decides that the decay of Sag Harbor after 1850 was the result of the decline of whaling. This elementary theory gives him a basis for synthesizing his facts.

In any ideal piece of history, no facts fail to possess some causal relation with other facts. Nothing should be left isolated or detached, and nothing thrown in simply because it is interesting or colorful. In some parts of John Bach McMaster's chronicle of the American people many pages have the appearance of a mere historical memorandum-book; confused masses of facts about social life in America are shot at the reader without due effort to relate them to one another, or to the general theme. However interesting in themselves, they lack significance because they are not synthesized, and in such passages McMaster ceases to write history at all. But a word of warning must be added as to some books. Various ingenious authors show great skill in giving a mutual relationship to matters which on the surface have no relation at all, and the appearance of haphazard disconnection in some subtly-written books is misleading. At first glance G. K. Chesterton and Thomas Beer appear to gain many of the effects of their quasi-historical works by sheer irrelevance. In *The Mauve Decade* Beer passes lightly from topic to topic, and frequently throws into otherwise coherent passages some details which seem as alien as the birds that sing in the spring. It is only when his art is more carefully studied that the reader perceives that there is really little irrelevance, and that both his satiric and historical aims have been furthered by the interjected details.

In the third and last place, it is important that the main architectural elements of any historical work be brought out in bold relief, and the minor appurtenances left in a clearly subordinate position. The commonest defect in the work of novices of history is that they never let the reader see the wood for the trees. They fill their monographs with facts which are all given approximately the same value; they pile dates, statistics, quotations, and assertions upon each other without subordinating them to any key statement; in short, they lose their way. The facts of the past are indeed sometimes a rather confusing maze. But a good history is like a good map; it possesses plenty of detail, but the important features stand out in large type. In any clear presentation of New York State the great cities, New York, Buffalo, and Albany, the principal rivers and mountain chains, are lifted in bold relief; in any good history of the Revolution in New York the great main forces are kept prominent, though the volume may contain an exhaustive statement of minor events as well.

As a means of attaining this necessary proportion, the best advice which can be given the beginner is that he should not be afraid of generalizations, but cultivate them; that he should keep general premises and general conclusions always in mind. If he does this, the petty details will soon assort themselves. When he writes, he should always try to proceed from the general to the particular, or the particular to the general — never merely from the particular to the particular. He will note that nearly all good historians do this. Élie Halévy, for example, begins each section of his *England in 1815* with a clear general statement which strikes the key for all that is to follow:

(1) "Three and only three possible methods are conceivable by which a people could govern itself; and all these three forms of government existed side by side in the British Constitution at the beginning of the nineteenth century."

(2) "Is it not perilous for a nation to sacrifice its agriculture to the development of its industries, and thereby to become dependent upon the foreigner for the satisfaction of its most elementary needs?"

(3) "During the opening years of the nineteenth century Methodism and Evangelism had imbued English society with their *ethos*."

It will also profit the student to study a number of volumes in which broad and intricate subjects, full of confusing detail, are brought into small compass in a clear, luminous fashion. The English language is well endowed with such works. Everyone will agree that the history of the Holy Roman Empire is one of the thorniest and most baffling of subjects, involving a huge mass of dry details; a jungle in which any writer might easily lose himself and his readers. But Lord Bryce's *Holy Roman Empire*, written when the author was twenty-six, makes the whole map of the wood as clearly visible as if we were in an airplane taking a lofty survey of it. In still briefer compass, an excellent treatment of an even larger subject is afforded by J. B. Bury's *History of Freedom of Thought*. Carl Becker's *Beginnings of the American People* shows in striking fashion how the intricate web of colonial history, rent eventually into thirteen segments, can be simplified, and its principal features disengaged from the minutiae that surround them.

V

High literary merit ought not to be confused with mere entertainment. Some of the most amusing historical writers have no enduring value, while the really conscientious historian does not pass by important subjects because they are essentially dull. Macaulay remarks in his essay on Horace Walpole that this graceful, shallow writer was never tiresome and never tempted readers to skip. He showed a superior talent not in learning, not in accuracy, not in logic, but in writing what people would like to read. "He rejects all but the attractive parts of his subjects. He keeps only what is in itself amusing, or what can be made so by the artifice of his diction. The coarser morsels of antiquarian learning he abandons to others, and sets out an entertainment worthy of a Roman epicure, an entertainment consisting of nothing but delicacies, the brains of singing birds, the roe of mullets, the sunny halves of peaches." But Walpole, and the writers who like him select only what seems diverting, have no standing as historians. The tendency of some authors to take only the juicy parts of an historical era — the anecdotes, the striking personalities, the picturesque social scenes, the bits of drama — is to be condemned. It is not this but something deeper which is implied by the phrase "literary excellence." Similarly, we should condemn the all too prevalent tendency of writers of popular history to seek enter-

tainment by the device of excessive dramatization. Since bore-
dom is a common ingredient of all human life, since some
monotony and tedium attend even great events, a high degree of
dramatization insidiously falsifies the record of past times.

Yet in political and military history especially, such dramatization is all too frequent. The color even of battles, sieges,
and forced marches can be heightened beyond all reason.
Guedalla remarked of the Australian author of *How England
Saved Europe*, a tub-thumping history of the Napoleonic Wars,
that his night encounters were more nocturnal and his scaling
parties more scaligerous than any others in literature.[1] Yet
Guedalla's own *Second Empire* is not free from the vice of over-
dramatization. Probably no subject in recent American history
has been treated in more histrionic fashion than the impeachment of Andrew Johnson; Mr. Claude G. Bowers, for one,
exhausts his descriptive powers to make it as striking as the
impeachment of Warren Hastings. That it was a momentous
trail, and that it had qualities of grim suspense as men waited to
learn whether a two-thirds vote could be mustered against
Johnson, is undeniable. But the proceedings themselves were
drab and tiresome. Johnson did not appear in person. Ben
Butler prosecuted the case, in his own words, "just as he would
a case of petty larceny in Massachusetts." Save by Evarts, not
one brilliant speech was made. Young Moorfield Storey, whose
perceptions were keen and whose feelings were strongly enlisted
against Johnson, might have been trusted to feel any drama in
the affair; yet writing at the time, he called the trial "a fearful
bore," with "very mediocre displays," and "eternal speeches
all on the same subject." And in its midst he grumbled: "I
feel not a little disgusted with the Congress of the United
States. The debates in the House for the last two days have
been utterly disgraceful." A highly dramatized account quite
misrepresents the event.

It is by more sterling means that literary distinction is at-

[1] Philip Guedalla, *Supers and Supermen*, p. 19

tained. No doubt the central structure of history is a plain square edifice built solidly upon the bedrock of factual research. But in its best manifestations history is a capitol with two wings, one looking toward the domain of ideas, the other toward the domain of imagination. Without these wings history would lack all grace, all inspiration, all depth of interest, and would be in fact unworthy of the name of history; it would be annalistic writing alone. Ideas must be combined with research to produce interpretation. Imagination must be combined with research to produce vividness, human warmth, and poetic truth. Add these wings to the edifice, and the reader can pace the halls of history with a sense that all his faculties, intellectual and aesthetic, are being satisfied. He not only feels a granite foundation under his heel, but he can gaze out at one extremity upon the mountain-peaks of thought, and at the other extremity upon the crowded, multicolored stage where fact is stranger than fiction, and where human destinies challenge the pictorial and narrative powers of the greatest artists. From one set of windows, clear as air, he can see the philosophy of history merging with the abstract philosophy of Kant, Hume, and Hegel. From the other, set with prism-panes, he can see the drama of history merging with the plays of Shakespeare, its romance with the novels of Scott and Hugo, its poetry with that of Dante, Milton, and Goethe. It is only a rare writer who offers in the fullest degree this sense of the richness, spaciousness, and elevation of history; but such writers have appeared in the past and will be given us by the future.

CHAPTER FOURTEEN

THE READING OF HISTORY

E VERYONE WILL agree, theoretically, that "the horrid tale of perjury and strife, murder and spoil, which men call history," should be read. But just how? — what is the best method of attacking it? The failure to answer these questions properly explains why so much good history remains untouched on library shelves while fiction and travel are worn to tatters. History may be read for entertainment. It may be read for instruction about the past, and (though as Coleridge said, most of it is like the sternlights of a ship, illuminating only the course that is past) for guidance to the future. Above all, it may be read for inspiration. "Show me," Walter Savage Landor makes Pericles exclaim, "how great projects were executed, great advantage gained, and great calamities averted . . . Place History on her rightful throne, and at the sides of her Eloquence and War." But there are generalities. To the ordinary reader, even the ordinary college graduate, history is a dim uncharted sea, her ports doubtless full of rich spoils but her waters rough and her headlands forbidding. The amateur goes to the shelves. He plucks down a volume of Tacitus, and turning to the first book, finds himself wandering in a half-understood revolt against Tiberius in Pannonia (where is it?) and Germany; takes down Buckle, and is promptly plunged into a long, dullish, and clearly outdated examination of resources for investigating history; opens Prescott's *Conquest of Mexico*, and is daunted by what at first glance seems a highly archaeological chapter on primitive races and institutions. He concludes that those who call history fascinating are indulging in empty rhetoric.

But are they? Is not the fault rather with the reader who fails to use a little common sense and show a little patience? The idea that fifteen minutes a day, or ten times fifteen, of aimless, undirected reading among good books will make a man well-read is one of the most pernicious ever disseminated under high authority. The idea that much history is "fascinating" in the sense of offering easy entertainment for a casual hour is equally fatuous. But if approached with as careful preparation and precaution as any sensible man uses in approaching a symphony, a masterpiece of art, or the handling of bicycle or skis, and if a little persistent effort is applied to it, ere long it will offer one of the most interesting, varied, and profitable — one of the most truly fascinating — of all employments.

There is but one golden rule in reading history: it should be read by the blazing illumination of a thoroughly aroused intellectual curiosity. Much fiction may be absorbed in lackadaisical mood; pictorial writers like Herodotus and Froissart may be so approached; but nearly all history worthy of the name requires application. Fortunately, the kindling of intellectual curiosity about the past need not be a matter of self-stimulation. Any alert citizen of the modern world should find it constantly aroused by a variety of factors. They include current events at home and abroad — for every newspaper carries great signposts pointing back into history; political issues, which run back to Lincoln and Jackson, Hamilton and Jefferson, Locke and Hobbes; conversations with friends who are interested in ideas and institutions; fresh discoveries in the past as bruited abroad, whether a Tutankhamen's tomb or an unpublished letter by Grover Cleveland; the wave of interest created by any controversial new interpretation of past events, any new fashion in writing history or biography. A self-stimulated interest, one based upon a fixed ambition to master some select period of history, and to do it by systematic, intensive reading, is of course far more valuable. It represents a steady, disciplined impulse, not a transient appetite. But some intellectual curiosity, some inner dissatisfaction leading to effort, is indispensable.

In certain minds intellectual curiosity plays like an unceasing fountain. That fact explains the rather jaunty tone of Theodore Roosevelt's observations upon reading history. In his impetuous, offhand way he wrote that every serious man should apply himself to serious books. "He ought to read interesting books on history and government, and books of science and philosophy; and really good books on these subjects are as thrilling as any fiction ever written in prose or verse. Gibbon and Macaulay, Herodotus, Thucydides, and Tacitus, the Heimskringla, Froissart, Joinville and Villehardouin, Parkman and Mahan, Mommsen and Ranke — why! there are scores and scores of solid histories, the best in the world, which are as absorbing as the best of all the novels, and of as permanent value." Roosevelt could write like this because he knew an immense deal upon certain eras of European and American history, and his incessantly active mind was eager to extend this knowledge. But other men do not have his grounding; even if they have part of his incessant mental activity, it may normally be channeled into non-historical directions — whereas Roosevelt began life as a writer of history. It is usually necessary to take a small flame of intellectual curiosity, and feed it higher and brighter. It may be necessary to take a distinct channel of professional activity and relate it to the nearest branch of history. The business man has every reason to be interested in economic history and the careers of industrial leaders; the lawyer, in Constitutional history.

Those who seek entertainment in history will have no great difficulty in finding it. They should be warned that Clio has never given up much of her domain to mere diversion. Yet by careful selection a good deal of pure description and pure narrative, delightful to peruse, can be found. Herodotus certainly falls in that category; he hardly penned a paragraph that is analytical. Many of the memoir-writers of medieval or early modern times are also found there. Take the chronicles of the crusades by Villehardouin and Joinville mentioned by Roosevelt. They are picturesque and stirring accounts by eye-witnesses of different aspects of one of the most striking movements in history, the effort of the Christian world to recapture "those holy fields over whose acres walked the blessed feet" of Christ. Philip de Commines is often analytical and much of his detail is dull; but in Froissart we see all the brilliancy of court life, all the glamour of chivalry, and dimly in the background, the bloody misery of battles, sieges, and spoliations, in the period when feudalism was fast decaying. Some of Hakluyt's voyages, not so much travel as history, are irresistibly entertaining, while they convey the very essence of the Elizabethan era. Thus we come down to the modern period, with whole shelves of interesting memoirs, and an increasing number of writers who bring to history a brilliant style and a desire to interest large popular audiences. Several of Parkman's books, notably his *La Salle and the Great West*, and his masterpiece *Montcalm and Wolfe*, are written with the rarest descriptive and narrative power, and are difficult to surpass in interest. Trevelyan's three histories of the campaigns of Garibaldi are rich in adventurous incident. Gabriel Hanotaux's *Contemporary France*, with its clarity of style, its rich gallery of personalities, and its flashes of insight, is — despite an inadequate translation — full of diversion to almost anyone.

One way of making the past entertaining is to approach it through historical novels. A course of reading in the American Revolution may be prefaced by *Janice Meredith*, with its portraits of Washington, Hamilton, and other heroes, showing their faults as well as virtues; by J. P. Kennedy's *Horseshoe Robinson*, a romance which culminates with the battle of King's Mountain; and by Cooper's classic *The Spy*. It ought to be difficult for anyone to read *The Cloister and the Hearth* without wishing to know more in general about the years which ushered in the Renaissance, and in particular about Erasmus; to read the two parts of Stevenson's *David Balfour* without a curiosity about Scottish affairs just after the rebellion of 1745; to read Dumas's *Marguerite de Valois* without keener interest in the massacre of St. Bartholomew. Who has closed Joel Chandler Harris's *Free Joe, and Other Sketches* without wondering exactly what slavery was like in the old South? — a wonder that might well lead on to the ante-bellum travels of Frederick Law Olmsted, and the histories of Ulrich B. Phillips. Who has finished the earliest and best tales of Bret Harte without an interest in California civilization in the days of its lawless beginnings? To be sure, most historical fiction does not carry us far into history, and the invented elements are frequently misleading. But some of it is really admirable — Scott's *Fortunes of Nigel*, for example, contains the best portrait of James I to be found anywhere; Shorthouse's *John Inglesant* reproduces the manners, ideas, and religious feeling of seventeenth century England and Italy with accuracy and artistry — while much of it may whet an appetite for more solid fare.

So also may the newspaper. It is as true to say that current events cast their shadows backward as that coming events cast their shadows before. No informed man read of the abdication of Edward VIII without thinking of previous dethronements — Richard II, James II — and some must have gone to J. R. Green's *Short History* and to Macaulay, if not further. The civil war in Spain, with the participation of Moors and Italians — what vistas these events call up! Several of them have been ably treated by American writers. No one needs to be reminded of Irving's *Conquest of Granada*, that lively work of the fictitious Fray Antonio Agapida which catches so faithfully the spirit of the final struggle between Cross and Crescent in the Peninsula. Not many people, unfortunately, are acquainted with the almost equally interesting and far more scholarly sequel, Henry C. Lea's *Moriscoes of Spain, Their Conversion and Expulsion;* a book which takes up the sad history of the conquered Moors, tracing their chequered fortunes from the fall of Granada in 1492 to their expulsion in 1609, and describing the heavy economic and artistic loss which their ejection cost Spain. Prescott's *Ferdinand and Isabella*, probably his masterpiece, covers a much broader canvas. It relates how the various States into which Spain had long been divided were brought under one rule; how the kingdom of Naples was conquered; how the ancient empire of the Moors was overthrown; how the New World was discovered; how the dire engine of the Inquisition was set up; and how the Jews, with all their wealth and culture, were banished. In short, it gives us a secure grip upon many threads which run down to the present-day position of Spain. And if the reader wishes more light upon Italian-Spanish relations, he need only turn for a beginning to two other American books: W. R. Thayer's admirable *Dawn of Italian Independence*, and his *Cavour*.

The newspaper, the weekly magazine, the monthly review, are indeed full of hints which ought to send alert men delving occasionally into the past. Is Abyssinia in the news? For a mere general background, the reader may begin with Sir Harry Johnston's *Opening Up of Africa*, a standard work by one who helped in the opening; go on to Charles P. Lucas's *Partition and Colonization of Africa;* and conclude with a realistic analysis of the selfish factors at work, L. S. Woolf's *Empire and Commerce in Africa, a Study in Economic Imperialism*. Has a Polish statesman died? Well, Georg Brandes wrote an eloquent book on Poland — the land, the people, the literature — full of sympathy for her long struggle for freedom; in its English translation it is still well worth reading. The brilliant and stimulating book by the Pole, Kazimierz Waliszewski, on the unknown Poland, offers a defence of the nation's history against hostile Russian and German interpretations. And Monica Gardner's well-known biography of the great national hero, Kosciusko, is supplemented by her book on the nineteenth century poets, Mickiewicz and others, who held the torch of national feeling aloft in the country's darkest hours. Are the origins of the American Constitution being debated? Someone might care to look up a really vivid but neglected historical novel of Shays's Rebellion, Edward Bellamy's *The Duke of Stockbridge*, and thence go on to McMaster, McLaughlin, Beard, and other writers who have treated the Constitutional Convention. Historical reading born of passing events is likely to be haphazard and sketchy, but it is certainly better than none.

Somewhat better is the type of curiosity kindled by a striking new historical or biographical work, which sets critics quarreling and dinner-tables talking. Works full of vitality are likely to do precisely this. Many of the great nineteenth century histories did not slip into the world, but exploded upon it. So it was with the nationalistic histories, the democratic histories, the communistic histories, of Europe. While some of the old quarrels are completely dead, others still reverberate with diminishing thunder. No one cares much today about the battle between Freeman, who held the Germanic theory of the origin of the village community, and Frederic Seebohm, who in *The English Village Community* retorted by defending Roman influences. But other disputes are unending. Froude's *The English in Ireland in the 18th Century* reflected, along with a liking for the Irish people, a contempt for their political activities; Lecky made an able rejoinder to it in the second volume of his history of eighteenth century England; books as old as Goldwin Smith's *Irish History and Irish Character*, and as recent as Stephen Gwynn's and Shaw Desmond's bear on the controversy, in which anyone may easily immerse himself. New quarrels are constantly beginning. In American history, how many myths about the Revolution have been struck down, and how many keep their defenders! How many myths about the Constitution have been shattered, and how many new ones have been substituted in their places! The writers who maintain, and plausibly, that Andrew Jackson sprang from an aristocratic instead of democratic social background; that Polk and the United States had ample justification for war with Mexico; that Supreme Court majorities have usually obeyed their masters standing in the background; that tariff battles after the Civil War were a disaster because they diverted popular attention from the great issues of business control that should have been faced promptly; that Taft was really an efficient and constructive President — these all arouse controversy. Has our literary history been as rich as Van Wyck Brooks believes, or as thin and poor as Ludwig Lewisohn intimates? Is the value of our cultural traditions as slight as many young radicals assert, or as great as Vernon L. Parrington and Bernard De Voto suggest? These are disputes which ought to provoke people to reading.

Yet reading thus provoked is likely again to be too topical, too hurried to be valuable; it will lack depth, consistency, and steady purpose. The world is so full of a number of things that those who do not exercise some discipline in controlling their interests will remain superficial and scatterbrained. Anything that arouses intellectual curiosity is praiseworthy. But the man who is inspired by the latest archaeological find to take up Breasted's history of Egypt, by some church celebration to tackle Williston Walker's life of Calvin, and by a club dispute over the battle of Jutland to hurry through Winston Churchill's *World Crisis*, is likely to suffer from intellectual dyspepsia. Interest in the past should be marked by a sensible dichotomy. Part of it should certainly be based upon the present, for the man who does not do *some* historical reading with reference to the problems of the day misses a great deal. But after all, the more solid magazines exist in part to relate the present to the past — to indicate the larger implication of current issues; and in any event no one should read too much with his eye on the passing show. Part of his reading should deal with the past as welded into the substructure of the present, not as related to its superstructure.

A casual, *ad hoc* type of reading is far from likely to yield the deeper results of historical study. The best fruits of such study do not lie in mere information, but in the wisdom taught by combining long and accurate historical views with reflection. It is often said that reading history enlarges the mind, and makes the spirit broader and more tolerant. But why and how? This end cannot be achieved by dipping here and there, but only by the planned study of considerable periods in the life of populous and important nations.

Only by such study, to begin with, are streams of tendency, economic, social, and cultural, to be discerned in history. These can be defined in brief textbooks, but they can be illustrated only by rich and ample narratives. As an example, we may take Motley's *Rise of the Dutch Republic* and *United Netherlands:* works which, with some superficialities and many inadequacies and inaccuracies, nevertheless furnish an impressive and instructive panorama. The titles are somewhat unfortunate. They have led many people to think of these works as essentially Dutch history, whereas Motley deals with Spain, France, and England almost as fully as with Holland. His seven volumes go far beyond an eloquent and vivid record of the struggle of the Dutch people against civil and ecclesiastical tyranny. They were intended to illustrate some great philosophical truths. In effect, he offers us a history of all Western Europe during a crucial period—a history of the later phases of the Reformation, of the triumph of religious freedom in various lands over clerical absolutism, and of the emergence of Europe from the Middle Ages into the full light of modern times. He presents the birth of a new era in religion, social life, and politics. No one can read the work through without feeling his spirit as well as mind enriched.

Motley's stage is well set; he presents Philip II and William the Silent as the two principal antagonists in a complex struggle in which, directly or indirectly, half a dozen nations participated. After an introductory description of the land, people, and civilization of Holland during the first half of the sixteenth century, *The Rise of the Dutch Republic* begins with the abdication of Charles V as Holy Roman Emperor in 1555. Motley relates how Philip II took up the reins of government in Spain and Holland, how the Reformation, the true cause of the Dutch revolt, spread steadily, and how the Inquisition, which he paints in rather too ghastly hues, scattered oil on the flames it was meant to quench. In the background, at this beginning of the story, we see many elements of a feudal civilization still persisting: Holland enchained, England weak, Spain holding sway over a vast empire; pre-Copernican ideas of this world and medieval ideas of the next still in the ascendancy. From this point the story proceeds with graphic and original detail drawn by Motley from every available archive. He traces the activities of Egmont, Horn, and the Prince of Orange; tells of Philip's resolve to enforce the decrees of the Council of Trent; describes the popular storm aroused by his torturings and executions; relates how Alva was sent into the Netherlands to crush the revolt; and tells of the years of war that followed, with the heroic feats of the Dutch, the defense of Haarlem, the defeat of Alva's fleet, and other stirring events, till, when freedom was in sight, William of Orange was assassinated. With this calamity of 1584, the first three volumes end.

The four volumes of the *United Netherlands* cover the second great epoch in what Motley expected to be his record of "the eighty years' war for liberty." They open with the independence of Holland practically achieved, though not recognized, and extend from the murder of William the Silent to the Twelve Years' Truce in 1609. The first half of the work is as much English history as Dutch. It deals with the period when the alliance of England and Holland against Spain was almost a political union, the Earl of Leicester becoming governor of the United Provinces; and it culminates in a stirring chapter on the defeat of the Great Armada. Motley never wrote anything better than his description of the tragic siege and loss of Antwerp, or his narrative of the destruction of the great Spanish fleet in 1588. The second half of the *United Netherlands* is somewhat inferior in interest. It contains no events which catch at the heart like the relief of Leyden or the cruel massacre at Naarden, and no personalities which win our regard as do William of Orange and Leicester. Still, Philip and Queen Elizabeth and Bloody Mary are present, and the story reaches a logical conclusion with the Dutch triumph of 1609. In the background, as the history closes, is a very different scene from that described at the beginning. The modern lineaments of society, such as town life, are distinctly marked; science is making steady progress; while Holland has been gaining her freedom, England, triumphant over the Armada, has been reaching the front rank of nations; France has become the political leader of the Continent, and Spain is sinking toward decay. The great central gain of the period, the triumph of Protestantism in most of northern Europe, seems assured. Motley meant to go on with the history of the Thirty Years' War in Germany, a continuation of the titanic religious struggle, but death intervened.

Now Motley's seven volumes have many faults. His research was sometimes far from exhaustive. His strong prejudices, especially on the Protestant side, carried him away and made him unfair to Philip II and Spain. Even Froude, as it has been said, saw the golden thread in the gown of the Dominican monk, but to Motley the gown seemed wholly black. Nevertheless, he told a magnificent story, with half of Europe as a background and some of the main forces of modern civilization hanging in the balance; and he told it admirably, for his style always has force and a dignity that sometimes rises to eloquence. The reader of these volumes gains more than information. He obtains a broad new view of a great critical period of European history, a deeper insight into some of the central tendencies of Occidental civilization. He rises from the work with judgment a little more matured, with wisdom a little riper. So, in still greater degree, readers of Mommsen's *Rome*, of Gibbon's *Decline and Fall*, of Michelet's *History of France*, gain an understanding of the main streams of tendency in history, and a wisdom born of that understanding.

Another object of historical reading is to obtain a view of the conditions, limitations, and potentialities of leadership in any sphere, whether political, economic, or cultural. Of necessity, it must be a view with a good deal of breadth and depth. Here again extended and planned study is almost essential; a considerable period in the life of a considerable civilization must be given thorough examination. In the political sphere, the history of mankind is strewn with instances in which true statesmanship has produced prosperity and happiness, while the lack of it has brought about the most terrible calamities. Was it possible for wise leadership in Washington to have averted the Civil War, which ruined half the South, degraded the whole country morally for years, and left upon American life debilitating effects which are still plainly visible? Not in the eyes of the best observers of that day; Hamilton Fish declared that if about 1850 a large carriage had been filled with the worst of the Northern and Southern extremists and plunged for ten minutes beneath the surface of the Potomac, the nation might have been spared that staggering calamity. The best scholars today equally believe that true statesmanship, especially at the South, might have prevented it. Or the American Revolution, which from the point of view of the British Empire was certainly a calamity — could it have been avoided? On this point we have the measured judgment of the British historian who wrote one of the very best studies of the event. Lecky tells us that "there has scarcely been a great revolution in the world which might not at some stage have been averted, materially modified, or at least greatly postponed, by wise statesmanship." He goes on:

Take, for example, the American Revolution, which destroyed the political unity of the English race. You will often hear this event treated simply as if it were simply due to the wanton tyranny of an English Government, which desired to reduce its colonies to servitude by taxing them without their consent. But if you will look closely into the history of that time — and there is no history which is more instructive — you will find that this is a gross misrepresentation. What happened was essentially this. England, under the guidance of the elder Pitt, had been waging a great and most successful war, which left her with an enormously extended Empire, but also with an addition of more than seventy millions to her National Debt. That debt was now nearly 140 millions, and England was reeling under the taxation it required. The war had been waged largely in America, and its most brilliant result was the conquest of Canada, by which the old American colonies had benefited more than any other part of the Empire, for the expulsion of the French from North America put an end to the one great danger which hung over them. It was, however, extremely probable that if France ever regained her strength, one of her first objects would be to recover her dominion in America.

Under these circumstances the English government concluded that it was impossible that England alone, overburdened as she was by taxation, could undertake the military defence of her greatly extended Empire. Their object, therefore, was to create subsidiary armies for its defence. Ireland already raised by the vote of the Irish Parliament, and out of exclusively Irish resources, an army consisting of from twelve to fifteen thousand men, most of whom were available for the general purpose of the Empire. In India, under a despotic system, a separate army was maintained for the protection of India. It was the strong belief of the English Government that a third army should be maintained in America for the defence of the American colonies and of the neighboring islands, and that it was just and reasonable that America should bear some part of the expense of her own defence. She was charged with no part of the interest of the National Debt; she paid nothing towards the cost of the navy which protected her coast; she was the most lightly taxed and the most prosperous portion of the Empire; she was the part which had benefited most by the late war, and she was the part which was most likely to be menaced if the war was renewed. Under these circumstances Grenville determined that a small army of ten thousand men should be kept in America, under the distinct promise that it was never to serve beyond that country and the West Indian Isles, and he asked America to contribute £10,000 a year, or about a third part of its expense.

But here the difficulty arose. The Irish army was maintained by the vote of the Irish Parliament; but there was no single parliament representing the American colonies, and it soon became evident that it was impossible to induce thirteen State legislatures to agree upon any scheme for supporting an army in America. Under these circumstances Grenville in an ill-omened moment resolved to revive a dormant power which existed in the Constitution, and levy this new war-tax by Imperial taxation. He at the same time guaranteed the colonists that the proceeds of this tax should be expended solely in America; he intimated to them in the clearest way that if they would meet his wishes by themselves providing the necessary sum, he would be abundantly satisfied, and he delayed the enforcement of the measure for a year in order to give them ample time for doing so.

Such and so small was the original cause of difference between England and her colonies. Who can fail to see that it was a difference abundantly susceptible of compromise, and that a wise and moderate statesmanship might easily have averted the catastrophe?

To understand properly this failure of British statesmanship no summary view will serve; the reader must go through some work as thorough and searching as Lecky's *History of England in the 18th Century*. So to understand properly the failure of American statesmanship just before the Civil War it is necessary to read some history of the fifties as extensive as James Ford Rhodes, and to supplement it by at least a few biographies. The extremes to which the French Revolution was pressed constituted a terrible calamity to Europe. They too cannot be understood by a few days over a brief treatise, but only by sustained examination of several volumes; a process more absorbing by far, once interest is fully aroused, than any dilettantish excursion into the period.

Still another utility of the *sustained* reading of history — of following a nation through many mutations and over a considerable period of time — is that this alone exhibits the rise, development, and decay of institutions; and what is more important, shows how much institutions depend upon national tradition, character, and habit, as well as upon physical and economic circumstances. Men untrained in history are wont to take contracted views of institutions. They suppose that because universal suffrage works well in Australia, it would be a great blessing in Egypt. They think that because modern legislatures have almost always been bicameral, they ought never to become unicameral. They believe that the American Constitution is a model of perfection, and that if it were introduced into other lands (perhaps with free schools and free speech thrown in), order, liberty, and prosperity would result; though they need only look at Cuba and some of the South American republics to see that this is not so.

People who read little history seldom comprehend, again, how greatly the different nations of men differ — how widely the average psychology of the Spaniard diverges from the average psychology of the Russian; or how much variation there is between different human types within the same nation. They are therefore nonplused by the extreme divergences of motive, the apparent eccentricities of conduct, often displayed in world affairs. They seldom realize, in consequence, that the institution which in one nation proves highly successful may be a calamity in another. Parliamentary institutions work well in the various nations of the British Commonwealth but almost nowhere else. The Presidential system of government has on the whole served the United States admirably, but south of the Rio Grande it has been an easy stepping-stone to dictatorships. A failure to grasp this elementary truth leads European dictators into foolish denunciations of democracy, and some democratic leaders into only less shortsighted denunciations of the totalitarian forms.

But the greatest lessons of history, as writers from Thucydides to Woodrow Wilson have pointed out, are the moral lessons; and here again some sustained reading is absolutely essential to a full grasp of truth. Such reading helps men a little to measure time against eternity; to rise above the heat and dust of ephemeral issues into a serener atmosphere. Who wins the next election may *seem* a matter of desperate concern; who wins

the war of really overwhelming importance. But the first may
be trivial in its bearing upon national destiny, and the second
of no lasting significance in its bearing upon human destiny.
In moments of party triumph or national exaltation, history
teaches a wise humility; in moments of darkness, confusion, or
pain it teaches a wise patience. It shows Americans that the
corruption, greed, and hatred of Reconstruction days were but
an evanescent obscuration of the true national spirit; it shows
them equally that the strut, fanfare, and arrogance of 1898 was
an inglorious rather than a glorious moment in the national
record. History has a moral lesson, again, in demonstrating
that the immediate results of a national policy are frequently
of slight account compared with the remote results. It is for
this reason that those who prefer principle to expediency in the
conduct of human affairs are usually right. The immediate
gain from seizing upon expediency may appear greater than any
possible loss; but respect for tradition, the value of continuity
in affairs, the importance of dependable habits to a community
as to a man, the close connection between principle and rectitude
— all this weighs heavily in the balance. When a Napoleon III
or Mussolini arises who charts his course by expediency alone,
his nation is in grave peril.

Not least of the moral lessons derived from any prolonged
perusal of history is that which relates to the character of
nations. No one can read much in this department of literature
without being profoundly impressed by the mutability of all
human fortunes, the constant alternations of prosperity and
disaster in the record of nearly all peoples. Nor can anyone
read much of it without feeling the hollowness of a vast deal
that is called glory and greatness. Little Athens may be more
truly great than Rome, little Denmark than imperial Germany.
When even the greatest Powers are essentially insecure, when
military disasters, economic collapses, territorial losses so frequently befall the strongest nations, it behooves a country to
seek its enduring welfare in quarters not too grossly material.

Americans rightly pride themselves upon the idealism of their national character; Britons upon their national integrity and steadfastness; Frenchmen upon their devotion to light and culture. The permanent well-being of peoples, one historian assures us, "is essentially the outcome of their moral state. Its foundation is laid in pure domestic life, in commercial integrity, in a high standard of moral worth and of public spirit; in simple habits, in courage, uprightness, and self-sacrifice, in a certain soundness and moderation of judgment, which springs quite as much from character as from intellect." [1] There is a great deal in history, read *in extenso*, to support this thesis. It is not difficult, over long periods, to tell when a nation is rising or when it is decaying, and almost invariably the rise or decay is connected with a development or deliquescence of the national character.

This thesis is nowhere better expounded than in the famous introduction of Polybius to the first book of his history. The Greek author, who had stood by Scipio's side while Carthage was burning, and had been at Corinth during or just after its sack by Mummius, knew the Romans of his day thoroughly. Writing about 150 B.C., he called the attention of Greek readers to the immense change wrought in half a century in the Mediterranean world. Who does not wish to understand just how "the Romans in less than fifty-three years have succeeded in subjecting nearly the whole inhabited world to their sole government — a thing unique in history"? In these fifty-three years the entire face of the known earth had been altered. If Rome was not everywhere sovereign, at any rate she was everywhere dominant. Polybius remarks that a man must be not only a dullard but morally deficient if he does not wish to understand this amazing achievement, this "spectacle so striking and grand." What is the explanation of it? To supply an answer is the purpose of his history. It is not mere events, he writes, that are interesting, but their causes. The causes of the rise of

[1] W. E. H. Lecky, *Historical and Political Essays*, 38

Rome were primarily moral, and these moral causes he elucidates.

To plan the extensive reading of history offers no great difficulty. It is not old-fashioned advice to say that the best step
that the ordinary amateur can take is to provide himself with
complete sets of some of the classic historians, and read them
through. Such sets are cheap. Judicious skipping may assist
in reading some of them, but not many require it. Thus the
amateur may make himself acquainted with large periods, with
great convulsions and their causes, and with vast changes for
good or ill in the fortune of nations. What, he may ask, read
all of Prescott? He wrote nothing that is not worth reading;
in fact he wrote but four books, each of which might nowadays
be printed in one volume. Read all of Parkman? He also
wrote nothing, save perhaps the *Conspiracy of Pontiac*, that
is not worth reading. Read all of Mommsen's *Rome* or Macaulay's *England?* Why not? Is not Gibbon a little too difficult
for the plain man? His style is certainly a little tiring in its
pomposity, and may best be taken in moderate quantities. But
two plain hardfisted men of affairs, Cecil Rhodes and Tom
Johnson, made Gibbon almost a Bible, and the latter could
quote the *Decline and Fall* with word-perfect familiarity. Let
readers but experiment a little — let them take Milman's
History of the Jews, or Thierry's *Norman Conquest*, and see if
when fully launched they can lay it down unfinished; if the experiment fails let them take up something else till their taste
is met.

Apart from this initial reliance upon the great standard
writers, it is usually a common sense rule to approach any
historical period by reading trustworthy books in the order of
their literary attractiveness. There are recent books upon the
American Revolution which possess greater authoritativeness
than any of their predecessors, but which are not precisely
delightful to read. One older work, however, is fascinating in
style and presentation. No man, however scant his knowledge

of the period or his interest in history in general, ever expressed disappointment in George Otto Trevelyan's volumes; hundreds of thousands have expressed the delight which led Theodore Roosevelt to invite the author to visit America and stay in the White House. Why not, then, take Trevelyan first? It is also a wise rule to follow any vein of ore for some distance by the connected but not necessarily systematic reading of various books, one suggesting another. A man may begin with John Addington Symonds's brightly colored and beautifully written work on the Renaissance, purchasable now in two volumes for less than that many dollars. From this he may go to other books upon the same beguiling period. Or, with equal logic and in some instances greater profit, he may turn into some side-road. Symonds's account of the cruelties and crimes perpetrated by church and state in the age of the despots may send him to a biography of the reformer Savonarola; then from that to Henry C. Lea's *Superstition and Force*, a striking record of the conflicts and exertions, the advances and defeats, by which the progress of humane legislation and exact justice was slowly forwarded; and then to Sir James Fitzjames Stephens's history of the criminal law in England, with its impressive exhibition of the growth of equity and justice in the land in which they have attained their greatest security. The large number of feasible and attractive roads through the domain of history will soon impress any diligent reader; and presently he will begin to find how frequently they offer stimulating inter-sections.

But after all, the essential advice is,— Read! There are the varied shelves, rich in works from Herodotus and Thucydides to the ten thousand writers of today; there are guides and handbooks which anyone can find. There is wealth it were a shame to neglect — wealth

> Compact of Rainbow Gold and of Fire
> Of sorrow and sin and of heart's desire,
> Of good and of evil and of things unknown.

APPENDIXES

AN HISTORICAL READING LIST

These lists of readings are divided into two groups, "Standard Works" and "Recommended Works." Generally speaking, the "Standard" authors are so designated because the scope, literary distinction, and influence of their writings have given them an especially high place in historiography. They are entitled to be regarded as classics. Some of them are to be used with care, for their conclusions have been modified by later writings; in using each standard historian the reader should, if possible, refer to a recent critique of his work. But their place in the development of historical knowledge, their methods, and their style and ideas are worthy of special attention.

I ANCIENT HISTORY

STANDARD WORKS

Ancient: Herodotus, *History;* Livy, *History of Rome;* Polybius, *Histories;* Thucydides, *History of the Peloponnesian War;* Xenophon, *The Institution of Cyrus, The Expedition of Cyrus, The Affairs of Greece, The Defence of Socrates, The Memoirs of Socrates;* Sallust, *The Conspiracy of Catiline, The Jugurthine War;* Ammianus, *Roman History.*

Modern: G. Ferrero, *Greatness and Decline of Rome;* George Grote, *History of Greece;* Sir Gaston Maspero, *Egyptian Archaeology, The Dawn of Civilization, The Struggle of the Nations, The Passing of the Empires;* Eduard Meyer, *Geschichte des Altertums;* Theodor Mommsen, *History of Rome;* M. I. Rostovtzeff, *The Ancient World, The Social and Economic History of the Roman Empire;* Fustel de Coulanges, *The Ancient City.*

RECOMMENDED WORKS

Ancient: Dio Cassius, *History of Rome;* Plutarch, *Lives;* Appian, *Foreign and Civil Wars;* Cicero, *Letters.*

Modern: J. Beloch, *Griechische Geschichte; Cambridge Ancient History;* J. H. Breasted, *Ancient Records of Egypt, History of the Ancient*

Egyptians; Edward Bevan, *Egypt under the Ptolemies;* H. R. H. Hall, *Ancient History of the Near East;* M. Jastrow, *The Civilization of Babylonia and Assyria;* W. W. Tarn, *Hellenistic Civilization;* A. Holm, *Greece;* S. Gsell, *Histoire ancienne de l'Afrique du Nord;* E. S. Bouchier, works on Spain, Syria, and Carthage; O. Seeck, *Geschichte des Untergangs der antiken Welt;* T. Gomperz, *Greek Thinkers;* Gilbert Murray, *The Rise of the Greek Epic;* J. B. Bury, *The Ancient Greek Historians;* J. A. Froude, *Life of Julius Caesar;* W. E. Heitland, *The Roman Republic;* H. Dessau, *Geschichte der römischen Kaiserzeit;* J. B. Bury, *History of the Later Roman Empire.*

II MEDIEVAL HISTORY

STANDARD WORKS

Medieval: Bede, *Ecclesiastical History of England;* Eusebius, *Church History;* Froissart, *Chronicles;* Gregory of Tours, *History of the Franks;* Guicciardini, *History of Italy;* Villehardouin, *Memoirs;* Joinville, *Memoirs;* Matthew Paris, *Works;* Orosius, *Works;* Otto of Freising, *Chronicle.*

Modern: Edward Gibbon, *Decline and Fall of the Roman Empire;* Thomas Hodgkin, *Italy and Her Invaders, Charles the Great, Theodoric;* Henry C. Lea, *History of the Inquisition, The Moriscoes of Spain, Superstition and Force, Sacerdotal Celibacy;* Fustel de Coulanges, *The Institutions of Ancient France;* F. Gregorovius, *The City of Rome in the Middle Ages;* K. Lamprecht, *Deutsche Geschichte, Deutsches Wirtschaftsleben im Mittelalter;* P. Vinogradoff, *English Society in the Eleventh Century, The Growth of the Manor, Villeinage in England;* F. W. Maitland, *Constitutional History of England, The Domesday Book, English Law before Edward I;* H. Pirenne, *Medieval Cities, Histoire de Belgique, Belgian Democracy;* Henry Hallam, *The Constitutional History of England; State of Europe During the Middle Ages.*

RECOMMENDED WORKS

Medieval: Einhard, *Life of Charlemagne, Letters;* Marsilius of Padua, *Defensor Pacis;* Pierre Dubois, *On the Recovery of the Holy Land;* Machiavelli, *History of Florence;* G. de Villehardouin, *Conquest of Constantinople;* John of Salisbury, *Polycraticus;* Salvianus, *On the Government of God;* The Paston Letters.

Modern: *Cambridge Medieval History;* E. Lavisse and A. Rambaud, *Histoire générale;* James Bryce, *Holy Roman Empire;* W. T. Waugh,

Europe from 1378 to 1494; G. B. Adams, *Civilization during the Middle Ages;* J. B. Bury, *History of the Eastern Roman Empire;* J. J. Döllinger, *The First Age of Christianity;* A. Harnack, *Expansion of Christianity;* A. Hauck, *Kirchengeschichte Deutschlands;* A. F. Gfrörer, *Papst Gregorius VII und sein Zeitalter;* P. Villari, *Life and Times of Girolamo Savonarola;* A. Luchaire, *Social France in the Age of Philip Augustus, Histoire des institutions monarchiques de la France, 987–1180, Louis VI, Innocent III;* H. H. Milman, *History of Latin Christianity;* W. E. H. Lecky, *History of European Morals from Augustus to Charlemagne;* C. H. Haskins, *The Normans in European History, The Rise of Universities, Studies in the History of Medieval Science, Renaissance of the Twelfth Century;* W. Giesebrecht, *Geschichte der deutschen Kaiserzeit;* F. von Raumer, *Geschichte der Hohenstaufen und ihrer Zeit;* C. Stephenson, *Borough and Town;* G. G. Coulton, *Five Centuries of Religion, The Medieval Village;* J. W. Thompson, *Economic and Social History of the Middle Ages;* P. Sabatier, *Life of St. Francis of Assisi;* E. Kantorowicz, *Life of Frederick II;* F. Schevill, *History of Florence.*

III MODERN EUROPEAN HISTORY

STANDARD WORKS

T. B. Macaulay, *History of England;* G. M. Trevelyan, *British History in the Nineteenth Century, Lord Grey and the Reform Bill, The Age of Queen Anne;* W. Cunningham, *Growth of English Industry, Monuments of English Municipal Life, Essay on Western Civilization in its Economic Aspects;* Lord Clarendon, *History of the Rebellion;* L. Pastor, *History of the Popes;* L. von Ranke, *History of England, History of the Popes, The Reformation in Germany;* H. von Sybel, *The Founding of the German Empire;* J. R. Green, *Short History of the English People;* H. von Treitschke, *History of Germany in the Nineteenth Century;* P. J. Blok, *History of the People of the Netherlands;* M. M. Kovalevsky, *Modern Customs and Ancient Laws of Russia, Russian Political Institutions;* S. R. Gardiner, *History of England, 1603–1656;* J. Janssen, *History of the German People at the Close of the Middle Ages;* A. Aulard, *The French Revolution;* E. Lavisse, *History of France, History of Prussia, Louis XIV;* W. E. H. Lecky, *History of England in the Eighteenth Century, Ireland in the Eighteenth Century, The History of European Morals.*

RECOMMENDED WORKS

General: *Cambridge Modern History;* E. Lavisse and A. Rambaud, *Histoire générale; Cambridge History of the British Empire;* A. Stern,

Geschichte Europas 1815–1871; A. Debidour, *Histoire Diplomatique de l'Europe; Cambridge History of British Foreign Policy;* C. Bulle, *Geschichte der neuesten Zeit.*
Renaissance and Reformation: J. C. Burckhardt, *Civilization of the Renaissance in Italy;* M. Creighton, *History of the Papacy;* Preserved Smith, *Age of the Reformation;* F. von Bezold, *Geschichte der deutschen Reformation;* J. E. Sandys, *Harrard Lectures on the Revival of Learning;* K. Burdach, *Reformation, Renaissance, Humanismus;* John Addington Symonds, *The Renaissance in Italy.*
Sixteenth and Seventeenth Centuries: J. A. Froude, *History of England to the Death of Elizabeth;* E. P. Cheyney, *History of England from the Defeat of the Armada to the Death of Elizabeth;* W. Stubbs, *Constitutional History of England;* H. D. Traill, *Social England;* J. Thorold Rogers, *History of Agriculture in England;* R. B. Merriman, *Rise of the Spanish Empire;* J. L. Motley, *Rise of the Dutch Republic, History of the United Netherlands;* W. H. Prescott, *Ferdinand and Isabella, Philip II;* A. Cosci, *L'Italia 1530–1789;* B. Erdmannsdörffer, *Deutsche Geschichte vom westfälischen Frieden;* Otto von Zwiedineck-Südenhorst, *Deutsche Geschichte im Zeitraum der Gründung des preussischen Königtums;* Noël Aymés, *La France de Louis XIII;* F. M. A. de Voltaire, *Histoire du siècle de Louis XIV;* Dmitri S. Mirskii, *Russia: a Social History;* V. O. Kliuchevskii, *History of Russia;* A. Rambaud, *Histoire de la Russie;* K. Stählin, *Geschichte Russlands;* C. H. Firth, works on Cromwell and the Protectorate.
Eighteenth and Nineteenth Centuries: C. von Noorden, *Europäische Geschichte im 18. Jahrhundert;* G. Robertson, *England under the Hanoverians;* J. R. Seeley, *Growth of British Policy;* A. T. Mahan, *Influence of Sea-Power upon History, 1660–1783, Influence of Sea-Power, 1793–1812;* G. O. Trevelyan, *Early History of C. J. Fox;* Charles Oman, *History of the Peninsular War;* J. H. Clapham, *Economic History of Modern Britain;* É. Halévy, *History of the English People in the Nineteenth Century;* Spencer Walpole, *History of England from 1815;* Herbert Paul, *History of Modern England;* F. A. Gualterio, *Gli Ultimi rivolgimenti italiani;* F. Bertolini, *Storia d'Italia 1814–1878;* W. R. Thayer, *Dawn of Italian Independence;* Bolton King, *History of Italian Unity;* B. Croce, *History of Italy 1871–1915;* J. Droz, *Histoire du règne de Louis XVI;* H. Carré, *La France sous Louis XV;* L. Madelin, *The French Revolution;* A. Sorel, *L'Europe et la Révolution française;* H. A. Taine, *Les Origines de la France contemporaine: I, l'Ancien Régime; II, la Révolution;* A. de Tocqueville, *L'Ancien Régime et la Révolution;* Lefebvre, Guyot, and Sagnac, *La Révolution française;* P. de la Gorce, *Histoire de la seconde république, Histoire du second empire;* Taxile

Delord, *Histoire du second empire;* E. Ollivier, *L'Empire liberal;* G. Hanotaux, *Contemporary France;* C. J. H. Hayes, *Historical Evolution of Modern Nationalism;* L. Hausser, *Deutsche Geschichte vom Tode Friedrichs des Grossen;* K. T. von Heigel, *Deutsche Geschichte vom Tode Friedrichs des Grossen;* W. Oncken, *Oesterreich und Preussen im Befreiungskriege;* A. Stern, *Geschichte Europas seit den Verträgen von 1815 bis zum Frankfurter Frieden von 1871;* H. Blum, *Die deutsche Revolution 1848–1849;* P. Lehautcourt, *Histoire de la Guerre de 1870;* E. Brandenburg, *Von Bismarck zum Weltkriege;* W. H. Dawson, *German Empire, 1867–1914;* W. Oncken, *Das Zeitalter des Kaisers Wilhelm;* E. Denis, *Fondation de l'empire allemand;* A. A. Kornilov, *Modern Russian History;* G. T. Robinson, *Rural Russia under the Old Régime;* W. H. Chamberlin, *Russian Revolution, 1917–21;* P. Miliukov, *Skizzen russischer Kulturgeschichte;* L. Kulczycki, *Geschichte der russischen Revolution;* J. R. Seeley, *The Expansion of England;* A. Zimmerman, *Die europäischen Kolonien;* P. Leroy-Beaulieu, *De la colonization chez les peuples modernes.*

Twentieth Century: S. B. Fay, *The Origins of the World War;* B. E. Schmitt, *The Coming of the War;* G. P. Gooch, *History of Modern Europe 1878–1919;* Ramsey Muir, *The Political Consequences of the Great War;* C. R. Cruttwell, *History of the Great War.*

Biographies: Preserved Smith, *Erasmus;* James Mackinnon, *Luther and the Reformation;* Frederic Seebohm, *Oxford Reformers: Colet, Erasmus, and More;* Mandell Creighton, *Queen Elizabeth;* Thomas Carlyle, *Cromwell;* Basil Williams, *Lord Chatham;* Lord Morley, *Edmund Burke;* J. Holland Rose, *Life of William Pitt;* A. T. Mahan, *Nelson;* Lytton Strachey, *Queen Victoria;* Graham Wallas, *Francis Place;* H. C. Bell, *Palmerston;* Lord Morley, *Gladstone;* W. F. Monypenny and G. E. Buckle, *Disraeli;* G. M. Trevelyan, *Lord Grey and the Reform Bill, John Bright;* Ruth Putnam, *William the Silent;* Paul Van Dyke, *Catherine de Medici;* James B. Perkins, *France under Mazarin;* Hilaire Belloc, *Danton, Robespierre;* A. Fournier, *Napoleon;* John M. S. Allison, *Thiers and the French Monarchy, 1797–1848;* W. R. Thayer, *Cavour;* Bolton King, *Mazzini;* Thomas Carlyle, *Frederick the Great;* Guy S. Ford, *Stein and the Era of Reform in Prussia, 1807–1815;* Charles G. Robertson, *Bismarck;* Joseph Redlich, *Emperor Francis Joseph of Austria;* Eugene Schuyler, *Peter the Great;* Sir Edwin Pears, *Abdul Hamid.*

Appendix

IV AMERICAN HISTORY

STANDARD WORKS

H. L. Osgood, *The American Colonies in the Seventeenth Century, American Colonies in the Eighteenth Century;* John Fiske, *The Discovery of America, The Dutch and Quaker Colonies, Old Virginia and her Neighbours;* George Bancroft, *History of the United States;* William H. Prescott, *The Conquest of Mexico, The Conquest of Peru, Ferdinand and Isabella, Philip II;* Henry Adams, *History of the United States under Jefferson and Madison;* Edward Channing, *History of the United States;* John Bach McMaster, *History of the People of the United States;* Francis Parkman, *Works;* James Ford Rhodes, *History of the United States from the Compromise of 1850;* James Schouler, *History of the United States;* F. J. Turner, *The Frontier in American History, The Rise of the New West.*

RECOMMENDED WORKS

Histories: *The American Nation Series; Chronicles of America; A History of American Life;* V. L. Parrington, *Main Currents in American Thought;* J. T. Adams, *Founding of New England, Revolutionary New England;* G. L. Beer, *Old Colonial System, British Colonial Policy;* Evarts B. Greene, *Foundations of American Nationality;* C. M. Andrews, *Colonial Period of American History;* S. E. Morison, *Builders of the Bay Colony;* C. H. Van Tyne, *Causes of the War of Independence, The War of Independence;* G. O. Trevelyan, *The American Revolution;* C. W. Alvord, *Mississippi Valley in British Politics;* C. A. Beard, *Economic Interpretation of the Constitution, Economic Origins of Jeffersonian Democracy;* Claude G. Bowers, *Jefferson and Hamilton, Jefferson in Power;* F. L. Paxson, *The American Frontier;* U. B. Phillips, *American Negro Slavery, Life and Labor in the Old South;* Frederic Bancroft, *Slave Trading in the Old South;* J. H. Smith, *Annexation of Texas, War with Mexico;* J. F. Rhodes, *History of the Civil War;* J. G. Randall, *Civil War and Reconstruction;* E. P. Oberholtzer, *United States since the Civil War;* David S. Muzzey, *From the Civil War;* J. D. Hicks, *The Populist Revolt;* W. P. Webb, *The Great Plains;* A. C. McLaughlin, *Constitutional History of the United States;* S. F. Bemis, *Diplomatic History of the United States;* Charles Warren, *Supreme Court in United States History;* Charles O. Paullin, *Atlas of the Historical Geography of the United States.*

Biographies: W. C. Bruce, *Benjamin Franklin Self-Revealed;* Rupert Hughes, *George Washington;* A. J. Beveridge, *John Marshall;*

F. W. Hirst, *Thomas Jefferson;* J. S. Bassett, *Andrew Jackson;* Carl Schurz, *Henry Clay;* A. J. Beveridge, *Abraham Lincoln;* J. G. Nicolay and John Hay, *Abraham Lincoln;* D. S. Freeman, *R. E. Lee;* Frederic Bancroft, *William H. Seward;* George F. Milton, *Age of Hate (Andrew Johnson);* Allan Nevins, *Hamilton Fish; Grover Cleveland;* H. Adams, *The Education of Henry Adams;* Tyler Dennett, *John Hay;* Henry Pringle, *Theodore Roosevelt;* Philip M. Jessup, *Elihu Root;* Ray Stannard Baker, *Woodrow Wilson.*

V THE HISTORY OF THOUGHT

STANDARD WORKS

Sources: Aristotle, St. Augustine, Roger Bacon, Dante, John Locke, N. Machiavelli, Marsiglio of Padua, Montaigne, Plato, Thomas Aquinas, G. Vasari, Voltaire (works of each).

Secondary: H. E. Barnes and H. Becker, *Social Thought from Lore to Science;* C. R. Beazley, *Dawn of Modern Geography;* H. T. Buckle, *History of Civilization in England;* W. A. Dunning, *History of Political Theories, Ancient and Medieval;* F. Guizot, *General History of Civilization in Modern Europe;* H. Hallam, *The Literature of Europe in the 15th, 16th, and 17th Centuries;* W. E. H. Lecky, *The Rise and Influence of Rationalism in Europe;* J. P. Mahaffy, *Greek Life and Thought, The Greek World under Roman Sway, What Have the Greeks Done for Modern Civilization?;* J. T. Merz, *History of European Thought;* H. Rashdall, *The Universities of Europe in the Middle Ages;* John Addington Symonds, *The Renaissance in Italy;* H. A. Taine, *Origins of Contemporary France, History of English Literature;* Henry Osborn Taylor, *Ancient Ideals, The Medieval Mind, Thought and Expression in the Sixteenth Century;* W. C. Dampier Whetham, *Science and the Human Mind.*

RECOMMENDED WORKS

Prehistoric and Ancient: W. G. Sumner, *Folkways;* R. H. Lowie, *Primitive Religion;* E. B. Tylor, *Primitive Culture;* A. L. Kroeber, *Anthropology;* J. G. Frazer, *The Golden Bough;* E. Zeller, *Introduction to Greek Philosophy;* J. P. Mahaffy, *History of Greek Literature;* H. N. Fowler and J. R. Wheeler, *Handbook of Greek Archaeology;* J. Singer, *Greek Biology and Medicine;* J. L. Heiberg, *Mathematics and Physical Science;* W. R. Livingstone, *The Legacy of Greece;* Cyril Bailey, *The Legacy of Rome;* James Muirhead, *Historical Introduction to the*

Private Law of Rome; F. de Coulanges, *The Ancient City;* A. E. Zimmern, *The Greek Commonwealth;* H. J. S. Maine, *Ancient Law;* A. A. Goldenweiser, *Early Civilization;* F. Cumont, works on Roman religion; M. Schanz, *Geschichte der römischen Literatur;* J. W. Mackail, *Latin Literature.*

Medieval: W. P. Ker, *The Dark Ages;* H. B. Workman, *Evolution of the Monastic Ideal;* Lynn Thorndike, *History of Magic and Experimental Science;* H. C. Lea, *Superstition and Force;* Alfred Kremer, *Culturgeschichte des Orients unter den Chalifen;* W. R. Lethaby, *Mediaeval Art;* Walter Pater, *The Renaissance;* J. E. Sandys, *History of Classical Scholarship;* A. A. Tilley, *Literature of the French Renaissance;* P. Monnier, *Le Quattrocento;* J. Huizinga, *Waning of the Middle Ages;* G. Scott, *The Architecture of Humanism;* F. J. C. Hearnshaw, *Social and Political Ideas of Some Great Thinkers of the Renaissance and the Reformation;* J. K. Ingram, *History of Slavery and Serfdom;* R. A. Nicholson, works on Arabic literature; D. B. MacDonald, works on Islam; H. A. Giles, *History of Chinese Literature;* T. F. Carter, *The Invention of Printing in China;* G. H. Putnam, *Books and Their Makers during the Middle Ages;* C. A. Beazley, *Dawn of Modern Geography;* G. Sarton, *Introduction to the History of Science.*

Modern: Galileo Galilei, *Dialogue Concerning Two New Sciences;* Preserved Smith, *History of Modern Culture;* H. Hallam, *Introduction to the Literature of Europe in the Fifteenth, Sixteenth and the Seventeenth Centuries;* Sir Thomas More, *Utopia;* F. A. Lange, *History of Materialism;* George Saintsbury, *History of Criticism;* E. A. Burtt, *Metaphysical Foundations of Modern Physical Science;* G. M. Trevelyan, *British History in the Nineteenth Century;* F. S. Marvin, *The Century of Hope;* J. T. Merz, *History of European Thought in the Nineteenth Century;* A. D. White, *History of Warfare of Science with Theology;* F. S. Marvin, *The Unity of Western Civilization;* E. W. Byrn, *Progress of Invention in the Nineteenth Century;* A. P. Usher, *History of Mechanical Inventions;* G. T. F. Raynal, *A Philosophical and Political History of the Settlement and Trade of the Europeans in the East and West Indies;* A. Reichwein, *China and Europe;* E. T. Williams, *China Yesterday and Today;* Georg Brandes, *Main Currents in Nineteenth Century Literature.*

BIBLIOGRAPHICAL AIDS TO RESEARCH

I GENERAL GUIDES TO BOOKS

Isadore G. Mudge. *Guide to Reference Books.* Chicago, American Library Association, 1929. A standard work, extremely helpful.

Library of Congress. Card catalogue of printed books, magazines, and pamphlets. A fairly complete file is kept in the Columbia University Library; another in the New York Public Library, and in many other college and city libraries. Authors, and titles for periodicals and anonymous works.

British Museum. Department of printed books. *Catalogue of Printed Books.* London, Clowes, 1881–1900. 393 pts. in 95 v. Supplement. London, Clowes, 1900–1905. 13 v. Chiefly authors, but some subjects.

British Museum. Department of printed books. *Subject Index of the modern works added to the library, 1881–1925.* London, 1902–27. 8 v. An excellent index to subjects.

Paris. Bibliothèque nationale. *Catalogue générale des livres imprimés.* Auteurs. Paris, Imprimerie nationale, 1900–1929. v. i–97, A-Liek.

United States Catalogue; Books in Print January 1, 1928. 4th ed. New York, Wilson, 1928, 1929–32. Continued by the *Cumulative book index* (monthly) and the *Publisher's weekly.* None of these is absolutely complete.

English Catalogue of Books published 1801–1925. London, Low, 1864–1901; Publishers' circular, 1906–26. 12 v. Lists books issued in the United Kingdom, 1801–1925. Continued by annual volumes.

William Swan Sonnenschein. *The Best Books; a reader's guide to the choice of the best available books.* 3d ed. pts. 1–4. London, Routledge, 1910–26. Classified by subject.

II GENERAL GUIDES TO PERIODICALS

Poole's Index to Periodical Literature, 1802–1907. Boston, Houghton, 1891–1908. 6 v. A subject index of about 12,500 volumes of 470 American and English periodicals.

Reader's Guide to Periodical Literature (cumulated), 1900 to date. New York, Wilson, 1905 to date. A careful modern index of important magazines published in English.

International Index to Periodicals, devoted chiefly to the humanities and science. 1907 to date. New York, Wilson, 1916 to date. v. 12, 1907–19, issued under title Reader's guide to periodical literature supplement. v. 4 covering 1924–27 indexes 277 periodicals of which 97 are foreign. There are more specialized periodicals not indexed in the *Reader's Guide.*

Annual Magazine Subject Index, 1907 to date. Boston, Faxon, 1908 to date. 1907 has title Magazine subject-index. Indexes more English periodicals than other American indexes.

Book Review Digest, 1905 to date. New York, Wilson, 1905 to date. Annual cumulated volumes. Summarizes and indexes important book reviews in more than fifty periodicals and newspapers.

The *Times,* London. *Palmer's index to the Times,* 1790 to date. London, Palmer, 1868 to date.

The *Times,* London. *Official index to the Times,* 1906 to date. London, *Times* office, 1907 to date.

New York Times Index. 1913 to date. New York, *New York Times,* 1913 to date. An excellent quarterly index. Beginning with 1930, is appearing monthly and cumulating quarterly.

III GUIDES TO GENERAL HISTORY

George M. Dutcher, Henry R. Shipman, Sidney B. Fay, and others. *A Guide to Historical Literature.* New York, Macmillan, 1931. A selected, classified, and critical bibliography of the whole field of history.

Charles Victor Langlois. *Manuel de bibliographie historique.* Paris, Hachette, 1901–4. 2 v.

Jahresberichte der Geschichtswissenschaft. Edited by J. Jastrow (later by Berner). v. 1–36, 1878–1913. Berlin, Mittler, 1880–1916. Discontinued with v. 36, 1913. Appeared annually two or three years after the year covered. Embraces the whole field of history, and attempts to list all books and articles of value.

Henri Stein. *Manuel de bibliographie général; bibliotheca bibliographica nova.* Paris, Picard, 1897. Not confined to history. Arranged by subjects with subdivisions. Brief notes on some works. Kept to date in *La bibliographie moderne,* edited by Henri Stein.

IV GUIDES TO ANCIENT HISTORY

George W. Botsford. A syllabus of Roman history. New York, Macmillan, 1915. A brief manual, with good selections of sources and secondary material.

Cambridge Ancient History, edited by J. B. Bury, S. A. Cook, and F. E. Adcock. Cambridge, England, University Press, 1923–33. v. 1–9, v. 1–3 of plates. A standard coöperative work. Good bibliography arranged by chapters.

Mikhail Ivanovich Rostovtsev. *A History of the Ancient World.* Oxford, Clarendon Press, 1926–27. v. 1–2. Bibliographies at the end of each volume.

Rudolph Klussmann. *Bibliotheca Scriptorum Classicorum et Graecorum et Latinorum.* The literature from 1878 to 1896 inclusive. Leipzig, Reisland, 1909–13. 2 v. in 4 pts.

August Friedrich von Pauly. Pauly's *Real-Encyclopaedie der classischen Altertumswissenschaft.* New Edition . . . published by G. Wissowa. Stuttgart, Metzler, 1894–1930. v. 1–14, 2d ser. v. 1–3, Supp. v. 1–4.

Charles V. Daremberg and Edmond Saglio. *Dictionnaire des antiquités grecques et romaines.* Paris, Hachette, 1873–1919. 5 v. and index.

George W. Botsford, and E. G. Sihler, *Hellenic Civilization.* New York, Columbia University Press, 1915. Full bibliographical apparatus.

V GUIDES TO MEDIEVAL HISTORY

Cambridge Medieval History, planned by J. B. Bury, edited by H. M. Gwatkin, J. P. Whitney, P. Orten, *et al.* New York, Macmillan, 1911–36. 8 v. had appeared by the beginning of 1933. Has good bibliographies arranged by chapters.

Friedrich Christoph Dahlmann. *Dahlmann-Waitz. Quellenkunde der deutschen Geschichte.* Edited by Paul Herre. 8th ed. Leipzig, Koehler, 1912. "The most perfect of all bibliographies of national history." Includes medieval and modern history. Lists sources and secondary works. Indexed.

Louis John Paetow. *Guide to the Study of Medieval History*, for students, teachers, and libraries. 2d ed. Berkeley, University of California Press, 1930. Lists sources and secondary works, with an adequate index. See pp. 1–10 for special bibliographies.

August Potthast. *Bibliotheca Historica Medii Aevi.* Wegweiser durch die Geschichtswerke des europäischen Mittelalters bis 1500. Berlin, Weber, 1896. 2 v. Confined to primary sources, but lists modern works which explain sources. Part I describes all important printed collections of sources. Part II contains alphabetical list of medieval authors and their works. Indispensable to the advanced student.

Gabriel Jacques Jean Monod. *Bibliographie de l'histoire de France;* catalogue méthodique et chronologique des sources et des ouvrages relatifs à l'histoire de France depuis les origines jusqu'en 1789. Paris, Hachette, 1888. Pays special attention to modern works.

James W. Thompson. *Reference Studies in Medieval History.* 3d ed. Chicago, University of Chicago Press, 1923–24. 3 v. All references are to works in English. Cites a large amount of periodical literature.

Bibliothèque de l'école des chartes, revue d'érudition, consacrée spéciale-ment à l'étude du moyen âge. Vol. 1 to date. Paris, 1839–40 to date. Contains bibliographies of recent publications in its successive issues.

VI GUIDES TO MODERN HISTORY

Cambridge Modern History, edited by A. C. Ward, G. W. Prothero, and Stanley Leathes. New York, Macmillan, 1902–12. 14 v. A standard work with full bibliography for each chapter.

Dahlmann-Waitz. See above.

Eugène Saulnier and A. Martin. *Bibliographie des travaux publiés de 1866 à 1897 sur l'histoire de la France de 1500 à 1789.* Paris, Les presses universitaires, 1928 to date.

Pierre Caron. *Bibliographie des travaux publiés de 1866 à 1897 sur l'histoire de la France depuis 1789.* Paris, Cornély, 1912.

Répertoire méthodique de l'histoire moderne et contemporaine de la France, pour les années 1898–1906, 1910–13. Paris, Rieder, 1899–1918. v. 17, 9–11.

Répertoire bibliographique de l'histoire de France, par Pierre Caron et Henri Stein, 1920–23. Paris, Picard, 1923–27. 2 v. Nos. 4, 5, and 6 constitute the most satisfactory bibliography of French history from 1789. Sources and secondary works included.

F. von Wenckstern. *A Bibliography of the Japanese Empire;* being a classified list of all books, essays, and maps in European languages relating to Dai Nihon (Great Japan) published in Europe, America, and in the East from 1859–93. Deiden, Brill, 1895. A second volume with similar title covers the period 1894–1906. Tokyo, Maruya, 1907. Continued by: Oskar Nachod. Bibliography of the Japanese empire, 1906–26; being a classified list of the literature issued in European languages since the publication of Fr. von Wenckstern's Bibliography of the Japanese empire. London, H. Goldston, 1928. 2 v.

E. Calvi. *Biblioteca di bibliografia storica italiana.* Catalogo tripartito delle bibliografie finora pubblicate sulla storia generale e particolare d'Italia. Rome, Loescher, 1903. Supplement for 1903–6. Rome, Loescher, 1907. Includes sources and secondary works.

Alonzo B. Sánchez. *Fuentes de la historia española.* Madrid, n.p., 1919. Secondary works. Does not include relations with America.

Robert J. Kerner. *Slavic Europe:* a selected bibliography in the western European languages, comprising history, languages, and literatures. Cambridge, Harvard University Press, 1918. Includes sources and secondary works; lacks critical commentary.

VII   GUIDES TO BRITISH HISTORY

Henry L. Cannon. *Reading References for English History.* Boston, Ginn, 1910. An introductory survey.

Charles Gross. *The Sources and Literature of English History from the Earliest Times to about 1485.* 2d ed. New York, Longmans, 1915. By far the best book of its kind.

Cambridge History of the British Empire, edited by J. Holland Rose and others. New York, Macmillan, 1929–. 8 v. had been published by the beginning of 1938. Excellent bibliographies by chapters.

Cambridge History of British Foreign Policy, 1783–1919, edited by A. W. Ward and G. P. Gooch. New York, Macmillan, 1922–23. 3 v.

Godfrey Davies, editor. *Bibliography of British History, Stuart Period, 1603–1714.* Oxford, Clarendon Press, 1928.

William Hunt and Reginald L. Poole. *The Political History of England.* New York, Longmans, 1906–07. 12 v. Full bibliographies at the end of each volume.

VIII   GUIDES TO WORLD WAR HISTORY

M. E. Bulkley. *Bibliographical Survey of Contemporary Sources for the Economic and Social History of the War.* Oxford, Clarendon Press, 1922. (Carnegie endowment for international peace. Economic and social history of the World War.) Confined to printed primary sources.

George W. Prothero. *A Select Analytical List of Books Concerning the Great War.* London, H. M. Stationery Office, 1923.

Encyclopaedia Britannica. 14th ed. Vol. XXIII, pp. 788–92. A careful and full list of works topically arranged.

Sidney B. Fay. *The Origins of the World War.* New York, Macmillan, 1928. 2 v. The footnote references constitute an exceptionally good bibliography.

IX GUIDES TO AMERICAN HISTORY

Edward Channing, A. B. Hart, and F. J. Turner. *Guide to the Study and Reading of American History.* Revised edition. Boston, Ginn, 1912. Standard guide. A helpful discussion of classified bibliographies on pp. 28–44. A new edition edited by members of the Department of History in Harvard University is (1938) about to appear.

The American Nation: a history, edited by A. B. Hart. New York, Harper, 1904–08. 27 v., with an additional volume which brings the narrative to 1917. A critical essay on authorities at the end of each volume.

Justin Winsor, editor. *Narrative and Critical History of America.* Boston, Houghton, Mifflin, 1884–89. 8 v. Excellent bibliographical notes.

J. N. Larned, editor. *Literature of American History.* Boston, Published for the American library association by Houghton, Mifflin, 1902. Contains estimates by competent authorities of a large number of works of American history.

A. P. C. Griffin. *Bibliography of American Historical Societies, the United States and Canada.* 2d ed., revised and enlarged. Washington, 1907. (In American historical association. Annual report, 1905. v. 2.)

Grace G. Griffin, comp. *Writings on American History, 1906–26.* Government Printing office, Washington, 1908–11, 1918–30. Volumes 1912–17 published by Yale University Press. 21 v.

American Historical Review. Decennial indexes, 1895–1925. New York, Macmillan, 1906–26. 3 v. A helpful guide to important articles and to reviews of historical books.

Cambridge History of American Literature, edited by W. P. Trent and others. New York, Putnam, 1917–21. 4 v. Exhaustive bibliographies appended to each volume.

Evarts B. Greene and Richard Morris. *Guide to the Principal Sources for Early American History* (1600–1800) in New York City. New York, Columbia University Press, 1929.

Arthur M. Schlesinger and Dixon Ryan Fox. *A History of American Life.* New York, Macmillan, 1927–. 10 v. had appeared early in 1938. A full essay on authorities at the end of each volume.

X GUIDES TO THE HISTORY OF HISPANIC AMERICA

Cecil K. Jones. *Hispanic American Bibliographies*, including collective bibliographies, histories of literature, and selected general works. Baltimore, *Hispanic American historical review*, 1922. Supplement in *Hispanic American historical review*, v. 6, pp. 100–133, February-August, 1926.

Hayward Keniston. *List of Works for the Study of Hispanic American History*. New York, Hispanic Society of America, 1920.

José T. Medina. *Biblioteca Hispano-Americana* (1493–1810). Santiago, Chile, printed by the author, 1898–1907. 7 v.

Herbert E. Bolton. *History of the Americas*. Boston, Ginn, 1928. Good chapter bibliographies.

XI GUIDES TO THE HISTORY OF THOUGHT AND CULTURE

Lynn Thorndike. *A Short History of Civilization*. New York, Crofts, 1926. Good chapter bibliographies.

Preserved Smith. *A History of Modern Culture*. v. 1, *The Great Renewal*. New York, Holt, 1930. A good general bibliography, pp. 609–53.

Isis. Bruges, the Saint Catherine Press, 1913 to date. Founded and edited by George Sarton. A quarterly international review devoted to the history of science and civilization. Publishers' critical bibliographies, of which no. 27 appeared in September, 1929.

W. T. Sedgwick and H. W. Tyler. *A Short History of Science*. New York, Macmillan, 1917. A list of reference books is given at the end.

A. G. S. Josephson. *A List of Books on the History of Science*. Chicago, John Crerar Library, 1911.

XII GUIDES TO JEWISH HISTORY

Jewish Encyclopaedia, edited by Isidore Singer and others. 12 v. New York, Funk & Wagnalls, 1901–06. Innumerable references to the literature of the subject.

Jüdisches Lexikon, edited by G. Herlitz and B. Kurschner. 5 v. Berlin, 1927–30. Also numerous references.

S. Dubnow. *Weltgeschichte des jüdischen Volkes*. 10 v. Berlin, 1925–29. Serviceable bibliographies at the end of each volume.

Quirvath Sepher. Jerusalem, 1925–. A current bibliographical quarterly covering most publications in Jewish studies.

WORKS ON THE STUDY OF HISTORY

I HISTORICAL METHOD

The best brief introduction is C. V. Langlois and C. Seignobos, *Introduction aux études historiques*, which is available in a good English translation. A more elaborate work, never translated, is Ernst Bernheim, *Lehrbuch der historischen Methode*. Five of the best books in English are: John M. Vincent, *Historical Research* — most of its illustrations drawn from medieval history; F. M. Fling, *Outline of Historical Method* and *The Writing of History* — most of their examples drawn from modern European history; Allen Johnson, *The Historian and Historical Evidence* — most of its illustrations drawn from American history; and Homer C. Hockett, *Introduction to Research in American History*. Among useful volumes of a more general character are: James Harvey Robinson, *The New History;* Benedetto Croce, *History: Its Theory and Practice;* Jusserand, Abbott, Colby, and Bassett, *The Writing of History;* F. J. Teggart, *The Processes of History;* W. W. Davies, *How to Read History;* and G. M. Trevelyan, *Clio, The Muse, and Other Essays*. Some suggestive papers may be found in James Ford Rhodes, *Historical Essays*.

II THE PHILOSOPHY OF HISTORY

See R. Flint, *History of the Philosophy of History;* G. W. F. Hegel, *The Philosophy of History;* Auguste Comte, *Positive Philosophy* (Harriet Martineau's translation), Vol. II especially; H. T. Buckle, *History of Civilization in England;* Herbert Spencer, *Study of Sociology* (especially Ch. 3, Nature of the Social Science); Walter Bagehot, *Physics and Politics;* John Fiske, *Outlines of Cosmic Philosophy*, vol. II; Oswald Spengler, *The Decline of the West*, especially volume I; J. B. Bury, *The Theory of Progress;* Vilfredo Pareto, *Mind and Society;* Arnold J. Toynbee, *A Study of History*, vols. 1–3; Karl Marx, *Contribution to the Critique of Political Economy*, preferably used with M. M. Bober, *Karl Marx's Interpretation of History;* James E. Thorold Rogers, *Economic Interpretation of History;* E. R. A. Seligman, *Economic Interpretation of History;* Shailer Mathews, *Spiritual Interpretation of History;* Henry Adams, *The Degradation of the Democratic Dogma*.

III SCIENCES AUXILIARY TO HISTORY

Anthropology: Sir Edward Tylor, *Anthropology;* also his *Primitive Culture;* Franz Boas, *Mind of Primitive Man;* also, his *Anthropology and Modern Life;* A. A. Goldenweiser, *Early Civilization;* R. H. Lowie, *Primitive Society;* F. H. Hankins, *Racial Basis of Civilization;* A. C. Haddon, *Wanderings of Peoples.*

Archaeology: W. F. Petrie, *Methods and Aims of Archaeology* (see especially the fine chapter on the nature of archeological evidence); D. G. Hogarth, *Authority and Archeology;* Sir G. C. C. Maspero, *Egyptian Archeology;* Adolf Michaelis, *Century of Archeological Discoveries;* H. R. H. Hall, *Aegean Archeology;* T. E. Peet, *Stone and Bronze Ages in Italy and Sicily;* S. B. Platner, *Topography and Monuments of Ancient Rome.*

Geography: H. B. George, *Relations of Geography and History;* Ellen C. Semple, *Influences of Geographic Environment;* Lucien Febvre and L. Battaillon, *A Geographical Introduction to History;* Ellsworth Huntington, *Civilization and Climate;* also, *Principles of Human Geography;* James Fairgrieve, *Geography and World Power;* Franklin Thomas, *The Environmental Basis of Society;* A. P. Brigham, *Geographic Influences in American History.*

Philology: Otto Jespersen, *Language, Its Nature, Origin, and Development;* Edward Sapir, *Language;* Henry Sweet, *The History of Language;* Joseph Vendryes, *Language, A Linguistic Introduction to History.*

Diplomatics: Hubert Hall, *Studies in English Official Historical Documents;* Arthur Giry, *Manuel de Diplomatique;* Oswald Redlich, *Allgemeine Einleitung zur Urkundenlehre.*

Paleography: Sir E. M. Thompson, *Introduction to Greek and Latin Paleography;* Philippe Berger, *Histoire de l'Ecriture dans l'antiquité;* Charles Johnson and Hilary Jenkinson, *English Court Hand;* Charles T. Martin, *The Record Interpreter.*

Numismatics: Stanley Lane Poole, *Coins and Medals: Their Place in History and Art;* George F. Hill, *Coins and Medals;* George MacDonald, *Coin Types.*

Sociology: Franz Muller-Lyer, *History of Social Development;* Benjamin Kidd, *Social Evolution;* William F. Ogburn, *Social Change;* William Graham Sumner, *Folkways;* Alexander M. Carr-Saunders, *The Population Problem;* Graham Wallas, *The Great Society;* C. C. Ellwood, *The Psychology of Human Society;* W. McDougall, *The Group Mind;* Andrew D. White, *History of the Warfare of Science and Theology;* Gustave LeBon, *The Crowd;* E. D. Martin, *The Behavior of Crowds.*

Statistics: R. Mayo-Smith, *Science of Statistics;* H. Secrist, *Introduction to Statistical Method;* R. E. Chaddock, *Principles of Statistics;* E. E. Day, *Statistical Analysis;* R. A. Fisher, *Statistical Methods for Research Workers.*

IV THE HISTORY OF HISTORY

See James T. Shotwell, *Introduction to the History of History;* J. B. Bury, *The Greek Historians;* H. Hallam, *Introduction to the Literature of the Middle Ages* (sections on history); Robert Flint, *Historical Philosophy in France and French Belgium and Switzerland;* Edward Fueter, *Geschichte der Neuren Historiographie* (also in a French translation); John B. Black, *The Art of History: Four Great Historians* (they are Voltaire, Hume, Robertson, and Gibbon); G. P. Gooch, *History and Historians in the Nineteenth Century;* Charles A. Beard, *Introduction to the English Historians* (a book of selections, with good editorial matter); J. F. Jameson, *History of Historical Writing in America;* John S. Bassett, *Middle Group of American Historians;* chapters on historians in the *Cambridge History of English Literature* and the *Cambridge History of American Literature.*

INDEX

INDEX